18⁰⁰AA

LORD ACTON
AND HIS TIMES

Portrait of Lord Acton, by F. von Lenbach
Reproduced by permission of National Portrait Gallery

LORD ACTON
AND HIS TIMES

DAVID MATHEW

UNIVERSITY OF ALABAMA PRESS

University, Alabama

First published in the United States of America
by the
UNIVERSITY OF ALABAMA PRESS
1968
Library of Congress Catalogue Card Number 68-23459

*FOR
ALICK DRU*

Contents

Preface

Lord Acton was a great historian. He was born in 1834 and he died in 1902. He held the regius chair at Cambridge and dominated the field of history throughout the later part of the Victorian Age. He gathered a mass of materials and laid plans for a *History of Liberty* that he never wrote. This would have been the last of the universal histories by a single hand. He was to be a founder of the *Cambridge Modern History* and of the *English Historical Review*. He belonged to the period that has now passed into history. He died in the year that I was born and this is the first attempt to provide within a larger study an extensive biography.

Anyone who attempts to deal with a life which has so many facets as Lord Acton's is bound to have some assets and some drawbacks. The historian had adopted early in life a rather old-fashioned and doctrinal Liberalism. This and other matters brought him into conflict with the Vatican of his day. On the asset side I am a life-long member of the Roman Church and am in consequence familiar with the tensions that exist within that body. I have a knowledge of its higher *échelons*. On the other hand I have always been a member of the Liberal Party in this country. As a lesser point I can well understand his tendency to go on amassing detail. These combined cover much of Acton's life. One is never certain of the conclusions that one draws and I think it possible that I have exaggerated the character of his anti-clericalism and dislike of bishops. I feel that one needs to be an Anglican to understand the nature of the appeal which higher ecclesiastical appointments in England made to him.

Lord Acton is now principally remembered for his celebrated statement, made in a letter to Dr Creighton, that 'power tends to corrupt and absolute power corrupts absolutely'. A few of his other

9

aphorisms will serve to give a further impression of his mind. 'No
secret lasts longer than twenty-seven years. . . . A wrong opinion
is never conquered until it has reached its most perfect expression.
And we are never masters of it until we have seen it at its best.'

'He will put on no more steam than the thing is worth.' He
was always interested in steam, whose working he does not seem
fully to understand. 'Clearness, a French disease' is found in one
of his notes and gives some food for thought. 'A man afraid or
being bored is as unfit for an historian as a fisherman.' Although
he did not possess Tocqueville's remarkable prevision, he has left
a phrase which has a bearing on the coming century, 'The modern
danger . . . state absolutism, not royal absolutism'. Lord Acton
was not accustomed to revise his opinion; his notes at Cambridge
he left unchanged.

His origins apart, which lay in the German aristocracy and in
the English squirearchy, Acton was essentially a clubman, a
Londoner and a Victorian historian. In spite of his two landed
estates, one in Shropshire and the other in the Rhineland, he
seems to have had no interest in farming or knowledge of estate
management. At a moment in his later life when he looked back
on his home at Aldenham he found that what he had enjoyed were
his conversations there in the long evenings. As a shot he was
poor and he never hunted. In fact there seems no evidence that
he ever rode. These elements cut him off from the young Whig
aristocracy whose interests were in hunting and in racing.

As far as out-of-doors recreations were concerned he enjoyed
walking, traversing the lower slopes of the Bavarian mountains or
wandering on the lip of the Alpes Maritimes, where they fall
towards the sea. He was of middle height and as he grew older he
developed a full figure. He was renowned as a conversationalist,
but his talk was on the German model, full of facts and references,
a rather more civilized and more European version of Lord
Macaulay. His talk, it is to be noted, was most *gouté* in two circles,
that where clubland bordered on the universities and at the Court.
Queen Victoria had this in common with her most learned subjects that they both appreciated the German model. It is also to be
noted that he had his full share in that German contempt for the
Italian mind, which went back in one form or another to the

distant days of Martin Luther. The fact that he was entrusted to the guidance of the Roman Catholic clergy and his disenchantment with them will appear later.

Much of this book will deal with Lord Acton's relations with Mr Gladstone, who gave him a long apprenticeship and then confided absolutely in his knowledge of history without evincing great interest in his judgment upon politics. This also is another constant theme. Mr Gladstone was a simple-hearted man with certain complications in his manoeuvres – it was only Lord Wolseley, sweating in the heart of the Sudan by the fourth cataract, who would ever describe him as a crocodile.[1] Acton's relations with Gladstone were a parabola, which reached their summit when the latter was in office.

Acton's old-fashioned Liberalism derived from Burke. In spite of the fact that he was Lord Granville's stepson, it had very few Whig affiliations; nor do I think that the influences of his background and education meant very much to him, except for Döllinger. It was a long time before he freed himself from that teacher and the specialized outlook on Germany that Döllinger brought to him. The establishment of his library and his great amassing of historic fact came to him early.

His earlier life included the brief six years as a member of Parliament and his work on Roman Catholic reviews. It can be said that 1864 was a turning point for it marked the final quarrel with his Episcopate in England, the closing down of his Catholic reviews and the publication by the Pope of the *Syllabus Errorum*, which appeared to him to be directly aimed at his politics. His membership of the House of Commons ceased the next year.

The whole of the period 1864–70 is concerned with Acton's contacts with Rome, the last years of the Temporal Power of the Popes and his attitude towards this and his approach towards the first Council of the Vatican. In 1869 he was created a peer. Then came the Gladstone years, his hopes for office or for some diplomatic post and finally his appointment as a Lord-in-Waiting. In 1895 he was appointed to the regius chair of modern history at Cambridge. He died in 1902 in Tegernsee in Bavaria of a paralytic stroke.

---

[1] Cf. Wolseley's Diary printed *in Relief of Khartoum*, ed. Adrian Preston, p. 169.

It was back in 1938 when I first began working on Acton's biography. During all that time I have had the guidance and judgment of my brother Gervase. I am also grateful for consultations
with Alick Dru throughout the years of our long friendship. I am
likewise deeply indebted to Lord Acton's grand-daughter Mia
Woodruff.

I should like also to give a list of the new sources that I have
used. I am grateful in the first place to Miss Margaret V. (Mar-
gery) Bryce for access to the Bryce MSS left by her uncle and now
lying beautifully arranged in the Bodleian Library. The collection
contains a number of letters from Lord Acton, which are particularly illuminating for aspects of the last twenty years of his
life. I have used, through the courtesy of the Superior of the
London Oratory, the mass of correspondence addressed by Father
Faber to John Brande Morris during the latter's chaplaincy to
Sir John Acton. They throw a vivid light on Acton's life at
Aldenham after he came of age. I must express my gratitude to the
Archbishop of Cardiff, who gave me access to the Aldenham
material in the archives of the diocese of Shrewsbury where he
was at that time the Bishop. I also give my thanks to the Superior
of the Birmingham Oratory for the use of the letters which Acton
sent to Dr Newman, and to the Abbot of Downside for the opportunity to examine the heterogeneous body of Acton material
assembled in part by Abbot Gasquet. I am grateful to Douglas
Woodruff for access to the series of letters addressed to Acton on
historical subjects during the years in which he held the Cambridge chair, and to the Warden of Keble for the chance to study
the Liddon MSS preserved in the library of that college. I have
used, through the courtesy of the Master of Pembroke College,
Oxford, the interesting collection of Renouf MSS bequeathed to
the college. In addition to hitherto untapped sources I have, in
common with all other Acton students, made use of the great
mass of notes and papers at the University of Cambridge.

During the years that I have been working on this subject many
of the older witnesses have died. Among them I have a particular
gratitude to Lady Galway, who was the daughter of Lady
Blennerhassett and a grandchild of the Countess von Leyden.
She had seen the later phases of the Acton-Döllinger relationship

and she had gained her mother's view of Acton's life. She thought that his loss of faith was more complete than I can accept. She had an unfriendly attitude to Mrs Drew (Mary Gladstone).

G. M. Trevelyan, then Master of Trinity, described the historian's life at Trinity and also the lack of contact between Sir George Otto Trevelyan and the other Whigs and Hawarden Castle. Sir Edmund Whittaker explained the admiration evoked by Lord Acton in a Trinity undergraduate. On the other hand Margot, Lady Oxford was not attracted to him when on a visit to Hawarden; she thought him over-deferential to Mr Gladstone. Sir Maurice Powicke and Sir Charles Oman and also A. J. Carlyle described to me the Oxford history school of Acton's later years. Lord FitzAlan, who was among all those to whom I spoke the nearest in age to Acton, gave me an idea of how the historian was seen from the rather unfriendly angle of Norfolk House.

I have been enabled to study two of the principal settings of the historian's life in England. Lord and Lady Acton showed me Aldenham Park, then still in their possession, and Mr Gladstone Hawarden Castle. No member of the Acton family of my time, with the exception of his daughter Mrs Herbert, had any personal memories of the first Lord Acton. I must express my gratitude to Professor Alexander d'Entrèves for his illuminating comments upon nineteenth-century Italy. I am deeply grateful to Sir Philip Magnus for his kindness in discussing Mr Gladstone and I have made use of the admirable biography that he has published of him. It was Gladstone who introduced Acton to Lord Camoys and I am grateful to the Hon. Mrs Sherman Stonor for the use of letters from the Stonor MSS. Sir Shane Leslie has kindly provided me with a letter of some importance from Lord Emly's MSS. I am indebted to Mrs George Villiers for an interesting account of her grandfather Sir Henry Howard, who was Minister at Munich in Acton's time. It is worth noting that except for meeting with denizens of the London clubs and for his later contacts with professional historians, Lord Acton never moved outside a single social *stratum*, whether he was living in England or on the Continent. This gave a certain channelled character to his ideas.

Under one aspect this book is a study of a varied range of

nineteenth-century ideas. It is my hope that character studies of his contemporaries may help to define the situation of the central figure. I am grateful for discussion and correspondence on this subject over the years with the Archbishop of Glasgow, Mr Douglas Woodruff, Mr E. E. Y. Hales, Mr Robert Speaight, Mr Graham Greene, Sir Llewelyn Woodward, Mr Maurice Gorham, Dr Marcel and Dr Tessa Hornik, Mr Roland Hill and Frau Emmy Wellesz.

Acton, with his deeply civilian mind, looked out upon a world of steadily increasing liberty. There was still, especially on the Continent, a certain limitation on the suffrage. He could not fore-see the blood-stained century that was to come and the rash of military dictatorships.

Five chapters from this volume have appeared in print before that is to say, the seventh, eighth and ninth chapters of Part One. These have formed part of my earlier study, *Acton, the formative years*. One chapter is reprinted from *Blackfriars* (Part One, Chapter 6) and one from *Chiese e Stato nell'Ottocento* (Chapter 1 of Part Three), a miscellany in honour of Pietro Pirri.

Stonor Park   DAVID MATHEW
January 1968.

PART ONE

ALDENHAM

Introduction

Acton inherited Aldenham, his Shropshire estate, and his father's baronetcy in 1837 when he was three years of age. That same year he came to England for the first time. He was an only child in what was to a great extent a house of women, his mother and his maternal grandmother and from time to time his father's mother. On leaving Aldenham he was brought up by priests first at Oscott and then at Munich with Dr Döllinger. There is no doubt that these years in Germany were crucial in his education. Although they became separated in much later life, Dr Döllinger remained for more than thirty years first his revered teacher and then his standard of reference. It was in his house that Acton learned German and came to accept so much of his German standard of values. It is worth stressing to what a great extent Sir John Acton was surrounded by priests, first under their authority and then with a priest under his control. Very slowly his views about the priesthood began to change as did his attitude to Dr Döllinger.

He was inevitably in contact with the three English Cardinals. The first whom he experienced was Wiseman, who was in control at Oscott. It clearly was not Wiseman's foreign quality that was out of tune with the young partly foreign boy. The Cardinal was assertive at an age when a schoolboy would welcome his assertions. The difficulty lay in another sphere. Nicholas Wiseman had been born in Seville, the son of an Irish merchant there. He had been many years in Rome, latterly as vice-rector and then as rector of the English College. His views of Church authority and on oriental scholarship were what he had learned in the papal capital. It is not surprising that his views on this second subject had a somewhat narrow range. He had a feeling for Roman language and a respect for the Roman system within which he was long assured that some high place had been reserved for him. He had quite buoyant dreams and a tolerant and ignorant good will towards the Church of England. His character was a difficult and not unusual combination of sensitiveness and intransigence. There was not very much place for lay activity within his world.

The two other Cardinals were in every way much greater figures. In regard to Dr Newman it was unfortunate that Acton never had the faculty for discipleship, nor did he understand until much later the Newmanian standards of reference, the recent history of the Church of England and the way of life represented by the Oriel common room. In fact he never knew the Oxford which had seen Newman's heyday; the University was very changed when he at last came to it.

Among the whole range of the Tractarian converts who followed Newman into the Church of Rome there were only two who ever received Acton's intimate friendship, Simpson and Renouf. It will be seen that neither had much connection with their old master. The Acton-Newman relations can be traced in the later sections of this part of the book. It will be noted from some friendly correspondence about him in 1873 that Newman, who was by thirty years the senior, always looked on Sir John Acton as a young man.

This brings us to the difficult case of Cardinal Manning. Much more than Newman, he was deeply remote from both Acton's interests and his ways of thought. The Cardinal had a schematic mind and in the years that we are now considering he gave Sir John Acton a certain weight as a fairly wealthy Catholic baronet and still more when he became one of the few members of Parliament of his Communion. There is indeed a point at which Acton refers to Manning as one of his few supporters in the world of the high ecclesiastics. It is the third section of this book that will describe his hostile action. At the same time it was only the official or perhaps rather the juridical sides of Manning's character that Acton knew. The Cardinal had, besides, a great feeling for the poor and especially for the Irish poor of his own flock and for Ireland. His crowded life was filled with energy and skill in matters which were very far from Acton's interests, the intricate administration of the see of Westminster at first on Wiseman's behalf and later on his own. It was Acton's misfortune that Manning was a stranger to him in their final conflict.

The failure of the relationship between Sir John Acton and Newman needs more consideration than the fact that he soon outgrew Nicholas Wiseman and failed to penetrate behind Manning's iron courtesy. It seems to me that in the last analysis Döllinger was at least in part to blame. He had given the young Acton the heavy engine of his German approach to all religious questions, while John Henry Newman was as insular as only an Oxford common room could make him. His rain-swept thought was seamed by hesitations. He was vague and tentative. It is interesting to note that, as far as I can discover, two of his contemporaries never made any reference to Newman's *Apologia pro vita sua*; they were Bishop Samuel Wilberforce and Sir John Acton.

An unusual influence on John Acton's life was introduced by his mother's second marriage in 1840 to Lord Leveson, the eldest son of Lord Granville, then ambassador in Paris. He was only nineteen years his stepson's senior and he dominated the Foreign Office whenever the Liberals were in office until almost the end of John Acton's career. Here it need only be said that he did not care for his serious and unathletic stepson. The intimacy, such as it was, only lasted until Acton's mother Lady Granville died in 1860; but the hostile judgment was not eradicated. Granville's sister, Lady Georgiana Fullerton, was a convert to Catholicism, who helped to form his literary tastes and the beginnings of his Catholic Liberalism. As a young man Sir John Acton was too serious to get on with his generation in the great Whig world.

It was Granville who persuaded him into politics and the account of his election for the borough of Carlow provides one of the lighter touches of those early Acton years. Sir John was young and soon in trouble; it must be said that this combination does not make for easy reading. The influence both of Burke and Tocqueville upon his early thought is set out here. An account of Tocqueville is brought in to give a kind of balance to Döllinger.

There are accounts of Acton's writings, mainly reviews, and of his library. This is important for these books remained the stay of his thinking all through his life. The turning point of his early

years was the refusal of Cambridge to admit him as an undergraduate because he was a Roman Catholic. If he had gone to
Cambridge and avoided the years in Munich with Dr Döllinger
his life would have been different. Had he been tempted to
finance an historical review, it would have consisted like the
E.H.R., that was to come, of reviews only, and articles whose
context was solely historical. As it was the influence of Döllinger
and to a less extent that of Newman led him into the field of
Roman Catholic small reviews which were already in existence.
These lay within the field of authority of the Roman bishops. The
influence of Liberalism in his case has already been assessed. He
was operating in a restricted zone and his work was broken up by
Cardinal Wiseman. This was in 1864, the year of the publication
of the *Syllabus Errorum*.

However, it was the House of Commons which opened to him a
wider sphere. It is true that he hardly spoke during the six years
of his memberships from 1859 till 1865; but he made an occasional
friend among his colleagues like Sir Mountstuart Grant Duff.
He was, rather uneasily, a Whig and had nothing in common with
his own leader. These were the last years of Lord Palmerston's
ascendancy. 'A gay old Tory of the older school,' so the Press
wrote of the Whig prime minister, 'describing himself as a Liberal
and hoaxing the Reform Club.' The jaunty manner, the intense
masculinity of the aged buck, the large sophisticated ignorance
were all abhorrent to John Acton. There in the House of Commons the premier would sit in his place with his white hat pulled
down over his eyes, pretending to be awake before he left to go
to his dinner, the turtle soup, the cod, the oyster sauce.

He certainly felt little more respect for the Tory leader, the
fourteenth Earl of Derby, than he did for his own chief. A note
made by a Tory henchman invited to Knowsley can describe him.
'As a leader of a party he [Derby] is more hopeless than ever –
devoted to whist, billiards, racing, betting.' It was not in the
historian to develop a Newmarket side. Acton was to prove himself in middle life an adept courtier on the German model. He was
already an easy conversationalist with a rather heavy sense of
social *nuances*. If we seek for an explanation of his failure to accom-
modate himself to either House of Parliament, the reason would

seem to be that he was too professorial for that assembly. There were, however, two of the ministers who showed a real interest in the young Acton, Lord Clarendon and Mr Gladstone. The Earl of Clarendon can be dealt with briefly. He was foreign secretary and nearing the end of his career; he would die in 1870. He was a man of virtue, a trifle dull, bitterly and almost surprisingly anti-Roman. He soon grasped the unusual breadth of Sir John Acton's knowledge of the foreign scene. Gladstone was of real importance to this story for henceforth his life and that of Acton were to be intertwined. He was pious from his youth and came from a rich Evangelical and commercial background. He retained throughout his life a curious and heart-warming innocence, which went with a tendency towards the devious which he apparently did not recognize. His contacts in his youth with the great household of the Duke of Newcastle at Clumber in Nottinghamshire show how far he was from the world of high privilege. Gladstone's was a different setting from that of Acton, who had known all his life his stepfather's uncle the old deaf Duke of Devonshire. It is worth noting that Gladstone, who was already a firm Tractarian, had first got to know Acton through the numbers of his own periodical the *Home and Foreign Review*. He was at this time fifty-six years of age and held the office of Chancellor of the Exchequer.

At the end of this period in the summer of 1865 Sir John Acton married. His wife was one of the cousins whom he had long known in Munich, Countess Marie Arco-Valley.

I

Acton's Background

John Emerich Edward Acton was born in the last days of winter in
Naples on 10 January 1834 in the Palazzo Acton all'Chiaja and
was christened in his father's private chapel. He was the only son
of Sir Ferdinand Richard Edward Acton by his young wife, the
daughter and heiress of Emerich, Duke of Dalberg. Although
descended from a long line of Shropshire baronets, whose title
and possessions he inherited, John Acton had much that was continental in his ancestry and upbringing. This was, however,
German and not Italian. His links with the kingdom of the Two
Sicilies were fragile: he had no South Italian blood and he was
without contact with the Bourbon dynasty. When that regime
fell in 1859 his cousins, the Baroni Acton, were by no means
Legitimist. His almost exact contemporary the Barone Ferdinando
was a frigate captain in the Navy of the Two Sicilies and passed
to the Sardinians; he commanded the *Principe Umberto* at the
defeat of the Italian fleet at Lissa by the Austrians.

The German heredity was a different matter altogether and this
pressed in on him from various angles. His mother belonged to a
great Rhineland family and his father's grandmother was a
Berghes von Trips from Düsseldorf. There was, however, this
transformation that while his ancestral links were with the old
Electorates of Trier and Cologne, his education and his marriage
and his friendships with his wife's family were all Bavarian. It was
the fact that he was seeped in German overlaid on French, his
mother's favourite language, that made his English expressions
sometimes *outré*. He was an English gentleman brought up on
German scholarship.

The original links with the old Italian scene were evanescent.
His uncle Cardinal Acton died in Acton's boyhood; the relative

on that side of the family whom he really knew with intimacy in adult life was the Italian secularist politician Marco Minghetti, who had married his cousin the Princess of Camporeale. Sir Ferdinand Acton died when he was three years old. Both he and his son adopted the name Dalberg-Acton in view of the Dalberg inheritance. His one set of English relations were the Throckmortons of Coughton Court in Warwickshire; but none of the sons was his exact contemporary. They were an old Catholic stock, country bred and unintellectual; he lost touch with them in later years. In 1843 he was sent at the age of nine to Oscott College outside Birmingham where the then president Bishop Wiseman had a strong influence on him, which did not endure. For many years and well past the period of Acton's parliamentary candidature Wiseman, now a Cardinal, had a diffused good will for the young Catholic baronet.

He left Oscott aged fourteen and passed two years at Edinburgh under the private tuition of Mr Logan, formerly vice-president at his old school. At sixteen, in 1850 he went to study with Dr Döllinger at Munich.[1] It seems that it was during the following year that he attempted through the help of John Shaw-Lefevre to obtain admission at Magdalene and at two other Cambridge Colleges. He was rejected as a Roman Catholic. His period at Munich was of profound importance in his development. He came of age in 1855. By this time he had a deep knowledge of German, which was in any case his mother's second language.

There was a further strand in his early background. Acton's widowed mother had married in 1840, as her second husband, Lord Granville, who later became the well-known Liberal statesman. John Acton had accompanied his stepfather on his special embassy to the Court of Russia in 1855 and had also gone as an *attaché* on Lord Ellesmere's journey to the United States in 1853. The influence of the Whig social world on Acton can be exaggerated. He lacked that interest either in horse-racing or in sport which would have made him acceptable within that circle. Lord Granville had acted as adviser to his wife who was Acton's

---

[1] Following the dates ascribed to two letters in Figgs and Laurence, eds, *Selections from the Correspondence of the first Lord Acton* (1917), vol. i, pp. 6–8, I gave in my book, *Acton, the Formative Years* 1848, as the date of his arrival. The same error is found in the *D.N.B.*, Suppl. 1901–11, p. 8.

guardian; but, after Lady Granville's death in 1860, her son passed away from the Whig world.

There is no evidence that Acton retained any friends from his school days, although in later life he used to speak of one or two with cordiality. There are no signs that he ever met them. Catholicism was never in his life a binding link, and there was nothing except their shared religion to link him with the other Catholics who lived with Döllinger. His contacts with Dr Newman were necessarily unsatisfactory. In a sense Acton was never a young man but passed directly from his retarded boyhood to that form of maturity verging on middle age which he displayed when editor of the *Rambler*. The long continuance of his boyish modes of expression can be illustrated from the American Diaries, written when he was nineteen, which give a pleasing expression of John Acton's tastes. They have all the delightful unforced innocence of a boy who had never been to a public school.

A few examples will explain their character. 'The ices,' he writes[1] for instance, 'are skilfully made, not too sweet, in order not to excite thirst, and they give you as much as two London ices for less money.' These were, of course, of the cream variety, for Acton remarks twice in the diary[2] that water ices seem unknown. 'This was,' he notes,[3] 'the hottest day I ever spent, Tuesday, June 20. Such heat is very rare here. It makes cooling drinks very necessary.'

He also made a comment at St Nicholas.[4] 'The wines are dear, and they have Madeira at fabulous prices. I have seen it at $12 a bottle.' This may be compared with a note made some five years later,[5] 'How often have I drunk Salvator Bier, at the Salvator Brau, at Munich.' Acton also had the practice, which he shared with Queen Victoria, of comparing the countries to which he came with German scenes. Thus the entrance into the mountains above Tappan Bay[6] on the eastern shores of the United States

---

[1] 'Lord Acton's American Diaries' have been printed in the *Fortnightly Review*, 1921, December, pp. 727–42 and 917–34, and 1922, January, pp. 63–83.

[2] *Ibid.*, pp. 742 and 928.

[3] *Ibid.*, p. 928.

[4] *Ibid.*, p. 734.

[5] Dated 11 June 1858, printed in 'Gasquet and the Acton-Simpson Correspondence', *Cambridge Historical Journal*, vol. x, p. 81.

[6] 'Lord Acton's American Diaries', p. 919.

reminded him of the Taunus above Mainz and he compared[1] the cars of his train at Albany with the second-class carriages in Württemberg. There was also a comment made as his ship slowly steamed up New York harbour. 'There was a look,' he writes,[2] 'that reminded me of the Giudecca at Venice; but the buildings are very different from the Venetian palaces, and are surrounded with ships. It is rather like Birmingham in the lagunes.'

Two short passages[3] describing his visit to Niagara give a very clear idea of the young Acton. 'The roar and the foam had a fine effect at night. Campbell (a travelling companion) and I had the same room, and before we fell asleep I discoursed upon the principles of historical criticism, and the facility with which truth is exaggerated. It was such a glorious night as to fill me with exultation, and yet with a feeling of melancholy at not being able to comprehend it adequately.' Still, after this foreshadowing of the future, he came back again to his youthful manner. 'We gathered,' he went on, 'wild strawberries on Goat Island and took an ice there. While I was on the tower a man was there writing verses. I did not feel poetical, which I seldom do, but boisterously happy. In the evening we played at prisoner's base in a field close to the Falls. Here I lost my hat.' That seems to give a complete and rather an appealing picture.

Acton kept through life to the stereotyped routes of travel of the upper classes of that time. His voyages to Russia and to the United States were not repeated. Spain he never visited[4] until old age,[5] and for the Spanish forms of Catholicism he retained through life a sharp dislike. He was familiar with England and Naples and the routes which lay between them. Known points of his movements were Vienna and later Biarritz. From his mother's death in 1860 until 1883 he owned the Dalberg *Schloss* at Herrnsheim in the Rhineland. He had a feeling for wide views

[1] *Ibid.*, p. 920.
[2] *Ibid.*, p. 730.
[3] *Ibid.*, pp. 922 and 924–5.
[4] About 1862, for the relevant letter to Newman is undated, Acton planned a journey; there is no reason to suppose that he carried out this project. Cf. Birmingham Oratory, Acton MSS, vol. i, f. 32.
[5] Cf. 'I left Biarritz on Saturday 27. Indeed I had spent most of my time there in making a hurried visit to Madrid, which was my first, and very pleasant.' Letter to Lord Bryce dated 7 February 1894, Acton-Bryce MSS, f. 82.

like that from La Californie across the coast line of the Côte d'Azur. He was born just too late for the need to make long journeys by *diligence*; he liked train travel. In his essays he often used metaphors derived from steam.

From the American Diaries there is also evidence that he had early come in his judgments to that tone of 'severity', which never left him. It is true that he was early used to English as used in social intercourse. But where did his 'severity' come from, and his later habit of piling up almost contradictory adjectives, sometimes of surprising harshness, in his assessments of character? It does not seem that this could have emerged from his early experience of English conversation. Lord Granville had nothing in common on this point with John Acton. His comments have an easy going, sophisticated laziness. It seems that it was in the German years with Döllinger that Acton developed his expressions. As a practice it is obviously a translation from some foreign language, although the old professor could never match the severe outlook to which Acton came in time.

It was Acton's misfortune that he did not come across his English equals in the field of scholarship until late middle life. Richard Simpson is, perhaps, the only one among his early associates in England who had something of a share in his own avid approach to knowledge. He was early at his ease with the cultivated Londoner of rank and with all women. It seems that he owed this last quality to the teaching of his cousin Countess Arco-Valley, who became his mother-in-law. In particular he understood ladies of position of German stock; he was perfect in his approach to Queen Victoria. He grasped, as so few English courtiers could really grasp, all the royal and ducal Saxon genealogies, and the various complicated inter-marriages which linked the Lutheran Courts. He had a very detailed knowledge of the eighteenth century.

In his early manhood he was already building up his library and in fact much of it seems to have been purchased between his coming of age and his marriage, for instance the whole library of Professor Ernst von Lasaulx of Munich who died in 1861. The library building at Aldenham, whose interior was remarkably ugly with its iron gallery, was constructed in 1865. Acton had, and this is not surprising, the taste of the men who planned the Great Exhibition of 1851. He had learned from Döllinger to value pictures for the scenes they represented, not for their quality.

He had at this time certain contacts which he would later lose. He was an eligible *parti* in the eyes of Catholic mothers of his own class. The estate at Aldenham was over six thousand acres in extent and the property had been husbanded through a long minority. It probably made him happier that he married a Bavarian rather than an English bride. He had so little in common with the Tory landed gentry.

He had a parliamentary career, but this was not important. He sat as M.P. for Carlow from 1859 until 1865, but he hardly ever spoke in the House of Commons. It does not seem that he undertook any work there in the interests of his constituency or his constituents. He stated later[1] that there was something that he disliked about the Carlow election. It is possible that his agents used bribery on his behalf without his knowledge.

It must be remembered that he had been an only child and had an essentially very lonely childhood. His first visit to Rome had taken place when he was nine years old and his mother and stepfather had rented an apartment in the Palazzo Simonetti in the Corso for the winter of 1843. It was at this time that he made an intimate friend of Granville Fullerton, his stepfather's nephew. This boy was six months younger than he was, a sensitive and moon-faced only child, fond of Macaulay's *Lays of Ancient Rome*. He was clearly dependent upon John Acton; later he went into the Army and died, aged twenty-one. Apart from this journey and his schooldays and visits to certain country houses, his childhood was passed at Aldenham.

It was, apart from his stepfather, a house of women, his mother and her visitors, her sister-in-law Lady Georgiana Fullerton and his two grandmothers, who both survived till he was thirty. Acton's Italian blood came from the Duchess of Dalberg, who brought in the Genoese family of Brignole-Sala and through whom he was related to the Marescalchi and thus to the Arco-Valleys, the family of his future wife. More accurately the Italian character came from his grandfather General Acton, the prime

---

[1] Cf. Letter to Dr Newman dated 4 June (1861?).

minister of the Two Sicilies. His portrait hung at Aldenham; an elderly man, still slender, with careful eyes. The star of St Januarius, the Russian Orders and the Gold Cross of Malta on his breast showed against the wide pattern of the braiding, and below this were the stiff vermilion facings. On each gold button was stamped the Bourbon lilies. He is painted standing on a terrace and behind him are seen the cupolas of the churches and beyond them the roadstead of Palermo and a great ship riding smoothly on a pale blue sea below the cliffs of Monte Pellegrino. It appears, although there is little direct evidence on this point, that John Acton disliked the memory of this grandfather. He was so very different in his love of money and disregard for truth from Mr Gladstone.

Aldenham, to which Acton came after his father died, dated from 1691, the period of the Acton prosperity when they were all 'tall men and Tories'. It was a long deep house, dignified and heavy, with high-pitched roofs and wooden corbelled eaves above the stonework. The fruit gardens, beyond the north-west angle of the building, seem to have dated from this time with their wrought-iron gates and the stone urns spaced upon the walls. The long slope of the avenue stretching away from the main front of Aldenham House was probably planted during these years.

There was no park land and the house stood squarely on rising ground in the midst of its own territory in the south-eastern part of Shropshire to the east of the turnpike road which ran from Bridgnorth to Shrewsbury through Astley Abbots.

The return to Aldenham, which took place in the year of the accession of Queen Victoria, resembled in some ways the coming of Prince Albert; for Lady Acton brought to the English countryside a taste in building which suggested a very different age and climate. The chapel with its light lines and its smooth white surface appears inspired by the classical taste of the Italy of the 1830s as does the monument to Sir Richard Acton with his son and widow mourning beneath the lintel. But the changes made in the house itself were very different. They were apparently later in date and have that heaviness that came from Coburg: the front of the house was modelled in a thick smoothed grey stone with rounded window-dressings which set off the new plate-glass. A formal garden, geometrical and gravelled, was laid out between the chapel and the house. The drawing-room was lovely with the air of the early thirties and a great chandelier and mirrors.

It was with his arrival at Munich in 1850 that Acton's true education first began. He was a questioning boy and he there found a tutor, who would answer everything that he might raise with him. This tutor was able to convey to him a sense of his own vast German knowledge and to assist him in that piling up of fact on fact which was the historian's lasting characteristic. It is worth noting that at this time Dr von Döllinger had been for many years a secular priest in Bavaria and was an old-fashioned Conciliarist, that is to say that he thought that a Council should control all papal action. Two comments, both made by John Acton – one before he went to Munich and the other after his arrival there – are worth recording. '*J'ai lu la lettre du prof. Döllinger avec la plus grande joie . . . Je vois que c'est un homme dans lequel je pourrai avoir la plus parfaite confiance, et je mettrai avec plaisir toute la direction de mes études et de ma conduite entre ses mains.*'[1] The next letter runs as follows: 'He [Döllinger] is unquestionably the most coolheaded man I ever knew, and probably the most dispassionate.'[2] This was John Acton's real beginning.

[1] *Correspondence*, p. 6.
[2] *Ibid.*, p. 8.

2

Oscott

There are, however, certain other points which should be touched on before describing that meeting of John Acton with Dr Döllinger which lay at the root of his education. In particular an analysis is required of his mother's influence. He was always a dutiful and, indeed, devoted son. It was not that Lady Acton was unconventional; she knew England very well, but as a foreigner. It was a knowledge something of the kind of that possessed by Princess Lieven, the celebrated Russian ambassadress. In spite of her second marriage, John Acton remained throughout her life her only child.

It is possible to overstress the Neapolitan inheritance. General Acton was born in Besançon, the son of an English surgeon in that place by his Burgundian wife. Sir Richard Acton, the last of the senior line, had died in 1791 and at that time General Acton had inherited the baronetcy, which dated from the Civil Wars. Sir Richard's only daughter, Mrs Langdale, had, however, a life interest in the Aldenham estate. Sir Ferdinand died in Paris of pneumonia very unexpectedly in the early part of 1837 and in the same year his widow and her son returned to Aldenham, where the great re-modelled house must have dominated all his early memories.

At this time there were only two adult members of John Acton's branch of the Aldenham family, his mother and her brother-in-law Charles Edward Januarius. This last-named figure had only an indirect influence on John Acton's life. He was one of the young cardinals whom Gregory XVI loved to create; he entered very much into the old pontiff's views of increasing and extending the missionary field. He was promoted in 1842 when he was thirty-nine. He certainly wished his nephew to receive an English education. His health was always delicate, for he was threatened with consumption. The Cardinal of Santa Maria della Pace died in 1847 in the Jesuit house at Naples. It is not likely that he would have had any serious influence on his nephew had he survived. A meek, unsmiling prelate nurtured in an ecclesiastical Conservatism of a Metternichian tinge would have had nothing in common with John Acton.

Unlike her intimate friend Mrs Augustus Craven, who had her own influence on John Acton, his mother had not been brought up to venerate the principles of legitimacy. She was the daughter of the Duke of Dalberg, the head of one of the aristocratic families in the territory of the ecclesiastical electorates. His career had been made through a more significant figure, the last of the Electors of Mainz, better known as the Primate Dalberg, who had entered fully into Napoleon's policies. The family of the Metternich-Winneburgs came from just this region, Johannisberg in the neighbourhood of Coblenz. Like Metternich, the Dalbergs were far-ranging and the duchess came from Bologna in the Papal States. Her uncle Count Ferdinando Marescalchi had been in charge of the foreign affairs of the Cisalpine Republic. This side had in the past embraced some Liberal principles. Thus Marescalchi had written *Catechismo politico Italiano*. Dalberg had represented the grand duchy of Baden at Napoleon's Court. The careers of both these men had been made on the basis of the Napoleonic Empire. All the same it is, perhaps, worth noting that among the writings of his later life John Acton refers relatively seldom to Napoleon Bonaparte.

Both the Duchess of Dalberg and her daughter were *dévote*. The former had expressed her belief[1] in the miracle of the liquefaction of blood of San Gennaro to visiting English Protestants. Lady Acton had come back to reinforce the sparse Catholic landowners of the county of Shropshire. The most considerable local figure of that grouping was Sir Edward Smythe of Acton Burnell. Lord Stafford came from time to time to his house at Shiffnal. Both lived about fifteen miles away from Aldenham, within carriage distance.

[1] Passage from an account of a dinner with the 'D. and Dss Dalberg at Mme Rumford's, 18 June 1821', *Journal of the Hon. Henry Edward Fox*, pp. 73–4.

A portrait of Lady Acton by the Dutch painter Ary Scheffer used to hang in the drawing-room at Aldenham. She is painted standing with her reddish hair, a frank and rather serious countenance, pale skin, her dress very *décolletée*. She does not look as if she had ever been a very pretty woman. There is no trace of the French or the Italian, the Rhineland blood predominates. Years later, when Acton was to be considered for the post of a lord-in-waiting, the Queen remarked that he was the son of Marie de Dalberg. The sovereign had a perfect knowledge of a subject which bored her courtiers, the genealogical implications of the German scene. The language which Lady Acton always spoke was French. We can imagine her with her small son on the terrace at Aldenham Park speaking French in the warm weather.

There was, however, one figure who must now be introduced, her second husband. In 1840 Lady Acton married in a double ceremony at Devonshire House and in the Spanish Chapel a young man of twenty-five, Lord Leveson, who the same year was appointed as under secretary of State for Foreign Affairs. He was the eldest son of Lord Granville, then ambassador in Paris, and the marriage had been arranged there; he was also a nephew of the Duke of Devonshire. He had at that time no house of his own for he only inherited 16 Bruton Street on his father's death some six years later. He settled down at Aldenham.

Lord Leveson was of great importance in his stepson's life. He had that distaste for Catholicism which belonged to his Whig background; it was not a religious point of view that he took with any seriousness. He had all the education that he required; he spoke French perfectly. A superficial interest in aspects of French history is made clear in a letter that he later wrote to his friend Lord Canning.[1] 'I have begun a life of Madame de Chevreuse in the *Revue des Deux Mondes* by Cousin. It seems very amusing.' He had a remarkable quality of laziness. If it is asked how he managed what was to be his fine career and to reach and retain the post of foreign secretary, the answer would seem to be that he had a quiet determination that he would not be put down. Nevertheless he had a considerable influence, if not on Acton, at any rate on

---

[1] Letter dated 9 December 1855, in the Granville-Canning correspondence, printed in *Life of the Second Earl Granville*, by Lord Edmond Fitzmaurice, i, p. 129.

Acton's life. He would be foreign secretary when his stepson was considered for posts abroad. By that time he knew him thoroughly, lazily and without affection.

Soon after the marriage Lord Leveson was the means of introducing Johnny Acton into the stream of English public life. He had held the borough of Carlisle and wished to transfer to a constituency which was more convenient. Lichfield fell vacant and Leveson was returned as a Liberal at an uncontested election. 'I began my political life in 1841,' Acton once said later,[1] 'I canvassed at that election.' Leveson fitted in with his wife's wishes. They travelled expensively upon the Continent. The education of a Roman Catholic boy was something that Lord Leveson left to his wife to devise.

'I never,' said Lord Acton in later life,[2] 'had any contemporaries.' This is a fact, stated with perfect accuracy, which has a bearing on the whole of the historian's boyhood and education. In the Throckmorton family, with whom the Actons were in constant contact, the eldest son, Richard, was three years his senior, the second, Nicholas, four years his junior; unbridgeable distances in childhood. Thus isolated, and subject to his mother's very imperfect knowledge of Catholic education, John Acton grew up speaking both French and English, living apparently mainly at Aldenham, until it was decided to find a school for him.

In the first place it would appear that Lady Granville, as Lady Leveson would become in 1846, was only looking for what would in later times be called a preparatory school for her only son. She had, already, later plans for his further education.

Stonyhurst was at this date incontestably the first of the Catholic schools in England; but there is no evidence that Lady Granville was ever within the circle of the influence of the Society of Jesus. Her neighbours the Smythes of Acton Burnell were among the then small group of the old Catholic squirearchy who believed in a Benedictine education. Her brother-in-law Sir Robert Throckmorton and her other Catholic neighbour Lord Stafford both sent their sons to St Mary's, Oscott, under the control of the secular clergy. We are fortunate in having two advertisements which give

[1] *Notes from a Diary*, 1892–5, by Sir Mountstuart Grant Duff, ii, p. 124.
[2] *Correspondence*, introduction, p. ix.

B

an account of the scope of the curriculum at this establishment.

> The new College [begins one of these announcements] has been built expressly for its present purpose, in a most healthy and cheerful situation, and is provided with every thing requisite for a place of education. The system pursued in it embraces, besides the classical languages, French, Italian and German, which are taught to all who pursue the ordinary course of studies, Mathematics and Natural Philosophy, assisted by very complete apparatus, as well as History, Geography, Elocution and other branches of learning, becoming either a scholar or a gentleman.

A rather earlier notice[1] is very similar.

> The course of education comprehends every species of instruction which is necessary for those who are destined to independence, in or out of Parliament, for any of the learned professions or for business. Arrangements are in progress by which the students of this College will have the opportunity of obtaining degrees in Arts or Law, and the other advantages held out by the newly-created University of London . . . Students are admitted at any age from eight to fourteen.

The school at this time consisted of the sons of the landed gentry and medical practitioners of the Midland countryside reinforced by the prosperous middle class which was now developing in the London area. The new buildings not far from Birmingham had been completed by Pugin and the president of the college was Dr Wiseman, who combined this post with the coadjutorship of the Midland district. It is of course true that John Acton left his school when he was only halfway through his course. It is therefore not surprising that he made no permanent friendships with those who had been boys with him. There are few references to any of his tutors. The one marked exception was Bishop Wiseman.

This prelate was of Irish descent and Spanish upbringing; but Rome had laid her mark on him. He belonged essentially to the papal city of the days of Pope Gregory XVI. The best memorial is,

---

[1] This second notice appeared in *The Catholic Directory and Annual Register* for 1840, while the first notice came from the 1848 edition of the same publication.

perhaps, the Ushaw portrait which shows him tripping with contented dignity, a mitre on his head and his full cope billowing, nervous, assured and very sanguine. The boy Count of Torre Diaz holds up his train. A great dignified, rather disordered presence, he fostered projects of the widest scope. It is worth noting the comments that Acton made on him.

'We were proud of him,' wrote Lord Acton at the end of the century to Wilfrid Ward,[1] 'we were not afraid of him; he was approachable and generous and no great friend to discipline.' His was an intermittent but a lasting influence. 'He was,' declared one of his pupils, Canon Smith,[2] 'much away from the college visiting at great houses, Protestant and Catholic.' There was much in him to inspire a child of quick intelligence. 'He was looking far afield,' wrote Lord Acton,[3] 'and these other things were what characterized him. We used to see him with Lord Shrewsbury, with O'Connell, with Father Mathew, with a Mesopotamian patriarch, with Newman, with Pugin, and we had a feeling that Oscott, next to Pekin, was a centre of the world.' With the boys, too, Wiseman would shake off that sensitiveness veiled by a pompous manner which so much hampered him. His difficulties with his colleagues were concealed from the children and his sanguine plans enveloped them. 'How seldom,' says one of the Bishop's *memoranda*,[4] 'has a word been spoken which intimated that those who entered the college considered it as more than a mere place of boys' education, or [saw in it] a great engine employed in England's conversion and regeneration.'

Upstairs in his study on the first floor Dr Wiseman would sit tracing plans with his swift easy pen. Downstairs young John Acton wrote to his mother:[5] 'I have had a pound taken out of my dormitory so I have no money scarcely left.'

Yet the child was soon writing generously:[6] 'I am very happy here, and perfectly reconciled to the thoughts of stopping here some more years.' The strange adult vocabulary sounds unusual

---

[1] *Life and Times of Cardinal Wiseman*, by Wilfred Ward, i, p. 348.
[2] *Ibid.*, i, p. 350.
[3] *Ibid.*, i, p. 349.
[4] Memorandum printed in *ibid.* i, p. 448.
[5] *Correspondence*, vol. i, p. 1.
[6] *Ibid.*, i, p. 1.

in a boy of his age; a child fitted by his training to respond to the Bishop's panoramic visions.

It was during these years that the Oxford Movement was developing and that Newman made his submission. He and a number of his companions came to Old Oscott in the winter of 1845, and Acton, now twelve, duly noted their arrival:[1] 'There are so many new converts here that I do not know half their names.' Still, it was not these conversions that then or later seem to have appealed to him. It was rather Wiseman's encyclopaedic approach to history.

It is perhaps as well to indicate here how remote Acton was to remain from the impact of the Oxford Movement. He came from a world in which, until the Tractarian secessions, the notion of conversion was relatively unfamiliar. The changes of allegiance among the Acton-Dalberg circle were occasioned primarily by marriage. The brand of English Tory politics which so many of these new converts maintained would likewise be profoundly unappealing. The processes of conversion as such would always appear to him unsympathetic. It was history of a very different kind which brought out all his single-minded zeal.

With Wiseman's ultramontane views there also went an attitude to world history which could not fail to be encouraging to a developing mind like that of the young Acton, a mind awakened but of course uncritical. In Wiseman's view all history was a paean to the Church's progress. 'What struck me most,' wrote Lord Acton of the Bishop in later years,[2] 'was his extraordinary facility.'

Certainly no writer could marshal his facts more rapidly or with such an assiduous *empressement*. 'And he secured,' went on the historian in the same letter, 'a very great library – Marini's or Garampi's, I forget which – and sent for a monk of Monte Cassino, who pasted little coloured patches in the books and perhaps arranged them.' The grandeur of Wiseman's whole conception found a ready response in young John Acton. 'I am going,' he wrote, aged thirteen,[3] to his mother with that strange vocabu-

---

[1] *Ibid.*, i, p. 2.
[2] Letter quoted in Ward, *op. cit.*, i. pp. 352–3.
[3] *Correspondence*, p. 2.

lary which makes one ponder, 'to write a compendium of the chief facts, in history, for my own occasional reference.' The attractive taste for the construction of such a compendium is surely a major factor in the historian's development.

It has occurred to me that perhaps Acton's curious habit of calling on strange bishops and cross-examining them, which comes out clearly in his journey to the United States, may have arisen from Wiseman's kindness to the little boy. Two points, however, should be made about the statements that have been quoted. Without questioning their sincerity, they referred to happenings at least half a century earlier. May they not have been composed with care in view of the official character of the biography in which they are destined to appear? The other factor is this. These happy contacts all occurred when Acton was still under fourteen years of age.

A letter written by Wiseman some years later will explain how he dazzled the young Acton as well as how he failed to hold the adult Liberal. 'It,' he is referring to his novel *Fabiola*,[1] 'had one good effect. It is undoing some of the mediaeval frostwork which late years have deposited round English Catholic affections to the forgetfulness of Rome and its primeval glories.'

There appear to be no records or correspondence relating to the next phase of John Acton's education. At fourteen he went to live in Edinburgh under the private tuition of Mr Logan, formerly vice-president at his old school. Two years later in 1850 he was transferred to the care of Dr Döllinger in Munich.

[1] Ward, *op. cit.*, ii, p. 191.

3

Dr Döllinger

Dr Döllinger and his background were to leave an indelible impression on the future historian. At two o'clock in the afternoon came dinner and converse with Acton's new teacher. 'I see him then for the first time in the day.'[1] It is worth examining what the young Acton would find after his arrival in Munich, when he went down to the drawing-room, as it was called, in which Dr Döllinger and his guests always took their midday meal.

It was not a large room, but from the accounts which have remained to us it seems congested. There were vases of yellow wallflowers, if in season, a dark green velvet sofa in the style of Louis-Philippe, every available space crowded with pictures. Arranged between distant views of Rome and Paris was a lithograph of the members of the Frankfort Diet of 1848. Copies of the portraits of Bossuet and Fénelon from the old *Pinakothek* balanced each other and were flanked by a reproduction of Giotto's Dante. There was a head of Christ in oils.

The professor, sitting at the head of the table, had the water-carafe beside him. A preciseness of manner and of taste survived from the early days of Würzburg. Some of the older articles of furniture had come, like his cook, from his father's house. He was fifty-one years of age and very settled. We can picture that slender figure with the careful bearing, the wrinkled priestly face, the bony hands. Dr Döllinger had a distaste for beer unusual in a Bavarian, and he found the taking of tobacco painful. He would not permit it in his presence. In the evenings the water was replaced by a tall jug of lemonade. Items of autobiography fell from him. 'Perhaps if I had gone to Berlin and heard Savigny and Eichhorn I might not have forsaken the study of law.' He had a great

[1] *Correspondence*, p. 8.

feeling for painting, and especially for Van Eyck; he would consider the elements which charmed him in each composition.

In the big library, to which the young John Acton went to borrow books but did not sit, there were more pictures, including engravings of Raphael's portraits of Julius II and Leo X. There the boy could stand and marvel at the thirty penholders in their cardboard case, at the massive black inkstand and the sandbox.[1] In the late afternoon the professor would on occasion invite him as his companion on the daily walk to the *Englischer Garten*, past the ornamental water to the Chinese Tower. Döllinger had a townsman's love of birds and flowers and sunshine. This was how he envisaged Tegernsee and the repose of a Bavarian summer. Master and pupil would speak English when together. '*M. Döllinger*,' we read,[2] '*me plaît infiniment. Il a les connaissances les plus étendues dans l'histoire et la littérature de tous les pays et tous les temps.*' The next phrase is worth noting: '*Je ne sais pas s'il est fort dans les sciences physiques.*'

In such an atmosphere Acton grew to manhood, reading with that copious enthusiasm which never left him. He could not only borrow from the professor's own great store, but the whole of the Royal Library was open to him and he could borrow from that source twenty volumes at a time.[3] The other students in the house were often young men debarred by the then statutes from attending an English University. It may be hazarded that their principal gain from this sojourn in Munich was a knowledge of German. It would seem that neither Döllinger nor Acton had much in common with such co-religionists.

Dr Döllinger was a man of simple tastes and preconceptions and of a wide discursive scholarship. Nothing that came within the scope of literary history and mythology was remote from his concern. He had always a high grand simplicity, and the romantic mood of early nineteenth-century German writing had marked him deeply; his standards would remain those of the frugal contented *bourgeoisie* from which he sprang. In his father's house at

[1] All the details of the furnishing of the house come from Luise von Kobell's *Conversations of Dr Döllinger* (ed. 1892).

[2] *Correspondence*, p. 9.

[3] In a letter to Lady Granville from Munich dated '*le jeudi, 4 décembre*', Acton wrote '*je suis obligé d'avoir toujours une vingtaine de livres de la bibliothèque royale*', *ibid.* p. 10.

Würzburg, as the son of the professor of anatomy in that University, he had imbibed the political and social maxims which he never questioned.

The professor's attachment to the House of Bavaria was very strong and his links were perhaps closest with Maximilian II. He was royal chaplain to this sovereign and to his son. In a sedate fashion the Wittelsbachs would flatter him. It was the custom to ask him for explanations of the Scriptures. 'Louis II,' we are told,[1] 'seemed to be especially interested in passages of the Bible having reference to the Kingly office, and in portions of the Song of Solomon.' In spite of his enthusiasm for English customs, Döllinger was insistent that ministers should be responsible not to Parliament but to the Crown. Two expressions of opinion, which belong to a later stage of the professor's life, seem worth recording here for the bearing that they have upon his outlook. He is found speaking of General Gordon as a figure of heroic proportions. 'Second to none,' so runs the telling sentence,[2] 'in moral grandeur, and worthy to be placed by the side of Bismarck and of Moltke.' He had, too, his own romantic vision. 'Out of all the nations of the modern world, the German people, like the Greeks of old, have been called to an intellectual priesthood, and to this high vocation they have done no dishonour.'[3] It was always what he conceived of as the Germanic nations which appealed to Döllinger. 'Vanity,' he observed tartly,[4] 'is an accepted characteristic of the French.' In simplicity he would roll out his unflagging and long quotations from Shakespeare and Walter Scott, Goethe and Schiller.

Dr Döllinger had had his own connections with England. Dr Cox of St Edmund's College, Ware, had made a translation of his *Church History* and Dr Pusey had visited him in 1840 and again in 1844. There had also been a visit from James Hope, who at that time shared Pusey's doctrine. It is interesting to see Döllinger through the eyes of this young Tractarian. 'There is,' he wrote,[5] 'about him [Dr Döllinger] a simplicity of thought and manner

[1] *Conversations of Dr Döllinger*, p. 45.
[2] *Ibid.*, p. 172.
[3] *Ibid.*, p. 206.
[4] *Ibid.*, p. 121.
[5] *Memoir of J. H. Hope-Scott, Q.C.*, by Robert Ornsby, i, p. 237.

which is most agreeable and which suits well with his great learning.' In his talks with Dr Döllinger and his friend Dr Windischmann, James Hope was shrewd and the priests kindly. They said that most of the clergy have something of the Fathers upon their shelves.'[1] To the quick Scotsman, with his intimate knowledge of civil law, the professor stood out as most impressive. 'I am,' he wrote on a second visit,[2] 'more struck with him than ever.' Another comment is perhaps worth recording. 'Notanda,' so runs one of the headings in Hope's journal,[3] 'the R. Catholic Church is not in a very flourishing condition in Bavaria. There is, moreover, a great want of clergy, the profession not being popular, though chiefly supplied from the lower orders.'

John Acton's knowledge came from Döllinger as through a sieve. In this connection it is worth considering how far the schools of German scholarship affected the young historian's development. In the first place, his knowledge of German soon became perfect, and to his death he retained an ease with that language and a tendency to fall back upon a German idiom. At the same time, all such influences were for many years only to come to Acton through conversations with Döllinger and through the latter's comments on his reading. During the long period of his training the German writers in especial would thus reach John Acton at second hand. Their work had first to pass the filter of Döllinger's specialized consideration. But it is worth noting that this was to stand him in good stead with the academic scholarship of an English century which possessed a particular reverence for German thought.

Writing in later life, Lord Acton was to stress the profoundly ecclesiastical character of the professor's interests. 'In early life,' explained[4] Acton in that study of Döllinger's historical work which was the only completed chapter in the biography of his master that he projected, 'he had picked up chance copies of Baronius and Petavius, the pillars of historic theology: but the motives of his choice lay deeper. Church history had long been the weakest point and the cause of weakness among the Catholics, and it was the rising strength of the German Protestants.' In the same connection

[1] *Ibid.*, i, p. 235.
[2] Letter dated 9th September 1844, *ibid.*, ii, p. 50.
[3] *Ibid.*, i, p. 233.
[4] 'Döllinger's Historical Work', *Essays on Liberty*, p. 379.

B*

a litany of the old high names among ecclesiastical antiquarians will by itself suffice to show how far Döllinger's interests ever lay from that new German learning which was to exercise so deep an influence upon Great Britain. 'In this immense world of patient, accurate, devoted research,' wrote Acton[1] of the beginning of the professor's training, 'Döllinger laid the deep foundations of his historical knowledge. Beginning like everybody with Baronius and Muratori, he gave a large portion of his life to Noris, and to the solid and enlightened scholarship that surrounded Benedict XIV, down to the compilers, Borgia, Fantuzzi, Marini, with whom, in the evil days of regeneration by the French, the grand tradition died away. He has put on record his judgment that Orsi and Saccarelli were the best writers on the general history of the Church. Afterwards, when other layers had been superposed, and the course he took was his own, he relied much on the Canonists, Ballerini and Berardi; and he commended Bianchi, De Bennettis, and the author of the anonymous *Confutazione* . . .' The names roll on, an ordered sequence. The shadow of Trent lay on such studies.

Acton goes forward with this account of Döllinger.[2] 'Hegel remained, in his eyes, the strongest of all enemies of religion, the guide of Tübingen in its aberrations, the reasoner whose abstract dialectics made a generation of clever men incapable of facing facts.' Among his masters Döllinger included Leibnitz and Burke.[3]

Still, there was in Munich another influence parallel to that of Döllinger in the household of John Acton's cousin and her husband, the Count and Countess Arco-Valley. Before considering this influence which in its different fashion was to be life-long, it is worth examining the nature of attachment to Catholicism then prevalent in Bavaria, and also in the German Hapsburg lands, among the men of the upper classes. The Romantic school of which Döllinger was a part-inheritor, considered as operating within the Catholic culture and with Munich as its geographical centre, was active, self-laudatory, urban and *bourgeois*. Religion was strong among the peasantry in most regions of Bavaria and had its element of support in the *bourgeoisie* and among women

---

[1] *Ibid.*, p. 387.
[2] *Ibid.*, p. 381.
[3] *Ibid.*, p. 393.

everywhere. The position among men of inherited position was somewhat complex.

In their outlook on the Catholic Church various trends of South German opinion at this time, both among the aristocracy and that section of the *bourgeoisie* involved in Government, were still regalian, that is to say that they granted to the State a controlling power in all Church matters. Implicitly it was considered that the new realms of knowledge opened up since the *Encyclopédistes* would be worked by the secular administration. The State was seen as the regulator of the expanding universe. The rule of the Wittelsbachs had already lasted without interruption for six hundred years. Bavarian governmental circles thus conceived that their ancestral State-form could absorb such ideas as might spring up in the liberated centuries. The religious outlook of this class, or rather of these two cognate classes, was tired and somewhat formal, since it seems accurate to maintain that it was the exhaustion of the Counter-Reformation, which had given birth to the Josephist form of *Étatisme*. This last position was so important as a frame of mind that it requires some definition. The fact that Acton's own teachers were arrayed against it only serves to emphasize its wide subconscious hold upon the general mood. It was of course only the *detritus* of official Josephism that was now in question.

This point of view derives its name from the Emperor Joseph II, who was the first sovereign to apply its principles. It was practical rather than theoretic and was under one aspect a German or rather a Central European variant of Gallicanism. But Gallicanism was an earlier phenomenon and implied a very strong, if national, ecclesiastical organization over against the sovereign State with which it was bound up. In the Josephist period the emphasis was placed on that secular power which was seen as covering each useful activity and as the well-spring of all human philanthropy. Gallicanism had had great Churchmen, like Bossuet, as its protagonists. The Josephist prelates, on the other hand, were in general men of little character, nerveless and hesitant. Their role as *philosophes* sometimes implied an interest that was fresh and vital, but always kept quite distinct from their fatigued hereditary Churchmanship. The eighteenth-century Church seemed pale beside the virile monarchy.

The actual expression of the Josephist or Febronian theory, for it is known by both these names, dates from 1763. This was the year of the publication of *De statu praesenti Ecclesiae et legitima potestate romani pontificis*, a work written by the coadjutor of Trier and issued under the pseudonym of Justinus Febronius. Behind this mood there lay the fact of Jansenism considered not as a doctrine but as a temper of mind. It is perhaps this that accounts for that note of aridity which dominates all this thought and its many variants. Port-Royal des Champs, that convent which fulfilled the role of the cool fortress of Parisian Jansenism, had been a purely seventeenth-century phenomenon, beautiful, unorthodox, not lasting. There remained always the tendency to Pharisaic virtues. This last characteristic went easily with the approach of the *philosophes*, which involved a high-minded seriousness of purpose and a standard of strict, but not specifically Christian, morality. But this was an eighteenth-century emphasis; the agony of the long wars would soon expel it.

The character of Febronius' work, as a recast of the Jansenist regalian position dealing with the subject of practical reforms, derived its significance from the passages in which reliance was placed on the secular arm as a safeguard against 'exaggerated foreign doctrine'. A national feeling was gradually making headway and the patriot was seen as defending his nation inspired by the motives that were held appropriate to the Greek or Roman. The characteristic features of the world of the high Renaissance and its Baroque succession were now being stripped away. The cultural values of the Counter-Reformation, including the whole Catholic-European solidarity, were by this time felt as alien.

At the instance of the Bourbon Crowns, Pope Clement XIV had in 1773 suppressed the Society of Jesus by the brief *Dominus ac Redemptor*. This was an event which ushered in, or more accurately recorded, a profound change in the climate of the thought of Catholic Europe. On the side of religious education nothing had come to replace the Jesuit education of a Roman Catholic nobleman, which had had its heyday in the Hapsburg lands of the seventeenth century. Expressed devotion to Rome was closely bound up with the dead Society.

In what may be called the governing classes, throughout the

Wittelsbach and Hapsburg lands, sacramental life reached a low ebb. The rigorist Jansensist theories had in the first place discouraged approach to Communion save after a most searching preparation. In the now chilled atmosphere an emotional element in worship was doubly suspect. The Lutheran Pietism of an earlier time had fallen into clear discredit, and within the Catholic Church the reaction against Quietism had carried far. Among the men, within these groupings, the custom of religious practice could founder slowly. Catholicism was part of the furniture of a carefree and neglecting mind; it was in the climate of their long inheritance. This was the background of so many of John Acton's friends and relatives.

It is possible that some of these points are overstressed, for the high tide of Josephism was far away. We are on safer ground in dealing with the clergy. Those who came out from the seminary at Freiburg-im-Breisgau, even as late as 1840, supported Febronian ideas; it was such men who were for so long the chaplains in the schoolrooms of the princely families in Baden, Württemberg and Old Bavaria as well as in the Austrian provinces.

It is always difficult to place ideas in immediate opposition to one another, because so many movements imbibe elements from the thought of those to whom they are in rigid opposition. Thus at this date we can see that the Romantic school in so far as this centred upon Munich had its own regalian element. The shadow of Louis XIV of France fell, so to speak, on the just and on the unjust. King Louis I of Bavaria, who ruled from 1825 until 1848, was generous to the endowed Catholic body, but also to the Old Lutherans. He had a royal view of the privileges of his own family; his mind oscillated as to contacts with Rome and the value of sending students to the German College. He had a distaste for the Jesuits, now reconstituted, and disapproved of 'rigorist' confessors. In spite of all that has been written about Joseph II and successive Kings of Prussia, it was not those sovereigns only who deserved the title of *rois sacristains*.

There were other elements in Bavarian politics which carried implications distasteful to Acton, the future Liberal. The Abel Ministry represented a bureaucratic-professorial outlook grateful to the conservative mind of François Guizot. The *bürger* world, as

Acton was to find, was very loyal, but the old South German aristocracy looked tranquilly upon the Wittelsbachs. It was only a generation since the mediatized families had lost their status as rulers. In 1803 their little sovereignties had been engulfed by Württemberg, Bavaria or Baden. It was natural that they and their friends and cousinage should be a little guarded, a trifle distant and remote in their attitude towards these royal stocks.

In effect Bavaria had a profound influence on Acton's life. His mother had chosen for him Dr Döllinger as a tutor and priest-adviser. The time would come when Acton would no longer accept this guidance. There was present in Bavaria among his family connections and their friends an interest in Catholicism which was both faint and neglectful, a certain distaste for the Court of Rome and for the reigning Pontiff. He would in time be at home in Bavaria.

4

Attitude to Catholicism

It is difficult to trace the origins of Sir John Acton's approach to Catholic ecclesiastics. He was a lonely boy and asked his own odd questions. Did he ever discuss the matter with Dr Döllinger? It seems unlikely. The American journey is the first example of his sustained comment about the Catholic life of a foreign country. The entries here examined show quite clearly how he followed his own tastes; he was very solitary.

In Sir John Acton's case there is, perhaps inevitably, a certain contrast between his private comment and the public standpoint from which he would address his co-religionists. He was tolerant towards the ecclesiastics; they were a part of that great scheme of Catholicism on which all his beliefs were then bound up. In his early days he had a desire to call on Catholic bishops who were strangers to him, to hobnob with them and to cross-examine. Their prospects and their policies formed subjects of his conversation with his companions. This was an unusual pre-occupation for a young intellectual of just on twenty. The American Diaries throw a sharp light on this aspect of his approach.

Too much attention should not be paid to these entries for they are in the strict sense *juvenilia*. There is another point worth making. Some of the diarist's adjectives strike the ear curiously, especially when used in juxtaposition. It would seem likely that the years of French conversation with his mother, and still more the German conversations with Dr Döllinger, may have given him a certain insecurity in judging the meaning of the English adjective.

Whatever the view of his Protestant companions, Acton's interest in each facet of ecclesiastical life would have appeared as natural to Dr Wiseman. At the same time there is no doubt that the lack of respect in the approach would have seemed to him intolerable. The actual diary[1] records Acton's visit to the United States in 1853, when he was just nineteen. The occasion of this journey was the visit of Lord Ellesmere, a cousin of Acton's step-father Lord Granville, to the New York Exhibition. He seems to have accompanied the Ellesmeres as some form of *attaché*; they had sailed in the frigate *Leander* and the future historian had been accommodated in the gun-room. In a chronicle letter sent to Dr Döllinger he gives an account of the voyage out and his first impressions of the Ellesmeres. They had taken a month sailing westward through the summer weather and making a short stay at the Azores. He notes that he was only seasick for five days. 'From Lord Ellesmere's conversation,' he writes,[2] 'I have learned much, and I have learned to respect and like him very much. The girls were amiable and good-tempered. The eldest Alice [later Countess of Strafford] is very well read and fond of history. One of our games was to endeavour to discover some historical personage or event the others had thought of, and was to describe. I amused myself in describing St Dunstan, St Thomas, St Dominic, St Ignatius etc. to the horror of the company, tho' they are by no means offensively prejudiced, unless I except Lady Ellesmere.' The latter was a sister of Charles Greville and it is not difficult to imagine what that diarist would have thought of a young Englishman of position whose interests lay in the story of Italian and Spanish saints.

There now comes a sharp comment on the Royal Navy. 'I was particularly interested,' he continues,[3] 'in observing the working of the ship. I used to keep night-watches, gazing on the stars and phosphorescence of the ocean while five hundred men slept beneath the deck. I collected materials for a most severe judgment on the naval life. Tho' better than formerly, a ship seems full of drunkenness and shameful vice, and in war-time must be much worse. The officers were generally very pleasant.'

The next diary begins on 11 June 1853 when the ship had anchored off Staten Island. Franklin Pierce had been recently

---

[1] 'Lord Acton's American Diaries', printed in *Fortnightly Review*, 1921, p. 742.
[2] *Ignaz von Döllinger-Lord Acton, Briefwechsel, Erster Band* 1850–1869, ed. Victor Conzemius, pp. 25–6. This standpoint did not endure.
[3] *Ibid.*, p. 26.

elected as fourteenth President of the United States. The Gold Rush to California was just four years old and this was the time of growth of the Free Soil party, the group of those who wished to keep the new States free from slaves. Everywhere Acton made or attempted to make contact with the Catholic bishops.[1] 'I went,' he wrote[2] at New York, 'to call on the Archbishop, who was out of town for some time. The chief of our churches is near his house. It has much less pretensions than the Jesuits' church in Farm Street. A fine cathedral is in process of construction.' At Albany he called on Bishop McCloskey, who was likewise absent from home.

He was more fortunate at Boston. The Catholics in that diocese then numbered about 70,000, composed almost entirely of immigrants from Ireland. He secured an interview with Bishop Fitzpatrick[3] through an introduction from Orestes Brownson.[4] The account is rather dull, but it shows at least the point of view from which Acton started.

On Friday morning at nine [he wrote][5] I went to the bishop's. He is a fine looking man, not particularly pleasant,[6] but I was told that this was accidental and not usually the case. He talked much of Brownson, of the Irish, and of American public men. He holds Mr Laurence very cheap and ridicules Ticknor[7] and his coterie. In spite of what was formal or distant in his manner, I found him a real specimen of a kind of man whose existence I have always been inclined to doubt who, without mingling in public life or gaining literary reputations, possesses greater abilities and wisdom than those who do. . . . I suppose he has made good studies, but he is not a great theologian. Yet he knows a great deal; and judges events with great sagacity.

[1] Two references in the same letter to Döllinger indicate Acton's then point of view. 'I went up the splendid Hudson . . . hoping to see the Bishop of Albany, as I thirsted after a Catholic prelate' and 'at Emmitsburg, our great college in this country, I shall see plenty of ecclesiastics'. *Acton-Döllinger Correspondence*, ed. Victor Conzemius, pp. 27 and 31.

[2] 'Lord Acton's American Diaries', p. 737.

[3] John Bernard Fitzpatrick (1814–1866), third Bishop of Boston, 1846.

[4] Orestes Augustus Brownson (1803–1876), a Congregationalist by origin and then a Unitarian minister who submitted to Rome in 1844. From that year until 1865 he edited *Brownson's Quarterly Review*.

[5] *Diaries*, p. 70.

[6] By 'pleasant' Acton apparently means 'pleasant mannered'.

[7] George Ticknor (1791–1871), Smith Professor at Harvard, author of a *History of Spanish Literature*.

Throughout this passage there is an echo of the place which Cardinal Wiseman held in Acton's young esteem.

His judgments [he explains[1] in a further comment on the Bishop of Boston] are by no means wanting in severity. I perceive that he is not ready to approve Cardinal Wiseman's conduct. Neither is Brownson, though he does not like to say so. Archbishop Hughes (of New York), on the contrary, fully agrees with the Cardinal. Dr Fitzpatrick thoroughly approves Brownson. I spent an hour with him and he was called out at least twenty times by poor people who wished to see him. This goes on all day; he cannot shut his door. He is not such a good man of business as Dr Hughes. Perhaps he is wanting in energy.

The same diary contains an impression of Acton's dealings with his Protestant fellow travellers, who ventured to comment on the Catholic Faith.

I made also [he notes[2] at this time] Mr Clough's[3] acquaintance. He studied under Arnold and became a fellow of Oriel. He knew several of my acquaintance. He was Mr Bastard's tutor. He left Oxford about some religious difficulty, and has been in America about eight months. He writes for the *North American Review*. He passes for a good classical scholar. He said something about Catholicity which induced me to floor him about the Byzantine writers with Lasaulx's story of the Palladium in the vault at Constantinople. When I spoke of the passages proving this story, another convive said the passage he wanted was that into the vault. This was James Russell Lowell.[4]

Brownson had a great effect on the young man.

I therefore [he wrote[5] in the account of his visit to him] went to Chelsea, through the old part of the town (of Boston) and across the ferry. Elm Street is some distance off. I found Brownson a very different kind of man to what I had expected; he received me very well. I will put off describing him to a later

[1] *Diaries*, pp. 70–1.
[2] *Ibid.*, p. 72.
[3] Arthur Hugh Clough (1819–1861) returned to England in July 1853.
[4] James Russell Lowell (1819–1891), minister in London 1877–85, had published the *Biglow Papers* in 1848.
[5] *Diary*, pp. 66–7.

period of our acquaintance. . . . We spoke of his attack upon Newman. The book on development[1] was thought dangerous here for reasons connected with the characters of the clergy in the country, which were not felt in England. He was requested to refute it, but refused at first out of respect for Newman. At length the book began to do harm. It was taken up by the enemies of the Church. A New York paper printed parallel passages from it and Gibbon, and Newman's were found to be the worst.

This last statement is an example of the type of judgment which Acton from time to time recorded. His thought went forward in his private mind. It does not seem to have occurred to him how deeply he would wound the Oratorian, who was still a stranger to him.

Brownson went on to explain how his reluctance had been over-borne by Bishop Fitzpatrick.[2] They then went on to praise to-gether[3] Lady Georgiana Fullerton's novel *Grantly Manor*. At this date Acton was still affected by those pervasive Catholic influences which came to him through his mother's friendships and which, after her death, he would reject decisively. Lady Georgiana, even more than Mrs Craven, would have approved this search for bishops which is likely to have appeared to the Ellesmeres as a strange pastime.

There is another aspect of this journey which is worth noting. The self-contained young man held quite aloof from both his patrons. Lord Ellesmere was a nobleman of immense wealth and with a generalized good will in the Whig manner. Charles Greville wrote a character of him which shows how far away he was from his young *protégé*. He had inherited £90,000 a year from the Bridgewater properties. He had served as president of the British Association and the Royal Asiatic Society. 'Churches,[4] schools

---

[1] Newman's *An Essay on the Development of Christian Doctrine*, 1845.

[2] In this connection a passage in the *Diary* is revealing. 'He [Brownson] gave me a letter for the Bishop of Boston, who, he said, is the most intellectual bishop in the United States, and to whom he owes more than to any one as to advice concerning his *Review*. From the time that he saw my card he was anxious to know whether I was a relation of Cardinal Acton's. Indeed, that relationship is my passport with all the clergy here,' *Diaries*, p. 68.

[3] Cf. *ibid*, p. 67.

[4] *The Greville Memoirs*, ed. Roger Fulford, vol. vii, p. 270.

and reading-rooms rose around Worsley Hall. His benevolent efforts were crowned with success and he reaped his reward in the Blessings of the surrounding multitudes.' He was an author, and among his books and plays were a drama *Wallenstein's Camp* and *Bluebeard*, a tragedy. This very British literary world was far from John Acton's own concerns. The latter's attitude to the Ellesmeres seems to have become noticeably cool;[1] it is doubtful if he had really much in common with any of the Leveson-Gowers.

Among the unpublished material at Downside Abbey, which Gasquet used as the basis for his book *Lord Acton and his Circle*, there are letters of a slightly later date which show Acton's mind running on ecclesiastical appointments and movements. 'Why,' he wrote[2] in 1858, 'is H[is] E[minence] gone to Belgium? and will Cullen[3] be another Cardinal? He is of the wood out of which they make them.' By this time Acton had already professed to move away from the main contemporary categories. 'A Gallican,' he noted[4] on 4 July 1858, 'which is as bad, I think, as an Ultramontane. . . . In Theology, not of course in practice, Gallicanism as well as Ultramontanism seem to me the productions of an imperfect state of learning impossible nowadays to men who are up to the mark.'

His boyhood and youth were now behind him and we reach the comments which John Acton made as an adult. It is remarkable that, in so far as these relate to persons, there is hardly any change from the tone of his Diary in America. This was partly because, apart from the influence of Richard Simpson, which will be considered presently, he was still working at this time in solitude. Nothing in fact so much suggests the solitary character of his intellectual life as the correspondence which he was soon to begin with Dr Newman. It seems best at this stage to print an analysis of the Catholic position which he gave to Simpson some four years later. It has the advantage of setting Acton's ideas within a frame. It shows how he was beginning to see the parties.

---

[1] 'Lady E. was rather offended at his [the British Minister in Washington] not doing more in their honour,' *Diaries*, p. 738.

[2] 'Gasquet and the Acton-Simpson Correspondence', by A. Watkin and the Editor, printed in 1950 in *The Cambridge Historical Journal*, vol. x, p. 88.

[3] Paul Cullen, Archbishop of Dublin.

[4] *CHJ*, p. 81.

I believe[1] you will find only three parties. 1.° The old school, not warmed up by the C[ardinal] into devotion to Rome, and not intellectual or progressive – descendants of Milner, Lingard, and even Butler, so far as they all refuse, like Chaos, to be converted. Their strength is in the north and in the midland counties. 2.° Ourselves. 3.° The zealous converts and those of the old set who are under [the] C[ardinal]'s influence, the Romanists, lovers of authority, fearing knowledge much, progress more, freedom most, and essentially unhistoric and unscientific. But the elements are very various and the leaven of different sorts.

And then he enters, as he was so fond of doing, into an analysis and enlargement of his first section.

Ad 1.um The very old school of Berington, the 'Staffordshire clergy', long ago vanished. Something of its spirit survived in the Butlerites, who were simply Gallicans and lovers of lay influence. Milner had almost succeeded in prevailing over these tendencies before Emancipation. The idea of the liberty of the *Church* was his, as distinguished from the liberty of *Catholics*, which they all desired. Liberty of the Church in the State involves authority of the Church in her own sphere – all liberty means the free exercise of authority in whatever is its right sphere. This separates Milner from Butler, etc., who disliked the hierarchical system almost as much as the penal laws. To the Milnerite Catholics, pricked up by agitation and emancipation enter (with a flourish of trumpets) Dr Wiseman, cetera.

This at any rate sets out the background as Acton saw it.

The attitude of profound concern for the Catholic structure was bound up with Acton's training and with the long and deep effect of Dr Döllinger. It was a preoccupation which would separate him as much from Granville as from the world of English scholarship. It was in part strengthened by all that he gave in these years to Catholic journalism and to the reviews of his own Communion. In later life he would think back to these old days. An instance occurs in a discussion of *John Inglesant*.[2] 'Of the instances suggested', he explained,[3] 'one, the Cultus of the Blessed Virgin, was

---

[1] Letter dated by Simpson 6 October 1862, *ibid.*, p. 95.
[2] Cf. Pt. Three, ch. 3, pp. 252–3.
[3] *Letters of Lord Acton to Mary Gladstone*, ed. Herbert Paul, p. 132.

partly of later growth and would not seriously disturb a contemporary of Charles the First. It does not offend in the older,
classical literature of the Church, in the Imitation, the Exposition,
the *Pensées*, or the *Petit Carême*. Sixty years ago [he wrote in 1882]
a priest who is still living was sent as chaplain to Alton Towers.
At Evening Prayers, when he began the Litany of Loretto,[1] Lord
Shrewsbury rose from his knees and told him that they never
recited it.'

It is natural that references to the sacramental life, to confessors
and to the reception of Communion, should be sparse in Acton's
life. As far as confessors are concerned, Döllinger, in a letter
written[2] to Lady Granville on 12 August 1850, refers to the only
one of the Munich period whose name has come down to us, Dr
Friedrich Windischmann, the vicar general of the archdiocese of
Munich. 'Tomorrow,' he explains, 'I believe Sir John [Acton] is
to go to confession: I have chosen for him the best confessor, who
is to be found here, the same who has the confidence of the Arco
family. I am perfectly aware that the views and projects I have
mentioned [in regard to John Acton's education] are only
secondary in comparison to the one thing needful, which is to preserve that innocence and moral purity, with which I trust he has
come to Munich.' Acton was then sixteen years of age and in many
ways a late developer.

A small mosaic of quotations will give a further note of Acton's
attitude throughout the years of youth and early manhood. It has
this significance that John Acton was then using those expressions
and that point of view that he still shared with all his English co-
religionists. He describes[3] Mohler's *Symbolik* as '*wonderschön und
Catholisch*'. He questions[4] Lord Elgin about the Catholics in
Canada. The Catholic Poor Schools Commission of the Shrewsbury diocese brings him into contact with Sir Pyers Mostyn. He
goes to the committee set up to aid Catholic ex-prisoners. Some
time later he mentions[5] in a letter to Döllinger the conversions of

---

[1] This should have been Loreto. It was not a word that Acton often used.
[2] *Acton-Döllinger Correspondence*, p. 5.
[3] Letter dated 6 May 1855, *ibid.*, p. 71.
[4] Same letter, *ibid.*, p. 69.
[5] Letter dated 5 March 1863, *ibid.*, p. 296.

Lady Herbert of Lea and Lady Londonderry. He refers[1] to the religious approach of Cavour's elder brother '*ein guter Catholik*'.

In fact, as long as he remained working at explicitly Catholic journalism, he retained much of the standpoint and many of the ideas of the English Catholic community. What came to separate him from this grouping, apart from the religious changes which were to come, was partly the links that he formed with Hawarden and the whole atmosphere of Gladstone's household and, perhaps even more, his absorption in the Continental life which was bound up with the Arco-Valley family.

[1] Letter dated 30 June 1863, *ibid.*, p. 316.

5

Granville and Newman

Two experiences, the journey to Moscow in 1855 and the beginning of the transitory influence of Dr Newman, had a measurable effect on Acton. As far as the Russian journey is concerned, when I began to study Acton's life I feel that I attributed too much consequence to this brief episode. On the one hand it certainly represented the highwater mark of Lord Granville's influence. At the same time John Acton as a boy of twenty-one must have had but little contact with his stepfather upon this journey. Granville, then Lord President of the Council, was going at the head of an elaborate complimentary mission to the coronation of the Tsar Alexander II. A mass of honorary attachés, all necessarily his seniors, separated the young John Acton from the ambassador. The visit lasted for the months of August and September 1855. Throughout there were also present Lord Kimberley and the regular staff of the British Embassy whose work was separate. The journey was honorific and its consequences negligible.

I do not now believe that Granville had much influence on his stepson. He was at this time just forty; but he had been formed on one pattern of an earlier Whig generation. It was a consequence that Acton's young seriousness was outraged at almost every turn. In the first place there was an air of levity about the ambassador's approach which could not fail to exacerbate. Never very far away from all that he said and did lay an equable and kindly cynicism which would recall the eighteenth century. He mocked playfully at his posts in politics – never, of course at his place in English life. 'The house beautiful, the China of the softest paste, the wine excellent, the Lord President,' Granville wrote[1] of himself, 'rather drunk.' Beyond the Rhine, in Döllinger's circle with its gentle fun,

---

[1] Letter dated 28 November 1855, printed in *Life of the Second Earl Granville*, i, p. 128.

they would not understand that indolent and barbed self-mockery.

Unfortunately the opinion which he held of foreigners in general was not a high one. And then he had a frivolous literary taste which it must have been hard for Acton to condone. Not only did he find a Life of the Duchess of Chevreuse, 'very amusing,' Lord Granville[1] also thought Macaulay 'charming reading'; but such comment was *de rigueur* with Acton's school of thought. At Mr Gladstone he was inclined to mock. 'He is devoted[2] to Homer. He is going to *réhabiliter* Helen, whom he has found to be a much injured woman.' This was the vein of humour of a less serious period. There was a Corinthian element in Lord Granville's leisure. He would ride to view his farm at Golder's Green and enjoyed robust amusements. On the other hand, his attitude to the world of fashion was irksome in its half-charmed lightness. 'Coventry House,' he would exclaim[3] in the days of the coming of the crinoline, 'too gay and pretty. The society the refined essence of cream, with a beautiful buffet laid out. Some of the women could hardly get into the doorways.' There was almost too much sunshine in the life of 'Pussy' Granville.

There was present throughout a certain strain of French influence from which the old Whig circle would never really free itself. Inevitably this entailed a lack of interest in the German world into which Acton and the Liberals were bound to plunge. 'I have been reading to Marie,' Granville explained,[4] 'the Duc de Broglie's speech on his reception at the Academy. It is clever, as only a French speech is when spoken by a gentleman and a master of that extraordinary language for conveying shades of opinion.' Lord Granville's French was singularly perfect with certain echoes of the language of the *Ancien Régime*.

Although surrounded by immensely wealthy relatives, the Dukes of Sutherland and Devonshire as well as Lord Ellesmere, Granville was himself a man of moderate fortune. His father had died leaving £150,000 and there was a certain amount of land at

---

[1] Letter dated 9 December 1855, in the Granville-Canning correspondence, *ibid.*, i, p. 129.

[2] Letter in the same correspondence, *ibid.*, i, p. 135.

[3] *Ibid.*, i, p. 179.

[4] *Ibid.*, i, p. 176.

Stone in Staffordshire; there does not seem to have been a house. The lackadaisical quality, so notable in his public life, is seen reflected in his attitude towards money. In the great Whig houses at Trentham or Chatsworth he was only a visitor. It is not surprising that his stepson struck no roots in that philistine high Whig society.

Granville had come into the Cabinet very early under Lord Melbourne's aegis. He had begun, together with Lord John Russell, as a representative of the great Whig house. He was now leader of the Government in the House of Lords. He was in the easy prime of his career, a little troubled by the gout and needing Vichy water. Such was the background to the Moscow mission.

Correspondence between Lord Granville and Lord Canning well conveys the substance of the special envoys talks with Gortchakoff and the effect produced by audiences with the new Tsar. The Crimean War was barely over and the Russian complaint and *innuendo* would be countered by dignified rebuttal intended to be tranquillizing. This form of careful amelioration of relations between the Tsar and the imperial ministers on the one hand and the Court of St James's on the other was what Lord Granville practised and John Acton understood. It was part of the latter's background, an uninteresting heritage.

There was nothing in common between Lord Granville and Professor Döllinger. Acton's stepfather possessed that lighthearted approach which was intimately chilling to the serious student. Far removed from the fashionable young men of the ambassador's entourage, there was nothing in that set-up which might soothe the historian's immature and nettled pride. It was not the members of the English mission who, to quote the article in the *Edinburgh Review*,[1] were astonished by 'the vastness of his knowledge and his mode of exposition'. Acton was twenty-two and already so learned; around him his compatriots laid their bets.

There is little evidence that John Acton ever became deeply interested in Russia; it was a country with whose language he did not become familiar. It would seem that his keen interest was limited to the political development of that great empire and her

---

[1] *Edinburgh Review*, No. 404, p. 502.

relations with the German lands. Throughout his life he could grasp swiftly the type of contact that is formed on the level of the landed or bureaucratic ruling class. He never showed concern with the Russian Orthodox Church, neither in its history nor its institutions. This probably was caused by the linguistic barrier. It does not seem that his journey had great importance.

After his return from Munich one side of Acton's life was dominated by his long and unsatisfactory contact with John Henry Newman. It is important not to exaggerate the significance of this association. The two men were brought together by the accident of Newman's establishment at Birmingham surrounded by his group of followers. Acton, with his largely foreign background, was one of the most unusual phenomena which Newman found in the Communion he had joined. There seems reason to suppose that any alliance between these men was doomed to failure from the start; and it seems clear that their relationship was fundamentally unstable, and that during the sixteen fretting years of its continuance, it never achieved a genuine mutual confidence. Newman, with his delicate and sensitive approaches, was already gathering to himself the new disciples of his Catholic period. That affectionate bond, with its understood and careful intimacies, was one in which Acton could never be included. He kept his personal reverence for men very different from Dr Newman, and was wholly uninterested in what Oxford had meant to the quiet and tentative and sweeping mind of the Oratorian. A cast of mind as positive as Acton's must have remained alike unaffected by Newman's very English sentiment and his self-raillery.

The relations between them, carried on at first only by letter, had a comparatively auspicious opening. This was in 1854, when Newman was fifty-three and Acton twenty; the first year of the former's Irish journey and of his rectorship of the Dublin Catholic University. The proposal that he first put before John Acton was clearly a routine suggestion, brought forward as a consequence of the meticulous sense of duty which oppressed him. 'I now write,' began[1] Newman, 'to ask you [Sir John Acton] to

[1] Letter dated 5 June 1854, preserved in the Newman Correspondence, Acton volume, f. i. in the Birmingham Oratory MSS.

let me put down your name in the University Books. This involves nothing more except your goodwill to an institution which the Church has sanctioned . . . I also wish to be allowed to enter on the books the names of Dr Döllinger, Dr Windschman (I know I do not spell his name rightly) and Dr Phillips; and should be much obliged if you would[1] obtain them for me. Mr Hope Scott and Mr Baddeley in London are going to send me a number of London names, such as Lord Arundel and Surrey etc. etc.'

In reply Acton wrote back conveying his own and Dr Windischmann's satisfaction, and there began a desultory correspondence. In the summer of 1858 Dr Döllinger came to Aldenham and was brought to the Oratory[2] by his host, and in the same year there commenced those negotiations concerning the *Dublin Review* and the *Rambler* which have been described at length in Cardinal Gasquet's book, *Lord Acton and his Circle*.

From this long story, very tedious to unravel, certain facts emerge with crystal clearness. Few men can have been less at home with the leaders of the Oxford Movement than was John Acton. The converts had now been established in their new Communion for several years, and he had been too young to witness the circumstances of their arrival. Already his attitude towards certain authorities of his own Church was sharply critical. Very shy, but apparently never touchy, Acton held to a standpoint grounded on a profound submerged assurance and fortified by a reasoned belief in the coming victory of Liberal principles. Still very young, Sir John Acton required only one thing from his co-religionists, that most depressing of instruments, a *platform*.

The idea of using the *Dublin Review* for such a purpose had been mooted, and he put this before Newman. 'I have,' he wrote[3] from Aldenham on 5 July 1858, 'just been informed that a circular has appeared announcing that the *Dublin Review* is given up, and I am asked whether I would take it in hand myself. I do not entirely reject the idea because I think that it would be a pity that it should cease to appear, or that it should pass into the hands of

---

[1] This letter is torn at the edge, but the word in question appears to have been 'would'.

[2] Three letters among the Birmingham Oratory MSS deal with Döllinger's visit to the Oratory and a proposed visit by Newman to Aldenham, which did not materialize.

[3] Letter from Sir John Acton to Dr Newman, *ibid.*

unsatisfactory persons.' Newman replied dissuading him, but Acton on the contrary set out three arguments. 'I have often heard,' he wrote, 'that the *Dublin Review* advanced money to the Cardinal, and that expenses of this kind outweighed the advantage derived from his very uncertain and unequal contributions. Again, the adulatory and undignified tone of the Review has alienated a good many subscribers. The literary wants of our Catholic public are unfortunately easily satisfied.'

This was not the tone which might serve to reassure the Oratorian. In other quarters, too, Sir John Acton's concern for the presentation of Catholic thought could only receive a scant appreciation. 'I never converse,' he wrote[1] at this time, 'with any even of the best and cleverest converts, Dalgairns, Morris, Mc-Mullen, Oakeley, Allies, Marshall, Wilberforce, etc., without finding them stating what I hold to be most false. It is just the mistakes of these, our best men, that it will be best worth while to discuss.'

Acton could hardly realize what it involved in a relatively small but hierarchic body to have Fr Dalgairns and Canons Oakeley and McMullen, Mr Allies and Mr Marshall and even the gentle Henry Wilberforce aligned against him. It was a sad presage of the future that he should add: 'I cannot look for sympathy with my ideas in any considerable body of men. Hope and Manning are the only ones that I feel likely on most occasions to agree with.' If this was the situation, it becomes natural to enquire to whom Acton could look as his supporter. Very soon it becomes clear that this support was offered generously by Richard Simpson.

It is not easy to obtain a clear impression of Simpson. He was at this time forty years of age and had entered the Catholic Church in 1845. He came of a middle-class family of ample means. His father is described in the Oriel entrance register as William Simpson of Wallington, Surrey, Armiger. The elder Simpson held the advowson of the valuable living of Mitcham, to which his son was presented on ordination. After his conversion Richard Simpson had spent some years abroad. He had a certain private income;

---

[1] Letter from Acton to Simpson dated Aldenham Park 28 February 1858, printed in Gasquet, *Lord Acton and his Circle*, pp. 8–9.

Acton at one point refers to his house property. He lived modestly at 4 Victoria Road, Clapham. Acton hardly seems to have visited his family; there are very few references to his wife. He had a talent for foreign languages and worked regularly in the State Paper Office. His principal book was his biography of Edmund Campion, which was published in 1867. One gains the impression of a rather lonely life, perhaps lightened by a vigorous sympathy for Acton's Liberalism.

The only letter from Simpson, now in the Downside collection, is a draft letter to a bishop dated 23 April 1862 and beginning 'my dear Lord'. The opening sentence is much in character, 'Brought up as I was, I have no other resource but literature.' His significance in Acton's life lies in the fact that during these years he seems to have been the one Englishman to whom he wrote freely, quite heedlessly in fact.

Judging by the nature of the correspondence Simpson seems to have kept everything that Acton wrote to him. On his death these papers passed to his own family and at a much later date were handed over to Abbot Gasquet. They form the basis of *Lord Acton and his Circle*. The letters were not printed in full and the explanation is given in detail by Dom Aelred Watkin and Professor Butterfield in an article[1] printed in 1950 in *The Cambridge Historical Journal*. At the time of Abbot Gasquet's publication it was only forty years since the letters had been written and Mr T. F. Wetherall was still alive. The omitted passages were not of great importance; but their freedom of expression reveals Acton as a much more cheerful and lighthearted character, fond of jokes and nicknames, schoolboyish in some ways.

In his reference to the Catholic bishops Acton was most unburdened. It is to be remembered that he knew that Simpson, for his own reasons, did not like them. The first letter dated 19 June 1860 refers to the quarrel between Cardinal Wiseman and Dr Errington, his coadjutor, and to the Duke of Norfolk's cousin, Henry Howard. 'It's all up with the Cardinal. Manning writes that his resignation [of spirit] is admirable. Very different then from Errington. Howard is monsignoring it about the town re-

---

[1] 'Gasquet and the Acton-Simpson Correspondence', *The Cambridge Historical Journal*, vol. x, pp. 75–105.

splendent.' This was the beginning of the Cardinal's illness, which would end with his death some five years later. 'I wonder,' he wrote later of the Bishops of Newport and Shrewsbury, 'how the two Browns did at Sedgeley (Park) and whether they were done.' And again, 'Old Waterworks, a devoted friend and admirer, but in fear of bishops, told me in all secrecy that Newport was overcome by our last number.' There is a comment on Dr Grant. 'He [the Bishop of Southwark] is at the same time a holy man, and a weak man.' His note on Cardinal Pitra has more tartness. 'Pitra's elevation is really creditable, for he is as learned as so great a goose can be.'

In one comment Acton clearly misses his mark. It is in a post-script to a letter dated 6 March 1860. 'I wrote to Ullathorne [Bishop of Birmingham] pointing out eight mistakes in his speech, and got a very friendly and handsome letter of thanks saying that my corrections came just in time for the expensive edition – being the only one that Protestants are likely to see. If he is found out saying one thing to the poor Irish and another to the mixed public he will be in a famous scrape.' (Gasquet has omitted the final sentence.) It is worth noting that in these years Acton did not feel himself cut off from the Catholic bishops, even from Ullathorne. For in a letter written on 29 March 1862 he mentions that he is trying to get his German protégé, Dr Helferstein, a berth at Oscott.

The *Rambler*, which brought Simpson into Acton's life, had begun as a weekly in 1848 under the proprietorship and editorship of Mr Capes, a Balliol convert. Simpson, who had been assistant editor since 1856, accepted the editorship two years later. After difficulties with the ecclesiastical authorities, it was undertaken by Dr Newman in 1859. In September of that year he, too, resigned after he had produced two numbers, and Acton came upon the scene as editor. He had been interested for eighteen months previously and was now co-proprietor with Capes and Simpson. The *Dublin Review* throughout this period was in close touch with the episcopate.

In April 1862 it was determined to change the *Rambler*, which appeared bi-monthly, into a quarterly review. The *Home and Foreign Review*, as this was called, reflected the increasing seriousness of Acton's outlook. In a later section of this study specimens of his writing in both these periodicals will be considered. After eight numbers Acton decided that the *Home and Foreign Review* should cease publication with the issue of April 1864. He had come to the end of his difficult course as a Catholic journalist.

6

The Chaplain at Aldenham

A certain light is thrown on Acton's religious outlook by an account of his dealings with the chaplains who served Aldenham between his coming of age and the final closing of the chapel. During the eighteenth century such chaplaincies, which were then at the hub of Catholic life, had been for the most part served either by the Religious Orders or by some relative or dependant of the squire's family. With the development of the big industrial populations, it became harder to obtain suitable priests for work of such restricted scope. There were certain exceptional cases like Wardour Castle, where the Jesuits had agreed to make a permanent provision. Aldenham, however, normally depended on the priests available in that section of the old Midland district.

At this time the Aldenham appointment had a quite special significance. Lord and Lady Granville had now retired to London and the priest chosen would be the daily companion of the young baronet, who lived at Aldenham when in the country. It would, therefore, appear that the Bishop of Shrewsbury had allowed Acton to make his own suggestion.

Sir John Acton's first appointment seemed almost too good to be true. The priest chosen was of the highest standing and had gained his new patron's sympathy when teaching him for a few months during his schooldays at Oscott.[1] The Very Reverend John Brande Morris was at this time forty-three years of age and had recently been installed as a Canon of Plymouth, when the new chapter had been erected.

During the past three years he had acted as chaplain to Edmund Rodney Pollexfen Bastard Esq., of Kitley and Ashburton Court in

---

[1] In an undated letter addressed from Oscott to Lady Granville John Acton wrote, '*On commence à bruiter que dans les changements qui vont avoir lieu M. Whitehouse va redevenir professeur ici, et que notre maître, Mr Morris ne nous enseignera plus; nous le regretterons beaucoup comme maître*', Lord Acton's Correspondence, ed. Figgis and Laurence, p. 4.

the county of Devon, a wealthy and extravagant young landowner who had recently submitted to the Roman Obedience. Canon Morris had been an undergraduate at Balliol with Frederick William Faber, who remained until death his closest friend. His career had had a distinguished opening and he had held the posts of Petrean Fellow of Exeter College, Lecturer in Syriac in the University and assistant to Dr Pusey in the chair of Hebrew. He had been received with cordiality and respect by the senior Catholic clergy of the West Country. 'We hailed him,' wrote Canon Oliver,[1] 'an ornament and luminary of our body.' Before he followed Faber to Rome he had been a member of Mark Pattison's then circle. In 1843 he had received an award from the Bishop of Calcutta for the best method of proving the truth of Christianity to the Hindus.

On the other hand as against these advantages he was touchy and impecunious, and engaged at the moment in attempting to raise a loan from James Hope-Scott.[2] His life was starred with quarrels. He had left Kitley as the result of a complicated series of disputes. 'Matters did not run', explains Canon Oliver in his courtly way,[3] 'so comfortably and smoothly for him at Yealmpton (near Plymouth) as we could have wished.' His principal enemy there was a Mrs Orleans,[4] presumably the housekeeper. He had offered himself to other patrons, to Mr Murray at Danesfield and to Colonel Leslie of Fetternear, an aged Catholic roué. Father Faber, who has left so many letters addressed to Morris, has a characterization of him. 'Voluntas Dei,' he wrote,[5] 'You rascal! Do you think yr. sunshiny old phiz, & yr. eternal laugh can be in anybody's way.' A 'sunshiny old phiz' was not an object that was likely to make much appeal to Sir John Acton.

[1] *Collections illustrating the history of the Catholic Religion*, by George Oliver, D.D., 1857, p. 357.

[2] Cf. Letter from Faber to Morris dated at St Mary's, Sydenham, Christmas Eve (1855?), 'I am sorry to hear of the money affair. All the people I know are fairly cleaned out. Ld. A[rundel], Ward & all. But you know Hope-Scott well: wd. he do nothing? I wish to goodness the matter was off yr. mind', London Oratory MSS, vol. 17, f. 180.

[3] *Collections*, by George Oliver, p. 358.

[4] Cf. Letter from Faber to Morris, undated. 'Dearest Old Jack, You shall have a lot of Aves. How come you to be at Lyneham – are you turned out of Kitley by Mrs Orleans', London Oratory MSS, vol. 17, f. 181.

[5] From the same to the same from St Wilfrid's, 4 June 1847, *ibid.*, f. 114.

Faber at that date had no especial reason to be reserved with Sir John, but his instinct was already to be wary and he knew that Morris's departure from his diocesan Dr Errington had been stormy. 'I am,' he wrote in a note which throws a vivid light on the arrival of the new chaplain at Aldenham,[1] 'nonplussed about you. I did not understand the Bishop of Plymouth's letter to you as you did. It seemed to me nothing beyond an expression of kindness and regret. On the whole I *incline* to silence.' He then turned to his friend's own position. 'Would not Sir J. do up a priest's house for any one? & must not the chapel be done up? As to victuals, you are eating as chaplain. *Silence*, if you can.' This was not a very encouraging beginning.

Still, Jack Morris had two qualities which at first appealed to his young patron, a multifarious although ill-assorted erudition and a cheerful mockery of Dr Newman[2] which went with a low esteem for the new Hierarchy.[3] Such pretensions to learning as these prelates possessed were torn to shreds; this was a process which John Acton found grateful as they sat beside the fire at Aldenham. In other respects they had less in common. Morris was a cheerful soul with an unrequited liking for the Catholic gentry. He had been for a time tutor with Mr Simon Scrope at Danby; he also had a tendency to interfere. It should be explained that so many details of his life are known because he seems to have kept every letter that he received from Fr Faber. Those preserved in the London Oratory number 192; the other side of this correspondence has not survived.

In the early days of Morris's chaplaincy at Aldenham the name of Faber, the superior of the Oratory, had power with Acton. Thus Döllinger was sent to call on him[4] in the autumn of 1858 at

---

[1] From the same to the same, *ibid.*, f. 140.

[2] Cf. A letter from Faber dated at St Mary's, Sydenham, 14 June 1859. 'I'm glad you speak so affectionately of the Padre [Newman]. You used to rile me at St Wilfrid's by pitching into him. We often deplored your skits at him,' *ibid.*, f. 150.

[3] Mark Pattison has a comment on this trait. 'I became a declared Puseyite, then an ultra-Puseyite; I saw a great deal of men like Jack Morris, whose whole conversation was turning the Church of England into ridicule, and who adopted as their motto, "Tendimus in Latium". Jack Morris, however, took me by my student's side. He passed his whole day up the tower of Exeter College reading the Fathers', *Memoirs*, pp. 184–5.

[4] Letter from Faber to Morris dated at the Oratory 13 October, 1858, 'A very nice visit from Döllinger; he is both a striking and a taking man when you see him quietly', London Oratory MSS, vol. 17, f. 149.

the end of his Shropshire visit. Later these feelings changed and in particular Faber was affronted by Döllinger's article tracing back the origin of Jansenism to St Augustine. At the same time the work on which the chaplain was engaged was not likely to win the sympathy of his young patron. Part of his time was devoted to a translation of *The Months of May and November* from the Italian of Fr Alphonsus Muzzarelli, S.J., but the labour to which he paid most attention was a verse drama in four acts entitled *Talectha Koomee*, or the Gospel prophecy of Our Lady's Assumption.

Acton gave his view of this book in a letter sent to Simpson from Aldenham on 25 July 1858.[1] 'Jack Morris' poem is out, full of atrocious theology. If you mean to expose it, do it at once, when I'm away, 1st September.' He also made another reference in a letter written after Mass one Sunday at Aldenham some two months later.[2] He had sat in his tribune as was his duty. 'Jack Morris,' he noted, 'has just preached about our Lady – that "we ought to pray for a fervid desire of leaning on those beautiful breasts".' Both of these reflections suggest a curious attitude on the part of the young baronet towards the middle-aged priest, who was his chaplain. There is no evidence that Morris for his part ever cared for Sir John Acton. He would not settle down, would not unpack.[3] His mind went back to Kitley where Edmund Bastard was now dead. He thought he might go back to help his young successor.[4] An offer from Faber[5] to try to get him a post at 'Primate Cullen's new University' did not appeal.

Morris was homely, pious and bawdy; not a trinity of qualities that Acton liked. It was the last matter which proved his undoing. Apparently it was a question of dubious stories and an old-fashioned and gentlemanly coarseness[6] which would be accepted

---

[1] Letter printed from the Downside MSS in an article, 'Gasquet and the Acton-Simpson Correspondence', by A. Watkin and the Editor in *The Cambridge Historical Journal* (1950), vol. x, p. 86.

[2] Letter from the same source, dated probably by Simpson, 13 November 1858, *ibid.*, p. 80.

[3] Letter from Faber dated at the Oratory, 13 February 1857. 'I think you should unpack your books, and proceed to act as if you were "en permanence",' London Oratory MSS, vol. 17, f. 143.

[4] *Ibid.*, f. 153.   [5] Letter dated only 'Monday', *ibid.*, f. 170.

[6] Cf. a comment by Faber. It is reported that 'Mrs Bastard says that Baldwin (her young brother-in-law) can't bear Jack because he says Jack's talk is looser than that of a mess room', *ibid.*, f. 153.

in an Oxford common-room with its eighteenth-century tradition, but would not be tolerated in a Tridentine seminary. Faber made it evident[1] that there had been complaints about this matter at Oscott and that Morris could not return to St Edmund's for the same reason. A Catholic gentleman of strict opinions had refused to have him staying in the house. At the same time his criticisms were light-hearted; it did not amuse Acton to hear him referring to Bishop Burgess as Bishop Purges.[2]

The position was not modified until Lady Granville died, when Acton decided to take up the question of Jack Morris's tenure. The following letter from the Shrewsbury diocesan archives[3] is worth printing almost *in extenso*. The Bishop of Shrewsbury had asked Sir John to build a Catholic school. The reply was sent from London and dated 22 May 1860; a preliminary paragraph dealt with the parliamentary and other labours and the business which had devolved on Acton through his mother's death.

My dear Lord,
    I had hoped until the very last moment I should be able to come down and receive you at Aldenham, and was very unwilling to find myself obliged to give it up. I must, as I have so often done, trust to your tried indulgence to forgive my very great discourtesy. You speak of several things on which I should have been most anxious to confer with you, and which have very much occupied my thoughts.
    With reference to the school I believe Mr Morris is somewhat misinformed, judging from what your Lordship says. When I came of age it was one of the first questions to which I addressed myself, and in which I endeavoured most carefully to obtain the highest authority and advice, and to act most strictly in obedience to your wishes. . . . Your Lordship is probably not aware that the new school at Morville was not only largely aided by me at first, but is still supported by me, moderately indeed, because it is little if at all visited by Catholic children. . . . It would therefore be a breach of contract (Morville having been founded for both Catholics and Protestants) for me to set up a school drawing away Catholics from Morville school,

[1] *Ibid.*, f. 153.
[2] Undated letter, *ibid.*, f. 179.
[3] Diocese of Shrewsbury MSS under heading 'Aldenham'.

just as it would if it were to have an essentially Protestant character. . . .

Canon Morris has never appeared to take the slightest interest in the school. . . . From his extreme sensitiveness of feeling and obstinacy of opinion I have very rarely ventured to remonstrate with him about anything. . . . Yet these things of which you speak have been a continual source of apprehension and distress to me. The openness and coarseness with which things hardly ever alluded to among Christians were constantly discussed in his sermons and in catechizing children were really alarming. It not only awakened the curiosity of young people, and tore away the veil from their imagination but habituated all the congregation to hear the most sacred things, and Our Lady in particular, associated with ideas hardly ever expressed out of a medical school. I should never contemplate with any peace of mind Mr Morris staying at Aldenham after my marriage. Yet I cannot take any steps to hasten his movements. He has never considered himself settled, has never unpacked his books, and has refused to allow alterations to be made which he wished for at first but desisted from when he thought he should not stay. Once he wrote to me a couple of years ago saying it must be awkward for me to have a chaplain always on the move and asking whether he had not better go at once. I answered . . . that I should take no steps to supply his place until he announced to me the date of his intended removal. This he never has done.

This concludes the significant portion of the letter. Sir John Acton left the next move to Bishop Brown. Before closing he states that by his mother's death 'some money which had become totally disconnected with the diocese of Shrewsbury and paid its ecclesiastical tribute by other channels' naturally reverted and that he hoped he should be in a position where he might do something more than hitherto for the material support of religion. It is a curious letter with its refusal to change his position about the school; stately as if from one power to another; full of a laden Baroque courtesy. The point about the marriage was interesting for this did not then take place. The bishop and the squire were in agreement. What was to become of John Brande Morris?

We can see the position as Faber saw it. Thus he would write to his 'Dearest Jack'.[1] 'Laid up here at Sydenham with a fit of gravel. . . . Don't know enough about Bernard Smith or his intimacy with you, don't believe you will ever go back to Plymouth, think you wd. be more comfortable under Northampton than Shrewsbury. Not in a condition to say more. Obliged to dictate this. Most affectly, F. W. F.' Each bishop rigidly controlled his area and Faber would give the territorial titles, which to most Englishmen would sound odd and unnatural.

The summer was passing and he wrote again.[2]

Indeed my memory did not need jogging; for I constantly think of you and your uncomfortable position. . . . I have not been able to hear of any place for you. Yet I can't help thinking many bishops would be glad to have you. But I can do nothing amongst bishops. Though we have not stirred hand or foot in these rows, & have certainly no particular cause to fight the C[ardinal]'s battles who has never fought one of ours, yet we are considered his men, & Talbot tells me that all the bishops, Nottingham (Roskell) excepted, were agst the Cardinal. So you see I've no interest on the *bench*. Why not pick out a diocese, & write & ask the Bp. if he'll accept your services for the present. Plymouth it appears won't have you. So *for the present* that is closed. They want you away at Aldenham.

Later he returned to the same subject. 'I hardly know a bishop to recommend to you. We converts are sadly out of favour everywhere just now. Dr Errington gave very triste acc[ts] of us at Rome. I don't believe we have any friend but the Cardinal & he's a languid & oblivious one. Still priests are very rare, & a man of yr gifts must be a Godsend to many bishops. . . . *Anyhow* it seems you must act *now*. I suppose they want you away before Acton's marriage.' The third letter to 'Dearest Jack' was sent from the Oratory on September 19.[3] 'I dread yr going [to a convent chaplaincy] if it be to mope & be sad. Yet on the other hand *where* are you to go? And matters are urgent.' He offered to enquire about Blandford Square,[4] that is about the convent there.

[1] London Oratory MSS, undated, f. 188.
[2] Letter from St Mary's, Sydenham, dated 30 July 1860, *ibid.*, f. 153.
[3] Letter from the Oratory, dated 19 September 1860, *ibid.*, f. 156.
[4] Letter dated 7 November 1861, *ibid.*, f. 165.

Finally, Morris was taken in at Downside.[1] 'I am glad all is going on well and I shall be glad when you get amongst those kindhearted monks at Downside.' Morris was destined for a time to serve the mission of Shortwood near Temple Cloud in Somersetshire. Then for two years he acted as chaplain to Coventry Patmore at Heron's Ghyll. The last twelve years of his life were passed as chaplain in the convent of the *Soeurs de Miséricorde* at Queen Caroline Street in Hammersmith. He spent his time in weighing the movements of the Blessed Sacrament in Paradise; he studied whether it might not rest in Mary's bosom. He looked for a D.D. from Rome, which never came. Although he did not return to Aldenham, it seems that he left a mark on Acton's mind. One comment about him by Faber sticks in the memory. 'You had always some little screw loose at Oxford.'[2]

The successor whom the Bishop of Shrewsbury chose for Mr Morris was to exercise a considerable, but subdued influence on Acton's life. For one thing the priest now chosen was to stay for twenty-three years at Aldenham. Mr Thomas Green was at the time of his appointment still in his early sixties, but he struck the patron as already old. Two or three quotations will serve to outline the position. They all come from letters written to Richard Simpson. 'English,' wrote Acton in 1862,[3] 'has been in this neighbourhood and met old Green, whom the bishop put here as the gravest of his old priests to keep me in order.' Another letter touches on the chaplain.[4] 'Old Green is knocked completely off his legs by the new world opened out before him when he expected that we are going to make everything comfortable.' In the early years of their association Sir John Acton got to know his chaplain well. They spent one Christmas at Aldenham alone together and there is a light-hearted reference to him as 'Verdant' in one of the patron's letters.

Still, this period did not last long. 'I have had,' Acton wrote to Simpson in August 1863, in the last of his letters touching on this

---

[1] Letter dated (St Luke's Day) 1861. Also 'Dearest Jack, I congratulate you on being now under the roof of those dear kind Benedictines. The old-fashioned spirit of their Order is enormously to my taste', *ibid.*, ff. 161 and 162.

[2] Letter dated 15 December (1846), *ibid.*, f. 119.

[3] Letter dated 3 September (1861), Downside MSS, f. 423.

[4] Letter dated by Simpson, 1 October 1862, printed in 'Gasquet and the Acton-Simpson Correspondence', *Cambridge Historical Journal*, vol. x, p. 93.

subject,[1] 'the house full of guests. I have been instructing a local architect to build my library, and I have effected a revolution in the management of the estate involving an immediate increase of rent – besides all of which I am obliged to take care of poor old Green, who has had a paralytic stroke. So don't be too hard on me if I have postponed a great many other things.' Henceforward Mr Green was noted as a priest of good character, who had had a stroke. Life was quiet at Aldenham, the pastoral work could well be easy there. For many years there would be no change in the chaplaincy at Sir John Acton's home.

It is a difficulty of arranging John Acton's life that his interests, although channelled, were so diverse. The account of the historian's religious development and personal life is resumed after the three succeeding chapters which deal with the development of Edmund Burke's ideas upon his thought.

[1] Letter, Downside MSS, f. 304.

C*

7

Tocqueville

Any study of Acton's early life is difficult because the layers of influence to which he was exposed were both simultaneous and successive. He seems never to have turned away from any of those who influenced him except from certain Catholics in the years between 1865 and 1870. Thus Döllinger was always with him as a friend, although his direct effect was never quite so great after the end of Acton's tutelage.

In a sense the ending of his legal minority proved a real turning point. He was master of Aldenham and its estate. He entered then upon a period in which he was the patron rather than the friend of those who came to him. These were the years of his first conducting of Reviews and also of the foundation of his library at Aldenham. It was an unhappy era in which to have to play the young Maecenas, and can be said to have ended with the historian's submission to Mr Gladstone's guiding star. These years, when Acton was approaching thirty, also cover the earlier of the two phases of his life in which his concern for current politics was acute. They further witnessed the development in Acton's thought of a political doctrine drawn from Burke and from those who looked to that thinker as their master.

The aftermath of the Crimean war was followed by the twelve years of intermittent struggle which ended in January 1871 with the proclamation of the King of Prussia as German Emperor in the *Salle des Glaces* at Versailles, while beyond the *Pickelhaube* of the German garrison lay a sullen and defeated France. On 19 April 1859 France and Piedmont declared war upon Austria. Three days earlier, as the southern spring came to the lemon groves above the Mediterranean, there died in a rented villa behind the

Bois de la Croix des Gardes a French historian who more than any of his contemporaries foresaw the shape of things to come. In the days before the creation of the Riviera the eastern border-lands of Provence were very tranquil; the villa was only a few miles from Saint Laurent-du-Var, the Piedmontese frontier. Down near the sea-shore in the Villa Eléonore-Louise lived old Lord Brougham, the former chancellor, but Cannes was as yet far from the great world. The invalid historian was only fifty-three. He read the Memoirs of Count Miot de Mélito, and quite till the end his thoughts were bent upon the literary exposition of his doctrine. Two sisters of charity nursed him as he still poured out replies to his correspondents. He had a consuming care for the arrangement and completion of his work, for he had a body of thought to communicate and a message for the theorists of politics, and not least for John Acton. On 16 April his life, so long en-dangered, flickered out, and his generation was left to assimilate the teaching of Alexis-Charles-Henri-Clérel de Tocqueville.

This teaching had a peculiar importance for Acton, who was well fitted to understand the basic conceptions and the *milieu* of a writer whose world had very little in common with that of his admiring English friends Nassau Senior and John Stuart Mill. The influence exercised on the English historian was in some ways all the more powerful for being purely literary. In fact, in the days of Tocqueville's last visit to Paris, Acton is found writing to Richard Simpson:[1] 'Have you made Veuillot's acquaintance? You pass by his door daily, 44 Rue de Bac, and Bonnetty is to be found hard by, 10 Rue de Babylon.' Apart from his mother's fashionable friends, Acton was still in a measure tied to those to whom Döllinger had introduced him. He did not make effective contact with the circle where M. de Tocqueville received his intimates in the Rue de Castellane.

Before discussing the influence of the author of *La Démocratie en Amerique* and *L'Ancien Régime et la Révolution* it is worth quoting some comments made by Acton in 1861 which show how seriously he was affected by his mentor. He was writing from Buckland, that great grey Georgian house lying in the Vale of the White Horse, and had found Tocqueville's life in the Throckmortons'

[1] *Lord Acton and his Circle*, p. 22.

library. 'To describe,' he began in some notes upon this writer,[1] 'what formed his mind and how it grew in power and how it developed in its views from American democracy to his last work, in which he stands in opposition to modern popular ideas far more than at first sight people suppose. Then to compare him to other Frenchmen – to show the very distinct limits and the very broad gaps of his genius and of his knowledge – how he occupies nearly the position of Burke to his own countrymen, minus the greatness and vastness of the other's mind, but plus much colder observation.'

One phrase of Tocqueville's is most familiar:[2] '*Je n'ai pas de traditions, je n'ai pas de parti, je n'ai pas de cause, si ce n'est celle de la liberté et de la dignité humaine.*' Two other expressions,[3] both recorded by Nassau Senior, place this statement in its setting. 'The great misfortune of France is the preference of *égalité* to liberty. I have long been convinced that the social soil of France cannot at present [1850] offer a solid and permanent foundation to any government.'

This last sentence well indicates that undercurrent of sadness in Tocqueville's outlook which went with an incapacity for working with colleagues in political affairs and a strange desolated sense of the extinction of his class. Through all his life, for all its great success, he has the quality of a *revenant*. An unremitting observation filters through his own remote, exact, astringent mind. In this connection Chassériau's crayon-drawing well conveys the delicate slight physique and the chiselled features, the long dark curling almost d'Orsay hair, and that quiet manner which was at once contained and very easy. One can see that list of dinner guests which Senior sets out:[4] 'Duc de Broglie, Monsieur de Viel Castel, the Baron de Billing.'

Alexis de Tocqueville came, like most men acutely conscious of their rank, from the less prosperous section of his class, the Norman *noblesse de campagne* who would keep besides their *château* a small *hôtel* in some country town – in this case Valognes, the centre of

[1] *Ibid.*, p. 223.
[2] *Correspondence and Conversations of Alexis de Tocqueville with Nassau William Senior*, ed. M. C. M. Simpson, i, pp. 90, 92.
[3] *Ibid.*, i, p. 86.
[4] *Ibid.*

society in the northern Cotentin. His financial circumstances were
easy and he was devoted to his granite *château* with its deep windows and the little careful park, and the new billiard-room and
the luxuriant creepers. In the coach house the family coach stood
with its armorial panels. Some dull days the sea mist would
wreathe in across the heavy pastures, but usually the sun shone on
his small constricted paradise.

Tocqueville's parents had been imprisoned during the Terror
and his mother was a grand-daughter of Chrétien de Lamoignon
de Malesherbes, who had defended Louis XVI at his trial. At the
Château de Tocqueville there was neither regret nor nostalgia but
a sense of the loss of values. In Senior's journal there is a character
of Napoleon drawn by his friend which bears this out. 'Napoleon's
taste,' asserted Tocqueville,[1] 'was defective in everything, in small
things as well as great ones; in books, in art, and in women, as
well as in ambition and in glory.' Here we have the pointed arid
comment and the sense of a mould broken. He drew himself back
into his own closed circle.

He had an approach to corruption which was both typical of
the country *noblesse* and also French. In particular he detested the
conception of the *pays légal*, the two hundred thousand voters who
formed the electorate under the *bourgeois* monarchy. 'With his
[King Louis-Philippe's] two hundred thousand or rather four
hundred thousand places, all the middle classes on whom his
government rested, were his tools. He made the middle classes
objects of hatred and contempt, and the people trampled them
and him underfoot.'[2] The next idea is expressed in a phrase particularly lucid and bitter:[3] 'Bribery has enervated and degraded
the middle classes, and filled them with a selfishness so blind as to
induce them to separate their lot entirely from those of the lower
classes whence they sprang.'

He would then turn back to his own position. 'When I talk to a
gentilhomme,' Tocqueville explained,[4] 'though we have not two
ideas in common, though all his opinions, wishes, and thoughts
are opposed to mine, yet I feel that we belong to the same family.

[1] *Ibid.*, i, pp. 113–14.
[2] *Ibid.*, i, p. 78.
[3] *Ibid.*, i, p. 37.
[4] *Ibid.*, i, p. 69.

I may like a *bourgeois* better, but he is a stranger.' Nassau Senior, whose reporting is so reliable, here makes a contribution. They had been discussing the statement of a very sensible Prussian *bürger* himself, who maintained that it was unwise to send out any ambassador who was not noble. 'You may be sure that when any of our *bürger* ministers meets one who is *von Adel*, he does not negotiate with him on equal terms; he is always wishing to sneak under the table.'[1] So did Tocqueville think. He had been elected to the *Académie Française* in 1841 and had been Minister for Foreign Affairs for four months in 1849; but his mind would return to the powerlessness of his own class. 'The people feel that as a political party the gentry are extinct.'[2] Guizot had said that in 1848 when the July monarchy fell the *Peuple* treated the aristocrats not as enemies but as slaves, as a class to be kept in preserves, and consumed from time to time as the wants of the *Peuple* required. In this connection Tocqueville had remarked, we read in Senior's journal,[3] 'that the comment was very just and that he had himself perceived the gradual transition in the minds of the people from dislike to indifference and ultimately to the sort of affection which one feels for one's milch cows'.

At this point Tocqueville produces one of his ideas upon which Acton early seized, the notion of the Revolution of 1789 as a gradually developing event. He believed that after seventy years the Revolution still continued; it was an uncompleted process passing from stage to stage. 'I have long seen that the Orléans family were mere actors, whose exit was approaching, and I fear that more actors have followed them.'[4] The French aristocrats were very different from the other elements of the *noblesse* in Europe, for they alone were both physically and mentally dispossessed. Under a grey sky and from an immense distance Tocqueville viewed his times. His work was marked by a character essentially Latin, that swift and successive, that serial disillusionment.

Phenomena passed very slowly as in a kaleidoscope before that patient and unexpectant observation. Tocqueville saw men in their categories. One morning he was speaking to Senior of the

[1] *Ibid.*, i, p. 69.
[2] *Ibid.*, i, p. 51.
[3] *Ibid.*, i, p. 50.
[4] *Ibid.*, i, p. 89.

influence of women. 'Formerly every young artist, or poet, or preacher, or even politician, must come out chaperoned by some patroness.'[1] This sentence with the word 'preacher' so carefully placed by one who was most conscious of each *nuance* can serve as an introduction to an examination of Tocqueville's attitude to religion. He was in the first place a Catholic by that social inheritance which to him was inescapable. He attended Mass at Tocqueville as an obligation in the landlord-peasant relation, and he received the Sacraments in his last illness. At Sorrento he was accustomed to go to the country chapels, it was a pleasure to him to witness the peasant faith. 'The *curé* dined with us. He took scarcely any part in the conversation at dinner or in the drawing-room. This, Tocqueville said,[2] was *convenable*.' One cannot help sensing that here was a world in which gravity of treatment sometimes took the place of faith.

The position was put to Senior very clearly. 'The aristocracy tried to revive Christianity as a political engine. Accordingly no gentleman in the present century writes, or even speaks, irreligiously. None but the lowest classes now profess irreligion.'[3] On another occasion we find that the same metaphor is used again.[4] 'A much greater proportion of priests . . . are constantly working on the minds of their flocks with the popular eloquence of a Catholic pulpit and the powerful engine of confession. The Pope,' he observed,[5] 'was most to be feared when he acted most silently.'

It is an interesting position, for it has resemblances and contrasts with John Acton's. It has the same quality of the inescapable, but touched by a realism which is quite stripped of sentiment. Alexis de Tocqueville came from the matrix of a Christian tradition which had created the great age of France. But his political and religious outlook both suggest an atmosphere of quenched hope. He was planted in Catholicism as in the midst of a moon landscape. It stretched away behind and all about him, but did much live in it?

In a letter to Henry Reeve, the first editor of the Greville

[1] *Ibid.*, i, p. 51.
[2] *Ibid.*, i, p. 116.
[3] *Ibid.*, i, p. 106.
[4] *Ibid.*, i, p. 185.
[5] *Ibid.*, i, p. 179.

Memoirs and a friend of Lady Granville, Tocqueville makes an illuminating comment. 'That aristocracy,' he explains in regard to the class from which he sprang,[1] 'had ceased to exist, and one can be strongly attached only to the living.' Few men were more conscious of the desolate character of their own world. This scepticism as to the vital element in all old forces was reinforced in Tocqueville's case by a complete absence of regret and a clear lack of interest in history. In his view the *Ancien Régime* must have been extremely bad because it evoked such detestation. Tocqueville's conversation never dealt with times earlier than those which his old friend Royer-Collard could remember. It is the characters of men of the generation of Danton and Lafayette and their successors which are alone passed in review. The whole bent of his mind was a-historical. He was influenced by the classic writers, and especially by Pascal. But they were regarded as timeless and as elements in the formation of the great tradition. He took for granted the *Grand Siècle*, which had moulded his own class. Discussion of the Middle Ages does not appear.

His taste was not aesthetic but for a manner of life. His own *château* was a jumble of easy and unsorted styles. He was very far from Gothic feeling or Romanticism, whether French or German. He was utterly remote from the spirit which would lead his younger contemporary, Viollet-le-Duc, to embark upon his restorations. At Carcassonne the sharp grey towers of the restored *Cité* would have seemed trivial to one whose mind was concentrated on the shadow of the mass age. It is only partly true to say, as Acton did,[2] that Tocqueville was 'no historian because he could not see things in their flow, *im Werden*'.

In certain aspects *L'Ancien Régime et la Révolution* follows Burke's thought in the *Reflections* very closely. In a sense it may be said that Edmund Burke's position is Tocqueville's starting point. The latter, in fact, foresaw the development of the powers which his great predecessor feared and analysed. It is worth pausing upon this question since in varying degrees both Burke and Tocqueville influenced John Acton's mind. Burke wrote in the *Appeal*:[3]

---

[1] Tocqueville, *Oeuvres*, vi, p. 67.
[2] *Lord Acton and his Circle*, p. 226.
[3] *Appeal from the New to the Old Whigs*, p. 169.

When the supreme authority of the people is in question, before we attempt to extend or define it, we ought to fix in our minds, with some degree of distinctness, an idea of what it is we mean, when we say, the people.

In a state of *rude* Nature there is no such thing as a people. A number of men in themselves have no collective capacity. The idea of a people is the idea of a corporation. It is wholly artificial, and made, like all other legal fictions, by common agreement.

Fragments from the succeeding pages stress this point.

When men, therefore break up the original compact or agreement, which gives its corporate form and capacity to a state, they are no longer a people. . . . They are a number of vague, loose individuals, and nothing more. With them all is to begin again. They little know how many a weary step is to be taken before they can form themselves into a mass which has a true politic personality.

He then came to his view of the rights of a majority; this should be established because of its influence both on Tocqueville's and Acton's thought.

We hear much[1] about the omnipotence of a *majority* in such a dissolution of an ancient society as hath taken place in France. But amongst men so disbanded there can be no such thing as majority or minority, or power in any one person to bind another. The power of acting by a majority . . . must be grounded on two assumptions: first, that of an incorporation produced by unanimity: and, secondly, an unanimous agreement that the act of a mere majority shall pass with them and with others as the act of the whole.

From these statements there follows one of the most familiar of all Burke's sayings.[2] 'Liberty, too, must be limited in order to be possessed.' With the contractual basis of the commonwealth upon

[1] *Ibid.*, p. 270
[2] *Letter to the Sheriffs of Bristol.*

which his suppositions reacted it was natural for the Whig statesman to write:[1] 'I flatter myself that I love a manly, moral,
regulated liberty as much as any gentleman.' There is one element
in this picture that must be noted. 'We have,' he asserts in the
Appeal,[2] 'obligations to mankind at large, which are not in consequence of any special voluntary pact. They arise from the
relation of man to man, and the relation of man to God, which
relations are not matters of choice. . . . In some cases the subordinate relations are voluntary, in others they are necessary –
but the duties are all compulsive.' A companion statement is set
out on the preceding page of the same tractate.[3] 'Much the
strongest moral obligations are such as were never the results of
our option. I allow, that, if no supreme Ruler exists, wise to form
and potent to enforce, the moral law, there is no sanction to any
contract, virtual or even actual, against the will of prevalent
power.' It is such sentences as these which led Dr J. P. Mayer to
the conclusions which he stated in his study of Tocqueville. 'Both,'
he writes in speaking of Burke and Tocqueville,[4] 'are profoundly
religious, and are agreed that states lacking the secure foundation
of a religious belief are doomed to destruction.' There were at
that time in Western Europe few exceptions to belief in a Christian
or in a Deist world.

The judgment which has just been quoted, is one which might
well be extended to include John Acton's name. The term 'profoundly religious' sits ill upon the elder thinkers. It was rather,
surely, that they were both in a stream of thought which in France
had been interrupted by the *Encyclopédistes*. They belonged to the
old tradition of Europe in which the nature of man's obligations
had been fixed for so long.

An element which is present in Burke's thought but absent from
Tocqueville's is the note of regret. This corresponds to that 'colder
observation' which Acton discerned in the Frenchman when
making a comparison of the two writers. Such a consequence is in
part a result of the fact that Tocqueville throughout his life was
never without his disillusion. Beneath a heavy sky he looked out

[1] *Reflections on the Revolution in France.*
[2] *Appeal from the New to the Old Whigs*, p. 166.
[3] *Ibid.*, p. 165.
[4] *Prophet of the Mass Age, a Study of Alexis de Tocqueville*, p. 154.

on the waste of waters. A letter to his friend M. Stoffels dated 28 April 1850 makes this point clear.[1]

> You wish for political prognostications; who can venture to make any? The future is as black as night; the most far-sighted admit that they cannot look forward. As for me, I see a tolerably clear outline of what seems to me to be the future destiny of this country. . . . What I see clearly is, that for sixty years we have been deceiving ourselves by imagining that we saw the end of the Revolution. It was supposed to be finished on the 18th Brumaire and again 1814; I thought myself, in 1830, that it might be over when I saw that democracy, having in its march passed over and destroyed every other privilege, had stopped before the ancient and necessary privilege of property. I thought that, like the ocean, it had at last found its shore. I was wrong. It is now evident that the tide is rising, and that the sea is still enlarging its bed; that not only have we not seen the end of the stupendous revolution which began before our day, but that the infant just born will scarcely see it. Society is not in process of modification, but of transformation.

In this connection a conversation with Nassau Senior which took place in 1850 is worth recording. 'He is,' said Tocqueville in speaking of the depression of spirits of the Duc de Broglie,[2] 'one of a numerous class who at each successive phase of our Revolution have believed that it was over, and that a settled state of things was to ensue. . . . The revolution of 1848 came, and these illusions were dissipated in an hour. The line along which they had been travelling since 1830 turns out to be only the segment of a circle.'

The general conception of this movement is set out in the preface to *L'Ancien Régime et la Révolution*.

> Amidst the darkness of the future three truths may be clearly discovered. The first is, that all the men of our time are impelled by an unknown force which they may hope to regulate and to check, but not to conquer, a force which sometimes gently moves them, sometimes hurries them along, to the

[1] *Memoir, Letters and Remains of Alexis de Tocqueville*, English edition, i, p. 423.
[2] Nassau Senior, *op. cit.*, i, p. 89.

destruction of aristocracy. The second is, that of all the communities in the world those which will always be least able permanently to escape from absolute government are precisely the communities in which aristocracy has ceased to exist and can never exist again. The third and least is, that despotism nowhere produces more pernicious effects than in these same communities.

It is only a step to the conclusion. 'Despotism . . . deprives its subjects of every common passion, of every natural want, of all necessity of combining together, of all occasions of acting together. It immures them in private life.'

It was Tocqueville's great merit to detect that tendency towards absolutism inherent in a search for political equality. In this matter it was the plebiscitary dictatorship of Napoleon III which moved him. He had a special horror, akin to Burke's, as to what might be thrown up by a 'mere majority'. This led to his tempered dislike of universal suffrage.[1] The suddenly enfranchised elements might find their own needs mirrored in a dictator who proclaimed himself the enemy of property and the scourge of vested interests. A comment on Henri Martin 'with his Asiatic democracy' is illuminating in regard to one angle of this subject. 'He belongs,' wrote Tocqueville of that publicist,[2] 'to the class of theorists, unfortunately not a small one, whose political *beau idéal* is the absence of all control over the will of the people. Equality, not liberty, or security, is their object. They are centralisers and absolutists.' In general, this record of opinion conveys Tocqueville's standpoint in regard to Europe; but its consequences can only be drawn out when Napoleon III, who was the exemplar of so much that he distrusted, is seen through his eyes. This also has importance in the development of Acton's thought, for the Emperor of the French was the first political figure upon the Continent to loom across the threshold of his adult life.

Few moods slid away more rapidly than the revolutionary sentiments of 1848. They had few traces when John Acton left his boyhood. By the time he came of age the Second Republic had evaporated and Louis Napoleon had become Prince President and

[1] *Ibid.*, i, p. 69.
[2] *Ibid.*, i, p. 185.

then Emperor. He was to rule France from 1852 until 1870. During that period he incurred a dispassionate and remorseless opposition such as few princes reap. Tocqueville, to take one instance, came to regard him with an ice-cold distaste. A friend and one whom he regarded as a great authority upon this subject stated the case. 'He is,' said Lanjuinais of the Emperor,[1] 'not a man of genius or even a man of remarkable ability. . . . He is ignorant, uninventive and idle. . . . His great moral merits are kindness and sympathy. He is a faithful attached friend, and wishes to serve all who come near him. His greatest moral fault is his ignorance of the difference between right and wrong.' And then Tocqueville himself took up the running. 'He does not belong,' he explained,[2] 'to the highest class of hypocrites, who cheat by frankness and cordiality.' With the admirable point that never left him, the great sociologist passed judgment on those who opposed Louis Napoleon: 'Our conspiracy was that of the lambs against the wolf.' In a talk with Nassau Senior he spoke on another occasion for that world to which the travelled classes in both countries belonged. 'We cannot bear,' he began, and his words were surely Acton's,[3] 'that the fate of France should depend on the selfishness, or the vanity, or the fears, or the caprice of one man, a foreigner by race, and education, and of a set of military ruffians and of infamous civilians, fit only to have formed the staff and the privy council of Catiline. We cannot bear that the people which carried the torch of Liberty through Europe should now be employed in quenching all its lights. But these are not the feelings of the multitude.'

There is here present a distrust of the judgment of the mass of men which is very striking. It was the plebiscite after Louis Napoleon's *coup d'état* which was responsible for the bitter quality of such a sentiment. That absolutism should be guaranteed by a popular vote on a wide suffrage seemed the death-knell of liberty. It was thus the plebiscitary dictatorship which instilled into Tocqueville that acute dislike which Acton in time would come to share. Both felt, and Tocqueville especially, that the peasants must

[1] *Ibid.*, i, pp. 204–5.
[2] *Ibid.*, ii, p. 12.
[3] *Ibid.*, ii, p. 7.

support a continuing revolution, while the huge new industrial populations, with which the old classes had so little contact, were unpredictable. Acton's own mind was normally not dramatic. The absolutism of the Second Empire was to him a bad principle in action. If Russia blanketed freedom, the new Imperial France imposed fresh fetters upon liberty.

In certain respects, and notably in regard to the actual new technique of State control, Tocqueville saw further than his pupil. He could imagine mass action and its strange consequences, and in a general way perceived the stair up which the national dictatorships would haul themselves. He felt acutely the insufficiency of that *bourgeois* monarchy which Acton valued on account of the measure of liberty which it supported. Guizot, who was not only the minister of Louis-Philippe but also the incarnation of his system, in particular had gained the young historian's admiration.

Broadly speaking there was, however, identity between Tocqueville and Acton in their approach to the Second Empire. A review which was published in 1863 in the *Home and Foreign* can mark the point at which the latter's outlook stabilized. The following sentences appear in a notice of *Le Fils de Giboyer* by Emile Augier:[1] 'The things which he honours and believes are political views not moral laws. . . . His comedy is the savage protest of the men of 1789, translated into imperial materialists, against morality and religion. . . . The sum of the author's philosophy is that love of equality which is not only compatible with the love of distinctions, but a strong incentive to it, and the worship of the *fait accompli*.'

The notice then continues with an examination of the popular absolutism then extant in France: 'In the following words he [M. Augier] vindicates the imperialist theory of equality. "Equality is not a level . . . the great word can have but one sense, to every one according to his works" '. Conceding to this authoritarian *régime* the term democracy, Acton probes further,[2] 'What is it that this democracy hates, if it tolerates wealth, desires distinctions of honour and worships power?' He arrives at the answer that the hatred is brought to bear on aristocracy. This is important, for it is around this conception of a natural aristocracy

[1] *Home and Foreign Review*, 1863, p. 667.
[2] *Ibid.*, p. 719.

that the thoughts of Acton and his two teachers gather. The qualifying adjective is introduced to show that only the core of such an element would be hereditary. To Burke this was the corner-stone of the Whig policy; to Acton this was in its Whig sense the air that he had always breathed; to Tocqueville it was his own shell broken. Among these three men only Tocqueville was a sociologist, and he alone believed that his own world had gone out to a waste land.

It is at this point that we should consider with more care the influence of Edmund Burke, for this would penetrate and colour each aspect of John Acton's thought. In some sense it was, perhaps, those elements in the Burkian view which came to him direct that left most impression. Their impact was more immediate than those that filtered through Tocqueville's mind or Döllinger's.

In this connection a few propositions may be considered before examining that *Appeal from the New to the Old Whigs* which contains the teaching on the nature of liberty which was so crucial to Burke's thought. At any rate during his early life the *Appeal* was John Acton's favourite among Burke's writings. Here are three sentences whose effect would in their different ways prove durable.[1] 'Abstract liberty, like other mere abstractions, is not to be found.' And again, 'Individuals pass like shadows; but the commonwealth is fixed and stable.' Finally, with a note that has more in it of realism than disillusion, there comes this phrase: 'The march of the human mind is slow.'

These lines of thought lead up to two expositions of doctrine that are familiar and memorable. Throughout his writings Burke displayed a temper in dealing with institutions which was both exact and serene. 'But the liberty, the only liberty I mean, is a liberty connected with order: and that not only exists with order and virtue, but which cannot exist at all without them. It inheres in good and steady government, as in its substance and vital principle. . . . We are members,' he went on in another of his speeches to the Electors of Bristol to which he would look back as his testament,

for that great nation, which, however, is itself but part of a great empire, extended by our virtue and our fortune to the

[1] *Speech on Conciliation with America*, Everyman series, p. 91.

farthest limits of the East and West. All these widespread
interests must be considered – must be compared – must be
reconciled, if possible. We are members of a free country; and
surely we all know that the machine of a free constitution is no
simple thing, but as intricate and delicate as it is valuable. . . .
A constitution made up of balanced powers must ever be a
critical thing.

And then in the *Appeal* itself there is expressed that view of the
constitution which Acton was always to find so grateful.[1] 'Neither
the few nor the many have the right to act merely by their will,
in any manner connected with duty, trust, engagement, or obligation. The constitution of a country being once settled upon some
compact, tacit or expressed, there is no power existing of force to
alter it, without the breach of the covenant, or the consent of all
the parties.' 'I am,' wrote Burke,[2] 'well aware that men love to
hear of their power, but have an extreme disrelish to be told of
their duty.' In fact, it was just Mr Gladstone's readiness to tell
men of their duty which in the future had such great appeal for the
historian.

It is here, perhaps, that a line of cleavage comes between the
German and the French mentality. The conception of duty was
indeed very central in the nineteenth-century German life. The
Prince Consort was himself in many ways an incarnation of this
sense of poised and weighted obligation. In Bavaria in a less self-
conscious fashion the same held good. With the greater lightness
of the South there was still a sententious concept of what was
owing from the German man. In time duty, conceived along
rather different lines, would expel freedom. In Germany the sense
of obligation would reveal itself in all the marching, riding, driving
armies and in all the men who thought for them. Still, on the professorial side of Acton's Bavarian world it was civilian duty that
appeared as freedom's guardian.

Compared to his deep understanding of the South German
temperament, John Acton's approach to trends of French opinion
appears as curiously superficial. He valued very highly the work of
various French thinkers; but there is no doubt that he was irritated

---

[1] *Appeal from the New to the Old Whigs*, p. 162.
[2] *Ibid.*, p. 153.

by certain tendencies which belonged rather to the sphere of mental habit. Thus he felt the absence of moral elevation, taking these words in their Gladstonian sense, and he was never to be at his ease with buoyant undefeated eloquence. This last factor may explain the lack of sympathy that Acton always felt for Dupanloup. It was the versatility and the quick fecund imagery of the great Bishop of Orléans that so repelled him. He believed in hewing and digging deep; he thought that rhetoric must expel learning.

8

Acton as a Reviewer

The influences described in the last chapter had their effect on Acton as a reviewer. To study his work at its early maturity, it is best to concentrate on the *Home and Foreign Review*. In this quarterly he had an independent control, which had for the most part been lacking in the *Rambler* and in 1862, when he took it over, he was just twenty-eight. He was at this stage still in isolation from the English academic world. There is a phrase in one of his letters at this time[1] in which he speaks of asking old George Finlay[2] to act as a reviewer; the younger men he did not know. It is ironic that Sir John Acton should have been prevented from entering upon his true country by the presence of two obstacles. The weight and presentation of his German learning was at this date a barrier, as was his politico-social position, which was smooth and impregnable.

This is the position in the light of which the *Home and Foreign Review* can be examined. We have now reached the stage of Acton's positive achievements and of his matured thought. His contributions to the new quarterly fall into two distinct sections: the reviews of books and the articles on contemporary foreign politics. In the articles which were a continuation of those printed in the *Rambler*, Acton considered the developments of foreign policy in the light of the principles which he held to be immutable. He harnessed his doctrine to these surveys just as his erudition came to bear on each book notice. It is perhaps simplest to begin with the examination of his reviews, which bring together a very rare body

---

[1] Cf. Letter dated 20 January 1863, printed in *Lord Acton and his Circle*, p. 397.

[2] George Finlay, b. 1799, d. 1875, published his *History of Greece* between 1844 and 1861.

of learning. After studying his work, we can examine that great library which was his workshop.

In the quarterly some sixty or seventy pages were devoted in each number to reviews of books. This was an entirely fresh departure, and it is seldom realized how much work Acton himself put into the new venture, for in fact it very well reflects his mind and thought. Thus in the *Home and Foreign Review* for January 1863 the historian himself contributed thirty-one reviews, most of them over a page in length. The remaining thirty-two book notices were divided among nine reviewers. The notices in this number indicate more clearly than the set pieces Acton's range of knowledge, which was already wide.

The clearest picture of his work at this time is presented by a discussion of Acton's attitude to those current books which caused him to define his own approach to history. It was a textbook for use in schools in which Professor Wilhelm Putz dealt with the Middle Ages that gave the first occasion for such comment. 'Nothing,' wrote Acton,[1] 'causes more error and unfairness in men's view of history than the interest which is inspired by individual characters. The most absolute devotion to certain ideas and opinions is less dangerous, for they may be perfectly true, while no character is perfectly good.' And then his mind would move to the teaching of history. 'An indiscriminate admiration and jealousy of criticism marks the feeling of a sect and a party towards its leaders. Now this is a disposition strengthened in early life by the manner in which history is generally learnt. The interest of biography awakens a thirst for knowledge long before history can be understood; and we have our minds crowded with objects of hero-worship before we can understand the intricacies of character, and before we can appreciate the sanctity of a cause.' Here we have the standpoint of the historian's maturity as he moved towards Gladstonian Liberalism. 'In this way,' the review continues, 'the imagination may be aroused and the memory stored; but the judgment is warped instead of being formed, and the historical faculty and habit, which is the most valuable fruit of historical study, and may survive even historical knowledge, is spoiled.'

[1] *Home and Foreign Review*, ii, p. 219.

Various factors had gone to form this judgment. There was the general approach to history which Döllinger favoured and the subjects about which his mind was exercised. There was again a sharp difficulty about Cardinal Wiseman's leadership. Praise which outstrips sincerity even by a little is liable to curdle and in Acton's mind, very critical and not yet poised, the notion of the Cardinal had turned sour. He had a young man's resentment at being patronized. At the same time there is another element which seems to have entered into Acton's plea that history should be impersonal. He could not rival those great scenes that Lord Macaulay painted with their built-up Titian colours; he had nothing of the scenario-contriver and it was difficult for him to value work so much at variance with his grey semi-tones. The deep contrasts that John Acton formed were in the world of thought and not in the sensibilities.

Macaulay in any case was in his mind, for among the books upon his desk for notice in this number there was a volume on that historian's public life by Frederick Arnold. It was now three years since his sudden death, and we feel as the review proceeds that Acton was clearing his thought upon the subject of his predecessor.

> Lord Macaulay [we are told[1]] was by the character of his mind averse to the niceties of political speculation. His own views on all public questions were free from the exaggerations of absolute Liberalism; but he was unable to discern the speculative origins of these errors, or to ascertain the necessary application of first principles. Hence he is not always just in describing the doctrines of different parties, nor always consistent in his own relations towards them. For the party to which he belonged has a double pedigree, and traces its descent on the one hand through Fox, Sidney and Milton to the Roundheads, and on the other through Burke, Somers and Selden to the old English lawyers. Between these two families there was more matter for civil war than between Cromwell and King Charles.

We are away on one of those surveys which through his mature life would always fascinate John Dalberg Acton.

[1] *Ibid.*, ii, p. 258.

He went on with that gathering assurance that was so much in character:

The divergence between any two systems that result in arbitrary power cannot be so great as that between either of them and a system which subjects the sovereign in law; and there were more principles held in common by Falkland and Selden, when one was Secretary of State and the other the colleague of Pym, than by Fox and Burke when they were in office together.

According to one theory[1] the King as well as the people was subject to the law, and both were bound to prevent or to avenge the breach of the constitution by the other. The men of the other school maintained the contrary principle of the right of every people to choose, and therefore to change, its own rulers. Not only a revolutionary but also an unpopular act on the part of the King might forfeit his crown. The legitimacy of resistance was to be tested not by the laws of the land, but by the consent of the people; and the cause which justified rebellion was not the arbitrary violation of unquestioned rights, but opposition to an arbitrary caprice.

Acton here sets out his views, with that opposition to dynastic Legitimism which was so deep seated, and then places his subject with great neatness.

Macaulay began life, we are told, as a Tory and was converted by distinguished friends. The Whiggism that prevailed at that time in the society to which he was soon introduced, was the Whiggism of Holland House – the Foxite school of Lord Grey and Lord Russell.[2] This is the school which he always acknowledged as his own. He would 'defend with unabated spirit the noble principles of Milton and Locke'. Again and again the utilitarian notion of government recurs in his writings, and the writer seems as sincere a believer in the sovereignty of the people as Sidney, or Paine, or Lord Russell. 'The Whig theory of government,' he says, 'is that kings exist for the people, and not the people for kings.' It is evident that he never mastered the real point at issue between the Whigs and all other parties: for

[1] *Ibid.*, ii, p. 259.
[2] Lord John Russell had been created Earl Russell of Kingston Russell in 1861.

in all these passages he overlooks the fundamental distinction
between sovereignty and authority, and between rights in the
sense of power and rights which imply duties. He was not
acquainted with the political writings of Plato and Aristotle, in
which he would have found more of the Whig doctrine than in
the men he delights to quote. But he was guided throughout,
and preserved from many errors to which his superficial treatment of principles would have exposed him, by an unswerving
admiration for the writings of Burke.

Upon Acton's desk there also lay a *Manual of English Literature,
Historical and Critical* just published by Thomas Arnold, the
younger son of the Headmaster of Rugby and at this time a
Catholic. We can see Acton's mind running on his former subject
as he turned the pages.

Political truth is identified with Whiggism, and the other
schools exhaust the various forms of error: the Cavalier Tories
represented by Filmer; the philosophical Tories by Hobbes;
the Puritan Whigs by Milton and Sidney; the philosophical
Republicans by Harrington. This exclusion of Milton and
Sidney from the ranks of the true Whigs shows that Mr Arnold
is fully conscious of the difference between the highly con-
structive positive and definite theory of Whiggism and the
generalizations of an ordinary Liberalism. Speaking of Johnson
he [Arnold] identifies Conservatism and Whiggism. 'His influence upon England was eminently conservative. . . . After
his death Burke carried on the sort of conservative propaganda
which he had initiated.' He is not quite true to himself when he
places Locke in the line of the Whig tradition.

Here we meet again the doctrinal emphasis that Acton favoured.
He explains:

Now the essence of Whiggism is the acknowledgement of the
supremacy of the divine Will, or as we should say, if the term
has not been degraded, of divine right over the will of man,
whether represented by the sovereign or by the people, in the
institutions of the past or in speculative theories. It is the
absolute exclusion from politics of the arbitrary element which
asserts itself in Toryism by denying the claims of principle, and

in Radicalism by rejecting the authority of fact. In this way Selden shared in the Great Rebellion, Somers justified the Revolution, and Burke defended the constitutional idea in the American and the revolutionary wars. But Locke derives civil society from a voluntary contract and thus introduces a principle as arbitrary in its nature, and as dangerous to right in its consequences, as the maxim that kings are above the law.

Acton's mind was now running upon systems and he turned to a volume which MM. Schauer and Chuquet had just edited containing the letters exchanged during 1792-97 between Kirchberger and Louis Claude de Saint-Martin. The latter had played a part in influencing Döllinger's thought,[1] for Baader had brought the young professor to a study of Saint-Martin's writings. Acton's note is interesting partly on account of the exhaustive examination of Saint-Martin's reading and also possibly as indicating a sympathy with those whom the orthodox Catholic world did not appreciate.

> Frederick Schlegel [Acton explains[2]] who described Saint-Martin as the greatest master of a spiritual philosophy in his time, anxiously vindicates him from the charges of a silent and passive opposition to the Church to which he belonged. . . . Kirchberger was a Swiss Protestant, who had studied deeply some of the mystics of the seventeenth century – German writers whom Saint-Martin could not understand, and especially Madame Guyon whom he had not read. He [Saint-Martin] declared that up to the age of fifty he had known nothing of the writings of Jacob Böhme, and that when he became acquainted with them through the English translation of Law, he discovered his own system in a much more perfect form of development.

These extracts in particular throw light on Acton's determination always to *place*. Whether it was in the descent of ideas or in the wider field of literary or political inheritance, he would always bring his ranging information into a clearly marked schematic frame. It seems reasonable to claim that this was a new conception in English history.

[1] Cf. 'Döllinger's Historical Work', pp. 376-7.
[2] *Home and Foreign Review*, ii, p. 241.

Acton was especially keen to trace the unexpected intellectual filiation. An example of this interest is provided in a generally unfavourable notice[1] of a biography of Freiherr von Wessenberg. 'Baron Wessenberg,' so runs this extract dealing with the Josephist administrator of Constance, 'was educated for the priesthood at a time when the reforms of the Emperor Joseph, the writings of Febronius and the later Jansenists, and the influence of Rationalism and Illuminism, had conspired to reduce the religious spirit of the clergy to the lowest point of fervour. He studied under the celebrated Sailer.'[2] It is the next note[3] that contains the special point. 'The man,' we read, 'to whom Wessenberg owed his promotion and with whom during many years he was most intimately connected was the Primate Dalberg. . . . Dalberg had grown up in the same school as his younger contemporary, and he had imbibed more deeply than any Catholic ecclesiastic the tone and ideas of the rising literature of Germany, which had its centre in his own neighbourhood at Weimar.' Acton was particularly drawn to study lines of influence that intersect the national and religious boundaries. Thus he would map out the effect of Goethe's work, the Goethe of *Hermann und Dorothea*.

And then Acton's notice returned once more to those who were almost his own contemporaries. Here we find again that standard by which he would always judge political ideas. The Burkian concepts were not forgotten, and to them was fitted that new emphasis which nineteenth-century experience had brought the later writer. The leaven of his views on sovereignty was always working in John Acton's mind.

In a series of studies Alfred von Reumont, who was for so long Prussian minister to the then grand ducal court of Tuscany, devoted a volume to Cesare Balbo.[4] Two sentences from this notice are worth quoting: 'In his hatred of revolution he [Balbo] seems to have invested legitimacy with some of the virtue of legality.' And again: 'The germ of his later opinions was laid by Châteaubriand's *Génie du Christianisme* – a work the success of which is a decisive measure of the intellectual condition of the period in

[1] *Ibid.*, ii, p. 248.
[2] Bishop Sailer was b. 1751, d. 1832, and Wessenberg was b. 1774 and d. 1860.
[3] *Home and Foreign Review*, ii, p. 250.
[4] Cesare Balbo was b. 1789, d. 1853.

which it was admired.' A certain tartness of expression was seldom very far from Acton's mind.

The historian also possessed two other qualities as a reviewer which these notices will serve to bring out. He liked to let the wide sweep of his thought play on the sources as they were calendared in the great collections or appeared in the archaeological transactions which were so marked a feature of mid-nineteenth century writing on this subject. Thus in this number of *Home and Foreign* he greeted the publication of the Calendar of Letters, Despatches and State Papers relating to the negotiations between England and Spain in the reign of Henry VII.[1] Dr Bergenroth, the editor, was placed in his setting: 'A scholar who has shown a very eminent capacity for the study of English history which already owes much to his countrymen Lappenberg, Ranke, Phillips and Pauli.' Then came the note on sources: 'The archives of Simancas . . . are in good order and prodigiously rich.'

To this subject Acton would return as he surveyed the report made by Anton Gindely to the Imperial Academy at Vienna.

Dr Gindely[2] was at Simancas at the same time as Mr Froude and Dr Bergenroth, who is making researches on behalf of the English Government. For a hundred and fifty years, from the death of Isabella to the Peace of Utrecht, the archives of Simancas are the richest in Europe. . . . The most interesting documents they contain are the correspondence from Rome, and the report of the deliberations of the Council [of Castile]. We can believe our author when he says that the publication of these reports will topple over the current views of history like a house of cards. But we have reason to expect that they will not present the government of Philip III and Philip IV in a more favourable light.

Here we find again that liking for a wide canvas and the striking and far-reaching implication. He drew attention to a comment by Professor Wilhelm Roscher:[3] 'The war of the Peasants, whose rising and defeat in 1525 I [Roscher] consider the turning-point which occasioned all the misery in the following centuries.' It is,

---

[1] *Home and Foreign Review*, ii, p. 227.
[2] *Ibid.*, ii, p. 235.
[3] *Ibid.*, ii, p. 234.

perhaps, the concentration on *political* history which dates such a remark.

Acton would thus place in juxtaposition a view of Charles V and of the great Peasants' Rising in his reign. One is tempted to believe that at this time the historian's mind was deeply occupied with the main lines of German history. To the *Mémoires de Luynes* Acton was cold,[1] and to the French translation of Dom Ruinart's travels, published by the Archaeological Society of Lorraine, even colder.[2] One phrase in his review of Gindely seems to forecast the future:[3] 'If we are not misinformed, a complete elucidation of the intrigues and the mysterious end of Wallenstein will be the most interesting fruit of his labours.' When he abandoned impersonal history, it was to the weakness of political man that Acton turned.

A final thread running through these notices is that unstrained bibliographical erudition which we have come to expect. In this respect Acton's criticism of vol. xl of the *Nouvelle Biographie Générale* is very damaging. 'For instance,' he writes,[4] 'out of fifteen Lives of Pius V only three are named, and they are not the three best.' And again: 'Ritschl's edition of Plautus, and Sillig's edition of Pliny are not spoken of; in the article on Pliny a book is referred to which the writer cannot have seen, and he knows nothing of the important fragment of the *Natural History* discovered a few years ago by Mone.' Acton was nothing if not categorical. His tone towards Hugo Laemmer's work is lofty.[5] 'His only real defect as an editor of unpublished manuscripts is an immaterial one. He does not always know what has been printed among the papers he finds. Thus he gives an account of Bellarmine's discourse to Clement VIII on the office of the Pope, without being aware that it is to be found in at least three printed and not uncommon books.'

It may be noted that in general he was already somewhat severe towards contemporary ecclesiastics. He is not particularly kind in his review of Dom Gams's first volume of *Die Kirchengeschichte von Spanien* which he describes as mainly a summary of the com-

[1] Cf. *ibid.*, ii, p. 239.
[2] Cf. *ibid.*, ii, p. 238.
[3] *Ibid.*, ii, p. 235.
[4] *Ibid.*, ii, p. 275.
[5] *Ibid.*, ii, p. 232.

mentaries already made by the Bollandists, by Ruinart in *Acta Sincera* and Tillemont in *Mémoires Ecclesiastiques*. It is in this notice that Acton cites the German Benedictine against the English Cardinal who always riled him.[1] 'Father Gams proves that all the so-called African words which the Cardinal [Wiseman] found in the pre-hieronymic version were in use in Rome and in the Roman provinces of Europe.' It is surely remarkable that all this learning and these vivid judgments are found in Acton's book reviews in a single number of one quarterly.

The *English Historical Review* was only founded in 1886, but more than twenty years earlier Sir John Acton was ready and equipped to play his part in working up a technical quarterly. One final quotation from these notices has an especial interest in view of the writer's lifelong ambition.[2] 'Raleigh's History of the World, though quite valueless in execution, is perhaps in design the greatest conceived by an historian.' Acton sat in his library at Aldenham. There lay spread out before him the many stones with which he would plan and never build his great History of Liberty.

[1] *Ibid.*, ii, p. 209.
[2] *Ibid.*, ii, p. 254.

9

The Library at Aldenham

Before considering the great library which Acton was now steadily building up, it is worth examining the method of his work and the form in which he wished to present it. Above all, he loved to penetrate sequence of thought. Parallel to such an exploration, he would track down the successive formulation of policy; it was almost a recreation to open one Chinese box after another. One example which shows how he would use his serried folios is in his celebrated study of German schools of history. 'Much,' Acton wrote,[1] 'has come lately to light touching the partition of Poland. Who proposed it? It was Catherine or Prince Henry in 1771, Bibikoff at Christmas 1770, Joseph II in July, Wolkonsky in March. It was Count Lynar in 1769, or a mightier person wearing his mask. Or it was Kaunitz in 1768, if not Choiseul in the same year. Panin started the idea in 1766, Czernitcheff or the electress of Saxony in 1763, Lord Stair in 1742, the King of Poland himself in 1732, or the crown prince of Prussia one year earlier.'

It is in such sequences that the reader feels a lightness of touch which is seldom revealed in Acton's published letters or in his more elaborate works. In this instance he seems to give himself up to the joy of the chase. It may be suggested that it was the necessity for giving judgment which expelled his humour.

In regard to the method of Acton's work Mountstuart Grant Duff has preserved a note. 'His usual rate of book-consumption,' he explains, 'was a German octavo *per diem*, and he had one of those faultless memories on which everything imprinted itself at once and remained for ever.' Grant Duff, however, goes on to draw attention to the complete system of cross-reference and notes that the historian built up, although he did not seem to need this

---

[1] 'German Schools of History', *Essays on Modern History*, p. 366.

apparatus. Macaulay had the prodigious memory of the nineteenth century, but in his case it was, so to speak, pure memory and took in every kind of list and fact; Acton's was a memory of erudition. Both men would seem to have strengthened this faculty by a continual exercise. Thus Acton never would allow the instrument to grow rusty; as his letters show, he kept it for ever at a stretch. Moving through the masses of his books, he probed and probed. He had a feeling for encyclopaedias.

No study is yet available of his great library, which now rests at Cambridge. It is simplest to pursue quite briefly a few lines of enquiry. A first impression gives rise to the belief that the books which were at Aldenham, when John Acton was a boy, were never brought into his historical library as we know it. Certainly they were sharply contrasted. Thus it would seem that the library which the family found when they returned from Naples to their Shropshire seat was more extensive than might have been expected. A few items will indicate its scope. There was the Livy, in an Amsterdam edition of 1661, inscribed 'W. Acton'. Then Sir Whitmore had added a copy of the first part of Jeremy Taylor's *Antiquitatis Christianae*, a rather fine edition of a *Dictionnaire Royal, François-Anglois*, had been purchased for the young girl who would marry Sir Whitmore's heir. It is inscribed 'This is the book of the Lady Anne Gray'. The whole effect produced is of a true country-house library.

Against such a sober background stood the volumes brought from Italy. There was a *Specola Astronomica* bought when John Acton's father was fifteen. It is marked 'Richard Acton. Londres, 21 April 1816'. In the year after the historian was born some recent purchases, thirty-one volumes in all, were sent to be rebound. They included Botta's *History of Italy*, Lingard's *History of England* and the first part of the *Dictionnaire analytique d'Economie politique*. Lives of the saints were kept in Aldenham chapel, and Elizabeth Acton on her marriage had left behind the edition of La Fontaine's *Fables Choisies* which she had been given as a child. A list of books possessed by the Chevalier Acton at Naples includes the *Mémoires de Mirabeau*, Madame Campan's *Correspondence* and an Italian edition of Benvenuto Cellini. So much for the Acton background.

By contrast the books from Herrnsheim seem to have been incorporated into the historian's general store. At Cambridge there are neat little volumes, *Oeuvres de Montesquieu*, *Oeuvres de Machiavel*. Each carries a small plate, 'Bibliotheque de S.E. Mr le Duc de Dalberg'. Lady Granville's contributions include four volumes of S. Alfonso Liguori and a rather elaborate copy, labelled 'M. D. Granville Aldenham 8 Sept. 1848', of the proceedings of the Court of Peers when taking evidence relating to the assassination of the Duchesse de Praslin.

With this beginning and urged by Dr Döllinger's example, John Acton set about his great collection. This has been described as a library from which a history of liberty might be constructed. It is, perhaps, more accurate to consider it as primarily devoted to the elucidation of law and custom, a purpose supported by a mass of biography and correspondence and by the existing encyclopaedias in all European languages.

The library is incomparably rich in regard to French local history, a richness reflected in the appreciation which Acton always showed for the work of the eighteenth-century French historians and chroniclers. It is equally extensive in matters both ecclesiastical and secular, a remote province such as Quercy being much better covered than most English counties. There are various reasons which may account for this tendency towards a French preponderance in the collection of an historian whose main interests, as well as his sympathies, lay elsewhere. In the first place, it is clear from the actual volumes that Acton employed three or four booksellers in Paris. They must have searched and brought many volumes to the notice of so persistent and valuable a customer. Another factor was that great interest which Acton inherited from Döllinger in the religious controversies of the seventeenth and eighteenth centuries whose literature was, in great measure, French. The *Bibliotheca Dollingeriana*, a printed catalogue issued in 1893, contains the titles of nearly 20,000 volumes in the professor's collection. A very considerable number of these books were acquired by Dr Döllinger in later life, but in each case the date of publication is provided. Under the combined heading 'Molinismus, Jansenismus und Gallikanismus' there are listed some 450 titles. This interest is well-reflected in Lord Acton's library and constitutes another reason why this book-buying was so largely concentrated on Paris.

After the very remarkable French section, which includes printed works on every school of thought and on most subjects, one of the pleasantest portions of the library is the collection of Italian and Spanish Church histories, ecclesiastical constitutions and synodal laws. The printing and the general production of the Italian volumes of the *settecento* is particularly lavish. Both these sections are close to the spine of Acton's interest, which was at one time so concentrated on the legislative framework of religion. Parallel with those sections is a series of small works dealing with the reigns of Pius VI and Pius VII or with that of Clement XIV. The latter turn upon the controversy relating to the suppression of the Jesuits. It is worth noting that Acton was at pains to collect every type of book and pamphlet relating to the history of the Society of Jesus.

Few private libraries have contained such a rare series of local Church histories, the synodal constitutions of the dioceses of Calahorra and Cuenca, the catalogue of the Bishops of Cordova, Martin de Ximena's *Annals of the Church of Jaen*. We must underline Acton's tendency to purchase the complete works of standard authors; the forty-two volumes of Antoine Arnauld are a case in point. The books bought were not necessarily expensive. Seven volumes of Beaumarchais cost £1. Inevitably many books had come from the secularized religious houses of South Germany and Austria. The Benedictine monastery of St Stephen at Würzburg provided several volumes, a work on Richelieu came from the Munich convent of the Augustinian Hermits, Greiderer's *Germania Franciscana* had belonged to the Franciscans at Bözen. In this connection a copy of *Florus Anglo-Bavaricus* can be traced to Benediktbeuren. The suppressed houses of the Society of Jesus provided their own quota. Laureto de Franchis on the controversy between Bishops and Regulars had made its way from the episcopal seminary at Culm. Some books, including Armellini's *Bibliotheca Cassinensis*, had belonged to the Electoral, later Royal Library at Munich; these in general were duplicates.

Books from French monastic sources were much more rare. There is a fine copy of Jean Besly's *Histoire des Comtes de Poictou* from the Benedictine abbey of Moyen Moutier in the diocese of St Dié. The Carmelites of Turin had owned one volume, while the magnificent edition of the Consistorial Orations of Innocent XI from the Marucelli Library is, perhaps, the most distinctive of the few Italian works whose *provenance* can be traced. The ecclesiastical antiquities of the town of Brunswick come from the library of 'Stadt Stralsund'. The classical section of the library at Aldenham incorporates the books of Ernst Lasaulx purchased in 1862.

The standard English political histories and memoirs were all included. Acton was not content with one copy when the subject interested him. There are no less than six variants of Platina's *De Vitis Pontificum*. The historian's copy of Wiseman's *Recollections of the Last Four Popes* in the edition of 1859 remains uncut. Inevitably the library has some of the limitations of the period in which it was assembled. Ranke's *History of Servia* has a prominent place in the section devoted to Eastern Europe. There were on the whole not many books of travel. The three volumes of Lord Valentia's journeys stand out in this respect.

The majority of the books were purchased between John Acton's coming of age in 1855 and his construction of the library some ten years later. This building was described by Henry Tedder, who was librarian at Aldenham in 1873, as a fine cruciform apartment lit by lantern lights and large french windows. An iron gallery, also shelved with books, ran round the walls. The restrained gilding and the moulded iron beadwork recalled the British Museum reading-room.

After this quick impression of the library, a note can be inserted of one aspect of the use that its possessor made of it. At the University Library at Cambridge there are preserved a large number of boxes containing a card index of a special subject. They vary greatly in size and contents. One labelled 'Burke' contains a series of notes of that statesman's sayings, without, however, giving any impression of Acton's views of these propositions. The box entitled 'French character' contains only two cards. One of these carries this sentence: 'When Burke says that a man has a right to the fruits of his labour, he gets behind the north wind, and accepts the Revolution.' The box described as 'Monacensia' gives a considerable number of brief details of Baader and the Munich school. The very interesting series entitled 'Döllinger's table talk' belongs for the most part to a later period.

There is, however, another approach which throws light not so much on Acton's commentary as on the essentially solitary character of his great knowledge. Viewed from one angle, the notices which date from this period form a most valuable illustration of Acton's attitude towards the library and its use. A careful study will suggest those periods of western history in which he was most at ease as also those in which his erudition ground forward somewhat heavily. Across the period one can observe a very gradual shift away from ecclesiastical history, a change of emphasis which goes with the development of that flair for the distant paternity of ideas.

Beyond the monumental character of Acton's erudition there was a certain adventurous element in his study. The quality of adventure in his nature was in fact poured out into research. Here he was, perhaps, the stronger because he had no companions. Nothing was less static than his history and his mind. This is possibly the reason for his impatience with Macaulay's high polemic. With all its merits the *History of England* was what Acton never cared for, a narrative without surprises. This note of adventure was Acton's own; it did not come from cautious Döllinger, still less from the Whig world. It was a quality which needed for its fruitful exercise a range of erudition such as Tocqueville did not possess.

There was also always present an experience of the world which is most refreshing. Naturally this operates most easily where the subject matter belongs to his own or to the preceding century. The approach has a realism which is singularly encouraging. A passage in the *Home and Foreign Review* will give an example. 'Maria Theresa,' we read in a notice dealing with the eighteenth century in Austria,[1] 'introduced a new system of government . . . which is a remarkable instance of the absolutism of the eighteenth century, aggravated rather than tempered by the sovereign's regard for morality, and, as in most cases where absolutism is not intensified by centralization, neither oppressive nor unpopular in the more remote dependencies.' Here lay the background of Acton's thought as he embarked for the first time on public life.

[1] *Home and Foreign Review*, 1863, p. 703.

D*

10

The Years in Parliament

The first change in the setting of John Acton's adult life was the result of his mother's death. Lady Granville had been taken to Brighton for the improvement of her health. In the early spring of 1860 it was clear that she was dying and her mother, the Duchess of Dalberg, came over to England to be with her. Sir John Acton wrote[1] from 9 Royal Crescent to Richard Simpson to tell him that 'my mother is lingering on in a painless and almost insensible state. . . . Her mother has arrived from Germany.' He soon wrote[2] again to the same friend. 'I am sure you will say a *De Profundis* for my mother, who died last night at twelve o'clock without a struggle. She is lying in her coffin now and will be at Aldenham on Friday. I go there to-morrow with her mother.'

Acton had promised Lady Granville that he would marry his cousin, who was at this time a girl of just nineteen. The marriage in fact did not take place for some five years. It seems reasonable to suppose that, when he made his proposal to her, she at first refused him. The marriage was eventually celebrated from the Arcos' house at St Martin in Upper Austria in August 1865. Much was to happen in his life between these dates. During this time he lived in London, when the House was sitting, and alternatively at Aldenham. It was a period in which he undertook relatively little foreign travel.

The search for a constituency for Sir John Acton began shortly after he came of age. He was necessarily inexperienced and also a Roman Catholic. Everything combined to indicate an Irish seat. Lord Granville was in no hurry and he was also somewhat

---

[1] Downside MSS, Acton Correspondence 1858–61. Original letters to Richard Simpson, f. 265.
[2] *Ibid.*, f. 267.

hampered by his ignorance of Irish political topography. Thus his first idea had been the great constituency of the County Clare, which O'Connell had represented. 'I am trying,' he wrote[1] to his friend Lord Canning, 'to get Johnny Acton in for some seat in Ireland. I am glad to find that although he is only a moderate Whig, he is also a very moderate Catholic.'

Later Acton was proposed unsuccessfuly for Cashel, Waterford City and for a Dublin seat. It was at this stage that the constituency of the Borough of Carlow came into view. The sitting member was a Conservative, a Protestant landowner Mr John Alexander of Milton, a relative of Lord Caledon's family. He had never spoken in the House of Commons. The Liberal interest was managed[2] by the Reverend James Maher, P.P. of Graigue, a neighbouring parish. He was an aged and powerful man and an uncle to Cardinal Cullen; he was not an elector. The borough had a slowly diminishing population of rather over eight thousand; but the electorate was based on an £8 household franchise, which gave a total of only 236 voters. In the event 16 persons could not be brought to the poll and only 220 voters exercised their rights. It was an important factor that voting was at this date still open. The smallest Irish constituency was Portarlington with only 99 voters. Seats of this character were not difficult to manage. Two Liberal candidates had already appeared in the constituency and then retired. Sir Thomas Redington was under consideration. It was at this point that Sir John Acton's letter induced Fr Maher to give him his support.

Carlow was a market town with a small manufactory of coarse woollen cloth. A horse barracks had been built there. Ecclesiastically it was in the southern portion of the diocese of Kildare and Leighlin, and in recent years a cathedral had been constructed. Beside it stood the seminary St Patrick's College. In those days of the Protestant ascendancy the Catholic influence was perhaps stronger than in busier places. It was a grouping of small white houses, some of them unoccupied, and was centred on Dublin

---

[1] Letter dated from London on 10 March 1857, quoted in Lord E. Fitzmaurice's *Life of Lord Granville*, vol. i, p. 227.

[2] Cf. for an account of this affair the admirable note by James J. Auchmuty, 'Acton's Election as an Irish Member of Parliament', *English Historical Review*, vol. LXI (1946), pp. 394–405.

Street where the road from the capital ran into the town. It lay off the main line of traffic some fifty miles south-south-west of Dublin in the broad valley of the Barrow, a little to the eastward of those limestone hills which surround the Leinster coal measures at Castle Comer.

The election day was now approaching and Sir John Acton was expected hourly. There were two newspapers in the town, the *Carlow Post* which applauded and the *Sentinel* which abused the absent candidate, nor was the situation improved by the fact that the Liberal agent, Mr Norton, was likewise a stranger to Carlow. In a speech on Election eve Edward Flood Esq. described the Liberal candidate as 'a distinguished scholar who promises to be one of the first literary men of Europe'. This was received with groans and with shouts of 'Where is he?' from among the crowd. Mr Flood went on to explain that 'he is a man of a princely income and respectable lineage – the most respectable in the United Kingdom'. This statement was met by cries of 'Oh, Oh, Oh'. The railway line had recently reached Carlow coming south from Mageney across the water meadows. It was felt that Sir John would surely take the packet service and then come down from Kingsbridge Station by the new railway. 'Crowds of anxious "friends" were to be seen on the look-out for him on the arrival of each train "but to no purpose".' This was the caustic comment in the Dublin *Daily Express* on 2 May.

In spite of the absence of the candidate the election was a re-markable success, Sir John Acton securing 117 votes as against the 103 cast for John Alexander. There was much popular rejoicing, mainly by the non-vote holders, and a certain amount of damage to the property of the ten Catholics, who had voted Conservative. These included a printer working for the *Sentinel* and two butchers. In these last cases it seems likely that their custom among the surrounding Protestant landed gentry and among their more affluent fellow citizens meant very much to them.

On 3 June 1859 the new member at last reached Carlow. He was met at the railway station by Fr Maher, Dr P. J. Cullen and Mr T. Price, proprietor of the *Carlow Post*. There was a noisy crowd who, after the shouts of welcome, gave groans for Soupers, for the patrons of Soupers and for the patrons of Gavazzi the

Apostate. This last-named was an Italian ex-priest, who had been imprudently introduced into the town by the local Presbyterian minister to speak on the subject of Italian unity. Dinner took place at Cullen's Hotel. There were ten toasts and Acton was advised to take an Irish bride.

The *Sentinel* reproached the Liberals with bribery; it seems that Acton came to think that this was true. He very seldom referred in later life to this election[1] and as far as I have been able to discover there is no reference to Father Maher in all his writings. He returned to England immediately and on 10 June by his vote helped to end Lord Derby's administration.

The principal factor in the background of these six years before his marriage was Acton's duties and position as a member of the House of Commons. This period included almost the whole length of Lord Palmerston's last administration. There was no reason for Acton to have had any genuine personal contact with the old premier and the main interest of these years, as far as the side of politics was concerned, lay in his slowly developing intimacy with Mr Gladstone. These were the early days of that statesman's Liberalism. He had just returned from his post as high commissioner in the Ionian Islands. This was a time when he was shaping himself to new attitudes and towards new friendships.

In 1861 Mr Gladstone had lost his contemporary Lord Herbert of Lea, whose affectionate intimacy had meant so very much to him. Lord Aberdeen and Sir James Graham, both of an older generation, had died within the year, and he was soon to lose the Duke of Newcastle. There was, beyond his wife's relations, the Glynnes and Lytteltons, a kind of vacancy among his intimates and into this Acton would find his way.

William Ewart Gladstone was born in 1809; he was therefore twenty-five years John Acton's senior. He held the office of chancellor of the exchequer and his first recorded letter to Acton is dated from 11 Downing Street. The historian therefore became

[1] There is an interesting letter to Lord Granville about this matter. 'I am not sure that O'Hagan (then M.P. for Tralee) is right about the wish of my Carlow friends to see more of me, but I am sure he is quite wrong in thinking that I could possibly retain my seat there. For a long time passed I have completely dismissed the thought from my mind. It would be possible only on two conditions, neither of which I can accept – a profuse use of corruption and of patronage.' Printed in *Acton-Döllinger Correspondence*, I, p. 318, note 2.

the friend of an elderly, and later of an ageing, man. Mr Gladstone had found his equipoise. This fact ensured the steady growth of intimacy. The mood of Mr Gladstone's youth, his feeling for Clumber as an instance, was something with which Sir John Acton would surely not have sympathized. For Gladstone approached this large Tory stronghold from the outside. He had none of the familiarity with which Acton since his childhood had approached the great Whig homes. In fact, had Acton and Gladstone been contemporaries, it seems unlikely that their lasting intimacy could have developed. For Gladstone in his youth was a Conservative marked by a strange unworldly innocence. Clumber, however, explains an aspect of Mr Gladstone's character. He had been brought up in Liverpool in a home which was wealthy and Low Church; his approach to Clumber was his first contact with long-established political riches. The particular atmosphere has its significance and is in a way surprising.

Gladstone was only twenty-one when that 'great borough-mongering Leviathan,'[1] the fifth Duke of Newcastle, invited him to Clumber to offer him the Tory seat for Newark which was in his gift. The young Gladstone was taken into a house which dazzled him. He was always ready to be impressed by strict virtue and a modest intellect. The Duke of Newcastle's education had been sketchy. Five years at Eton 'learning[2] everything that I ought not to have known' and then four years as a prisoner in France caught by the rupture of the Peace of Amiens in 1803. His notes in Diary form[3] are most appealing. 'With a tender conscience, great inexperience and inadequate means I entered life.' His political and religious opinions were both tinged with severity. He was a strong supporter of the Protestant Church of England by law established. His attitude to the Roman Church was clear. 'I think,' he told[4] the young Gladstone, 'there can be little doubt that we ought to wish for its destruction.' On the other hand he refused to admit a gentleman of Dissenting principles to the commission of the peace in his own county. He constantly regretted

---

[1] Gladstone quoted in *Gladstone, a Biography* by Sir Philip Magnus, p. 15.
[2] Notes from a diary quoted in the *Life of Henry Pelham, fifth Duke of Newcastle* by John Martinson, p. 2.
[3] *Ibid.*, p. 3.
[4] Record of a conversation, Sir Philip Magnus, *op. cit.*, p. 15.

the absence of a parliamentary leader for men of his strict views. He deplored the Liberal tendencies of the Duke of Wellington and was deeply frightened by him. 'I had the will,' he noted,[1] '[to be a leader] but not the smallest portion of the ability.' This was, indeed, borough-mongering drawing to its close.

He was a stiff letter writer and an imprudent buyer. He had acquired the great estate of Worksop from the Duke of Norfolk partly for the purpose of pulling down the house. He quarrelled with the Duke of Portland about some water meadows. On the other hand he was in an Evangelical sense a perfect father to his ten children, early motherless. When he took them to the dentist, 'Mr Cartwright[2] drew eighteen teeth from five of them'. Ten such children, he once noted,[3] 'and I thank God for it, as I verily believe are not to be found together in one family in the whole world'. On his fiftieth birthday the Duke of Newcastle jotted[4] down, 'As a politician I am shunned and discouraged'. This was a very strange beginning for Mr Gladstone.

From such a world Acton was far removed. The intertwining of politics and religion in the Tory Protestant sense was deeply un-congenial. It was the appeal of Gladstone's Anglicanism that it was presented in a Liberal setting. At the same time it was a help for their developing relationship that Acton's mind moved over the whole sphere of government. Thus a letter to Simpson written from 16 Bruton Street on 15 April 1861 gives his view of the work of the chancellor of the exchequer. 'Gladstone,' he explains,[5] 'has brought forward his budget in a very tame straightforward speech, and it is on the whole well received. I rejoice at the con-firmation it contains of my view that he is not inclined to democ-racy, or to class legislation, but tries to carry out true principles of economy. He spoke very well on direct and indirect taxation, and balanced different interests by remitting a penny of direct taxa-tion and removing at the same time the paper duty.' It was one of Acton's charms for Gladstone that he was in a political sense always so serious.

[1] Martinson, *op. cit.*, p. 8.
[2] *Ibid.*, p. 11.
[3] *Ibid.*
[4] *Ibid.*, p. 5.
[5] Gasquet, *op. cit.*

In these years Sir John Acton was only finding his way in this new friendship. In the spring of 1861 he moved from his step-father's house to 37 Half Moon Street, which he refers[1] to as his 'new lodgings'. He was now from time to time at Gladstone's breakfast table. He began at last to move in the general intellectual world of the capital. Such contacts were not always fruitful. 'I have,' he wrote,[2] 'just been breakfasting with Pearson [*Spectator*] and Bagehot [*Economist*] and did not get much out of them.' This may have been because for Acton the successful method of communication was the *tête-a-tête*. The case of Walter Bagehot is interesting for in some ways they had much in common. Both men shared a wide and rather desiccated approach to problems of Victorian history. It was at this period, too, that John Acton first met Samuel Wilberforce.[3] The Bishop of Oxford was his fellow-guest at Gladstone's breakfast table.

There were certain explorations among the Catholic peers belonging to the Liberal party, who had hitherto been outside his circle. At the time when he was moving into his new rooms in Half Moon Street, Sir John Acton went down for a week-end to Stonor Park in Oxfordshire. The third Lord Camoys, now elderly, had been a Whig member of Parliament for Oxford City and later a Lord-in-Waiting during Liberal administrations. There is some reason to suppose that it was from Gladstone that Acton had heard praise of him. 'I have spent,' he wrote[4] to Simpson, 'an unholy Sunday with Lord Camoys and Sir John Simeon, who uttered many abominations.'

This is, perhaps, the point at which to draw attention to Acton's phrasing. He seems hardly to realize the distinction between criticism and invective. In these respects the English language was a foreign tongue to him. Sir John Simeon was a dull and rather uninteresting Newmanite baronet. It seems likely that he had been putting forward propositions for the Catholic members of Parliament to defend the temporal possessions of the Holy See. This use of the word 'abominations' throws a light on much of John Acton's private phrasing, nor should one forget his cheerfully

---

[1] Downside MSS, f. 396.
[2] *Ibid.*, f. 260.
[3] Cf. Letter noted as 2 May 1861, Gasquet, *op. cit.*
[4] Downside MSS, f. 399.

boisterous humour. The letter goes on to say that 'Camoys is not as intelligent as I had thought and heard'.

A little later there was a visit to a peer, who has not been identified. 'I have been wasting[1] my time on a visit to a crazy Lord in Cheshire.' There is one further reference to a Catholic gathering. 'I dined[2] and slept at Hornyholds – such a sleepy party. Walker of Oscott was there, vacantly amiable.' In this last case John Acton did not trouble to spell his host's name correctly for he was Mr J. V. G. Hornyold of Blackmore Park.

There were of course certain contacts with the Government. Thus in March 1863 there appears the note[3] 'Clarendon talked to me for two hours yesterday, only too confidentially, telling me many things he wants me to keep to myself'. It is possible that the foreign secretary wished to draw out his opinions about Italy. But this is a solitary example; there was always the burden on his time. 'I have lost,' he wrote,[4] 'one evening with Princess Murat – and must lose another for my cousin's coming out to-morrow.' And then there is a precisely dated letter 37 HMS, as he was accustomed to abbreviate his London lodgings, Monday 6 o'clock, noted 23 January 1863. 'I must tie my choker for an early (fashionable) dinner, and the Prince of Wales afterwards, shirking Poland.' There is here suggested Acton's long fatigue at sitting silent on the benches of the House of Commons. It was Aldenham for which he was homesick.

There is a note[5] to Simpson written from his house in Shropshire on 7 February 1864. 'I shall be in the dreary Halfmoon tomorrow.' A letter as early as December 1860 sets out the true position. Acton is writing[6] to Simpson about some literary work. 'If I could only get turned out of Parliament in an honest way and settle down among my books. I should soon bring to maturity my part of the plan.' The comments in his letters[7] on the members' speeches come from his earlier years in the House of Commons. 'Osborne, perfectly drunk, said some good things', and the

[1] *Ibid.*, f. 297.
[2] *Ibid.*, f. 304.
[3] *Ibid.*, f. 285.
[4] Gasquet, *op. cit.*
[5] Downside MSS, f. 318.
[6] Gasquet, *op. cit.*, pp. 155–6.
[7] Downside MSS, f. 261.

reference to Stansfeld's 'bow-wow platitudes'. The end came suddenly. At the general election in 1865 Acton had given up his Irish seat, he had had very little contact with his constituents, and instead stood for Bridgnorth the local seat in his own county. He had then just married. He won by a single vote and was unseated on petition. 'You may suppose,' he wrote[1] to Simpson. 'how we liked being beaten by such an opponent with his No Popery cry, and how strongly we begin by believing in the corruption as well as the iniquity of the Bridgnorth majority. Our grand point was to get me seconded by a clergyman Mr Ward, master of the grammar school.' Still, a problem arose over the difficulties made by his congregation at his giving such support to a Roman Catholic.

The first stage of Acton's political life was over. He gave up his rooms in Half Moon Street; his married life was now beginning. There is a letter from Brown's Hotel, 22 Dover Street, dated 21 February 1866 inviting Simpson 'to dine and make my wife's acquaintance at the St James'.' Acton was moving now in a new orbit. His contacts with Simpson inevitably decreased; they concerned his technical historical interests. He turned to him once more in the troubled years.

[1] *Ibid.*, an envelope containing undated letters.

II

Last Newman Contacts

In the years during which he sat in the House of Commons, Sir John Acton inevitably had a very varied series of contacts. The fact that he was a member of Parliament attracted the attention of Gladstone and Lord Clarendon; but it also gave a positive significance to his career in the eyes of Cardinal Wiseman and Dr Manning. Still these, in fact, incompatible relationships were not destined to endure. The publication of the *Syllabus Errorum* would lead John Acton to take his side.

The contact with Newman was of a different character. This was in a way likewise affected by Acton's parliamentary career. The intricate relationship of the *Rambler* period was now fading. Newman sought for support in the establishment of the Oratory School and Acton in his turn recommended that his cousin Paolo Beccadelli should be sent there. Their contact faded out almost insensibly. The letters now to be considered represent, with the exception of a single note written in 1877, the last stage of John Acton's correspondence with Dr Newman. A long letter dated from 37 Half Moon Street on 4 June is worth quoting *in extenso*. On the sheet the year 1861? is added in pencil. Acton, now in Parliament, was approached by the Catholic authorities in regard to various measures in which they were concerned. These were, too, the last years of his social contact with Dr Manning.

My dear Father Newman,
I have so many things to speak to you about that I must break my rule of not writing without absolute necessity. First of all I hope that you were not displeased with the May *Rambler*. Thompson has written with more vehemence than force against the chapter on Campion, accompanying his public with a private letter which Wilberforce showed me, in which he

says that Simpson will destroy the *R.* but that he thought my political summary interesting and respectful. Others think otherwise. You know that Faber had published his Whitsun sermon in which everybody says I am directly pointed at in a passage which Wilberforce has extracted for special recommendation. Others speak of a denunciation of the last number in Rome. Various attacks on it have appeared in the *Tablet.* The Cardinal has told a priest who told More O'Ferrall that C. Antonelli has written to inform him that I am to bring forward in parliament a motion against the Temporal Power which is to be supported by many Irish members, and he asked this priest whether he thought it was true.

Manning has got unfortunately upon the unsafe ground of prophecy, and dedicates to you a dissertation which he sent me, but he has never spoken to me on the subject. An attempt has been made at a meeting of the Club to coerce me into immediate action on the subject of prisons, as I intended to postpone it till after the Workhouse question was settled in our Committee. Manning and Bowyer proposed a very peremptory resolution, which the meeting adopted on Saturday and sent to me, demanding a reply for to-day. I replied by stating my reasons, and then surrendered my possession of the subject in deference to the general wish that it should be at once brought on, which I cannot consent to.

It is clear that Acton was a difficult member of Catholic Committees in the last years in which he served on them.

I hear [he continues] that to-day they resolved to ask me to keep it in my hands to bring on at my own time, but this of course I shall not do, and I shall abide by my promise to support any other member who undertakes it. I hope they will have the fairness to publish my letter, as they have attacked me on the subject, and you will then understand the character of this move, and the way in which I have successfully met it. More O'Ferrall and O'Hagan are however the only men who approve of what I have done. The suspicions and ill will excited against me would revive and continue if I accepted the conspicuous position in which the unskilfulness of the other party has placed me.

I hope you will allow me to explain to you why I am resolved to cling to my obscurity. Nothing would induce me to stand for Carlow again after certain proceedings which came to my knowledge long after my election. Moreover they are in other ways a constituency I cannot well represent. Besides my books have an irresistible attraction for me which make me miserable in London. In the House I find that I am perfectly isolated, and without hopes of obtaining any influence for my principles. I am sure I can do better in another sphere.

Besides, if you will recall to mind an announcement[1] I once prematurely made to you, you will understand me when I say that a private sorrow weighs on my health and energies. I took a short Whitsun holiday abroad and went to see Döllinger. He is expecting Father St John, and will I am sure take care of him. He was busy composing a book on the church and the world at the present time, a development of his lectures in which he discusses all the great and burning questions of the connexion between religion and modern society, and gives an elaborate apology of the church. I have the first 6 sheets. It is so well adapted for Protestants, and so likely to attract their notice that I am anxious to bring it out in English. Longman will not publish it. Do you recommend Burns?

I feel very painfully that I am altogether unworthy to be regarded as the champion in this country of the cause which is yours, and the cause suffers by its identification with me. Faber, quitting the grounds of argument, has set up his own claims as the sole teacher and authority on the grounds of sanctity and humility, and thus disturbs people's consciences. Very holy and distinguished priests, whom I shall name to you as soon as I am authorised, offer me materials and support, but refuse to share responsibility, and therefore to give the authority of their views which is wanting in my hands.

This is of interest as a record of one of Acton's last contacts with any body of priests of his own Communion.

Gratry and Lacordaire [he concludes[2]] are so intimidated that I found Montalembert ignorant of their real opinions. I shall have something of a somewhat spiritual kind in the July n°. and

---

[1] An undated letter from Acton to Newman from the House of Commons bears on this point. 'A great private trouble has come upon me very soon after my mothers' death, and I am longing for the recess in order to try and find some distraction and relief in a journey to Spain', Birmingham Oratory, Acton MSS, vol. i, f. 32.

[2] *Ibid.*, i, f. 43.

otherwise nothing on this question. We are still listening in vain
for the voice we most reverence and most love to hear. The
examination of Catholic witnesses before the Poor Law Committee has been very satisfactory and successful. Both Morris
and Bagshawe gave good evidence well, and there is a strong
impression in our favour.

Believe me,

Yours ever faithfully,

J. D. Acton.

The historian's next exercise in this interchange appears to have
been despatched on 9 June of the same year. The letter deals,
among other subjects, with Simpson's attack on Pope Pius V and
contains a further comment on Acton's position in the English
Catholic body. He was accustomed to switch rapidly from one topic
to another. The fact that Pius V was canonized had its importance.

Only a Jansenist [he begins[1]] can say that a pope or a saint
was not liable to sin or error, or that the church has the same
infallibility in government as in faith, where such personages
appear in a history they cannot be treated as subject to different
laws from other men, and in the life of a saint written even for
religious instruction and edification I suppose the account of his
faults is as instructive, or at least as necessary for instruction,
as the account of his virtues. Here however is a matter not
affecting his sanctity but his judgment as ruler of the church,
and nobody I suppose will say that saints are necessarily wise
in the wisdom of this world. . . .

I have no sort of personal quarrel [he goes on] with any of
the persons mentioned in your letter. Manning is on the best
terms with me, and gave me a sort of apologetic explanation of
the part he took in the first meeting on prisons. The second
meeting knocked under to my letter. I have not the letter to
refer to, but Wilberforce told me that he said that the pope's
declaration on the temporal power bound & determined his
own judgment. If so this is one of those phenomena which, I
think, make it idle to conduct controversy with the Protestant
world. I have not read Faber's sermon and spoke only from
what I hear is the general impression, shared, I know, and confirmed by the Jesuits.

[1] *Ibid.*, i, f. 44.

Acton was early unhappy in Parliament; it is recorded that he only made one speech and asked two questions during the whole time that he retained his seat. At the same time the fact that he was a member of the House of Commons gave him a certain weight in the eyes of Cardinal Wiseman and his advisers. The next three letters record the rather heavy courtesy with which the old prelate treated his former pupil. 'This evening,' Acton wrote,[1] 'I believe the Academia holds its first meeting at the Cardinal's, who is to deliver an inaugural address. I mean to be there and to do what I can for the undertaking, but without sanguine hopes.'

> You must not consider me a regular supporter of the Government. I should vote against their foreign policy, and I probably should not vote for them on a vote of confidence. But it seems to me equivalent to a falsehood to vote against the merits of a question, only from general sympathy or resentment towards a party. Antonelli told Blennerhasset of Catholic MPs selling the pope for paper, so I have had a hit at those who would give up paper for the pope.

Acton had written that 'Manning is on the best terms with me' and to this he had added the statement that he must not be considered 'a regular supporter of the Government'. In each of his three first years as a member of Parliament he had spoken once and usually during question time. The first subject was 'the condition of the Roman States', the second 'Catholic inmates of prisons' and the third 'the inspection of Roman Catholic schools'. After this last occasion he did not speak again. These questions[2] and perhaps especially the two last show the intention not to break with Manning's wishes.

It was natural that Acton's views should evolve gradually, and two comments in his article on 'The States of the Church' printed in the *Rambler* in March 1860 tend to reflect his then opinion. 'For more[3] than a century the temporal authority of the popes remained unchallenged and unaltered, and they enjoyed a period of repose such as they had never known in more Catholic times.

[1] *Ibid.*, vol. i, f. 47. Dated in different ink 29 June '61.
[2] These interventions took place on 4 May 1860, 7 May 1861, and 11 April 1862.
[3] Reprinted in *Essays on Church and State*, ed. D. Woodruff, p. 111.

Then, at the end of the eighteenth century, came a period of
disaster and decline, of which we have not seen the end nor, we
fear, the worst.' This same article concluded[1] with a quotation
from the Epistles of Pope Innocent III. 'The most powerful and
prosperous of all the successors of St Peter has said, that what he
relied on was not his own power, but the prayers of the whole
Church – *Non de nostra virtute confidimus, sed de universalis Ecclesaie
prece speramus.*' Acton's forecast of the future did not alter, but he
came in time to approve what he foresaw. However, his standpoint
in 1860 was to cause Lord Granville's complaint made in August
of that year that 'Johnny has thrown us over'.

It is worth for a moment to examine how Sir John's line of
action was then viewed on the Tory benches. It must be said that
there was something pleasant to Mr Disraeli's heavily furnished
imagination in the notion of a young Catholic baronet. He was
always ready to consider any grouping and he had spoken[2] of the
pope as 'an old man on a Semitic throne'. These were his happy
years; his authority with the Queen was now immense. His
phrasing clearly gave him so much pleasure. 'The great[3] Whig
Coalition that was to have devoured Her Majesty's Government
as an ogre does a child.' His efforts to bring Gladstone over to the
Tories had been fortunately unsuccessful. It would have been
terrible to have been saddled with Mr Gladstone as an ally. He
was now delivered for ever from what Lord Derby called[4] 'this
half-regained Eurydice'. The two men had now come into their
natural relationship. 'Gladstone,' he wrote[5] to his wife with cheerfulness, 'looked like a beaten hound and ate no ordinary quantity
of dirt'. His letter had a tone of irony. 'The old Aulic Councils,'
he told[6] Sir William Heathcote, 'which, full of prudence and
science, always conducted the Austrian armies to discomfiture.'
He had long gained the note to win the Court. He was prudent and
used the same expressions of the Royal Family whether he was
writing to or of them. It was two years since he had written to

[1] *Ibid.*, p. 122.
[2] *The Life of Benjamin Disraeli* by W. F. Monypenny and G. E. Buckle (1929 ed.),
vol. ii, p. 59.
[3] *Ibid.*, vol. i, p. 1549.
[4] Quoted, *ibid.*, i, p. 1555.
[5] Letter dated 16 July 1860, *ibid.*, ii, p. 15.
[6] *Ibid.*, ii, p. 33.

Mrs Brydges Williams that 'the Prince Consort and the Duc d'Aumale – the two most richly cultivated minds I ever met and men, too, of great abilities'. He knew so well the little ways to please them. In his grounds at Hughenden the German forest was growing up for the Queen's sake. It was not unnatural that he had taken the old Belgian King as a correspondent. A letter written[1] to Brussels on 23 August 1860 set out his views. Among other observations he made the following.

> This struggle [in regard to a Government proposal to repeal the duty on foreign paper] elicited another important feature in the relative state of parties: viz., the complete alienation of the Roman Catholic party from the present Government, avowedly caused by their Italian policy. On that occasion, while many independent Roman Catholic Irish members voted with the Conservatives, as has been their custom of late, the Whig Roman Catholic members for the first time evinced their disapproval of the Ministry, rose, and in a body left the House, including among many others the leading names of Lord Edward Howard, Mr More O'Ferrall, Mr Monsell and Sir John Acton.

With the world of Hughenden Acton was never to have the slightest contact, but the quotations from Disraeli are included to show how very far he stood from Acton's temperament. He was as far from him as was Lord Palmerston, his own jaunty leader. Sir John Acton's sympathies were bound up with the ethical seriousness of Mr Gladstone.

A curious episode which took place in this same session was a visit by Ralph Earle, Disraeli's private secretary, to Cardinal Wiseman, who was resting by the sea in the house that the Duchess of Leeds had purchased for the Holy Child nuns at St Leonards. It must be said in explanation of this interview that we have not got the Cardinal's words but merely a report.[2]

> In Ireland there is a very good feeling towards us, and some of those who declined his invitation to help us in 1859 held out hopes of eventual assistance, which is now likely to be realised.

---

[1] *Ibid.*, ii, p. 17.
[2] *Ibid.*, ii, p. 59.

Monsell, Bowyer and Hennessy, he thinks a very good combination, as they influence three different coteries. The first has great
influence with the Irish bishops and clergy. The Cardinal . . .
concluded by observing that we were quite right in looking to
the R.Cs for our majority, for they would give it to us.

The word Conservative had power with him and as a sick man he
still retained his love for the grand phrases. 'If,' he continued,
'there were any prospect of a Government being formed that
would carry out a respectable foreign policy, the Catholic constituents and their members would all support it.' Sir John Acton
had many worries and was now a firmly Liberal politician. It was
lucky that he does not seem to have learned of the existence of this
letter.

Meanwhile Acton was still involved with Wiseman's work. As
he explained[1] to Newman,

The academia held its first meeting at the Cardinal's the
week before last and he is well pleased with the event. A long
paper of his was read, of which everybody says that it is quite
in his old style, only a repetition, and without any power or
depth. You will see it in a few days. He seems to think that
Catholic science has only a great victory to gain, not great
problems to solve. He was looking well, and was very gracious;
but the selection of noblemen etc. was capricious and some are
jealous at their exclusion in favour of Feilding, Campden etc.
The worst of it is, Dr Rock starts next time with an archaeological dissertation.

One further note[2] refers to this same body. 'Meantime I have been
appointed censor to the Accademia,[3] together with Bagshawe
and, I think, 10 very reverends.' It was earlier in the same summer
that he had sent[4] to Newman his *cri de coeur*.

I have never been very zealous for particular views, but I care
above almost everything for one or two principles, or general
opinions. I cannot bear that Protestants should say the church

---

[1] Birmingham Oratory, Acton MSS, vol. i, f. 50. Dated in pencil 8 July 1861.
[2] *Ibid.*, i, f. 53. Dated 13 August, the year 1861 added subsequently.
[3] He spells this word indifferently 'academia' and 'Accademia'.
[4] Birmingham Oratory, Acton MSS, vol. i, f. 50.

cannot be reconciled with the truths of precepts of science, or that Catholics should fear the legitimate and natural progress of the scientific spirit. These two errors seem to be almost identical, and if one is more dangerous than the other, I think it is the last. So that it comes more naturally to me to be zealous against the Catholic mistake than against the Protestant. But the weapon against both is the same, the encouragement of the true scientific spirit, and disinterested love of truth.

A little later he makes his avowal.[1] 'Yet I cannot conceive how such a cause can be pursued without a collision with Rome, or how it can avoid being beset with difficulties in such a society as ours.'

And yet throughout this period there are evidences which go to foretell the line that John Acton would adopt. In regard to the foundation of the Oratory School at Edgbaston he gave the measure of conventional support which was expected from a wealthy Catholic layman, who had associations with Father Newman and had not experienced either the Jesuit or the Benedictine educational systems. Acton was brought to call at the Oratory upon this errand by Serjeant Bellasis, a man in his late forties, who was at that time trustee for the late Earl of Shrewsbury's estates and much busied in the affairs of the community. It was the expected grouping with the fourteenth Duke of Norfolk supported by about a dozen laymen including Lords Campden and Feilding about whom Acton already had his reservations. There was one member of his close affinity, Sir Robert Throckmorton, who was married to his aunt.

A letter to Father Darnell, the new headmaster, is however in his accustomed vein. It is dated[2] at Aldenham on 3 February 1859. Acton begins by discounting the alleged opposition of the London Oratorians to the new school. 'People anticipate opposition from Brompton, but as I think erroneously. They object to the plan 1° as inconsistent with the rule. This prevents them from setting up an opposition establishment. 2° Because of the Padre's general incompetency.' It is curious that Acton should have described Newman in these terms in writing to one of his devoted Birmingham

[1] In the same letter.
[2] *Ibid.*, i, f. 22.

community. 'The confutation of this,' he then goes on, 'will be a practical one in your hands, but if they say anything too loud, I can quote Faber's express promise to me that he would not only tolerate, but assist the school. The promise of course is worthless, but the publication of it by a "well-wisher who is happy to know etc" might in case of need be of use. . . .' In one short letter Acton had committed himself heavily against the leaders of both the Oratories.

> I speak [he continues] as one personally interested in a high degree in the success of your undertaking, when I venture to mention what people will be most prepared to criticise in the execution of the plan. It is the discipline. They will be on the watch for a flaw in this respect and this is what an enemy can most effectually use to prejudice mothers against you. I have met with unfavourable anticipations in several places where I could not trace them to a hostile source – therefore I conjure you to be on your guard. A slip at first might be very injurious to the scheme. My recollections of the deficiencies of Oscott discipline are further than your school memories, but you can refresh your knowledge of *vitanda* by stepping over there any day. The system is worse now, but I think the boys were worse in my time. There are such fluctuations in schools. On the principle of setting a thief to catch a thief, I should like very much to have an opportunity of talking over several things with you some day. Believe only this, that people will look out for a peg on which to hang an accusation of lax discipline.

This letter shows how far away Acton already stood from Oscott College.

It was apparently in the next year that Acton began a desultory correspondence with Dr Newman concerning the acceptance and attendance at the Oratory School of his cousin's son Paolo Beccadelli, at that time 'not nine years old'. He described[1] the boy's father, the Prince of Camporeale, as 'a great Sicilian noble of opposition principles, who went out of his mind on hearing of the bombardment of Palermo'. Soon afterwards it appeared that Corpus Christi had been proposed as the time for him to receive

---

[1] Letter from 16 Bruton Street, undated but with an annotation '1860?', *ibid.*, i, f. 40.

Communion. 'I am sure,' wrote[1] Acton, 'that Paul's mother wishes him to make his first Holy Communion only at such time as you and his confessor may think proper.'

In these years between his mother's death and his own marriage John Acton was very close to his Throckmorton aunt and to his cousins. They shared in the general care for young Paul's future. 'I see,' he wrote[2] to Newman from Half Moon Street, 'from Paul's letters that he is quite reconciled to what you have decided for him. We are in great troubles for my uncle Sir R. Throckmorton, who has been in serious danger for two days, and lies now, somewhat better, but fully prepared for the worst.' This was in the summer of 1862 and he soon wrote[3] again.

> I came back to-day from my uncle's funeral, and thank you for your memory of him in the Mass yesterday. Dr Grant preached a short and very touching sermon. The daughters are going to spend some weeks at Aldenham with your old disciple John, who has just returned from Tübingen, where Kuhn, the great German developmentist, took care of him. The Princess Camporeale is at Naples. I write to her to-night to ask what she wishes to be done with Paul during the holidays. The house at Buckland is shut up, nobody will be living regularly at Coughton, and I cannot ask my cousins to have him with them at Aldenham, nor do I suppose he would enjoy being in a house of mourning.

These rather detailed notes are set down here for they reveal that Catholic family life and a care for the religious upbringing of the children which were typical of him. Although his tone would alter in later life, he always remained faithful to this care. In this, as in so much of his conduct in religious matters, he must be seen as a man of the Continent.

In 1865 Acton gave up his seat for Carlow in order to contest the constituency of Bridgnorth, his home ground. This brought him one of the last letters that he received from Dr Newman which reached him after his election by one vote but before he was unseated on petition.

---

[1] Date added in pencil June 17? 1860, i, f. 58.
[2] Added in pencil 1862 and June 26, *ibid.*, i, f. 59.
[3] Added in ink 'July 9? 1862', *ibid.*, i, f. 60.

I congratulate[1] you, or rather the Catholic body, on your
election – but *yourself*, as far as this – that you are in your proper
place, as Member for Bridgnorth, but you were not so exactly
as member for an Irish Borough. It is pleasant too that you are
the first to break through the impediment raised against
Catholics since the Hierarchy Bill – as Sir John Simeon will, I
trust, be the next; and the event comes with a curious fitness
after the recent decision about the Archbishoprick (he is here
alluding to Manning's nomination), which seemed to force the
action of the Catholics of England into one only channel. I
wish you & Sir John Simeon may be the rallying points of a
party, and that you may hit upon some means of being represented in the newspaper press. You will be looked after very
sharply, and your influence may be very great. I am not speaking of a political party in the House of course (which is absurd)
but a party among Catholics.

At the bottom of the sheet is added 'p.s. So Sir J. S. is elected.'

This was indeed a chimera. Sir John Simeon has left a faint
impression, a baronet with a nineteenth-century fortune and an
estate in his constituency, the Isle of Wight. He was a nephew of
the founder of the Simeon Trustees and was a convert and
protégé of Newman's. His contact with Acton seems to have been
slight and he was to die in 1870.

Two years later, and this was after the *Syllabus* had made its
deep impression, there was another brief exchange. This dealt
with Paolo Beccadelli, who had clearly been sent to other schools
and was to be taken back to the Oratory provisionally. 'As to
Paul,' wrote[2] Newman, 'we always liked him and got on with
him, tho', as you know he certainly had his faults. . . . When he
gets somewhat older, we should wish to put him on the list of boys
preparing for higher education (such as Towneley and Bellasis
are at present) who pay instead of eighty guineas £120 a year.'
And this brought him naturally to his plans for a house at Oxford.
'I sent you,' he continued, 'an application for a subscription to our
Oxford project some time ago, with (I think) a prospectus, direct-
ing "Poste Restante', Rome".' Acton at once sent him twenty-five
pounds. He also explained that his cousin and Marco Minghetti,

---

[1] Letter dated 21 July 1865, *ibid.*, i, f. 73.
[2] Letter dated 13 March 1867, *ibid.*, i, f. 75.

the Italian politician whom she had now married, were grateful for the arrangements for Paolo. He then makes a statement on Minghetti, which has a bearing on his own standpoint.[1]

> Minghetti, from whom you will hear more to the purpose, is a man who observes outwardly at least the duties of religion, and is politically a most decided supporter of religious liberty. Within the last year or two he has advanced a good deal in this direction and he is particularly unpopular just now, as a friend of the clerical party. I don't think he has any unbelieving theories, and he is not a scoffer, but his education must have been neglected as far as religion is concerned.

This may be the last example of Acton's interest in a neighbour's orthodoxy.

The ending of the intercourse was almost casual. Acton had called at the Birmingham Oratory on Christmas Eve of this same year 1867. Newman was away and wrote[2] to him on the following day saying that Father St John thanked Acton for the German Tract and says that 'I ought to express my acknowledgments to the author of it'. This brief note marks a very tranquil fading out of the relationship.

Three years earlier Acton had conveyed to Dr Newman an invitation to come to London and go with him to breakfast at Mr Gladstone's. 'He[3] has I know been long anxious to see you. He never speaks of your writings without great warmth.' This was an invitation which was not to be repeated. The fact seems to be that John Acton was never at ease with Dr Newman and had no sympathy with his admiring circle. There were other factors. He was no longer engaged in literary work in which he wished for Newman's patronage. Dr Döllinger was now losing interest in those English Catholic contacts with which Newman had supplied him. Sir John Acton was by this time very far from Archbishop Manning; he did not feel the need of the support of Dr Manning's opponents in his own Communion.

In the future he would take the same care of the Catholic up-

---

[1] Letter dated from Hotel Serny, Rome, on 26 March 1867, *ibid.*, i, f. 77.
[2] *Ibid.*, i, f. 77.
[3] *Ibid.*, i, f. 71.

bringing of his children as he had shown in the case of his cousin Paolo Beccadelli. Any other course of action would be considered reprehensible by all his Continental cousinage. It was from the *adult* Catholic groups in England that he drew away. There is every reason to suppose that after 1867 Acton's communication with the Oratory had almost reached its end.

Meanwhile all contact with Archbishop's House had ended. Cardinal Wiseman, after warning his clergy against the practice of the *Home and Foreign Review* in inaccurately reporting foreign news, had continued in these terms:[1]

> But this can hardly excite surprise in us who know the antecedents of that journal under another name, the absence for years of all reserve or reverence in its treatment of persons or of things deemed sacred, its grazing over the very edges of the most perilous abysses of error, and its habitual preferences of uncatholic to catholic instincts, tendencies and motives. In uttering these sad thoughts, and entreating you to warn your people, and especially the young, against such dangerous leadership, believe me I am only obeying a higher direction than my own impulses, and acting under much more solemn sanctions. Nor shall I stand alone in this unhappily necessary correction.
> But let me pass to more cheerful and consoling thoughts.

Acton had a certain literary purism and had been schooled in public exchanges to a grave politeness. It is from this period that there dates the implacable dislike with which he came to view the then accustomed range of ecclesiastical expression. It would seem that to his sensitive mind the Cardinal's words appeared to be both bland and vindictive.

The closing down of the *Home and Foreign Review* in 1864 was really the conclusion of his work in periodical literature of an effectively Catholic character. He contributed to the later ventures edited by T. F. Wetherall, the *Chronicle* which ran through 1867 and 1868 and the *North British Review*, which came to an end four years later. This last periodical was bound up with the defence of Acton's attitude to the Vatican Council.

[1] Cf. *The History of Freedom and other Essays*, pp. 448–53.

12

The Two Disciples

Sir John Acton's handwriting was really beautiful; he wrote always with a thin nib and the lines were spaced with careful accuracy. The letter 'a' in particular was broad and open. It was of course a trifle mannered and it must have taken time. It was a courteous style and in this a reflection of Sir John's own character.

The writing of his articles was a different matter. The gaiety of his American diaries found no reflection. His style was opaque and he was in some ways hard to read. A tendency to somnolence may overtake the earnest reader. These elements may perhaps seem to mark the pages of his work which have been quoted in the last chapter. There have been discussions on the subject of the great *History of Liberty*, which he planned and never wrote, but one question never seems to have been advanced, whether the public would in fact have found it readable.

As his life advanced, his style changed somewhat. In the 1870s it was at times and on certain subjects lit by those strange fires which smouldered in him. And at length he came to the useful, stiff, rather Germanic style of his later years.

These articles, just considered, also mark Acton's fondness for the antithesis. One rather wonders at this later date whether matters or tendencies divided themselves so evenly. But they have this importance that they mark the close of his English Catholic period. It seems that there were three main divisions in Acton's working life, first the run of years which ended in 1864, then the Anglo-German period which lasted roughly from the time of his Bavarian marriage until he was deeply committed to Mr Gladstone's world. The Gladstonian years had great significance, and his final period, when he held the Cambridge chair, can really

E

be regarded as post-Gladstonian. He was growing old and approaching death through all this decade.

We are not now considering his religious outlook, but in other matters there were also differences between his attitude when he gave up the *Home and Foreign Review* and that which he would adopt when he had been received within the Hawarden circle. Mr Gladstone, for instance, with his deeply Anglican ecclesiasticism, never showed any interest in the world of Science. The following wording in defence of Science would not recur. 'A Science,' wrote Acton, 'that for the sake of protecting faith, wavers and dissembles in the pursuit of knowledge [is an] instrument at least as well adapted to serve the cause of falsehood as to combat it.' There were aspects of thought from which, however imperfect his expression, he now turned away.

The year 1864 was crucial for John Acton. With the ending of the *Home and Foreign Review*, he did not again address an English Catholic audience with the hope that this might prove nation-wide. The other periodicals which he used in the succeeding seven years were merely intended to give space for the presentation of certain of his historical ideas. It will in time be seen that his place as a Catholic spokesman was destroyed by the publication of the *Syllabus Errorum*. In another fashion he vanished at first almost imperceptibly from the life of the rich English Catholic world. Until the time of his engagement to Marie Arco-Valley he was regarded by English hostesses of his own Communion as a *prétendant* for their daughters. Thus he would be invited to Thorndon Hall by Lady Petre. It was natural that this concern should not outlast his marriage.

This brings us to the names of the two men who, as he went forward on his lonely course, would still keep close to him. It is worth considering them before we come to those associations with papal Rome, which would for so long dominate John Acton's mind. Richard Simpson of course was in a sense his intimate and dependent friend. With Peter Renouf the situation was rather different, and the association was less close. Nevertheless, he appears like a recurring decimal through the very varying aspects of Acton's life.

Peter le Page Renouf, descended as his names indicate from two

Channel Islands families, was born in Guernsey in 1822. He was educated at Elizabeth College and then gained a scholarship at Pembroke, remaining all his life an undergraduate of that Oxford college. He had come up with the intention of taking Holy Orders; but he was swept into the current of the Oxford Movement and he actually joined the Church of Rome four years ahead of Dr Newman. He could therefore hardly be regarded as one of the future Oratorian's disciples, but he benefited for long from Newman's care. He was offered the post of English tutor to the Marquis de Froissard's son. Then in 1855 he was appointed by Dr Newman to the Chair of ancient history in the university in Dublin, to which was added later the professorship of eastern languages. In 1857 he married Ludovika Brentano La Roche, a relative of the poet Clemens Maria Brentano; it was a link with Acton that he became bi-lingual in English and German. He had through life a certain element of private means and a house in Guernsey at Ruette Brulée.[1] On 29 March 1860 he undertook to continue the translation of Dr Döllinger's most recent work, 'detecting the blunders etc.' His life was always marked by a Victorian self-confidence. He was also a contributor to the *Home and Foreign Review*.[2]

Renouf had forwarded Newman's ill-starred project for a Catholic college at Oxford and this brought him an interesting letter from Sir John Acton. The latter was taken with the idea of the beginnings of a college in the English countryside. His mind ran upon the details of Döllinger's house in Munich. 'For this purpose,' wrote[3] Acton from Aldenham on 6 November 1863, 'there is a very good, large house near here, which I am putting in repair and which would be suitable in many respects. It was inhabited by my agent's family and by the curate and besides their rooms and offices on the ground floor contains fifteen rooms upstairs, and might hold ten or twelve pupils. My library contains twenty-five thousand volumes.' The project did not materialize.

---

[1] He was residing there on 1 September 1863. All these details are obtained from the Renouf MSS at Pembroke College.

[2] On 11 June 1864 Dean Milman of St Paul's had written to Sir John Acton about an article by Renouf in the *Home and Foreign Review*.

[3] Renouf seems to have retained all the letters which he received at different dates from Acton.

This was towards the end of Acton's period of interest in joint Catholic enterprises.

Renouf was at this time beginning to move along a line of thought which was to some extent parallel to Sir John Acton's. In this year he resigned his chair in Dublin; Ireland was not a happy hunting ground for his new interests. These centred round the pontificate of Honorius I. This pontiff was at that time known to English antiquaries as the Pope who had conferred the *pallium* on the occupants of the sees of York and Canterbury; he had also given his commission to St Birinus. These facts were recorded in Bede's *Ecclesiastical History*.

It was, however, the pontiff's relation with Constantinople in the reign of the Emperor Heraclius which engaged Renouf's attention. It was the question of a letter to the Patriarch Sergius of Constantinople in which he appeared to countenance the Monothelite doctrine of the 'one will' in Christ. On the evidence of this letter he had been named among the Monothelites at the first Trullan council of Constantinople in 681, and had later been anathematized as a heretic. These ideas were roving in Renouf's mind as the Vatican Council approached and emerged in the *Condemnation of Pope Honorius*. Much depended on the weight and nature of the Pope's statements; but Renouf's work was placed upon the Roman Index. One present view of the question is described[1] by Professor Dvornik. 'The Patriarch Sergius promoted the doctrine of one will in Christ – Monothelitism – and succeeded, for a short time, in deceiving the vigilance of Rome, when Honorius I (625–38), although himself professing the orthodox doctrine, gave the impression in his answers to Sergius of being favourable to the Patriarch's views.' It is not surprising that Renouf retained a sharp sympathy for Acton's judgments.

Meanwhile there is no evidence that Sir John himself was primarily affected by the historical arguments advanced by those who wished to stop by these means any declaration of the papal claims. The case of Pope Vigilius (537–55), which was also raised, could be explained by irresolute character rather than heresy. Justinian's letter had been most explicit. 'We have condemned,' the Emperor declared, 'Nestorius and Eutyches, preserving in

[1] *The Cambridge Medieval History*, vol. iv, pt. 1 (1966), p. 440.

every way the unity of the sacred Churches with the holy Pope and Patriarch of Old Rome. . . . For we cannot tolerate that anything concerning the ecclesiastical order should be settled independently of his Holiness, since he is the head of all the sacred priests of God.'

Acton had a very clear knowledge of the history of the Church. The story of the Papacy was long and in a sense tangled. The circumstances of the papal elections had greatly varied; but Acton was well aware of the long line of the silent Popes. He also appreciated that very different world of the Middle Ages in which Boniface VIII had issued his famous Bull, the *Unam Sanctam*. No one had been more subject to attack in the world of the Reformed Religions than the second Borgia Pope. But the only intervention of Alexander VI in the field of the thought and practice of the Catholic life had been his liturgical introduction of the *Angelus*. It was not what the Popes had said, but what Pius IX was about to say that would disturb him.

PART TWO

THE ROMAN SCENE

Introduction

The second section of this book entitled 'The Roman Scene' deals with practically the whole of Acton's contacts with the papal capital. It therefore goes back a little in time and begins with Acton's first visits to Pope Pius IX, which began characteristically in the company of Dr Döllinger. This section commences with the election of that pontiff, which took place in 1846. Cardinal Mastai-Ferretti had been born in 1792 in Sinigaglia and he had held the sees of Spoleto and of Imola, all three cities in the States of the Church. He occupied the papal throne from 1846 until 1878, that is to say from the days of Acton's childhood until he was advanced in middle life. The ideas and life of the papal nobility of the States of the Church in which he was embedded are considered in some detail, and in particular what the Pope meant by Liberal institutions. An interesting comparison can be made with the family of the poet Leopardi. It was in many ways an inward-turning world.

An account is given of the States of the Church which remained after the greater part of the Pope's territory had been absorbed into the new Italian kingdom under Victor Emmanuel of Sardinia. The area that remained in the Pope's control from 1860 until 1870, which was known as the Patrimonium of St Peter, is described; its small towns and its pastoral land surrounding Rome, the one great city. Throughout this section a return is made again and again to build up different facets of that Roman life which depended on the papal palaces, the Vatican and Quirinal. An account is given of the great Roman papal families and the elements are stressed that separated them from their equals in the other European capitals. The breakdown of the papal administration in those provinces which the Pope had lost is noted, and it

E*   137

is made clear that the Vatican had now become a Court of priests. This policy is described in detail; it was the only State that Acton wished to see swept away.

The effect in Rome of the Liberal ideas of Count Cavour, an anti-clerical politician from within the frontiers of Italy, are considered. The character and objectives of Cardinal Antonelli, the chief minister of the diminished Papal States, are examined and the Roman political situation as seen from England. For this matter the despatches of the British representative Odo Russell, Lord Clarendon's son-in-law, are very useful. Mr Gladstone's visits to Rome are described; his long visits to the churches to hear sermons; his purchase of a white marble statuette of a brigandess. The circumstances leading up to the publication of the *Syllabus Errorum* and the reasons for this attack on current Liberalism are examined.

There follows an account of Acton's work in the approach to and during the first Council of the Vatican. His Bavarian affiliations are stressed, and his relations with Cardinal Hohenlohe and with his chaplain, Dr Friedrich. A suggestion is made as to Acton's share in the letters to the *Allegemeine Zeitung*. His mixed relations with the bishops at the Council who belonged to the Minority and regarded the definition of Papal Infallibility as inopportune are appraised. Acton's main difficulty seems to have been that all these bishops had accepted and many, like Dupanloup, had defended the *Syllabus Errorum*. A careful account is given of Bishop Dupanloup.

The description of the actual Council is foreshortened and only those debates which interested Acton are given in any detail. The point is made that as a layman he was always an outsider. Bishop Ullathorne's position is described as giving the views of a central member of the English Episcopate. Then comes Lord Acton's (he had been created a peer in December 1869) correspondence with Mr Gladstone and his hopes for the intervention of the Powers. This section ends with an account of his retirement to and sojourn in Bavaria and Austria. There is a chapter on the Tridentine Church, giving an account of Roman Catholicism in the centuries between the Council of Trent and the second Council of the Vatican.

I

The Roman Background

Some appreciation of the background to the pontificate of Pope Pius IX would seem essential to an understanding of the situation which John Acton faced. In a sober English sense Liberal values meant very much to him. Under another aspect this turned on the term Liberalism and the sense in which this expression was understood by the Cardinal Bishop of Imola, who was to be called to the papal throne, by the Italian thinkers with whom he was in contact and by the English and Gladstonian world. This can also be regarded as a study in the contrast of the German and the Italian mind.

Giovanni Mastai-Ferretti had been born and brought up in the city of Sinigaglia in the province of the Marches in the States of the Church. He returned to his birth place for the first years of his ministry as a priest. He came from the provincial nobility of that difficult region. He had charm and a kind of rippling merriment; he was *simpatico* and at ease with all who came to him. From certain aspects he was thus very much open to lay influence. He was spontaneous and light-hearted and singularly candid; he did not appeal to the Germanic North. The account that the Pasolini have left of him when he was Bishop of Imola reveals him as accessible to new ideas. His spontaneity made small appeal to Metternich, nor was it of the kind to draw the Dalbergs.

He belonged essentially to that provincial nobility, which in the Marches and the neighbouring province had given all the recent Popes except for Gregory XVI, who came from the then Austrian territories of Venice. It had been a long succession. Pius VI and Pius VII both came from Cesena, Leo XII from Spoleto, and Pius VIII from Cingoli. The last-named pontiff had also ruled the diocese of Cesena in the Marches. There had thus been formed a close tradition of noble stocks, centred in the Papal States and for the most part relatively impoverished.

An impression of the life within the background of this circle is given in the autobiography of Count Monaldo Leopardi, who passed all his life at Recanati and was sixteen years older than Pius IX. 'To Monaldo,' writes[1] the Marchesa Origo in her biography of his son Giacomo Leopardi, 'as to most members of his caste, the boundaries of the Papal States were also those of the universe.' Pius IX, born into such a grouping, had also a swift Italian use of political ideas, an ease in discussing and absorbing and transmuting them.

It is this characteristic that lent significance to the evenings that the future Pope would spend at Montericci, the country house of the Pasolini family outside Imola. The setting was contented, perhaps rather wealthier than was usual in the same circle. The emphasis lay on the status. 'I never heard,' wrote[2] Count Pasolini, 'my father talk of any more remote ancestor than his own grandfather.' A further note[3] implies the same suggestion. 'A diligent collector of domestic traditions, he arranged all the dusty old family parchments, collecting also and hanging up the blackened portraits of our ancestors.' With certain stocks containing members of the higher clergy there was in a social sense a close alliance. The Pasolini were nephews of Mgre Antonio Codronchi, the Archbishop of Ravenna during Byron's visits to that city. At Fermo there were the allied and cardinalitial families of the Bernetti and the Brancadoro.

There was here a more political element than was found among the Leopardi where the foreigner was seen as the invader; the Frenchman; the Austrian. One must make allowance for certain Austrian sympathies among the older generation of the higher clergy; but, these men apart, the Marches were united in aloofness from the lands beyond the Alps. There had come down from the eighteenth century a sense that the patriciate should fill the key posts in the Papal States. This gave their anti-clericalism its quite peculiar flavour. Such a factor is set out clearly in the account of

[1] Iris Origo, *Leopardi* (1953), p. 3.
[2] *Memoir of Count Giuseppe Pasolini*, compiled by his son, p. 1.
[3] *Ibid.*, pp. 2–3.

the outlook of Pietro Pasolini. 'Although much attached,' it is explained,[1] 'to Rome and its associations, he took great pride in his ancient Romagnolo descent, and the sight of these new men, those upstart rustics, who as prelates or lawyers made so much noise at the Court of Rome, made him place still more value on his own birth and lineage. He was always most respectful to the Pontiff and to all ecclesiastical authority, but could never willingly bend himself before those whom he considered to be exalted in dignity and power merely by virtue of the clerical habit.'

Several factors are revealed by these last words. It is, for instance, worth noting how the privileged stocks in Europe tended to be allied against an episcopate recruited from outside their circle. Here was something that was an echo of Bavaria. The States of the Church indeed belonged to the old world. Changes had come rapidly, but the pre-Revolution era was very close. At the election which raised Cardinal Mastai-Ferretti to the papal throne there were seventeen cardinals who had put on the soutane before 1789. This time-lag between the governing circles of the Catholic Church and the heads of civil governments has seldom been so clearly manifested as in the last days of Gregory XVI.

It was during his years as Bishop of Imola that Cardinal Mastai-Ferretti developed his reputation as a Liberal; yet what the future Pope envisaged was not the doctrinal Liberal principles as these were interpreted beyond the Alps. The severance between the outlook of Pius IX and that of his predecessor was in the first place the natural contrast of generations. Gregory XVI had been born in 1765 and Pius IX in 1792; it was normal that the latter should share in the desire to take advantage of the material improvements which had so much impressed his generation. A passage[2] in Count Pasolini's book bears on this point. 'One evening in conversation with a noble of Ravenna he [Cardinal Mastai] said, "I cannot understand the captiousness of our Government in liking to persecute the rising generation who must needs breathe the air of the present century rather than of the past. It would be so easy to gratify their aspirations and to win their love." Neither could

---

[1] *Ibid.*, pp. 2–3. Count Pietro Desiderio Pasolini was born in 1782.

[2] *Ibid.*, p. 31. It must be noted that this conversation was reported very much later.

he understand the opposition to measures of material improvement, such as railways, gas, suspension bridges and scientific
associations. "There is nothing contrary to theology that I know
of in the advancement of science, industry and art; but then I am
no politician, and I may be mistaken".' The phrases attributed to
Pope Pius IX are not necessarily exact, but the general impression
seems convincing. It appears evident that what gained the Pope
his reputation as a Liberal and the support of the more traditional
circles of Italian Liberalism was in reality his belief in progress,
a different realm.

Allied to this belief in progress was a sympathy for all Italians.
This comes out strongly in the support that the Pope gave to
Vincenzo Gioberti's thesis set forth in his *Rinnovamento civile
d'Italia*, which he read when he was at Imola. In this work the
Holy See was conceived as the suzerain and guide of Italy. The
author did not consider what would be the position of the Pope
when Italy was at war with Catholic Powers. At this date Pius IX
was filled with a compassionate desire to relieve suffering. He
saw with simplicity of heart forms of progress which he could
support. He never really gave himself to those nations from which
John Acton's thought had been derived.

There was not a trace of cynicism in the Pope's disposition; he
believed all those who came to him with a certain right. Pius IX
was not without his Legitimist side, almost instinctive. He was in
these respects in fact a high Conservative; he never saw a flaw in
his right to rule his own possessions. It was this which brought to
and kept for him the rather desiccated attachment of all the arch-
duchesses of the House of Austria.

The opening months of his reign proved to be the smoothest in
his long and chequered contacts with the Catholic sovereigns.
These at first were principally with his neighbour kings, Sardinia
and the Two Sicilies. It is doubtful how much the pontiff had in
common with Ferdinand II of the Two Sicilies; but Charles Albert
was a different matter. This prince had gained his name Albert
from his Saxon mother and was in some respects northern in
temperament. He was shy, withdrawn and mystical and had a
bruised idealism. He had inherited to the full that rather *outré*
form of religion which marked the House of Savoy in the Restora-

tion period. The Pope was the godfather to his grandchild Maria Pia. This association did not last long. Three years after the Pope's accession, Charles Albert was to be driven from his throne. Pius IX was in time to be the sustainer of two successive Queens of Sardinia and then that house would pass away from the Pope's contact.

Another quotation from Pasolini is revealing.[1] 'Mastai's whole soul was stirred with fervent zeal for the peace of his country and of the Church of Christ. . . . In his enthusiastic moods he would often throw himself from one side to the other of his great armchair [at Montericci] repeating Gioberti's words.' In the calm chancelleries of Europe there was a solid determination that the Pope should not become the temporal ruler of all Italians.

It is stated[2] that the Cardinal carried to the Conclave the works of Gioberti and Massimo d'Azeglio's *Casi di Romagna*. He was in fact a generous-hearted nationalist, who wished to make use of progress for man's benefit. As far as political forces were concerned, he kept his mind upon the field of Italy and on the princes and their ministers who ruled them. It was a further consequence of the pre-eminence of Italy in his mind that he was always so conscious of Count Cavour, the Savoyard statesman.

Nevertheless, although Cavour was ultimately to prove the decisive factor in moulding both the future outlook and the resultant policy of the Pontiff, the immediate effect was that produced by Gioberti. It was in consequence of his warm-hearted patriotic appreciations that Cardinal Mastai-Ferretti could find this writer so attractive; it was in part the profound union of the Italian priesthood. A distinct factor was the sympathy which the future Pope could rouse so easily for the poor and the dispossessed; for Gioberti, when the Cardinal read his work, was an impoverished exile teaching in Brussels. The affection was a part of the Cardinal's generosity and good nature. Gioberti and the Cardinal shared a sense of the fatherhood of the Pope in the Christian world; neither seems to have foreseen Italy as a moderate power in the Concert of Europe surrounded by unenvious rivals.

The dangers of a situation in which the Pope was president in

[1] *Ibid.*, p. 33.
[2] *Ibid.*, p. 34.

an Italian Federation were naturally felt more acutely in the lands beyond the Alps. This point is worth making for it was with the Italian moderates and not with the French Liberals that the future Pope's thought would for a time be in accord. He had in fact a happy Italian patriotism which could not but exacerbate his French supporters. He seems to have been one of those characters in whom good will takes the place of imagination. He had been a pastoral bishop of a small diocese and was, perhaps in consequence, intensely personal in his reactions; personal in his sympathies and disappointments and also in his feelings towards those who had wronged him. These traits are seen after the breakdown of the brief Liberal period which opened the pontificate. The sequence of events remained sharply in his memory; the murder of his minister Pellegrino Rossi; the emergence of the Roman Republic; the Pope's own flight to Gaeta. He had returned to Rome under the protection of French bayonets in April 1850, but the impression of these days was ineffaceable. The change can best be expressed if it is suggested that the area of his sympathy had narrowed. He felt now for the Faithful, for the rich and the poor among them, for the converts and for the devout who would soon crowd to the Lourdes grottoes. He had still the same sympathy but its effects were circumscribed; he was generous to the suffering. He was bound to be affected by those who suffered from Mazzini's policies and from Cavour's. He consoled the exiled royalties; the Queen of the Two Sicilies who had come to die at Frascati; the princesses of all the Bourbon houses; the young archdukes of Tuscany. In the autumn of 1860 the Papal States had shrunk to the Patrimonium of St Peter. The rest of Italy had been absorbed by the King of Sardinia. These consequences were the outcome of Cavour's policies.

Camillo Benso di Cavour came, on his father's side, from the rural nobility of the Italian Courts to which the Pope was well accustomed. In his presence the Liberal notions were conceived as essentially anti-clerical; the Giobertian dream vanished for ever. There were also present in Cavour's character a coldness and a calculated prudence which were both antipathetic to the Roman Pontiff. Cavour owed much to the Genevan Calvinism of his mother's stock. He used and with expertness each phrase in the

Liberal vocabulary. This made it easy for Pius IX to come into accord with all those members of the Papal Court who were determinedly Conservative.

Another characteristic of the pontificate dates from the destruction of the papal rule over the States of the Church. As the Pope turned his mind from his obligations as a temporal sovereign, he became more inaccessible to those laymen who formerly advised him. He was surrounded almost exclusively by the clergy and by such of the laity as lived under their wing; the project of the Vatican Council filled his mind. The Pope's thought was less in *time*, while Acton's interests were markedly contemporary. The Papal Court remained, when the States of the Church vanished; but the most difficult period was that run of years when the temporal power was reduced to the Patrimonium. The mundane interests of the old Papal Court, the appointments to the governorships of the Legations, the apparatus of the clerical administration, the rights of sanctuary were all in process of being swept away. Motives that had attracted to the priesthood both the ambitious civil servants and the sons of the noble families of the provinces had ceased to operate. An ecclesiastically directed State was replaced by a Court of Ecclesiastics.

It was this last factor which surely had a deep effect on Acton. He did not believe that the virtues of Liberalism would be assessed with any clearness in that specialized *milieu*. It seems that he attributed the attack on Liberalism not to the Pope alone but also to his clerical courtiers.

They had moved far away from the eighteenth century in whose dry light Acton still had his being. There, in the Bavarian and Austrian noble households, the priest had been at hand to perform a series of necessary services but did not influence the patron's judgment. Benedict XIV had been the pontiff whose wit and poise had been appreciated. It seems that in the 1860s Acton hoped for a Pope who would prove urbane and civilized and motionless in politics.

A climate of opinion which was destructive of so much that Acton valued was now slowly gaining ground in the Papal Court. A warm devotion to the person of the pontiff and to his sufferings was manifested at this time by priest and nun and convert. It was not wholly new for it sprang in part from the Romantic movement of the early part of the century, but it placed the Pope in an unique context. It was deeply fervent and quite opposed to that calm and ruthless examination of each element which was for so long a characteristic of John Acton's thought.

It is an important factor in examining his outlook to note that Acton was at this time an anti-clerical as well as a Liberal. He was therefore not in any way in sympathy with the Liberal ecclesiastics. This lay at the root of his isolation in the coming years. He was opposed to certain doctrines of the papal power which were brought forward. He had a northern, perhaps what one might call a Cisalpine, liking for checks and balances, provided always that these were not in the hands of ecclesiastics. He did not prefer a Council of churchmen to the Pope; he was nothing of a Gallican.

The Pope had a sympathetic feeling for loyalty. His friendships were all lasting except perhaps for Cardinal Antonelli. He was playful and benign and had a quick understanding for those who suffered. His kindness won the converts and the clergy. He was encouraged by their warm applause. Acton had no respect for the Pope's mind.

It is at this point that Acton's earlier contact with the Pope should be considered. There survives an account[1] of three audiences with Pope Pius IX in April, May and June 1857. Acton was at that time twenty-three and visiting Rome for the first time since his childhood. He was travelling with Döllinger, who had been his companion on earlier journeys in North Italy and Switzerland. This was Dr Döllinger's first visit to Rome and he was perhaps not an auspicious companion for a papal audience. The Pope was cold about the Wittelsbach family with whose views the doctor was so closely connected. This was nevertheless the most successful of the three audiences. A detailed extract from a journal of the Roman visit will serve to bring out John Acton's standpoint.

Theiner [the Vatican librarian] present on Saturday [he wrote[2]] at the audience of the Pope. They spoke French, but

[1] 'Journal of Lord Acton: Rome 1857', edited by H. Butterfield and printed in *The Cambridge Historical Journal*, vol. iii, pp. 186–204.
[2] *Ibid*, p. 190.

the pope speaks it ill. He said that he had expected the professor [Döllinger] for some time. He made a confusion about my mother, thinking she was my sister. Spoke of the importance of unity in the church, for strength, and the professor told him no clergy were more thoroughly devoted to the Holy See than the German, which pleased him. . . . He thought King Max[imilian of Bavaria] had been injured by his prot[estant] mother. Spoke with great consolation of Wirtemberg [Concordat, 1857]. He said that the Holy See is head and chief of all authority and all other authority attacked in it, wh[ich] many princes do not see. The p[ope] gave the impression of great kindness and suavity, well acquainted with religious questions, but not so with the state of other countries. He is of a liberal family, so that Gregory XVI was unwilling to make him a cardinal, and his election was a concession to the liberal spirit. So that what followed was natural and to be expected. He knew like all Italians nothing of other countries, and there was not sufficient example in Italy of the failure of a constitution. When he thinks he is in the right he is very energetic and decided.

This is a fairly calm presentation of a more or less routine audience arranged primarily for Dr Döllinger through Dr Theiner. It is followed by various comments which reflect Acton's acceptance of each passing rumour.[1] The third audience had much the same character, although Acton appears to have been accompanied and introduced by Mgri. Talbot and Pacca. The most interesting part of this exchange is that concerned with Mr Gladstone's character. After discussing Palmerston's anti-Catholic proclivities, the visitor mentioned that his mother's husband was a minister. 'Oh, yes,' said the Pope,[2] 'you are the son of the Lady Gr[anville] who was in Moscow – well we have less to fear from Lord Gr[anville], but Gladstone I believe was better, and as a Puseyite near Cath[olicism].' It is interesting to note that criticism of Gladstone came from Acton. 'I said,' he continues, 'that ambition made him useless, as it was a very bad thing. Oh, he said, *secondo me ei passioni inubbriancono li uomini come il vino* and when it masters them, makes them incapable of good. Then I said

---

[1] Cf. for the Pope's alleged attitude towards the Jesuits, Cardinal Hohenlohe and Dr Theiner, *ibid.*

[2] Account of an audience at nine o'clock in the evening of 12 June 1857, *ibid.*, p. 199.

G[ladstone] was also unsafe in foreign affairs, and he said yes, he had been carried away and deceived in Nap[les].'

The illuminating account is that dealing with the second audience. This was a family party arranged by old Lady Acton, known as Nonna. It was very much the presentation of the nephews and nieces of a Cardinal by His late Eminence's mother. For Acton it seems to have been an experience both frustrating and exacerbating. There is no future difficulty between Pius IX and the historian which would surprise those who read this young man's diary.

Saw the Pope [the account begins[1]] with Nonna, the Throckmortons and Mlle Dal[berg]. . . . We waited under the tapestries: Hohenlohe very polite and pleasant. Count Medici came and spoke. My hat, sword and gloves allowed to pass – only our party present. Nonna introduced us as we knelt down successively – *una molto buona amica delle figlie* (Dal). He [the Pope] leaned forward and gave us his hand rather to shake than merely to kiss, very gracefully and raised us by it – without allowing us to kiss his red-shoed foot. He made us all sit down. I stood. Nonna alone spoke, until she turned to appeal to me, and the Pope attended to me for a little while. He saw my uniform and asked what it was. She said I had been in Russia – with the embassy – and that my mother whom he seemed to think N[onna]'s daughter, was ambassadress. This he remembered, but asked the ambassador's name. Had heard much of our brilliancy, and of my mother's religiousness from Chigi[2] – asked me if the story was true of his [Chigi's] coming to the sick servant, and said every priest must do the same – was the servant a Catholic? He said even the Pope must have done the very same. . . . Gave us his blessing, and his hand again, calling each up successively, with a wave of the hand, and stood by the side of the table till we were all out of the room, which I left last.

The next three sentences contain in germ all that Acton would come to feel about Pope Pius. He was wholly without that element

---

[1] Audience on Sunday, 3 May 1857, *ibid.*, pp. 192–3.

[2] Flavio Chigi-Albani (1810–1885), Archbishop of Myra and special envoy to the coronation of Alexander II of Russia; created Cardinal of Santa Maria del Popolo in 1873.

of respect with which the English Catholic gentry would approach the sovereign pontiff. One wonders how much was due to Dr Döllinger. 'Asked,' Acton continues, 'which was which among the girls – all greatly struck with his obesity and almost torpidity, and found him old and weak. He took a good deal of snuff, and spoke very quietly, distinctly and slowly, with no affectations whatever of impressiveness. My impression is not of any ability and he seems less banally good natured, than his smiling pictures represent him to be.'

Pius IX was then sixty-five; he would still reign for more than twenty years. Leaving aside the accustomed 'severity' of tone, it is evident that Acton already had a clear dislike for the warm enthusiasms which the Pope aroused. He wished to judge dispassionately of all phenomena. Acton was cold at heart towards the Roman Pontiff.

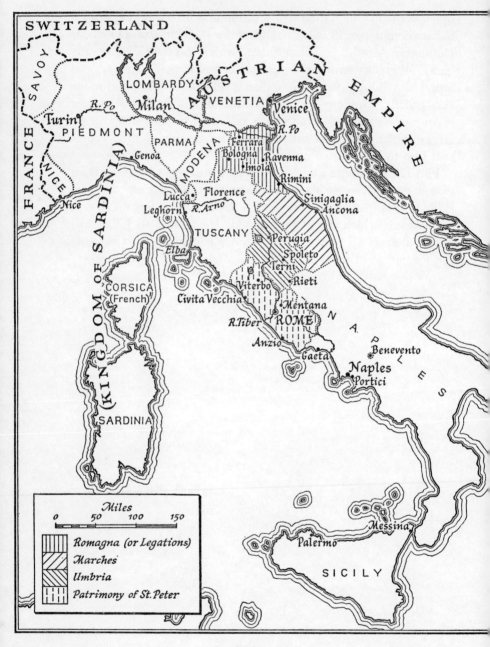

Italy 1860

2

The States of the Church

The politico-geographical setting of the Vatican Council was that area of the Papal States known as the Patrimonium of St Peter. The rest of the States of the Church had vanished after the Sardinian campaigns of 1860 and were now ruled by King Victor Emmanuel. They had formed a great block of Central Italy with more than two hundred miles of Adriatic coast-line from the mouth of the Tronto river to the flat lands of the Polesina. Within this territory there was included Umbria and the Marches and then Romagna, with the city of Bologna, and finally the duchy of Ferrara in the Lombard plain. But when the Council opened it was only the southern, the specifically Roman section of the old territories, which remained within the papal jurisdiction.

The Patrimonium of St Peter was hinged upon the papal capital. It is simplest in considering its extent to begin with the shores of the Mediterranean. In the first place there was 130 miles of shelving foreshore, which stretched from the Maremma Romana, along the Tuscan border, and reached through the whole malarial region of the Campagna. This area was bisected by the Tiber, which came through almost uninhabited country to the sea. A good many miles beyond its mouth there lay the little ports of Anzio and Nettuno along the narrow shore to the south-westwards of the Pontine marshes. The papal frontier lay beyond Terracina, where the high mountains, a spur of the Apeninnes, came down to meet the coast. Towards the northern extremity of this sea frontier lay the one defended harbour, Civita Vecchia, already connected with Rome by a railway line, which in these years was carried northwards to Pisa to reach the system of the Sardinian kingdom.

The area of the Patrimonium was roughly a quadrilateral with the further frontier passing some forty miles inland from the sea. It contained the city of Rome and the Campagna all around it, bounded by the Sabine mountains and the Alban hills. Away to the south-west lay the district of Frosinone. Here the Liri ran down past Sora and Isola Liri, a bandit-haunted country, to the edge of what had been the kingdom of the Two Sicilies where the sheltered fields of the county of Fondi fell in a narrow valley towards the sea. The northern portion of this area contained Ceprano sull'Liri, then the frontier station on a new railway towards Naples by Cassino, and the old stronghold of Anagni. Northwards again there lay the wild hill country around Olevano and Subiaco.

Beyond the foothills of the Sabine mountains the frontier lay for thirty miles along the Tiber. North-westwards out of Rome the Campagna ended quickly and at Storta Romana, the first post-station on the high road into Tuscany, one reached the first lip of the hills. Here were the good lands of the province of Viterbo, stretches of corn and vine. There were also the vineyards of the Castelli in the Alban hills; but generally speaking the land was poor.

Viterbo was a small city and the only one of the Pope's provincial capitals that still remained to him. There was a close self-centred town nobility. This pattern on a smaller scale was found again at Carpineto, behind the Alban hills, with such a family as the Pecci with their town palace. Cardinal Pecci, the future Leo XIII, was at this period at Perugia. In effect it could be said that the Patrimonium was little more than the hinterland of Rome. Across these lands lay the estates of all the papal families; fields and vineyards and a hunting box; they seldom lived there. Except in the height of summer they preferred their Roman palaces.

Ecclesiastically the map was simple. The bishoprics, of course, were numerous, a feature throughout central and southern Italy; eight to the south and seven to the northward of the city; there was no archdiocese. Closer in there were the so-called suburban sees, which were all held by cardinal bishops. Many estates were owned by monasteries, the summer houses of the headquarters of religious orders. There was hardly any industry. At the centre lay the great capital with a population of two hundred thousand. The whole countryside of the Patrimonium only contained just twice this number. The carts creaked down from north and west into the city; countrymen came to find their profit there.

The city lay unprosperous, inert and beautiful. The deserted Campagna formed a timeless setting. Across it stretched the paving stones of the Via Appia, then still uncovered. Within Rome itself the ancient churches rose among the trees and bushes. A view of the Roman Forum, now in the Louvre and painted by Corot a few years before this time, catches very perfectly the light on the wall spaces of the ancient city. The domes and towers and pine trees rose in the warm weather. There were many priests and monks; it was their kingdom.

The city was very crowded. The great palaces stood in teeming squares. From the Pincian one could see nearly the whole of urban Rome. Open country lay between the houses and the Aurelian walls. St John Lateran rose greyly in the fields. To the north-east the Porta Pia, with its stretch of walls, had gardens upon each side. On the waste ground beyond Santa Maria degli Angeli there stood the new and temporary railway station. The streets and houses within the city were now gaslit. There were open carriages plying for hire.

The largest foreign colonies would seem to have been the English, French and German. the last-named including some historians and archaeologists. Two Italian sovereign princes owned property in the State, the King of Naples held the huge and empty Palazzo Farnese and the Duke of Modena the Villa d'Este out at Tivoli; both memorials of those great extinct houses whose inheritance had fallen to the royal crowns. Rome of those days has been described by visitors who came for a few months in the spring and took apartments in the Via Sistina or in one of the old palaces. Still, they made little impact on the city. It had in certain ways been affected quite profoundly by the loss of the Papal States. The system of rule in every city by an ecclesiastic known as a delegate had now come to an end. These had formed part of the unified home service and foreign service staffed by the Holy See. There had in consequence never before been so many priests around the Vatican maintained and pensioned by the generous Pontiff. There was a gradual ferment taking place among the slow-moving, long-established families of the old Roman nobility.

When King Victor Emmanuel had annexed the northern provinces, his ally Napoleon III had sent a small French contingent to patrol the city and to protect the Pope's new frontiers. Since then the situation had developed a lack of movement. There were, of course, among the intelligentsia of the capital a certain number who hoped for or believed in some future Sardinian occupation. But it is on the whole likely that the peasants were not greatly affected by these problems, for the changes of political authority which took place in Italy in the mid-century were in essence variations in a *bourgeois* system of polity. Linked with the peasantry and in effect indistinguishable from them were the innkeepers and the local carriers and the lowest rank of the shopkeepers and contractors. To them it surely would appear that there was little difference between Pope and King. There was, too, a strange atmosphere of political tranquillity. And then there were the Roman nobility and all the land agents and men of business who worked for them and theirs. This aristocracy had always held a peculiar position. They were not particularly united, between some houses there were feuds which were very deep, but with hardly an exception they had been created as the nephews of some reigning Pope.

Among the court families there was one exception, the Sacchetti, who had come to Rome with the cardinal of that name who had been the candidate of the Barberini for the papal throne after their period of power. The Torlonia, a very rich banking family of French origin, had married heiresses of some of the branches of the papal lines. After the Pamphili heiress married a Doria, the main possessions of no papal family had passed by inheritance to a non-Roman.

As a group the great families were in the last stages of their magnificence. They accepted their pictures, their statuary and hangings; they were not patrons. Their palaces, scattered across the city, were very large but already old; they travelled little and passed their lives in them. There were separations, but no divorces. Up their great wide stone staircases, they never brought an Orthodox or a Lutheran bride. In these days they made no *bourgeois* marriages. Their court life did not tie them, except perhaps a period in the *Guardia Nobile* in early manhood. Alone among their caste they had no opportunity for service or display in foreign capitals. Where other sovereigns sent an ambassador, Rome sent a nuncio.

It was, therefore, a somewhat static life in a town which had no secondary nobility, entertaining ambassadors and the foreigners who came within their circle. They were not close in to the Holy See and for almost a century and a half no member of their caste had held the Papacy. It is curious that for some time before the fall of the Temporal Power they had ceased to provide cardinals from their own families. There is little information available upon this subject. Two points, however, may well be hazarded. The elder generation of the Roman princes for the most part belonged to the staid extreme right of the political spectrum. They had understood Gregory XVI and his young cardinals; but the first years of Pius IX must have proved disconcerting. It seemed that hazards had come upon the old profession. Viewed from another angle, the practice of the priest tutor had in recent years been discontinued. It is likely that the princes' sons now had a mild unintellectual Voltaireanism in their formation, a parallel to their equals in Austria and in Germany. And over all there was the papal government now under the control of Giacomo Antonelli.

Antonelli was at this time fifty-five years of age. He was Secretary of State and with the contraction of the papal power other offices had come to him. He was in effect the ruler of the Papal States. He had rather rough black hair, heavy eyebrows, a brave and sallow countenance. In origin he belonged to the *petite bourgeoisie* of Sonnino, a small town in the tumbled Volscian hills. His father moved south to Terracina and made a fortune as a contractor. He trained his son for the government service, for the official *cadre* of the rulers of the States of the Church. Already under Gregory XVI the young man had risen to be pro-treasurer-general and Pius IX promoted him to be Cardinal deacon of Santa Maria *in Via Lata*. He was only in deacon's orders and remained, in effect, a layman.

One gains the impression that he alone was truly outside the picture of that ecclesiastical society; he served the world in which he found himself. The Cardinal did not favour the calling of the Council when this was mooted. It seems that he long knew that the Sardinian Government would gain the victory. He had a cold and objective assessment of the Austrian reactions to each movement; he was without experience of the northern nations. The history of the world he knew was bound up with the Roman Church; he could not regard the multiplicity of the northern sects with any seriousness; he had never travelled. But he possessed something that the other members of the Roman Court did not possess, a clear understanding of the Voltairean in politics. And this applied especially to the Voltairean with Catholic roots like Count Cavour.

There was a curious love-hate relationship (if these terms are not too strong) with the Emperor Napoleon III. They were neither entirely respectable and they had both their unavowed financial side. The other members of the Sacred College did not take to the Cardinal, nor did the Roman princes. He had, however, stood by the Pope in the bad days before he went to Gaeta; the Pope never forgot this service. He did not receive too many at that time. He did not come within the orbit of the Pope's affection. From one angle, indeed, Cardinal Antonelli can be regarded as a courageous Italian politician, who was not accustomed to conceal his enmities. There was more than a touch of Mazarin about him, both men had cast their minds on jewels and cameos. The diplomats of the time appreciated him. In treating of public affairs he spoke their language. In a sense John Acton would understand him.

Since 1860 Pope Pius IX had given up the journeys into the provinces which had occasionally taken place in the earlier and more carefree period of his reign. His life in fact was now passed in his two city palaces, the Vatican and the Quirinal, and in his country house Castel Gandolfo. His court was primarily composed of ecclesiastics, the Cardinals *in Curia*, the *Monsignori* in attendance. There was room here for laymen, but hardly for lay interests. The *Guardia Nobile* were on duty in the range of ante-chambers leading on to the pontifical apartments. Their contact with the Pope was benign and distant. There were of course the nuns in the Pope's service; but it was a court from whose private life laywomen were excluded. They came in with their husbands and their children for those brief audiences that form the kaleidoscope of royalty. It is well to mark this point, for the Pope's lines were laid where his interests were channelled, in the recital of an immense mass of detail, the daily history of the Roman Church. He does not seem to have liked the rich and the kings were a disappointment to him. What gave him satisfaction was the pouring out of his flowing sympathy on priest and nun and bishop. His mind could turn from Italy to the Bishop of Tarbes' reports of the Lourdes apparitions. There were the first beginnings and the strong second generations of orders of nuns, for the most part French. This was the heyday of the *Missions Étrangères de Paris*; a time of martyrdoms in Indo-China and Korea. These problems and these difficulties were placed before the Pope as he sat by his desk with the big crucifix. They moved his heart. Day by day followed the providential design, as he conceived it, of the Church's progress. It was largely a French movement, vocations coming from the *petite bourgeoisie* and from those remote farms which sheltered for the last time a truly Christian peasantry. Each problem was in the framework of religion and he and those who sought him had their own fixed place. The Pope and every priest and nun were united by so many things and by their own simplicity. Relics piled up in the reliquaries and those of the virgin martyrs were most sought after. There was some discussion about the apparitions of La Salette.

What was the place of John Acton here?

In spite of all the Foreign Missions it was an inward-turning world. For example, Monsignor George Talbot, a younger son of Lord Talbot de Malahide, was for twenty years a prelate in attendance. As a young man he had been Vicar of Evercreech. His father, a revising barrister in the West Country, had married the squire's daughter, and George Talbot had received the family living from his uncle. Evercreech lay in the deep countryside on the edge of the county with one of the last of the lovely Somerset church towers. Mgr Talbot had now given himself to a special circle, which had involved a transformation. He was now absorbed in the life of the Roman Pontiff and was with him daily, soothing and cheering him, recommending good men, and above all keeping the Pope's mind on Dr Manning. It had become for him the only world that mattered, keeping undesirables off the stairways of success. There was an absolute lack of contact between this life and Evercreech. In the end the strain was too great for him and his mind gave way. '*Povero Giorgio*', said Pius IX as he visited the English College where Talbot's portrait was already hanging.

Such following out of each trace of the Pope's fancy was the actual antithesis of Acton's mood. It was a transient phenomenon found at this one period in certain circles in France and England, Veuillot and W. G. Ward. It was, too, a foreign and not an Italian characteristic. With all the phrases of somewhat honeyed reverence to which the Italian language lends itself so readily, there is a hard realism at the core of Italian thought.

Yet in the case of Pius IX there is so much evidence available that it is sometimes necessary to revise one's first opinions. Like many leaders he lived on different levels, and while his permanent concerns were all bound up with the development and the life oi his religion, the same buoyancy of his natural character becomes apparent in all his contacts. Episodes from a couple of the Pope's audiences granted in 1864 and 1866 to Odo Russell will make this clear. 'There is,' the Pope said[1] on the first occasion, 'a very bad newspaper published in Turin, called the *Fischietto*, but bad as it is the caricatures in it amuse me and the other day I saw a picture in it that made me laugh.' He then explained that the English envoy to the impending Congress was represented as holding a box in his hand containing a little devil who was cocking a snoot at Napoleon III. At the second audience there were two separate examples. The Pope began[2] by 'admiring the power and energy of Englishmen in the suppression of revolutions, such as in the Ionian Islands, India and lately in Jamaica, where they hung two thousand negroes and met with universal approval, while he could not hang one single man in the Papal States without incurring universal blame. His Holiness here burst out laughing and

[1] Noël Blakiston, *The Roman Question, Extracts from the despatches of Odo Russell from Rome 1858–1870*, ed., p. 281.
[2] *Ibid.*, p. 321.

repeated his last sentence several times holding up one finger as he alluded to hanging one man so as to render the idea still more impressive.' After some further talk His Holiness 'said he had heard of Mr Layard's visit to Rome and of his conversations with Cardinal Antonelli and he regretted he had not seen Mr Layard and talked with him on various subjects, among other things he would like also to have questioned him about Nineveh and heard his opinion of Queen Semiramis. His Holiness again burst out laughing and repeated his last sentence about Queen Semiramis four or five times, much amused at his own thoughts.' This is like the Pope's reference to a book that he had read while a young man at Montevideo. His thoughts came tumbling out. He was so natural and spontaneous.

This simple sense of fun welled out against the background of a life that was filled with sorrow. It is not suggested that even in this mood he could communicate with Acton; but in fact he very naturally turned back to those who followed him with warm devotion. In effect this meant the Court by which he was surrounded. The gaslight swung in the ground glass of the great fixed lanterns in the long stone entrances to the Vatican. The papal throne rose against a background of heavy scarlet which reached up towards the ceiling surrounded by gilded corn in rising sheaves. The walls were lined with hangings in vermilion silk, shadowed in silver. The Roman night came down on the great palace.

3

The Syllabus Errorum

It was now 1864 and the Pope had reigned for four years within the narrow frontiers of the Patrimonium of St Peter. The climate was changing in the world around him. It was a sad business to look out upon the Catholic kings.

Victor Emmanuel II and his prime minister were excommunicate. The phrase *il Re Galantuomo* well described the King of Italy. He was coarse and shrewd, with a ravaging sensuality. No wonder that, coming from the old exhausted lineage of his pious stock, it was rumoured that he was a changeling. One matter had separated him from Cavour. The minister's cool mind was devoid of superstition, the King was burdened by it. His second daughter, the Pope's godchild, was married to the young King of Portugal, another country where the Liberals had suppressed the monasteries. The idea of freemasonry attached itself to the House of Braganza. The King of Portugal's uncle, the Emperor of Brazil, so admired in Europe for his Liberalism, was certainly a Mason.

Maximilian, the young Emperor of Mexico, leaned the same way. As an Austrian archduke he was still affected by the Josephist ideals. The Prince of Roumania and the King of Greece had married Lutheran princesses and had promised that their children should be brought up in the Orthodox religion. The Pope had little confidence in the Wittelsbachs; he knew that family. Queen Isabel II of Spain was, perhaps, reliable in the political sense; there was little in her personal character to rely on. Saxony did not impinge on Rome. Lastly, there were two heads of monolithic States, Napoleon III and Francis Joseph.

From such unpromising material the Pope's mind turned away. His links with his bishops were always close and now, boxed up in Rome with its French garrison, he turned again to his devoted prelates. It was as an attempt to protect his flock against the errors of the outer world which pressed about them that he launched the *Syllabus Errorum*.

Two quotations from Acton's writings in 1862 and 1863 will indicate his outlook before the storm broke on him. The first indicates the historian's favourable attitude towards Catholic institutions, while he still felt at peace. The letter is addressed to Mr P. le P. Renouf. 'Here,' Acton wrote from Aldenham in the autumn of 1863, 'is a basis and an opportunity for the growth of something like a Catholic University such as did not exist in Ireland, when the institution which has passed through such pitiful phases was *octroyée*. . . . I have promised Newman land for buildings at Bridgnorth and explained to him the merits of the situation for an university – an agricultural country, a large river, a healthy position, a good feeling between Protestants and Catholics, and the vicinity of my very large library. I do not know whether it would be so suitable for a very limited number of Catholic students.'

Another account, this time of the congress at Munich, which was held in the autumn of the same year, has a similar note as the last example of a phase in his early life. This congress had taken place under Döllinger's chairmanship and at his invitation. It was a gathering of nearly a hundred professors, authors and doctors of divinity. There were present about a dozen laymen and the priests came for the most part from the archdiocese of Munich. They included two who would in the future become Old Catholic leaders, Dr Reinkens and the young Dr Friedrich. There were of course some of Döllinger's opponents like Professor Hergenröther, the future bishop. Acton himself seems to have been oppressed by the silence of many of the *conférenciers*. The meeting took place in the chapter house of the Benedictine monastery of St Boniface. An address of fidelity to the Holy See was voted unanimously and at the conclusion a telegraphic message was received from the Pope bestowing his blessing on all participants.[1] The words with which Acton concluded[2] his article are worth recalling. 'It [the Congress]

---

[1] Article in the *Home and Foreign Review*, January 1864, reprinted in *Essays on Church and State by Lord Acton*, ed. Douglas Woodruff, p. 160.

[2] *Ibid.*, p. 199.

F

will enable the Catholic writers of Germany to vindicate the Church from the reproach that faith is inimical to freedom, that we are hampered in our investigations, that we acknowledge a power which may prevent the publicity of truth, or impose untruths on our belief.' The last sentence marks the end of a period in Acton's life. 'Then indeed it will mark the dawn of a new era, and will justify the words of the Bishop of Augsburg, that, in giving the impulse to it, Dr Döllinger has set the crown on the splendid series of his services to the Church.' Acton never seems to have had any forewarning of the *Syllabus Errorum*.

With these two quotations there may be compared a statement made in 1872 to his friend Sir Rowland Blennerhassett. The letter dealt with the work of their mutual associate Eugène Michaud. 'I think,' explained[1] Acton in reference to the opinions of this inveterate opponent of the Vatican Council, 'very much worse of the *Vor Juli Kirche* than he does and better of the *Nachjuli Kirche*.' This comment on the position of the Church before and after the Vatican decrees is full of interest. What was it that worked this change of outlook? There seems little doubt that for Acton the decisive factor was the publication of the *Syllabus Errorum*.

It is not that this document should have come exactly as a surprise. Fourteen years had passed since the Pope had returned from Gaeta. The early period of the reign, when Pius IX had been in touch with the Italian Moderates, was now forgotten. A number of the sections of what would become the *Syllabus* had been printed by Mgr Gerbet, Bishop of Perpignan, in his *Instruction pastorale sur diverses erreurs du temps présent*. The real core of the difficulty lay in the fact that Acton was a believing Liberal.

Certain factors in the situation should be set out. The Liberals in the States of the Latin world were unamenable to clerical influence. They were for the most part convinced Deists coming from a *bourgeoisie*, which had viewed religious questions with indifference for at least a century. In many cases their wives and daughters were more or less Catholic; but they did not esteem the judgment of their womenfolk. The bringing to an end of monasteries and religious houses, although not their burning and destruction which was an effect of mob violence, had been an

---

[1] Letter, *Correspondence*, pp. 116–17.

axiom with Continental Liberalism. This went back as a practice to the days of the Emperor Joseph II, although it must be admitted that there was a difference in this field between the post-revolutionary Liberalism and the eighteenth-century form of *Étatisme*.

There was no contact and, partly in consequence, no possibility of compromise between the local bishops and these nineteenth-century Liberal politicians, so *doctrinaire* and so convinced. It was the appreciation of such reasons which led the Roman Curia to move forward. It was natural for the old Conservative churchmen to endeavour to keep intact the largely nominal Catholicism of the threatened regions.

It must also be said that those who recommended the Pope to issue the *Syllabus Errorum* were uniquely concerned with the Latin world. They were without any serious concern for the political forces in England or in Germany. It was likewise only in later papal reigns that attention would be paid to the standpoint of the laity. For some time the *Syllabus Errorum* was to prove a burden to those politically-minded Catholics in the northern world, who were not innately Conservative. In the years after its publication, the London Oratorians laboured to explain it to Liberal converts. But the *Syllabus* was not in fact to be covered by the Infallibility decree, although it remained for fifteen years part of the teaching system of the reigning pontiff.

This *Syllabus*, issued by Pope Pius IX in 1864, was described in its sub-title as a collection of modern errors. The portion of the document which produced so lasting an effect on Acton's thought was the sixteenth and last section entitled *Errores, qui ad liberalismus hodiernum referendus*. It is simplest to set out the four articles in this section and then to consider their bearings one by one.

77. *Aetate hac nostra non amplius expedit, religionem catholicam haberi tanquam unicam status religionem, ceteris quibusque cultibus exclusis.*

78. *Hinc laudabiliter in quibusdam catholici nominis regionibus lege caute est, ut hominibus illuc immigrantibus liceat publicum proprii cuiusque cultus exercitium habere.*

79. *Enimvero, falsum est, civilem cuiusque cultus libertatem itemque plenas potestates omnibus attributam quaslibet opiniones cogitationesque*

*palam publiceque manifestandi conduce ad populorum. more animosque
facilius corrumpendos ac indifferentismi pestem propagandam.*
80.   *Romanus Pontifex potest ac debet cum progressu, cum liberalismo
et cum recenti civilitate sese reconciliare et componere.*

These were the last four of the eighty propositions which were
put out with the Encyclical *Quanta Cura*. The date is important in
Acton's life for it was the year of the last number of the *Home
and Foreign Review* and the end of the historian's troubled connection with official Catholic journalism. The propositions were
found for the most part in periodical literature, much of it Italian.
Their condemnation was issued almost exactly midway between
the Sardinian occupation of the bulk of the Papal States in 1860
and the capture of Rome by Italian forces just ten years later.

A careful reading of the propositions is required owing to the
tendency to employ the double negative. The seventy-seventh
and seventy-eighth items can be related to the attempt to maintain the unique position of the Church in Spain and Portugal and
in the republics which had sprung up in the Spanish colonial
possessions. In particular they had a bearing on certain aspects of
the contemporary situation in these republics and in the empire
of Brazil. The first of these propositions stated that it is no longer
expedient in this our age that the Catholic religion should be the
only religion of the State and that other cults should be excluded.
The second proposition stated that it is desirable that in regions
belonging to the Catholic name immigrants should be permitted
the public exercise of their own form of worship. The opinions set
out in these two propositions were condemned.

The seventy-ninth item had a more universal application. It set
out that in truth it is false that civil liberty, liberty of worship and
the full power to manifest publicly all thoughts and opinions
tends more easily to the corruption of souls and of the customs of
the people and to the propagation of the pest of Indifferentism.
This opinion was likewise condemned.

The eightieth and last of the propositions is the well-known
statement condemning as erroneous the opinion that the Roman
Pontiff can and ought to reconcile himself with progress, Liberalism and modern civilization. There seems reason to suppose that

this last statement had a profound effect upon Sir John Acton's outlook.

Statements in the political field and actions in politics came home to him sharply. It would appear that it was the publication of the *Syllabus Errorum* and not the deliberations and outcome of the Vatican Council which caused him to become a settled antagonist of the pontificate of Pius IX. Henceforward he was a friend to all those who wished to weaken the political influence of that pontiff. From a critic of the new Italian Government he became its supporter. The year 1870, in which the Vatican Council assembled, was likewise memorable for him on account of the occupation of Rome and the ending of the Temporal Power of the Popes.

In the development of his conception of political sin Acton was to manifest a sincere conviction in the rightness of his own judgment. Later he attached a moral sanction to his judgments in the political field. Viewed from this angle it was as a force in politics that he wished to see the power of the Papacy curbed.

In his early years he had imagined the Church and State in harmony, the Church with her own great field and contribution. This attitude had been gradually modified during his struggles with his own ecclesiastical authorities; it was dissipated by the publication of the *Syllabus Errorum*. In general, doctrinal controversies concerned him little. It was the movement of political forces, and above all what he conceived to be the ethical content of political action, which captured his keen attention.

In all these matters the influence of Gladstone had its effect. To the English Whig or Radical, to those who belonged generally to the Liberal grouping, there were no two opinions as to the eightieth proposition of the *Syllabus Errorum*. Acton took his place beside them. His Tory Catholic contacts faded out completely. Whenever he was in London, and immersed in that club life which appealed to him increasingly, he found no one who would differ from his views of papal action.

Besides, there was in this question an especial link with Gladstone. It is notable that Acton was in general more severe than his new mentor; the historian had little sympathy with Gladstone's search for a good Roman Catholic ecclesiastic. To most of the

Whig world, which his stepfather Lord Granville represented, papal pronouncements were a matter of indifference. It was, perhaps, not altogether healthy for Acton that Gladstone should on the other hand have regarded them with such exacerbated concern.

4

Last Years of Papal Rome

In contrast with these burdened years for the believers, there was tranquillity among the non-Catholics who witnessed the last days of papal Rome. In this connection the evidence of Odo Russell, the British *chargé d'affaires*, is full of interest, all the more because his outlook has in the past been so often misconstrued. In this case it is as well to give a rather close description. Odo Russell was youthful and gay; he joined Signor Alari's music class and took part in Mrs Plowden's private theatricals to keep in touch with the English Catholics. He had not much money, a yearly charge upon the rents of the Bedford estate in Bloomsbury. As a member of an English governing family and as a nephew of the Prime Minister, Lord John Russell, he was welcome in the Roman palaces.

He had been born in Florence and educated for the most part in Germany and Austria by private tutors. A stay at Westminster School had hardly marked him. He liked to watch the working of men's minds. Thus he enjoyed the *expertise* of Manning's[1] outlook. That prelate was always more interested in what he said himself than in what was said to him. It was partly his mother's conversion that made the Roman world imagine that Odo was himself a sympathizer. But Lady George was an unconventional woman, who had become an easy-going continental Roman Catholic from long residence abroad. Odo Russell was deeply interested in all the diplomatic implications of a political situation then in flux. He was in fact an immaculate Protestant like all the then members of the House of Russell.

During this time there was an atmosphere of increasing tension. In November 1867 there took place that incursion of Garibaldians

---

[1] Cardinal Wiseman had died in 1865 and Dr Manning had replaced him.

into papal territory which was defeated at Mentana by the French troops armed with *chassepots*. The future began to seem less secure. A division was by now appearing among the great Roman families, the *Italianissimi* or *Bianchi* section separating gradually from the *Papalini* or *Neri* grouping. It was the latter body, the 'black' aristocracy, which alone would remain faithful to the papal monarchy. Separated both from the other prelates of the Vatican circle and from the old Roman world there stood the figure of Cardinal Antonelli dominating the now shrunken State as its prime minister.

Odo Russell was among the diplomats charmed by his talents. The Cardinal was *fine* and as Italian as Machiavelli. Three extracts from his talk will give its flavour. To Russell he spoke in rapid French with a rough accent. 'We were alarmed more than was necessary,' declared[1] the Cardinal, 'Rome is always full of false and contradictory reports, for although we have not like you the liberty of the press, we have the liberty of speech in the highest degree.' On another occasion he expressed[2] his views of papal policy. 'The policy of the Pope is unchangeable for it is subject only to the holy laws of religion and the sacred principles of justice. When Napoleon I wanted to carry out the Continental blockade, the Pope resisted him, not because he had any reason to be satisfied with the policy of England but simply because the course Napoleon proposed was unjust.' And finally,[3] in reference to the appointment of a British consular agent: 'We do not care whether he is a Protestant or a Roman Catholic, but we do attach much importance to one thing, namely, that he should prove to be an *honest man*.' The Cardinal had never travelled; but he had studied human nature. He knew the phrases that an English gentleman would need from him.

On his lighter side he invited[4] Odo Russell 'to come and see his collection of precious stones'. The final note[5] is rather pleasing. 'Cardinal Antonelli, ever cheerful and pleasant, finding I had no news to give him talked for an hour about his flower garden and

---

[1] *The Roman Question*, ed. Noël Blakiston, p. 6.
[2] *Ibid.*, p. 75.
[3] *Ibid.*, p. xxvii.
[4] *Ibid.*, p. 177.
[5] *Ibid.*, p. 101.

the fish of Lake Albano. His Eminence confided to me that his real vocation in life was the study of Nature, more especially Botany and Geology, that he hated politics and power and he prayed that Providence might relieve him of his duties to the Papacy.'

It would appear that the Cardinal had an unexpectant knowledge of what was coming. He did not favour any of the projects for the Pope's removal to Malta or to Würzburg or to the catacombs. Alone in the Vatican administration he saw the way in which the world was going. Like most men who are bent on the private accumulation of money he was very lonely, and he also lacked that piety which was an open sesame to the Pope's sympathy. One sees that in the warm relationship which his rival Mgr de Mérode developed with the Holy Father. Antonelli was, perhaps, a believer; but it does not seem that he approached the sacraments. Religious phrases garnished the Cardinal's discourse. In the end it appears that they had no meaning for him, he was bound up with the kingdoms of this world.

It was in these years that Cardinal Antonelli freed himself from the last of his internal political embarrassments. He had been troubled by the French, and not the French Imperialist, influence about the pontiff. The leader of this point of view was Mgr de Mérode, supported by General de Lamoricière and Colonel de la Vallée de Pimodan. In October 1865 he secured the removal of Mgr de Mérode from the office of Minister of War. These three were high Conservatives and de Mérode, who was of Belgian nationality and French education, was a brother-in-law of Charles de Montalembert. Their impracticable and chivalrous ideas were an irritant to the Cardinal's cold judgment. De Mérode was simple and straightforward and not an intellectual; he was no match for him.

A note in the diary of Ferdinand Gregorovius, the historian, gives an impression of how this situation struck the foreign onlooker. 'The day before yesterday,' he wrote,[1] 'the Pope sent de Mérode his dismissal as Minister of War. Rome is full of the event; everyone rejoices. With Mérode, the Jesuit-Legitimist faction is

---

[1] *The Roman Journals of Ferdinand Gregorovius 1852–1874*, ed. by Friedrich Althaus and trans. by Mrs Gustavus Hamilton (1911), p. 204.

F*

suppressed, and the national party under Antonelli returns to the helm.' This, of course, is not exact for the Cardinal had never given up his office. It was one of the consequences of the approaching end of the Temporal Power that the Vatican was increasingly Italian. Among foreigners the French in the nineteenth century were always the most unpopular. They spoke their own language and not Italian. Their Gallican inheritance was much disliked. They had no esteem for the Italian nation.

The next visit was from a statesman, who was outside the accustomed Roman orbit. It was in the autumn of 1866 that Mr Gladstone made the third and last of his Roman visits. The House was not in session, but he had been particularly busy with his duty as trustee to the late Duke of Newcastle at Clumber. Accompanied by Mrs Gladstone and his two elder daughters, he had come in by the new railway from Ancona. He had found the Lake of Lugano, which he now saw for the first time, the most beautiful[1] of the Italian lakes. They settled in an apartment, which he had used in the middle years of Gregory XVI, at the corner of the Piazza di Spagna and the Via Frattina. They found Lord Acton there. The family's day began with a reading of Dante by Mr Gladstone. The Dean and Lady Augusta Stanley were with them. They wandered round the city. Mr Gladstone, who did not show much interest in archaeology, went steadily from church to church listening[2] to the Italian sermons of priests and friars. In the evening they read through Old Mortality.

On 28 October they had their papal audience. This is described in Mary Gladstone's diary.[3] 'Mama went first, then Agnes, then me, then Lady A[ugusta], and lastly Papa; all in turn curtseying to the depths and kissing the Pope's hand. He then told us to sit on five stools which were arranged in a semi-circle round the table behind which he sat on a kind of dais. Then he began to talk and trolled on very goodnaturedly, laughing a good deal, for about 20 minutes, asking but few questions and carrying on the conversation (in French) almost alone; about Rome, the Italian language, poetry, Milton, Atlantic Cable, the Queen, Scotland

[1] Letter to the Duchess of Sutherland, dated 13 October 1866, printed in Morley's Life of Gladstone, i, p. 849.
[2] Ibid., i, p. 851.
[3] Mary Gladstone, her diaries and letters, ed. by Lucy Masterman (1938), p. 33.

etc., calling the Prince of Wales "Prince George" and com-
placently remarking that there were three or four hundred
thousand Catholics in Glasgow. Asking Lady Augusta whether
she was the daughter of the Lord in China.'[1] As to the final impression of this audience there is a certain variation. In writing to
the Duchess of Sutherland Mr Gladstone stated[2] that 'nothing
can be more pleasant than the impression made by his [the Pope's]
demeanour and language. He looks well and strong, but seems
to have a slight touch of deafness'. His daughter's comment was
more sharp. 'Altogether we were very much pleased with his
kindness and simplicity, but there was something excessively
ludicrous in the whole thing.' Perhaps it was a mistake for the old
Pope to receive those who came from so far beyond the Roman
circle.

During his stay Mr Gladstone had seen some striking pieces of
modern sculpture, in particular a remarkable bust of a brigandess.
In January he and the other Liberal leaders, the Duke of Argyll
and Mr Cardwell left Rome together. They immediately went to
Florence and called upon the King of Italy. The Papal Court
could not have felt that their visit had been successful.

In her old age Mary Gladstone wrote[3] to her daughter about
this journey. The letter gives a very clear impression of how remote the English visitors could be, even in the days of the Temporal Power, from papal Rome. At the same time it is not, perhaps,
a fair example. There is something in Mary Gladstone's writing
which conveys, wherever she may be, the impression of that cosy
and restricted world which centred round her father at Hawarden
Castle. Rome or Paris, it mattered little; she always was the
devoted Anglican expatriate. In the end one always feels that no
one mattered much save Mr Gladstone. The actual passage runs
as follows. 'Rome was extraordinarily romantic and lives in my
mind as a vivid personal experience; the three men we chiefly
consorted with – Sir Wm Richmond (in love with Agnes, my
sister, and she with him), Lord Odo [Russell] in love with me
(tho' he pretended), and then Lord Lorne, the most exciting, as I

[1] Lord Elgin.
[2] Letter dated 30 October 1866 printed in Morley's *Life of Gladstone*, i, p. 850.
[3] Letter from Mary Gladstone, then Mrs Drew, to her daughter Dorothy Parish,
dated February 1924 and printed in Mrs Masterman's volume, p. 490.

was what would now be called in love with him. The love duets with Lord Odo, the wonderful rides on the Campagna with Lorne – playing to Liszt and he playing to me. All with an accompaniment of Lord Acton's and Dean Stanley's talks with Papa.' It was long ago and 'Lord Odo' had in fact been Mr Russell. It all came to nothing. Sir William Richmond disappeared and Lord Lorne married a Princess of Great Britain. The troubles of the Temporal Power seemed far away.

These were the years in which the Roman Campagna as a resort was first discovered. Naturally the Italians never went there except for the few shepherds, who looked after the great herds of sheep. Across the wide and open country of the Agro Romano, which was very gently tilted towards the sea, ran the straight line of the Via Appia with the grasses pushing up between the Roman paving stones. It was very solitary. There were cypresses beyond the tomb of Cecilia Metella. The English visitors would drive out with their *vetturini* as far as the little church of *Domine quo vadis*. There one entered the Campagna, a silent land. There were no towns in sight except in the far distance on the northern slopes of the Alban Hills, and in the foreground a little group of buildings at Castel di Leva. The travellers would return well before sunset, for the night air was malarial. The Campagna was an aspect of the Roman scene which made a great appeal to foreigners. No *monsignore* trudged along the Via Appia.

Support was now building up in Rome for the extension of the new Sardinian kingdom. The politics of the House of Savoy had been agitated since the accession of the King's father. Before that there had been a century of quiescence and earlier still there had been efforts to extend the Savoyard boundaries eastwards across that wide quiet plain which lies between Piedmont and the *Milanese*. It would certainly appear that there was no feeling in Rome for any King of Italy except perhaps in certain *doctrinaire* circles among the urban middle class. There was Republicanism across the North Italian provinces and also an element in Rome, but there seems to have been no desire for the *farouche* figure of King Victor Emmanuel as such. Mazzini, of course, did not want him and nor did Garibaldi. At the same time in many quarters there was a conviction that the papal monarchy was doomed.

This seems to me a recognition that the time was strictly limited in which French bayonets would continue to protect the temporal possessions of the Holy See. There is a list sent by Acton to Dr Döllinger as early as May 1861 giving the names of nine Cardinals who even at that time were said to wish for the surrender of Rome to the Sardinian Government. This list sounds in certain ways convincing, although Acton did not possess authoritative knowledge. A list identical with that despatched to Dr Döllinger was conveyed by Odo Russell[1] to the British Government. Among the names set out there occurred that of one foreign prelate, Clement Villecourt, the Cardinal Bishop of La Rochelle. This name has small significance and Villecourt was dead before the summoning of the Council and the ending of the Temporal Power.

The numerous bishops of the *Regno* were unrepresented; they were all the nominations of the Bourbon years. Among those mentioned on the list was one of Sardinian noble stock and another had connections with the royal House of Savoy. They were all of them at the time in Curial offices and had nearly all been raised to the purple by the reigning Pope. Among them there was only one survivor, Amat di San Filippo, from Pope Gregory's young cardinals. Girolamo d'Andrea was the solitary example of an 'opposition' cardinal, that is to say of the type of prelate who openly or secretly favours policies which could only be put into operation in some later reign. They were in no sense a grouping and four of them were to die before the crisis had developed. One element in Acton's letter is of interest. 'Many more,' he states,[2] 'are supposed to hold similar opinions, but they fear the all-powerful Antonelli.' This is curious, for Antonelli in fact shared their views. He had a more lucid judgment than his fellow-

---

[1] The list runs 'Card, Santucci, di Amat, Grasselini, Silvestro, di Pietro, d'Andrea, Bofondi, Villecourt, Mertel'. The last-named Cardinal, deacon of Sant'Eustachio, was an Italian from Allumiere in the hills behind Civitavecchia. Two of them were to become Cardinal bishops of Sabina and Palestrina respectively, Girolamo marchese d'Andrea and Luigi Amat di San Filippo. They were at this time Cardinal priests of S. Agnese *fuori le Mure* and of S. Maria *in Via*. It seems likely that the name of Giuseppe Bofondi, Cardinal of S. Cesareo *in Palatio*, is correct and is not a mistake for Gaetano Baluffi, Bishop of Imola and Cardinal of SS. Marcellino e Pietro. Cf. *Acton-Döllinger Correspondence*, i, p. 203.

[2] *Ibid.*, p. 203, note 23.

members of the Sacred College. It did not seem to him that the rickety staircase by which he had ascended could last out; it was not a structure that accorded with the later nineteenth century.

Still, Acton was never at ease with members of the Sacred College. It seems that he very rarely met a cardinal. This also applied to his lack of contact with those who would in time be cardinalitial. In fact, among the future Italian cardinals, the only one that it seems he knew was the Oratorian librarian Capecelatro.[1] Indeed, it was through the side of librarianship that Acton made his contact with ecclesiastics. This becomes clear from a long chronicle letter sent to Döllinger during his stay in Rome in the early spring of 1865. After discussing the papers in the Angelicum and the Vallicelliana, Acton adverts to the Society of Jesus. '*Die Jesuiten haben ihr Papiere,*' he writes,[2] '*heimlich in einen sichern Ort gebracht, den Nieman kennen soll.*' This is one of the earliest of his suspicious comments. He saw the Jesuits as among the strongest supporters of the reigning pontiff. Henceforward he had a friendly echo for all those who disliked the great Society.

With the rich Italian laymen, it was another matter. Here he had easy contacts. Those who were close to the Papal Court had as little in common with him as the Duke of Norfolk; but there were others. We are fortunate to have Sir John Acton's comment on a most important Roman figure. It is no surprise to find from his correspondence that the Duke of Sermoneta was the Roman prince who alone awoke his sympathies. 'The head of the Caetani,' he explained,[3] 'is the only outstanding man among these aristocrats, with an extremely sharp penetrating eye.' The Duke of Sermoneta was just sixty years of age; the chief of a great house, whose male heirs throughout the nineteenth century were Liberal in politics and sceptics[4] in religion. By accident his house was free from the honorific offices at the Papal Court: for over two hundred years they had never had a cardinal. A true Roman family, they

[1] Alfonso Capecelatro del Castelpagano (1824–1898), Archbishop of Capua 1880 and Cardinal of Santa Maria del Popolo 1886.

[2] 'The Jesuits have brought their papers secretly to a secure place, which nobody is supposed to know', Letter from 5 Piazza di Spagna, Rome, *Acton-Döllinger Correspondence*, p. 405.

[3] Same letter, *ibid.*, pp. 396–7.

[4] These traits are noted under 1889 in *My Diaries 1888–1914* by Wilfred Scawen Blunt (1932), pp. 28–9.

lived in the Palazzo Caetani and on their large estates which stretched from the further end of the Via Appia to beneath the escarpment of the Latium hills. The Duke had married his heir to an English Protestant; he was different from the other Roman princes. On the political side he was quite close to Acton; he would welcome the King of Italy when he entered the Quirinal. He had an almost English interest in the political set-up which would control the new-born monarchy. Still, there seems to have been little contact between them. The Duke of Sermoneta was a whole generation older[1] than Sir John Acton and they had nothing in common in religion. Sermoneta had a clear lack of interest in all such questions; he was freed from religion as certain elements in the Italian Renaissance had gone free. But religion in a German sense was Acton's life-blood; he regarded some aspects of the Catholic system with a concern and a deep exacerbation.

I have so far set out certain aspects of the background to the Council, and Acton's own attitude will be considered in detail later. But it is important not to be too schematic. A comment in his long letter to Döllinger might have been made by some *flâneur* with quite a different outlook. '*In der hiesigen Gesellschaft,*' he explained,[2] '*ist eine Hauptperson der Dalmatinische Malteser Ritter Graf Gozze, ein geistreicher, gebildeter Mann.*' It must be remembered that the end of the Temporal Power was a process which moved forward very slowly.

In these last years of papal Rome the foreign visitors were increasing. The Mont Cenis tunnel was as yet not completed, but through trains ran from Rome to Turin, Florence and Naples. The *Hôtel de Russie* and the *Hôtel de Londres* were among those that were already open. There were inns at Tivoli and Frascati, both suitable for northern travellers. The *alle chiave d'Oro* at Orbetello was a first-class hostelry; its beds were draped with high silk curtains. Persons of distinction came with their archaeologist; Queen Victoria's stepsister, the Princess of Hohenlohe-Langenburg, with Herr von Klumpp; the young Prince of Saxe-Weimar

---

[1] Michelangelo Caetani, Duke of Sermoneta in the States of the Church and Prince of Teano in the Two Sicilies, was b. 1804 and d. 1882.

[2] 'A main figure in the present society is the Dalmatian Knight of Malta, Count Gozze, a clever, well-educated man', *Acton-Döllinger Correspondence*, i, p. 400.

with Kuno Fischer. There was Count Tolstoy and Liszt and the Princess of Sayn-Wittgenstein. But there was now little contact with the Roman churchmen, except for those who were given political authority.

In his judgments Odo Russell was still sharp. He was married now and Pius IX had given Lady Emily a mosaic paperweight as a wedding present. This acerbity throws into relief Russell's judgment on John Acton given, in the last days of 1869, in a letter[1] to Lord Clarendon, now his father-in-law, who was already one of Acton's strong supporters.

> You ask me what amount of consideration is shewn to Acton and whether he is thought to be too black a sheep to be of service to the cause of common sense? He is simply looked upon as *un diable dans un bénitier* at the Vatican because of his articles in the last *North British*, the 'Massacre of St Bartholomew' and 'The Pope and the Council', and his active interference to bring about an understanding between Monseigneur Dupanloup and the German Bishops. . . . I cannot say how deeply I admire his talents, virtue and learning and how much I delight in his society.

The personality and outlook of the Bishop of Orléans governed his relationship with Acton: they were in fact very much less close than Odo Russell appears to have believed. As far as their temperament and their opinions were concerned, Acton was as far apart from Dupanloup as he was from most of the prelates who would attend the impending Council. For Dupanloup was before all things an ecclesiastic.

He was at this time sixty-seven years of age. The natural son of a Savoyard peasant woman, it seems likely that he came on his father's side of noble stock. This would account for the way in which he was cultivated from his youth upwards by the families of the Faubourg St Germain. He was brought up by Conservatives and by the clergy of the *ancien régime*. He was confessor to the Comte de Chambord and also to the Orléans princes in their childhood. He remained all his life a devoted *protégé* of Saint Sulpice. He was opposed to the Bonapartists and was away to the

---

[1] *The Roman Question*, ed. Noël Blakiston, p. 375.

right in the changing policies of the Second Empire. From the moment he became a bishop he was always close to the reigning Pope; he had received innumerable laudatory briefs from him: he had a warm devotion to Pius IX. When still a simple priest he had been offered the diocese of Annecy by the King of Sardinia. He had been from the very first a champion of the papal retention of the full extent of the States of the Church.

He had a fine presence, his face like the mask of an old Roman Emperor. He was very French and his interests were in the politics of his day as a churchman would conceive them. As a member of the chamber of deputies he was to have all the talents of a tribune going from one politician to another, the blood coursing in his cheeks. Liberal personalities and in a certain measure Liberal sentiments served him in his later middle life as he examined the field to consider how best he could promote the interests of the Church. As an educator he remained attached to the old-fashioned ideas and methods, which the Sulpicians had taught him in his youth. He was their man.

These details will serve to explain the effect that he produced on Acton. There was in fact very little to unite them. In an undated letter, which seems to have been written on the occasion of the bishop's death, Acton gives[1] his own impression of Dupanloup to Lady Blennerhassett.

> He cannot have known Greek, for at Rome it came out that he had never seen a Greek Testament. He knew Latin fairly, not elegantly. The Hungarians were shocked at the Latinity of his protest and made many alterations. . . . 'Surtout, méfiez-vous des sources' is the most characteristic of all his sayings. When he came to Herrnsheim to see the Professor [Döllinger] in September 1869, I was appalled at his ignorance. After he was gone I said to the Professor, with some emotion: 'What is to be expected, if this is one of the best specimens?'

The conclusion in this same letter is marked by all Acton's severity. 'You may be sure that to a man accustomed *an das strenge Denken*,[2] to Scherer, Taine, St Hilaire, he appears a mere

---

[1] *Correspondence*, pp. 50–1.
[2] To rigorous thinking.

windbag – otherwise *pour les beaux esprits*, I can fancy Sainte-Beuve or Renan (his disciple) taking delight in him.' It has, of course, to be remembered that Dupanloup had hastened to make the best of the *Syllabus Errorum*. He was throughout attacked by Veuillot; but for Acton Veuillot's hostility was not enough. The Bishop of Orléans established himself early at Rome, taking up his quarters with a host of secretaries at the Villa Grazioli.

Among the other bishops, who were now slowly coming to the city, Acton does not seem to have had a close relationship with either the Austrians or the Germans. This may have been in part a consequence of his association with Dr Friedrich. He expresses his appreciation of Bishop Hefele and Bishop Strossmayer; the latter was one of the very few among all the prelates of the opposition with whom he kept up relationships in after life.

It was among the usual come-and-go of visitors that the preparations for the opening of the Council were completed. The workmen were at last finished in the late autumn of 1869. It had been decided to use the north transept of St Peter's. The seats for the cardinals were covered with red cloth and those for the bishops with green. The tall grey stone pillars rose from the lilac marble of the floor space. The sharp colours, the bright blue and the rich purple of the Flemish tapestries let for this occasion into the spaces of the wall, showed how the decoration of the vast cathedral had escaped both from ideas of taste and grandeur. The great window in the northern transept with its square panes, seven up and six across, was set in its grey stone framing above the altar. The general effect was one of high grey columns and pillars.

It was very silent. There was little traffic in the Via della Fondamenta, which ran beneath this northern window and brought the cardinalitial carriages up the inclined way from the Piazza Santa Marta to the tunnelled passages which led through to the Cortile di San Damaso. There were as yet no loudspeakers and it was felt that it would be difficult to hear the individual prelates. A hall at the Quirinal was examined but proved no better.

5

Acton and the Council

Two influences upon Acton's life, his friendship with Mr Gladstone and the effect of the *Syllabus Errorum*, prepared the way for the mood in which he now came to Rome. He had moved away from the ideas he had expressed when visiting the city in 1857 with Dr Döllinger.[1] His attitude to Pius IX had further hardened. He would no longer refer to the Pope's 'great kindness and suavity'. To Döllinger's criticisms there were added those that Gladstone now placed before him. The warmth and the devotion and the Conservatism of the English Catholic world was far away.

The whole English Conservative body was unprepared to enter into his objections to the *Syllabus Errorum*. In this matter the Tory squires among the Catholics had at least in some measure the support of the Anglicans who shared their own political allegiance. Both groupings were alike opposed to the subversive elements of Liberal forces in South America. In considering the bitterness which Acton came at one period to express, it must be remembered how inaccessible the English Catholics were to prove to him. In regard to the Council he was to some extent a solitary as far as the English Catholics were concerned. It was not only the priests who abandoned him, it was also to some extent his equals among the wealthy laity. The fears which beset him as to the outcome of the proposed Council meant nothing to them. Even the French moderates envisaged the development of some eventual declaration. He alone stood for papal inaction.

It must be admitted, however, that by this time Acton had

[1] An example of Döllinger's influence on him may be detected in a note made after a conversation with Mgr Modena during his visit to Rome in 1857. 'The Pope unfortunately has no knowledge whatever of theological matters, and this is very inconvenient in a personal point of view. Gregory XVI was a good theologian', *Journal of Lord Acton: Rome 1857*, ed. H. Butterfield, *The Cambridge Historical Journal*, vol. viii, p. 193.

developed a strong dislike for the Italian character, or to speak more exactly, for the Italian ecclesiastical temperament. He came to Rome from Germany, from the Cisalpine lands where suspicion of Italian rule had never died. He had always a clear distaste for Vatican machinery. Thus he describes[1] Dom Simplicio Pappalettere, the Abbot of Monte Cassino, as a *'tipo della furberia Romana'*, an example of Roman cunning. Long ago he had decided[2] that 'the *Civilta Cattolica* and the *Armonia* have revolted me with fearful falsehoods'. He described[3] Antonelli and Altieri as utterly bad, false people.

The list of pseudonyms[4] which Acton chose for his private correspondence with Döllinger is rather curious. It includes names for de Rossi, Friedrich, de Luca, Theiner, Tosti, Gladstone, *Janus*, Arnim and Tauffkirchen, as well as for those of the following six prelates who would be present at the Council: Dupanloup (Padre Giovanni), Schwarzenberg (Dr Jones), Hohenlohe (Walker), Maret (Ilari), Manning (Miranda) and Mermillod (Costa). There is no name set aside for the Pope, and the only member of his administration is Antonelli (Melander). Presumably, this was meant to be an early list and further names would be sent northwards later. One point is very characteristic of Acton's life, the presence of Miranda.

By this time there was already a certain divergence between Acton's views and those of Dr Döllinger. A letter to Simpson written in 1864 at the time of the death of Maximilian II of Bavaria bears on this point. 'I have been hoping,' wrote[5] Acton, 'to hear from Döllinger, in order that our course may square with anything he may intend to do; but I suppose he is wasting his time saying Masses for the late King and preaching his funeral oration.' Already the priestliness of his old tutor was a burden to Acton, and also his Royalism. This was a sentiment which the reigning house of Bavaria was able to evoke in many priests and prelates, who were brought into its circle.[6] But Acton's outlook was quite

---

[1] *Acton-Döllinger Correspondence*, i, p. 594.

[2] *Ibid.*, pp. 210-1.

[3] *Ibid.*, p. 397.

[4] *Ibid.*, ii, p. 33.

[5] Downside MSS. Cf. *Acton-Döllinger Correspondence*, i, p. 339.

[6] Cf. the illuminating notice by Dr Conzemius of Michael von Faulhaber (born at

different. He belonged to that high world which, especially upon the Continent, was cold at heart towards the persons of the sovereigns; they lived too near to them.

His actual stay in Rome on this occasion lasted some seven months. By the end of November 1869 Acton was established at 74 Via della Croce, and he moved in the following month to the Palazzo Chigi. He left for Florence early in July 1870 on his way northwards to his brother-in-law, Count Arco's house at Tegernsee. His journey had received the restrained publicity which that period afforded. An appreciative notice in the *North British Review* on the subject of *The Pope and the Council* had made clear the historian's general sympathy with the recent expression of Döllinger's views. At the same time Dr Pusey had written[1] to him from Christ Church sending copies of his book, entitled *Is Healthful Reunion Possible?*, and suggesting that they be given 'with my respects to any bishop to whom you should think it desirable'.

It would be an error to consider Acton as at heart favouring any of the varying definitions suggested by the groups of bishops who had been called to Rome by Pius IX to that Council whose main business was to the definition of Papal Infallibility. On the contrary, his only wish was that the Pope had been passive and that the Council had never been called. It was upon the Governments that he relied and not upon those bishops of the Minority who regarded the definition of Papal Infallibility as inopportune. In all this time he had a concern for governmental action, which would make sense to Mr Gladstone. He had a hostility to the contemporary papal rule which had something of the reflection of a modern Ghibelline. He saw the Roman scene, as an alien, a Bavarian. He could hardly have been more removed from the impulses and reactions of the English prelates.

Another element assisted in withdrawing Acton's interest from the sphere of present fact into the realms of history. He had a German feeling for cosmic merit and for cosmic weakness. He shows no understanding of the quality of homeliness. There he

Klosterheidenfeld in 1869), Cardinal of Santa Anastasia and the last Archbishop of Munich under the monarchy, *Dictionnaire d'Histoire et de Géographie Ecclésiastiques*.

[1] Letter dated Vigil of St Thomas, 1869, printed in *Correspondence*, p. 84.

worked at his fine desk in the Palazzo Chigi, while his sentences formed and strengthened themselves before his eyes. Down below in the Colleges there sat the bishops with their old cassocks stained with snuff and gravy.

The Bishop of Birmingham had earlier had his passages with Sir John. On the day of Acton's appeal to the Queen's Government, a matter which will be considered later, Dr Ullathorne made an entry in his diary.[1] That solid moderate man was enjoying the duties of the Council, staying at the English College and driving in those February afternoons with his friend and colleague Dr Amherst. The weather was now less inclement and he had recovered from an attack of dysentery.

> The Council [he noted] moves slowly on. We have had speaking or enrolled to speak, twenty-eight bishops on one single point, the number speaking in one day varying from four to seven. After our present *schema* is finished, we shall come to the *great point*, and then the interest will grow intense. But all is prepared for moderate measures. What I said in the letter to *The Times* I repeat; I am quite satisfied with the position of affairs. If we are not doing as much in the time as Rome anticipated, we are doing more. All sides are learning great lessons for future use.

Another entry, this time from Bishop Amherst's diary, will give a further impression of the members of that quiet hierarchy.[2] 'Feb. 24. We spent Shrove Tuesday at Frascati and enjoyed ourselves. Mrs Furse gave us an English dinner: roast beef and boiled turkey, but forgot the pancakes.' It became very chilly after sunset thus early in the year as the party drove down from Frascati through the olive trees past Villa Senni. The bishop was back in his apartments in Piazza di Spagna, with the blazing wood stuffed into the stove and the firelight on the red gilt sofa, before the church bells rang for the *Ave Maria*. At their friendly dinner parties the bishops poked fun at Mr Scott-Murray for his solem-

---

[1] Notes by Bishop Ullathorne, dated 16 February 1870, printed in *The Vatican Council* by Dom Cuthbert Butler, vol. i, p. 239.

[2] These details are from the diary of Dr Amherst, printed in the *Memoirs of Francis Kerril Amherst, Bishop of Northampton* by Dame Mary Francis Roskell O.S.B., p. 295.

nity. The John Dormers and the Vavasours and their children walked with the bishops on the Pincio under the new umbrella pines.[1]

There was another quarter of the city which had the same unchanging Catholic life. The English families of the Roman faith appear to be unaltered in 1840 or in 1880 because they were anchored to the Vatican; as foreigners the local administration passed them by. The *Trasteverini* also were a group apart; they were the bulk of the population that was then living under the protection of St Peter's dome.

They were established in that narrow quarter of the city which lay beyond the great sweep of the Tiber. There were fewer bridges in those days, only the Ponte Sisto and the Ponte Cestio, which linked them with the Isola Tiberina. The modern embankments were not yet in place and the big river went sweeping by above the normal level of the crowded streets. In the spring there could be flooding when the snows on the Apennines melted. Here there were no foreign visitors and no great palaces. The Palazzo Corsini was not then occupied by that rich family, and the Palazzo S. Callisto belonged to the Vatican. The streets and tiny alleys lay around the churches, Santa Maria in Trastevere and Santa Cecilia, Santa Maria dell'Orto and Santa Agata and San Francesco a Ripa. Steep above them rose the Aurelian walls and beyond these lay the open peaceful fields of Monte Verde. No roads out of the city lay through this quarter. The population was curiously static. They were said to descend from the Roman people. Great names were found there like Ottaviani, the family of the future cardinal. The churches were crowded with the women and the children. The men stood quietly in their small shops and little bars; they had a real benevolence towards religion. Politics did not touch these people any more than it touched the *lazzaroni* down in Naples. No conscription brought them into the armies of those days. Like the English visitors, these would remain.

By contrast Acton and his circle were really transients These were the relatively high-grade diplomats who were at that time at the Papal Court Here he was at his ease with laymen, often present in a diplomatic character, who were unamenable to the

[1] *Ibid.*, pp. 283–96.

Holy See. It came natural to him to act as a *liaison*, both with Gladstone and with Döllinger, and on the political side his presence in Rome at this time had come about so easily. For the Bavarian Minister, Prince Hohenlohe-Waldenburg-Schillingsfürst had all along entered into a policy of opposition to the Council and had been prepared to lend official aid. It is seldom realized that, looked at from this angle, the Vatican Council was but an interlude in Acton's prolonged Bavarian visits.

Bearing this fact in mind it is best now to assess John Acton's contribution to the writings of 'Quirinus'.

These were a series of sixty-nine long letters under this signature, the first dated December 1869 and the last 19 July 1870. They were contributed by Döllinger to the *Allegemeine Zeitung* and were based on communications sent from Rome by Dr Friedrich, Acton and apparently some other correspondents. An English translation entitled *Letters from the Council* was published by Rivington before the end of 1870. Both Acton and Friedrich were still young men; but the latter was temporarily attached to the Bavarian Embassy in Rome and held the post of theological consultor to Cardinal Hohenlohe. It is, in consequence, to his pen that the actual details of the working of the Council must be ascribed. The papers reflect certain Gallican sympathies which were far from Acton's outlook, and they all mark a concern for the action of the leaders of the 'German Church'. Thus Cardinal Schwarzenberg,[1] who belonged to the Austrian princely house of the same name, is described as a German. The comments on the prelates of other nationalities were much less detailed.

Certain passages have all the marks of Acton's signature. One comment[2] deals with various bishops. 'Those of French Switzerland, among whom Mermillod rivals Manning in his fanatical zeal for the new dogma: the Spanish prelates – men selected for promotion by Queen Isabella and the nuncio at Madrid, simply for their thorough-paced Ultramontanism.' Another sentence[3] refers to some proposal that the Council should hold meetings in the

---

[1] Friedrich Josef von Schwarzenberg, Cardinal of S. Agostino and Archbishop of Prague, was born in Vienna in 1809 and died there in 1885.

[2] *Letters from the Council*, first letter, p. 66.

[3] *Ibid.*, fourth letter, p. 99.

Sistine Chapel. 'The latter would be an ominous place for in the *Sala Regia*, which the bishops must pass through to enter the Sistine is Vasari's famous picture painted by order of Gregory XIII, for the glorification of the massacre of St Bartholomew's.' The comments on the English prelates, Manning excepted, are fairly rare. 'Bishop Brown of Newport,' so runs one entry,[1] 'an open and decided opponent of Infallibilism, is kept away by ill health.' A final passage[2] has all John Acton's flavour. 'For the Kingdom of God, wherein the least is greater than John and all the prophets, lies as is well-known between Montefiascone and Terracina.'

There are, however, two characteristics of the range of the 'Quirinus' letters which are worth noting in considering the development of Acton's thoughts. In the long introduction there is reference[3] to 'the practical results involved in making the *Syllabus* and Papal Infallibility into dogmas'. In fact the status of the *Syllabus* remained unchanged by the decisions of the Council. There is also another matter on which this correspondence throws some light, John Acton's relations with the Jesuits. The Roman *Curia* of the Society he did not like; but in contrast to his approach to various aspects of the Roman Church which had oppressed him, his casual references to the English province of the Society of Jesus had hitherto been favourable. He had discussed various of his periodicals with Fr Charles Weld, S.J., although this contact seems to have been carried on under a veil of secrecy.[4]

Dr Friedrich was a hearty young opponent of the Society and John Acton was ready to accept criticism of any ecclesiastical corporation which worked in closely with the Holy See. There is also Cardinal Hohenlohe, who, in certain respects, is a strange figure to find in Acton's range. There were no shared intellectual interests to link their minds. He was part of a small and very wealthy class, which was then on the frontiers of John Acton's experience. In fact he was really associated with a later period of

---

[1] *Ibid.*, fourteenth letter, p. 190.
[2] *Ibid.*, ninth letter, p. 141.
[3] *Ibid.*, introduction, p. 23.
[4] In Wetherall's notes, provided for Abbot Gasquet and now at Downside, there occurs this comment: 'Boeto and Weld. These names are to be kept profoundly secret', Downside MSS. Wetherall, f. 326.

Acton's life, when he was in contact with the Queen of England and with Bismarck's Germany. The details now set out were of more interest at Windsor than at the Vatican.

The Cardinal belonged to one of those great 'mediatized' families of South Germany which tended to associate with the royal stocks and with their own precise equals. This branch of the Hohenlohe complex was centred at Schillingsfürst in Middle Franconia; but they were ramifying. They had little in common with the Bavarian nobility, to which the Counts Arco-Valley belonged. The Cardinal's father had been an old-fashioned Catholic, a survivor of the period of the *Aufklärung*. His mother was by birth a Lutheran princess from Hohenlohe-Langenburg; his three sisters were Lutherans. It was this marriage which had brought in the connection with Queen Victoria,[1] which the house so valued.

Great properties had come to them; beside their hereditary estates they held the allodial lands of the extinct landgraves of Hesse-Rheinfels-Rothenburg, to whom they were the heirs. The area was wide and seemed to demand a German *Reich*, the duchy of Ratibor in Silesia and the principality of Corvey, formerly a secularized monastery, in Westphalia. These estates brought in their train the goodwill of the King of Prussia. Thus, although Prince Chlodwig, the Cardinal's brother, was in these years foreign minister of Bavaria, it was in the service of the Hohenzollerns that his career began and ended. Pius IX would refuse the *agrément* when the Cardinal was proposed as Prussian ambassador to the Vatican; he stood behind Bismarck in the *Kulturkampf*. This was a strange background for a Cardinal of the Holy Roman Church and the red hat, which Prince Gustav Adolf received in 1866, was one of the more surprising nominations of the reigning Pontiff. It appears that the new Cardinal's interest in theology was inconsiderable; no doubt his appointment was grateful to the House of Hohenzollern.

A brief impression of Cardinal Hohenlohe is given in the *Diaries* of his cousin, Princess Marie of Thurn and Taxis, the friend of Rainer Maria Rilke. They are the impressions of child-

---

[1] Princess Hohenlohe's elder brother, the Prince of Hohenlohe-Langenburg, married the Princess of Leiningen, who was the Queen's stepsister.

hood for the princess was at that time just fourteen. 'As he was very slender,' she wrote,[1] 'he looked taller than he was: he had fair hair, very blue eyes, regular features and his whole appearance was very youthful.' He was a typical *grand seigneur*. His ring was studded with enormous emeralds. His servants wore magnificent liveries – pure white, trimmed with red and silver galloons and embroidered with the leopard, the Hohenlohe crest. He was constantly in debt and had better carriage horses than any other member of the Sacred College. There are two other points which should be made. He had been a Cardinal for three years and he was just forty-six. He had the simplicity which often belongs to members of great families; he was the type of man whom Prince Bismarck used.

Acton and the Cardinal had little in common, yet one point seems worth mentioning, not for its intrinsic significance but because it seems to throw a light on Acton's outlook. 'When he [the Cardinal],' so relates[2] another comment, 'came to see my mother, which was fairly often, he refused even a glass of water for he was convinced that the Jesuits were going to poison him.' It is a strange fantasy and only of interest because it seems that at this time John Acton shared it. Lady Galway said that her mother, Lady Blennerhassett, told her how, during the Council, Acton used to speak of 'the chocolate of the Jesuits'. The chief impression that one gains of the historian in this winter and spring is of a marked aloofness.

Throughout the sessions he maintained a frequent contact with the Austrian and South German laymen, who found themselves in the papal capital, with them and with Dr Friedrich. He had no similar intercourse with English Catholics. His relations with them appear to have been superficial, nor does he seem to have maintained any real contact with the two English prelates who acted with the opposition, Bishop Clifford of Clifton and Archbishop Errington. The latter was an old High Tory with some Gallican propensities, and Bishop Clifford was an intimate disciple of Dr Newman.

---

[1] *Reminiscences of Princess Marie of Thurn and Taxis*, compiled by Nora Wydenbruck, p. 60.
[2] *Ibid.*, p. 61.

It seems that Acton found himself apart from all those who wished to guide a papal policy, whether it was that of the old Curia or that of the supporters of the specific which Dupanloup regarded as appropriate to the modern world. It was natural that all the bishops should have favoured some plan or other of papal action. No one in the ecclesiastical circle shared John Acton's *political* hope that the papal régime should be swept away.

In regard to the future there was not much doubt. From the beginning Acton did not exaggerate the number of those who considered the proclamation of the dogma as 'inopportune'. No man was less inclined to minimize the effect of the papal wishes upon the members of the Council. The close link of every bishop with the Pope was distasteful to this Anglo-German layman. As a layman, too, he could receive that steady trickle of authentic information which was conveyed to the outer world through many channels.

To explain the position in another way, some recently published comments on the Council indicate a position which was at once widely held and was as far away as possible from Acton's standpoint. This is the Diary of Léon Dehon, a French ecclesiastic, who acted as one of the stenographers at the Council. The Abbé Dehon was young, pious and deeply Roman. He would travel with the French bishops on their train journeys; he would be invited by these same prelates to sit in their carriages with his back to the horses as they moved through Rome; he had only one lay companion, Louis Veuillot.

In these last days the many bishops present for the Council served to emphasize the still continuing papal rule. The feast of La Luminara, which celebrated both the return of the Pope from Gaeta and his preservation at the accident at Sant'Agnese fuori le Mure, had a particular relevance for the reigning Pontiff. It is worth noting Veuillot's description.[1] '*Il y a dans le monde un peuple qui a resté inviolablement fidèle a son roi vaincu et depouillé . . . ce peuple, c'est le sage, pieux et véritablement auguste peuple romain.*' It was natural that all the members of the Council should pay homage to the papal sovereignty; not so John Acton. Perhaps too much attention has been given to all those varying opinions; henceforward we

---

[1] Printed in Léon Dehon, *Diario del Concilio Vaticano*, I, p. 122.

will keep strictly to the views put forward by Acton himself.

The degree to which he looked to those secular Governments, which appeared to him as the guardians of true liberty, can best be illustrated by some quotations from his correspondence. Thus a passage in his second letter to Gladstone, written in December 1869, throws light on the position. He is in this case deploring the influence of the Vatican in Paris. 'I cannot,' he states,[1] 'understand the position of a Liberal ministry in France which should continue to buttress and patronize an authority so misused.' Such ideas led rapidly to the notion of intervention by the British Government. The Liberal Power has in his eyes their duty. 'Each statement by the Roman Court,' so runs[2] his comment, 'has added to the danger and increased the need for prudent and intelligent action on the part of the States.'

It is within the framework of this historical conception that Acton now set his remedy. After describing the dangers which in the view of those whom he supported must result from the adoption of the dogma of Papal Infallibility by the Vatican Council, the historian comes to his panacea. 'They see,' he continued in reference to his associates, 'no human remedy for this peril other than the intervention of the Powers.'

This and the other phrases deserve careful study. The solutions proposed were impracticable and they also marked a transitory defect in Acton's Liberalism. In later life he would not invoke coercive governmental action. Now he pressed this course on Mr Gladstone. 'There can,' he wrote,[3] 'be no uncertainty as to the designs of Rome. We know that it seeks to be made absolute over the consciences of men, and we know for what civil purposes it will enjoy its power.'

It is not surprising that Mr Gladstone should have been stimulated by these letters which chimed accurately and severely with his own convictions. He had considered maturely the situation of the Roman Catholic episcopate and priesthood. 'It becomes really a little difficult,' the prime minister wrote[4] from Hawarden, 'to maintain in argument the civil right of such persons to toleration,

[1] *Correspondence*, p. 88.
[2] *Ibid.*, p. 89.
[3] *Ibid.*, letter dated 20 March 1870, p. 112.
[4] *Ibid.*, letter 8 January 1870, p. 97.

however conclusive is the argument of policy in favour of granting it.' To this Acton made a reply expressing his agreement.[1]

Acton was an opponent of absolute power and he feared that the Council, which was now opening, would give absolute power to the Papacy. Further, while the doctrine of Infallibility was still developing, he imagined that a Council would bind the ideas of the *Syllabus Errorum* upon the consciences of the Catholic world. It seems that this fear was germinating behind all that he wrote, while the Council was developing and in its course.

The laymen with whom he consorted in Rome shared his dislike for increase of the papal power, but they very seldom shared his Liberal doctrine. These were his lonely years and it was during the Council that his proposals were least pondered. He was later to become anchored in the Gladstone family circle, but to this he had not yet attained. He had now to be contented with the determined consideration of Mr Gladstone's public mind. The Liberal Party was indeed fortunate in securing for the advancement of its cause Acton's high-principled expositions. There was, strange as it may seem, something of the high priest about Lord Acton.[2] The Liberal principles showed forth as luminously real.

Seen from this point of view, Acton's intervention in the matter of the Council involved an affirmation of his political beliefs rather than his doctrinal creed. At this time Acton already pursued a path which was remote from that of Döllinger and had still less in common with Dupanloup. It may be defined as the affirmation of a Liberalism which he conceived to be in peril. He belonged to that aristocratic *milieu* which did not yet fear plutocracy. His hope was in the Governments which had accepted some measure of Liberal principles.

The theological interests of his early years evaporated slowly. They were, perhaps, replaced by a very mild concern for all such matters which went with an acceptance of the Church's framework. This included a permanent acceptance of the sacramental system. Thus, in an undated letter[3] from Aldenham to Mr Renouf, which from internal evidence belongs to the winter of 1874, Lord Acton

---

[1] *Ibid.*, letter dated 16 February 1870, p. 103.

[2] He had been raised to the peerage on 11 December 1869. See below, page 195.

[3] Letter in the Renouf-Acton correspondence among the Renouf MSS at Pembroke College, Oxford.

refers to 'Dr Green, who is my confessor here'. This was old 'Verdant' Green who still survived. Such sacramental practice tended to separate Acton from those elements of the Austrian aristocracy, who had never shaken free from a Josephist inheritance.

There were two further differences which served to set the historian apart. Lord Acton possessed a severe and questing judgment, and he had something that he owed to Mr Gladstone; a singularly ethical approach to each diverse subject. A sentence from the introduction[1] contributed by Dr Figgis and Mr Laurence to the *Essays on Liberty* has an especial relevance in this connection. 'His scholarship,' so runs the passage, 'to him was as practical as his politics, and his politics as ethical as his faith.' So far as can be judged at this lapse of time these words with all their implications ring absolutely true. They are closely followed in this appreciation by another paragraph. 'What wonder then,' comment[2] the editors, 'that he [Acton] should exhaust the intellectual and moral energies of a lifetime, in preaching to those who direct the affairs of men the permanent supremacy of principle.'

Acton, now in his middle thirties, had arrived at his conceptions as to the way in which constitutional rights and checks could achieve a moral purpose. His attitude to the new Italian State was only slightly concerned with its diplomacy and not at all with its social consequences. His mind was concentrated on its laws. This was a stage in which he gave to the State a power that in his later thought he disallowed. It is clear that in 1870 he considered that the regulation of the relationship of Church and State could be achieved by means of a unilateral legislative code.

This is borne out in that part of Acton's correspondence with Mr Gladstone in which he adverts to the attitude of King Victor Emmanuel's Government towards the Council. Since 1860 all the States of the Church, with the exception of the Patrimony of St Peter, had been annexed to the Italian kingdom. In consequence the situation was naturally delicate. It is unnecessary to enter into Acton's assessment of the various Italian ministers[3] for it is the

[1] Introduction to *Essays on Liberty*, p. xviii.
[2] *Ibid.*, p. xix.
[3] Two were from the kingdom of Sardinia, Luigi Federico Menabrea, born at Chambery in 1809, and Giovanni Lanza, born at Casale Monferrato in 1810. Quintino

question of principle that is significant. After an analysis of the attitude to the Vatican Council shown by Menabrea, Lanza and Sella, all then in office, he proceeds[1] as follows. 'He [the foreign secretary Visconti-Venosta] has already arranged with Lanza that he shall be free to use what means he can to assist the better portion of the bishops. Their property is still in the hands of the Government, and their position is very trying and unsettled. Arrangements will be made for regulating their affairs as speedily and as favourably as possible, giving the preference to those who best deserve it.' It is those last words that are worth a careful consideration. It would seem not unjust to say that he was somewhat severe to his episcopal opponents.

In any event it is not difficult to understand how it happened that Lord Acton never offered his friendship to the members of that group of bishops who considered the definition of Papal Infallibility inopportune.

It seems to have been rather as an exercise in contemporary history than as theology that the Council was to affect Lord Acton. The element of the judicial was always present in the curbed rhetoric of his Victorian prose. This is well illustrated in the account of the Vatican Council that he contributed to the *North British Review*. In the course of this article there occurs a pen picture of the character of Mgr Darboy, the Archbishop of Paris. 'He had,' wrote[2] Lord Acton, 'none of the conventional prejudices and assumed antipathies which are congenial to the hierarchical mind. He was without passion or affectation; and had good sense, a perfect temper and an intolerable wit.' Considered quietly, do not these phrases seem a little heightened? The writer seems to have had no hold on the precise meaning of his adjectives, whether of praise or criticism. This is a curious and recurrent factor.

In this case Lord Acton's admiration for the prelate was not persistent. The reason why his admiration faded was very simple. Acton could not abide the phrasing and approach even of the 'Inopportunists'. His own wording was Germanic and never

---

Sella was born in 1827 at Sella di Mosso, and Emilio Visconti-Venosta was born in 1829 at Milan.

[1] *Correspondence*, p. 94.

[2] Reprinted in the *History of Freedom and other Essays*, ed. Figgis.

dulcet. He had no feeling for the great influence of Bossuet on the Church of France and thoroughly disliked[1] the cast of mind which the following passage represents. '*Dieu vous a fait asseoir,*' declared Archbishop Darboy in his address to the Pontiff, '*sur la chaire apostoloque, entre les deux moitiés de ce siècle, pour absoudre l'une et pour inaugurer l'autre. C'est à vous qu'il appartient de réconcilier la raison avec la foi, la liberté avec l'autorité, le politique avec l'Eglise.*' An examination of those words will make it clear how Lord Acton came to feel as remote from the French bishops of the Minority as ever he had from Dr Manning.

[1] The greater part of this address is to be found in Abbot Butler's *Vatican Council*, i, p. 142.

G

6

The Definition

If Acton was isolated among the Roman bishops, it must be stressed at the same time that he had very strong support from his own Government. There are letters in the correspondence between Odo Russell and his father-in-law, the Earl of Clarendon, then foreign secretary, which prove this point. On 9 March 1870 Odo Russell wrote,[1] 'I have taken steps to protect Lord Acton, but I do not apprehend that he will be molested. He is of course watched by spies, but I do not for one moment believe that they will otherwise interfere with him in any other way for the present.' Twelve days later Russell sent[2] Lord Clarendon another letter. 'All Lord Acton's views appear to me admirable and I am glad to hear that he writes occasionally to Mr Gladstone and Lord Granville, for his advice is excellent in every respect. I fully agree with him that the source of all evil in Rome is the unconditional Protectorate of France.'

Clarendon's own judgment is made clear in a note to Lord Augustus Loftus, then ambassador in Berlin. Both men were strong supporters of the Church of England; Lord Augustus had recently built at his own cost the English church at Baden-Baden. 'I do not believe,' wrote[3] the foreign secretary, 'that the closer union or the more vigorous action of the Catholic powers would now arrest the steady advance of the Pope to victory over the reason of mankind.'

Acton had the company of his wife and children, although he was worried by his little daughter contracting measles. At the Austrian embassy to the Holy See was Count Ferdinand von

---

[1] Letter printed in *The Roman Question* by Noël Blakiston, p. 408.
[2] *Ibid.*, p. 411.
[3] Letter dated 16 March 1870, *ibid.*, p. 409.

Trauttmansdorff-Weinsberg, who had just come from Munich. Acton never seems to have minded, perhaps as yet he hardly realized, his isolation from his English co-religionists. It had been clear to him the way that things were going. Cardinal Antonelli remained the one prelate open to receive the complaints of various Governments; but by June 1870 the situation was in some ways becoming simpler. It was evident by that time that the Governments hostile to the decree would take no action. The French and Austrians would remain silent.

'Cardinal Antonelli', wrote[1] Odo Russell, 'is very cheerful and amiable, but diplomatists complain of his never speaking but of *la pluie et le beau temps*.' In the same month Lord Clarendon wrote[2] to the ambassador in Paris, then Lord Lyons. 'How right Odo has been throughout in declaring that the Pope would end by having his own way in all things. He has stood alone against all the representatives of the Catholic powers and all the opposition bishops *plus* Acton, who is worth them all put together.' On this note Acton's last long visit to Rome drew to its close.

It was in the first month of this stay in Rome that Acton had received his peerage. In the same month another had been conferred on the proposition of the Liberal Government, on Lord Edward FitzAlan-Howard, who had sat for Arundel and held the post of deputy earl marshal. He had this through the years of the young Duke's minority. Both men were Roman Catholics, had given parliamentary service and would have some difficulty in finding another seat. The Queen was especially insistent that the new peers should be possessed of landed property and Acton had, in addition to his Restoration baronetcy, an estate in Shropshire of rather over six thousand acres. It seems that the peerage was intended to secure Acton's continued service to the Liberal Party; henceforward his work as a politician was a continuing factor in his life. This promotion was also a reward for his work in Rome as this was seen by Mr Gladstone's Government.

We have now reached the time when the dogma was first publicly brought forward. The various elements in the Roman scene have been described; but before coming to the actual

---

[1] Letter to Lord Clarendon, dated 9 June 1870, *ibid.*, p. 442.
[2] Letter dated 15 June 1870, *ibid.*, p. 445.

Definition, it is worth giving a brief account of the position of the
bishops. It is, perhaps, best to begin by giving a list of those
prelates who formed the inner circle of those anxious to press
forward the dogma of Papal Infallibility. This list consisted of the
Archbishops of Malines and Westminster, the Bishops of Regens-
burg, Paderborn, Carcassonne and Nîmes, and Mermillod, the
coadjutor of Geneva. Among these prelates Manning knew Acton
well, and the Germans, Senestrey and Martin, were deeply
conscious of Dr Döllinger. These seven men were at the core of
that party[1] which secured the fourteen places on the deputation
de Fide, which studied and placed before the Council the documents intended to support the Definition of the dogma of Papal
Infallibility. The prelates who favoured this course of action were
known (for obvious reasons) as the Majority.

It is part of the difficulty of assessing the evidence relating to
this time that the weight of the Majority opinion tends to be
neglected by the laymen and others who, for different reasons,
placed their hope in the Minority. No careful examination has
yet been made of the nature of the Majority opinion. It may seem
strange that so many bishops approved a tendency which seemed
neglectful of their own rights; but they could not foresee that the
impending Council would be interrupted before the rights of the
episcopate could be discussed. There were variations of opinion
within the groupings of the Majority and the Definition, which
finally emerged, was bound up with the decrees of Trent. This was
the childhood's background of so many of the Fathers; it was not
Manning's. It must be stressed that the personal preferences of the
Archbishop of Westminster were not victorious.

Certain general considerations may be brought forward. There
were few bishops who were not aroused to sympathy with the
Pope's misfortunes. Their natural tendency was to aid the suffering pontiff. The presence of a living Vicar of Christ had a powerful
effect especially in the African missionary territories. It is notable
that among the fairly considerable number of bishops from the
mission field, support for the Majority opinion was unanimous.
These prelates were for the most part French; but their appointments had been free from Government interference and they were

---

[1] This is the general thesis of Abbot Butler's *The Vatican Council*.

closer in outlook to the French priesthood than to the French episcopate. What may be called the Majority opinion was honeycombed into many sections. The episcopal body in Spain and Portugal was strongly prejudiced against anything that savoured of Gallicanism. It may be said that in general the bishops of Latin America followed in their wake. The Italian bishops had *antennae* which linked them closer than the foreign hierarchies to currents of opinion in the Vatican. The bishops of the United States were not in the forefront of the struggle.

Whatever might be felt about the States of the Church, the bishops were always conscious that Rome had been the Pope's own city for a thousand years. Mundane issues had their effect. Many prelates for most diverse reasons were tempted to build up the Pope's position. These varying circumstances should be remembered as one studies Lord Acton's efforts to give help to the Minority.

There were only two bishops who can be said to have held the full Gallican position,[1] Maret, the dean of the faculty of theology at the Sorbonne, and Verot of St Augustine in Florida. Nevertheless, the old Gallican spirit still survived among all the French bishops of this section, that unassailable confidence that there was nothing to equal the *Eglise de France*. Politically some were Legitimists and others had rallied to the Second Empire. They were seldom in close touch with their own much more 'Roman' clergy. As a group they were untravelled and had small esteem for the Italian character. They gathered together at *Saint Louis des Français*. To such men the atmosphere of the Vatican was uncongenial. The German and Austrian bishops, who worked along with them, were for the most part strangers. These latter in most cases came from among the elder prelates of their own provinces and had had their seminary training under the old professors who viewed Rome in the dry light of the Febronian eighteenth century. There had also borne down on them the persistent influence of bureaucratic Josephism. The last-named Regalian influence, and also the memory of the Synod of Pistoia, were not without their effect on the rare Italian members of the Minority. Needless to

---

[1] Nevertheless, the expression Gallican was widely used by the Majority. Cf. '*Ni Mgr Dupanloup, ni aucun des gallicans militants ne passèrent*', Dehon, *op. cit.*, p. 64.

say these were not found among the bishops of the old Papal States.

Under another aspect the Austro-Hungarian bishops of the Minority had a more real contact with the Vatican than the French bishops of the same colour. Thus two of their leaders, Rauscher and Schwarzenberg, were already cardinals, while Haynald and Simor, the Archbishops of Kalocsa and Esztergom, would later receive the Hat.[1] Hefele of Rottenburg was, perhaps, the most scholarly among the prelates of this opinion. He had long been in touch with Acton and was a distinguished historian of a rather old-fashioned school; but he was a Württemburger and seldom in Munich. Bishop von Ketteler of Mainz, coming from a noble Westphalian Catholic family, had also visited Acton at Herrnsheim as his diocesan.[2] It seems that both men were now alienated by Acton's recent association with Friedrich. There were no German bishops who would have cared for this. The truth was he had very few episcopal associates.

The case of Bishop Strossmayer was, perhaps, the one exception. He was not so very far from Acton's age-group,[3] by origin an Austrian of the official classes; by choice the great defender of the Croat culture. He was burdened by the hostility of the Government of Francis Joseph; his hope lay in some improvement of relations with the Orthodox. There was little enough in common with Lord Acton and the two men were never intimate; but their contact, in fact, survived the Council. Strossmayer was possibly the only one of all the bishops of the Minority who in his heart would have preferred that the Western Church had been developed on a different model.

There were, however, many bishops of this grouping with whom Acton appears to have had no contact. Among the members of the American episcopate, Kenrick of St Louis seems to have been the only one he knew. He had nothing in common with the two English prelates of this opinion. The term 'Inopportune' has in

[1] Lajos Haynald became Cardinal of Santa Maria degli Angeli in 1879 and Janos Simor received the same promotion in 1873.

[2] There is among the Renouf MSS a letter from Acton at Herrnsheim dated only 2 September, but clearly coming from 1869. 'Hefele, Bishop of Rottenburg, tells strange things of what he saw in Rome, and is as straight as a pikestaff on the great question. . . . Ketteler was here the other day and is, I am told, perfectly resolute.'

[3] Strossmayer was born in 1815 and Acton in 1834.

any case a transitory significance. In regard to bishops from out-side France, its meaning was sometimes shadowy. Had the Vatican Council taken place in 1890 instead of in 1870, it seems likely that the 'Inopportunists' would have formed a quite small grouping. For the heart-land of the Opposition lay in France and the situation depended on the fact that the episcopate, as restored by Napoleon, was wholly Gallican.[1] With each passing decade this Gallican influence was receding.

There is here a certain problem of interpretation. The letters sent by Acton to Mr Gladstone (which were unpublished) and his share in the compilation of the letters of 'Quirinus' (which were unsigned) fit quite perfectly together as the productions of one mind. Neither series, however, seems really consistent with an active pursuit of the policy of the Minority within the Council. It would appear that Acton's interest in and assistance to any body of the bishops has been exaggerated.

It was during this period that Odo Russell left the papal capital. There has been a certain confusion as to his attitude owing to the account given in his old age by Cardinal Manning to his bio-grapher Purcell.[2] This suggests that Odo Russell accepted faith-fully the account of events that Manning pressed upon him. As a consequence the same idea is reflected in Abbot Butler's book on the Council. The quotations from Russell's writings show that this is false. It appears very clearly that what he admired in Manning was not the cogency of his arguments, but his power of expression. Like all the other members of the English governing world, he was case-hardened against Roman propaganda. Lord Odo, as he soon became, went forward on his great career.

Thus it would seem that Acton had a rather muted interest in the actual happenings of the Council, at whose meetings he was in any case not present. His mind was by now bent, and would be for several years upon its consequences. Meanwhile he waited in the Palazzo Chigi for the emergence of the propositions about the Papacy. Discussions on the use of various catechisms or the powers and rights of vicars general did not concern him. The *schema* on

[1] This fact was stressed by Mgr Darboy in a speech at the General Congregation of 19 January, Dehon, *op. cit.*, p. 74.

[2] Purcell's comments in his *Life of Manning*, ii, p. 436, were repeated in Abbot Butler's *The Vatican Council*, I, 62, p. 271.

Infallibility was not distributed to the bishops until 7 March and it was in fact 17 May before they began to discuss this question. The one real clash of personalities in the Council had already taken place.

It was in the General Congregation of 22 March that Bishop Strossmayer spoke to complain of the fifth paragraph of the *schema de Fide*. 'The Proem,' began[1] the bishop, 'ascribes to Protestantism all the errors of the day – rationalism, pantheism, materialism, atheism; but all these errors existed long before Protestantism. And there are among Protestants many grave men who are a great help to Catholics in opposing these errors, as in former times Leibnitz, in our day Guizot whose refutation of Renan I would like to be in the hands of all. I believe that there is in the midst of Protestantism a great crowd of men in Germany, England and America, who love our Lord Jesus Christ and deserve to have applied to them those words of Augustine, "They err indeed, but they err in good faith: they are heretics, heretics; but no one holds them for heretics".' After comments in interruption had been made by Cardinals de Angelis and Capalti, the Bishop of Sirmium went forward. 'I thank,' he said, 'Your Eminence for this instruction; but your argument does not convince me that all these errors are to be attributed to Protestants. I believe that there exists in Protestantism not merely one or two, but a crowd of men who still love Jesus Christ.' The bishop then got entangled in a discussion. The bell rang and he was ordered to come down from the rostrum. Some of the surrounding bishops called out against him. One shouted that he was *un'uomo pestifero, questo*.[2] Others said that he was another Luther, let him be cast out, and others, 'He is Lucifer, anathema, anathema'. There was no recurrence of such a scene; but the words of these Italian and Spanish bishops must have seared Lord Acton's memory. In the Vatican itself these words were not reflected; there they were always circumspect with the Protestant kings.

The debate on the question of defining the Pope's Infallibility lasted for just three weeks, from 13 May until 3 June. Objections

[1] The translation of this speech is taken from Abbot Butler's *The Vatican Council*, pp. 236–8.
[2] This phrase is printed in Dehon, *op. cit.*, p. 99.

were made in regard to the effect of the Definition on Protestants and Orthodox. Cardinal Rauscher said[1] that reference to Infallibility is not to be found in Scripture or in Tradition. In neither of these sources is there mention of the word. The Melchite Patriarch of Antioch hoped that the Fathers would content themselves with repeating the decree of the Council of Florence so as not further to alienate the Greeks. The Maronite Patriarch supported him in regard to the effect upon the Eastern Churches. Bishop von Ketteler expressed the view that Infallibility was a pious doctrine which he himself had always taught, but that it was not certain enough to be defined. The Bishop of Concepción in Chile said that all Latin America wished for the Definition. There was a long speech from Archbishop Manning.

Bishop Verot declared[2] that the Definition would be a sacrilege. The faith of the Irish proved nothing, they believed even in the infallibility of their priests. Monsignor Valerga, Patriarch of Jerusalem, compared Gallicanism to the Monothelites, and the objections of the Gallicans to those of Sergius and Pyrrhus. Archbishop Claret, who has since been raised to the altars of the Church, spoke in favour of the Definition.

On 2 June Bishop Strossmayer declared[3] that it was necessary to open the gates of the Church instead of closing them. Bishop Dinkel of Augsburg spoke of the difficulties that lay ahead in Germany. Manuals of theology in use had described Infallibility as a matter of controversy. Bishop Maret explained that the power of a Council was superior to that of the Pope. This caused[4] a great commotion. It was then announced that 150 Fathers had asked for a closure of the discussions.

In general I have concentrated here on the expression of opinions by the bishops of the Minority. No change would have been effected by a lengthier debate.

For the rest of the month the discussion turned upon the Primacy of the Roman Pontiff and the question of his immediate and ordinary jurisdiction. Here the Minority spoke again; but the subject was further away from Acton's interests. The text of

[1] *Ibid.*, p. 147.
[2] *Ibid.*, p. 151.
[3] *Ibid.*, p. 157.
[4] *Ibid.*, p. 158.

G*

the Infallibility decree was debated in the General Congregation beginning on 15 June. In these discussions the bishops of the Minority brought forward the formula of St Antoninus that 'the successor[1] of St Peter using the counsel and seeking for the help (or testimony) of the universal Church cannot err'. The Dominican Cardinal Guidi made an intervention which had effect on the final wording of the draft. The debate closed on 4 July.

Lord Acton had no access to the meetings of the Council. He and Monsieur Veuillot were both excluded from these gatherings. There only came before them the final public movements of the Pope through his own city. The Pontiff was seen through the glass of those great golden coaches which now went through the streets of Rome for the last time. Around the venerable figure dimly per-ceived, there pressed the crowds of his own subjects. The reactions of Acton and Veuillot to this spectacle must have been different.

Sixty-one bishops of the Minority left Rome before the final session to avoid the necessity of voting *non placet*. Without excep-tion these accepted the decrees when they were published. The formula ran as follows. The operative words appear at the close of the fourth chapter of the constitutions *de Ecclesia Christi. Itaque nos . . .* so runs the clause, *sacro approbante Concilio, docemus et divinitus revelatum, dogma esse definimus,* and then comes the central wording: *Romanum Pontifices, cum ex cathedra loquitur, id est, cum omnium Christianorum pastoris et doctoris munere fingens pro suprema sua Apostolica auctoritate doctrinam de fide vel moribus ab universa Ecclesia tenendam definit,* followed by the explanatory paragraph *per assistentiam divinam ipsi in beato Petro promissam, ea infallibilitate pollere, qua divinus Redemptor Ecclesiam suam in definienda doctrina de fide vel moribus instructam esse voluit; ideoque eiusmodi Romani Pontificis definitiones ex sese, nunc autem ex consensus Ecclesiae, irreformibiles esse.*

This wording will be examined in some detail when the matter comes up again in Acton's life.[2] At the moment it will suffice to give the English version as set out by Bishop Ullathorne in his October pastoral for the benefit of the Catholics in the diocese of Birmingham. 'The Definition,' he explains, 'is contained in these words. "We teach and define that it is a dogma divinely revealed:

---

[1] Butler, *op. cit.*, p. 352.
[2] See below, pp. 232–3.

that the Roman Pontiff, when he speaks *ex cathedra*, that is, when in discharge of the office of Pastor and Doctor of all Christians, by virtue of his supreme apostolic authority he defines a doctrine regarding faith or morals to be held by the Universal Church, by divine assistance promised to him in blessed Peter, is possessed of that infallibility with which the divine Redeemer willed His Church should be endowed for defining doctrine regarding faith or morals; and that therefore such definitions of the Roman Pontiff are irreformable of themselves, and not from the consent of the Church".'[1]

We know how these decrees were to be taken by all those who had been reared in a Protestant *milieu*, whether this had a strictness in matters of belief or had been buttressed by the Liberal principles of the northern nations. Acton, on the other hand, would share with all his neglectful Catholic world the background of the Tridentine decrees. It seems always to have been the historical rather than the theological angle which appealed to him in Döllinger's philippic, written under the name of 'Janus' against the Council. Theology lay out on the periphery of all the knowledge in his crowded mind.

It had been planned that the Council should resume its sessions and the rights of the bishops would be considered; but on 19 July the Franco-Prussian war broke out and the French troops were recalled to their own country. The Council terminated and the position of bishops in the teaching Church was not considered until the second Vatican Council, which opened in 1961. It should be stated that throughout Acton's life the great powers of the Papacy, defined in 1870, were never used.

On 20 September 1870 the Italian troops occupied the papal capital. The breach of the Porta Pia on this occasion was to Lord Acton a fortunate happening. The courteous disregard which many cardinals had displayed towards him became irrelevant. The destruction of the political status of the Papacy gave him a profound satisfaction. He settled down for the autumn with his brother-in-law in Bavaria at Tegernsee.

[1] From Ullathorne's Pastoral of October 1870, quoted in Butler, *op. cit.*, pp. 455–6.

7

Acton in Bavaria

The years that follow 1870 are the most scantily documented period of Lord Acton's public life. They were marked by a development of social activities in a time of carefree expenditure. In Bavaria, where he had been first a student and later the *prétendant* for Countess Arco's younger daughter, he was now accepted as a man of authority, weight and experience. At this period he moved in a different circle from that to which Dr Döllinger had introduced him. He fell back, perhaps almost insensibly, on the disordered, generous and lavish home life of the Arco family.

His headquarters were the houses of his brothers-in-law. These included the summer villa at Tegernsee, a small lake running north and south, lying between the Bavarian Alps and those smaller hills which masked the plain in which lay Munich. This appears to have been the house in which Lord Acton kept the largest of his continental libraries. At Munich there was the old Arco Palace, and at St Martin in Upper Austria, a large estate. Here the house lay on the downland which ran northwards from the Hassruck Hills. The nearest town was Ried, some twenty miles from the Bavarian frontier, which lay about it from north to south-west like the inner segment of a sickle moon. It was a great house in the Innkreis, large and white and square with an elaborate portico. There was metal work surmounted by small onion domes at the edges of the roof line. In winter time there was snow in that high country; it lay upon the roof and on the stone statuary along the garden terrace and on the upper surfaces of the onion domes. Frontiers meant little in those quiet years. Sankt Martin was nearer to Munich than to Vienna.

It was at this period that Acton came gradually to develop

those gifts which Queen Victoria was to prize so highly. These years saw the burgeoning of those qualities which he would display as a Lord-in-Waiting. It was, perhaps, as a relief from the strain of his mental life that he turned to intellectually unexacting friendships. In the absence of the relevant correspondence it is difficult to say quite how much his cousin the Countess Arco-Valley meant in his life, but it seems clear that her influence was singularly enduring. In her house he was never ill-at-ease, as he was with his stepfather, Lord Granville. Anna Arco, by birth a Marescalchi, guided and trained him; in 1865 he had married her daughter. In this circle John Acton was valued for himself and in a seemly way for his possessions, for Herrnsheim and Aldenham. Here he was in a *milieu* which had few intellectual concerns; he was accepted as a man of the world, well-informed and with wide connections.

His very absence of contact with the universities helped him, since this confirmed his satisfactory amateur status. Here he brought up to date his recent knowledge of the *minutiae* of German genealogies, whose eighteenth-century ramifications he had already studied. Together these would arouse a keen appreciation in his own sovereign. In South Germany these years after the wars were peaceful. Bismarck was much disliked and Acton's Liberal sympathies viewed with favour: in this circle there was always a strong dislike for the police-State. In that cultivated world, which a certain nervous tendency saved from being philistine, no difficulties were felt in regard to Lord Acton's religious standpoint in so far as this was apprehended. In this Bavarian circle there was little sympathy for Vatican politics as long as Cardinal Antonelli remained a leading figure. It may be said that there was no great change in this matter so long as the old Pope lived. In the political field the Papacy was still supported by the Legitimists and now began to draw the new Catholic *bourgeoisie*. The Arcos were remote from both these groupings. The new German political party, the *Centrum*, was in essence Clerical.

There is a point that is worth making about Legitimism. This seems to have had no appeal for the Wittelsbach dynasty. Apart from the old Duchess of Modena, the princes and princesses gave little support to such a standpoint. The kingdom of Bavaria was itself the fruit of an alliance with Napoleon.

Again, the religion of the royal family had its own emphasis. Catholicism as professed by the junior and ducal line was wayward and fanciful. This factor was not irrelevant in Bavaria, where the members of the reigning house, with its quality of brilliance and instability, were so close to the life of both the landowners and peasants.

It is also to be noted that Bavarian particularism had been rendered all the keener by the Prussian victory. The Bavarians had not recovered from the discomfort of the proclamation of William I of Prussia as German Emperor. This particularism manifested itself in a feeling for the native product. Döllinger, with his innate conservatism, his old Bavarian character and his sympathy for South German values, was bound to be regarded with approval. Certain ladies, Countess von Leyden for instance, looked on Dr Döllinger with hesitation; but this did not apply to their men-folk.[1] There was indeed little resemblance between the standpoint of Acton's Bavarian relatives and that of Archbishop Manning and the English Catholic body. Intellectual interests were not keen among either of these groups of Catholic laymen, but at Tegernsee there was nothing which resembled that warm reverence for the clergy which was so marked a feature of the Tractarian convert world. The Bavarian priesthood was taken for granted.

Viewed from one angle, Acton was now living within a family circle which, with their friends, was in some respects almost a closed society. Children had been born to him, a son and daughters. They would grow up with their cousins at Tegernsee and at St Martin; Acton was to all appearances deeply embedded. At the same time this way of life was obviously not calculated to press Acton on to publication, although it did not actually hinder the prosecution of his studies. This factor may have had a bearing on the drying up of his articles and his reviewing at this period. In the Arco circle there was considered to be something painfully middle class about the literature of anonymity. Liberty of speech

---

[1] This account of the reactions to Dr Döllinger was provided by Countess von Leyden's grand-daughter, Lady Galway.

was hardly paralleled by freedom of controversy in the public prints. Save for a thread of patronage, very tenuous in effect, there was nothing that linked the circle of the Counts Arco-Valley to that of the *littérateurs* and still less to the propagandists. The network of allied families shared certain characteristics; they were spendthrift, erratic, generous and wholly unself-seeking.

This goes some way to explain the fact that Acton at this time appears to have remained remote from the strictly political scene on the Continent. The Austrian politicians of that era were without contact with the Arco circle.[1] This is of some importance, for in that administrative world certain ideas were current which had a parallel with Acton's own. They were different, however, owing to the stress that such politicians placed upon the events of 1870. An example may be found in the ideas of Karl von Stremayr, the minister of worship in Austria, who persuaded Beust to denounce the Concordat with Rome because Pope Pius IX had become a different moral entity since the proclamation of Papal Infallibility. The other sides of the policy of the Beust chancellorship made small appeal to Acton. He does not seem to have developed any serious contact with administrative circles in the Austrian capital. He had no contact with the *bürger* element and it is clear that the Court of Vienna was uncongenial.

By the time that Acton was forty there were various links with England which had been weakened or transformed. His relations with the great Whig families had depended on his stepfather, Lord Granville. This contact had not, in any intimate sense, survived his mother's death. In 1865 Lord Granville had married again; there was only a distant suitable cordiality on Acton's part towards his stepfather's second family.

There was one of Acton's close Bavarian relationships which would soon be brought to an end by his absorption into the Hawarden circle. The years between 1870 and 1879 covered the period of his most intimate association with Charlotte von Leyden. It is a real misfortune that Lord Acton's correspondence with

---

[1] Their kinsmen, the Arco-Zinneberg family, were rather different. They were the children of Count Ludwig, the Obersthofmeister (d. 1854) by that archduchess who was the widow of the Elector Karl Theodore of Bavaria. They were thus close to the Court of Vienna and married into Austrian Court families. They were based on Maxlrain; their rather fey Catholicism and their literary patronage lay in the future.

Lady Blennerhassett, as Charlotte von Leyden became on her marriage in 1870, seems to have disappeared. All that appears to have survived are four early letters[1] printed in Lord Acton's *Correspondence*. There are also some others in the same collection from a rather later period when their relationship had become less intimate. She herself was a Bavarian, while her husband, Sir Rowland Blennerhassett, sat as Liberal M.P. for Galway City. He had known Döllinger since 1864 and found the money for starting the *Chronicle* three years later.

Lady Blennerhassett was a *littérateur* and many years later was to write two articles in the tenth volume of the *Cambridge Modern History*, one on the Doctrinaires and another on the Papacy and the Catholic Church, a careful excursus on the half century which ended with the death of Pope Gregory XVI. She was one of the rare women who sympathized with Lord Acton's religious pre-occupations. It was in these years, before he became so closely associated with the Hawarden family circle, that she stood nearest to him. She came from the world of the Arco-Valleys.

A spirit very different from this circle is shown in the approach to the Catholic Church maintained at this time by Lord Granville and Mr Gladstone. The examples to be given have admittedly a rather narrow range, but they are appropriate at this point, for they turn on the qualities required in a minister despatched from London and accredited to the Bavarian Court. In their impressions of Bavaria they almost seem to be dealing with a different world.

These were the years in which in their political association Lord Granville and Mr Gladstone were most opposed to Roman Catholics. Apparently Granville was for the most part actuated by a political dislike for anything which might prove detrimental to the Protestant constitution of his country. Even as far back as 1869 there is a curious expression in one of his letters[2] to Mr Gladstone. 'I shall leave it to you to discuss in conversation whether it will be wise as a general principle for the future to treat

---

[1] These letters are dated 12 July 1873, 17 February 1879 and another in the same month. One letter was apparently written in 1878, *Correspondence*, pp. 43, 52–7 and 70–2.

[2] Letter from Lord Granville to Mr Gladstone, dated at Balmoral Castle, 25 August 1869, *The Political Correspondence of Mr Gladstone and Lord Granville 1868–1876*, ed. Agatha Ramm, vol. i, p. 48.

R. Catholics with disfavour, in order to rescue the Protestant Religion.' This seems a definite alteration from the Whig scepticism of his earlier years. A private note[1] from Walmer bears on this point. 'How is Charles Barry to succeed in England [as a Catholic representing an English constituency in the Commons] when Edward Howard and John Acton failed?' It was just at this time that the Queen[2] refused to offer a vacant Garter to the Duke of Norfolk.

The Council had further soured both politicians. Neither wished to retain or to appoint a Catholic to the legation at Munich. On 30 November 1871 Lord Granville wrote[3] from Walmer to Mr Gladstone. He had received a despatch from Sir Henry Howard,[4] who had been minister at Munich for some years. 'As it was,' he explained, 'only Howard's opinion addressed to me, it is hardly worth while to argue with an ultramontane who has been recalled.' Sir Henry had been deeply settled in the world of Munich. He was something of a *bon viveur* and his Lutheran wife came from a family of Prussian officials. The term 'ultramontane' seems rather extreme; it appears unlikely that the Vatican would then regard an ordinary English diplomat as coming within that category.

Gladstone replied[5] immediately from Hawarden and his line has a certain interest. 'I do not know if Petre[6] has any of the same leanings as Howard.' Granville answered[7] this in a private note. 'Lytton (foolishly) has refused Munich. West does not wish for it. Petre has the next claim. But I doubt its being a good thing to send another Catholic to Munich. I therefore propose to transfer Morier, who desires it, to Munich and send Petre to Stuttgart.'[8] This city had a Lutheran Court and administration.

At this time both men were touchy on the subject of the Church

---

[1] *Ibid.*, vol. i, p. 72.
[2] *Ibid.*, vol. i, p. 73.
[3] *Ibid.*, vol. ii, p. 288.
[4] Sir Henry Francis Howard (1809–1898).
[5] *The Political Correspondence*, vol. ii, p. 288.
[6] Sir George Glynn Petre (1822–1905).
[7] Letter dated at Walmer, 4 December 1871, *The Political Correspondence*, vol. ii, p. 289.
[8] Lord Granville was careless about the spelling of foreign place names. He referred to William I as Emperor of Germany.

of Rome. The same spirit is alive in another letter[1] to Granville from Hawarden Castle It relates to a recent Roman convert. 'Lord Granard's[2] application to interfere with the Italian Government about the Convents has come from you without any mem. or minute – and *zero* seems to be about the proper answer.'

It is clear that by this time Lord Granville, from his rather specialized approach, had written off Lord Acton as a failure both as a politician and as an editor. Two letters to Gladstone bear on these points. The first is a note[3] sent in 1870 returning a letter from Archbishop Manning. 'I send you back Manning's letter. I presume there is no Protestant or Atheist whom he dislikes more than Acton. I am afraid, however, he may be right about the latter's success in public life.' The second letter[4] forms part of a correspondence written some four years later. 'Acton's friends are a mere handful. He never would raise the number of subscribers to the *Home and Foreign* beyond a thousand.'

This coldness was in contrast with the hearty warmth to which Mr Gladstone had now come in his approach to the historian. It is, however, noticeable that at this time neither of the leaders was concerned with Acton's usefulness in the sphere of politics. It did not occur to either of them to consider that Lord Acton might have stayed on in Munich as the diplomatic representative of the Queen of England.

[1] Letter dated at Hawarden, 8 November 1872, *The Political Correspondence*, vol. ii, p. 361.
[2] George Arthur Hastings, seventh Earl of Granard (1833–1889).
[3] Letter, *The Political Correspondence*, vol. i, p. 160.
[4] Letter dated at Venice on 10 November 1874, *ibid.*, vol. ii, p. 458.

8

The Tridentine Church

These early Bavarian years were also the time of Lord Acton's last contact with that world of the Catholic Church which, in his Hawarden period, was to mean little to him. It seems appropriate to conclude the study of the years in which he was in one way or another concerned with Church activity by giving an impression of the Tridentine Catholicism of the 1870s, from whose idiom he would become so much divorced.

The Council of Trent had presupposed a ruling Catholic State. Tridentine Catholicism, so called from the adjective for Trent, was therefore contained for the most part within the territories of Catholic monarchies. It appears to me that Iberian Catholicism, the religion of Spain and Portugal and of their former colonies throughout Latin America, was different in emphasis from the Catholic life in the other countries of Western and Central Europe. In Spain it was in some respects stronger and more evenly spread among the people; but it was veined with a fierce anarchical anti-Clericalism which had shown forth in the burning of the monasteries. In any case it lay outside Lord Acton's lines of travel and had no effect upon his life.

This being granted, the areas of the old Tridentine Church can be regarded as lying to the east of the Pyrenees and being bounded by the lines which separated the Catholic from the Calvinist regions of the Dutch countryside and from the Reformed areas in Northern Germany and in Franconia and Suabia. Its eastern frontiers were the furthest predominantly Catholic parishes among the Masurian Lakes and in Lithuania and Russian Poland. It extended in broad terms throughout the lands dependent on the Hapsburg Crown, except for the Calvinist pockets across Hungary. Bosnia and Herzegovina had not at that date been annexed to the

Austrian Dominions. The southern boundaries were the shores of
the Mediterranean running eastwards from Port Vendres in the
Roussillon as far as Ragusa on the Austrian shore of the Adriatic.

This was the area which had for the most part been occupied
at the beginning of the century by a deeply Catholic peasantry.
In France it was from the farming stocks that there had come the
greater part of the future missionaries who had gone crowding in
to the seminary of the *missions étrangères de Paris* and those of the
new societies. Throughout this area of Europe the villages were
served by priests from their own countryside. The large families
encouraged by unmechanized agriculture had always sons and
daughters for the Religious Life. It was only in archaic Spain that
there were no missionaries.

At this time Lourdes, as a centre of pilgrimage, was the discovery of the French towns and country districts; the crowded
trains with their old wooden carriages steamed slowly into the new
railway station from every corner of the French provinces. There
were certain regions, especially perhaps in Brittany and La
Vendée, where religion would unite the squirearchy in their old
manor houses with the surrounding country people. There were
still Legitimists among the young bishops like Mgr de Rovérié de
Cabrières. All the same, the coming of the Third Republic had
ushered in the final dissolution of this politico-religious world.
Legitimist Catholicism could not survive the death of the Comte
de Chambord, which would take place in 1883. With him died
the last of the senior line of the House of Bourbon, and the only
French prince uncompromised by the *bourgeois* monarchy. The note
of Legitimism could not attach to any member of the House of
Orléans.

The rest of this great region of Tridentine Catholicism was at
this date still ruled by Catholic dynasties, except for parts of
Germany, the newly-Prussian Rhineland and Baden, and the
territories beneath the Russian Crown. Across Europe there still
was to be found that static quality of peasant communities with
little travelling, save to and from the market town. This was the
period in which the complement of village churches was completed; the bells in their towers would still ring across a wholly
Christian countryside.

There were, of course, variations in this Catholic picture. The Walloon provinces had for long remained indifferent on religious questions, as had certain *départements* in southern and south-eastern France, where the Huguenot leaven had taken root most strongly. Throughout Catholic Europe there was found a surviving corporate religious outlook in which the local feasts and great Church festivals were deep among the habits of the whole community. These were bound up in those rural areas with the sense of the immediacy of the Gospels, with the corn growing on the hills of Galilee and the shepherds on the slopes by Bethlehem. In a word, the enemy and the solvent of this way of life was the Great City.

Linked with the peasants in their religious outlook there was that *petite bourgeoisie* of the country towns, which for the most part sprang from them. A rather extreme example is the life of Monsieur and Madame Martin at 'Les Buissonets' at Lisieux. He was a watchmaker and his wife came of a family of lacemakers from Alençon, the neighbouring town. They were both Legitimists, believing that there lay the best hope for the protection of religion in their country. Not far away on the borders of La Beauce and Perche was the little town of Illiers, where the Prousts had been long established as candle and taper-makers in the Rue du Cheval Blanc. Adrien Proust, the father of the novelist, was of this stock.[1] In many regions the *petite bourgeoisie* of the provinces would remain *pratiquante*.

When one comes to the more prosperous circles, and especially to the world of Paris, the scene changes. Here the Voltairean influences had long been present and in recent years a newly-current Positivism. In the circle of the industrialists and among other elements of the *grande bourgeoisie* it is in general the women who alone retain the practice of the Catholic Faith. The aristocracy in France was of relatively little consequence after the fall of the Second Empire and the renunciation of the Comte de Chambord. The only difference in the religious question between this section and the *grande bourgeoisie* was that the men of this high world found it unfashionable to deny the name of Catholic.

Going from Strasbourg across the Rhine the scene would change

[1] Adrien Proust was married in 1871, and St Thérèse de Lisieux was born in 1873.

again. Beyond the miles of forest land there lay the Catholic parts of South Bavaria, the territory of the old electorate and the suppressed prince-bishoprics. The northern section of the kingdom had a Lutheran peasantry in the lands of the former margraviates of Brandenburg around Ansbach and Bayreuth. Here in the South there was a Catholic peasantry and a peasant priesthood rather deeply separated from the wealthy landowners with their private chapels and private chaplains. There was also a Catholic *bürger* element from which Dr Döllinger had come. Industry developed slowly in these regions except for the great breweries at Munich.

Further to the southwards there was the Catholicism of the Alpine slopes, which was reflected in the passion play at Oberammergau, now growing famous. There was a mass of Catholic mountain parishes, which included the Swiss eastern cantons and the Tyrol. This was now the Austrian Empire, and across the German Hapsburg lands there still remained the custom of the wayside crucifix; but the peasant world grew less religious as one moved towards the East. There were, for instance, difficulties with the Czechs in the parishes in the Sudetenland.

Vienna was the political centre of this great complex. In general the city was marked by a rather negligent religious practice. This bore on all the circles of the city's life, arising rather from *insouciance* than infidelity. The men of the Austrian aristocracy had long since ceased to feel the need for worship. At a rather lower level there was that purely worldly life, just nominally Catholic, which marked the education of Marie Vetsera[1] and her Baltazzi uncles. At the crown of the Imperial city there was a formal Catholic order at the Hapsburg Court; the Emperor and the archdukes on foot and then the empty carriages with the cream-coloured horses, as they followed the Blessed Sacrament to the *Stefanskirche* on the annual feast of Corpus Christi. There was here an element of religious theatre. There was nothing durable in this whole picture. The horse-ploughs on the farmlands were as evanescent as the State procession; both in time would quietly pass away.

It was a weakness in the Tridentine system that, in spite of many tensions, it was too closely linked up with the State. This

---

[1] Marie Vetsera, the lover of the Crown Prince Rudolf, who died with her, was born in 1871.

was one of the several reasons why the working-class population of the great Continental cities were lost to the Catholic Church; their future was bound up with a secular-minded Socialism. But Lord Acton seldom viewed the working class.

In England the spirit of Father Faber lies over all this time. It is true that he had died, his heavy body destroyed by overwork, in 1864; but he was then only forty-nine and his influence was singularly enduring. He is a better example than John Henry Newman, for the latter was a genius. In a letter that Faber wrote to Lord Granville's sister, Lady Georgiana Fullerton, he said[1] 'I subjoin a list of books towards a little spiritual library. [The ten books included] Surin, Boudon, Grou,[2] Lallemant, de la Colombière, *Retraite Spirituelle*, St Theresa – French ed. of her works in 2 vols, *Esprit de S. François de Sales*. . . . Burns has all the above.' It was in the 1870s that the Carmel of Notting Hill was established, coming from the Rue d'Enfer in Paris. David Lewis produced the first English edition of the works of St Teresa of Avila and Père Ramière his edition of Père de Caussade's *Traité de l'Abandon à la Providence Divine*, omitting the passages which savoured of Quietism, about this date. This was the period of the full flowering of the French religious writing of the eighteenth century. If one wishes to obtain the flavour of the piety of the time one need only read the letters sent to the Visitandines at Nancy, and especially to Marie Thérèse de Vioménil and Charlotte Elisabeth Bourcier de Monthureux in this same volume. They have the security and that protected calm which marked the deeply settled Catholic community.

Another of Faber's letters, written this time to the Dowager Duchess of Argyll, has always seemed to me most deeply characteristic. He was referring to Ardencaple Castle.[3] 'I would gladly take one of my novices, & go & listen to ye blue Gareloch sobbing on its quiet shores, & walk out with ye peacocks, & talk to ye squirrels, & sit under ye larches in ye high wood, & fancy ye misty peaks of Arran to be ye "land beyond ye sea", whither we are all bound.' That approach to the next world, the conviction

---

[1] Oratory MSS, vol. 21, f. 117.

[2] Jean-Nicholas Grou (1731–1803), the author of *Maximes Spirituelles*, was chaplain for the last eleven years of his life to the Welds of Lulworth Castle.

[3] Oratory MSS, vol. 18, f. 14.

of a rewarded future life, was something that bound together the Catholic, the Baptist and the Evangelical. This idea was clearly linked with the Victorian certitudes.

We can see now that the last period of the heyday of Tridentine Catholicism was the second half of the nineteenth century, the period covered by the papal reigns[1] of Pius IX and Leo XIII. These were the years when no one envisaged, except for the Eastern Rites, any alternative to the age-old Latin Mass and to its long developed Liturgy. There were the ancient chants, the *Dies Irae* and the *Vexilla Regis*; the setting of the Mass by Palestrina. The *Adeste Fidelis* alone was modern. There was a long-encrusted and revered tradition. The calendar was filled with many saints; this was all clearly understood along the lines of a developing history. This was the old Tridentine Church which Newman knew.

There was something to be said on the other side. There was, perhaps, a plethora of relics, and in the villages of Calabria and Apulia, and to some extent also in Sicily, devotion to the local saint could be quite *outré*. Pious legends tended to proliferate. Old-fashioned notions dominated the Holy Office.

As has already been suggested, this was a period of deep concern for the Contemplative Life. In France, as in England, it was a time of Carmelite vocations. In right-wing military families of restricted means both Charles-Eugène de Foucauld and the future *Mère Elisabeth de la Trinité* were growing up. In 1867 Friedrich von Hügel first came to England as a boy, and from 1876 he lived at Hampstead. His great personality was still in germ. As a young clerk in the Education Office, Edmund Bishop was spending his spare time in analysing the 'Collectio Britannica' of papal letters which he was to print in 1880 in the *Monumenta Germaniae Historica*.

The spirit at the Vatican throughout this time was Roman and not Italian. There was no warmth towards the holder of the title of King of Italy. Across this Tridentine world there was little knowledge of the religion of the Protestants from the North, who came and spent their money there. Among the educated Catholics the attitude maintained to those who belonged to other Christian Communions was calm and incurious.

---

[1] Pope Pius IX reigned from 1846 until 1878 and Pope Leo XIII from 1878 until 1903.

These years, too, were marked by what was in effect Acton's withdrawal from the friendship of the English Catholics. Already he tended to regard the period of his intimate association with that grouping as a closed epoch. In time he was to gain something of the calmness and serenity of judgment in regard to their lay leaders which we find in the later Newman's approach to the Tractarians. To explain this clearly it is necessary to quote a letter written some ten years later.

It was occasioned, as so often was the case, by a biography. It was addressed to Mr Gladstone after the publication in 1884 of Ornsby's *Memoirs of J. R. Hope-Scott*. 'It strikes me very strongly,' Acton is found writing,[1] 'that we seem to remember two different men. Common to both are the charm of manner, a noble and amiable disposition, quick intelligence and a certain superiority. But I do not quite recognise a man capable of attracting and in-fluencing you so deeply in the indifferent, languid, self-contained Hope that I knew from 1851 to 1864, who showed no care to strive for any higher or more distant aims than those of daily life, and whose powers of purely disinterested mental work were gone.'

The background of this letter is the intimate friendship between Gladstone and Hope Scott, which was broken when the latter submitted to Rome in 1851. Later Acton went on to consider the time when he knew Hope Scott best, the years between 1851 and 1860. He described himself as living much with him and Badeley.[2] 'I do not think,' he continued, 'that I am confounding the impres-sion of different times when I say this. But there is no doubt that, when the Roman question came to the front, he took a further step in religious change and became an Ultramontane. We hardly ever met during the last ten years of his life because Norfolk House was uncongenial.' Hope Scott had married, as his second wife, Lady Victoria, the eldest sister of the young Duke of Norfolk. Since the accession of the fourteenth Duke in 1851, Norfolk House, a great grey stone Georgian building which stood at the East side of St James's Square, had been the centre of the English Roman Catholic social grouping.

[1] The letter printed in *Correspondence*, pp. 261–2, is only dated La Madeleine, 9 February, but states that the writer had not yet seen the Life of Hope-Scott. The death of James Robert Hope-Scott had occurred in 1873.
[2] Edward Lowth Badeley (d. 1868), the ecclesiastical lawyer.

It was true that by 1874 his letters to *The Times*, which will be considered later, had in effect closed Norfolk House against Lord Acton and that his relations with the fifteenth Duke never progressed beyond a formal minimum. Still, ten years earlier Acton had come to dislike the setting of Norfolk House; that profound reverence for Dr Newman in which the Dowager Duchess had brought up her two young sons; the ready appreciation which the Jesuits from Farm Street always found there; the presence, while he lived, of Father Faber. For this generation of the Howards was quite profoundly religious. The fourteenth Duke of Norfolk had been apparently brought up almost without denominational affiliation until he fell under the influence of Montalembert, and his wife, Augusta Lyons, was an ardent convert to the Roman Church. Their third daughter, Lady Minna, became a Carmelite. They accepted all those influences which have been described as emanating from the Brompton Oratory. They had antiquarian tastes and took a Roman view on all disputed questions. Their charity was cast within a Roman mould. And in addition there was a political[1] barrier between Lord Acton and the young Duke, which neither side ever wished to surmount.

At the same time Acton had little contact with the Catholic supporters of the Liberal Party. There is a correspondence between Lord Ripon and his cousin, Lady Amabel Cowper, who was approaching the Catholic Church, which Ripon had lately joined. Both of them, writing in 1874, felt a difficulty in regard to what might be the attitude of the Church towards Liberal institutions. Neither, at that time or later, would be found in Acton's world. There was one standpoint which none of the English converts could tolerate, indifference to the Papacy.

It is interesting that to Acton, looking back, the year 1864 should have appeared as a significant date in regard to his different social contacts. It was the time of his practical severance from Hope Scott and it also marked the breaking of his intimate association with his English co-religionists. It was the year of the publication of the *Syllabus*.

[1] The comment on the political divergence was put in conversation by the late Viscount FitzAlan of Derwent, who was born in 1855.

PART THREE

THE GLADSTONE YEARS

Introduction

The last sections of this book run on continuously, the first part centring upon Lord Acton's relations with Mr Gladstone and the second beginning with his appointment to the regius chair of modern history at Cambridge. In both periods his life, although much of it was spent abroad, was wholly centred upon England. These were the rich Victorian years with peace among the Great Powers in Europe. Such wars as Great Britain was engaged upon were all in essence colonial. In England it was for the possessing classes a period of deep tranquillity.

Abroad there were no revolutions, it was a time of stability for the European dynasties. It is, perhaps, as well to set out at this stage those domestic details of that life in which the richer English families were embedded. There were of course certain changes, but relatively not very many, in the next thirty years. This period saw Lord Acton move from the middle thirties to the middle sixties. He aged early and these were his central years. This was the time when a sedentary life would best fulfil itself.

In the volume of correspondence with Mrs Drew there is reproduced a photograph of a group at Tegernsee taken in the autumn of 1879. Lord Acton, in black coat and dull white trousers, is seen leaning back on an iron garden chair with his round black hat reposing on his crossed knees. His left foot rests on a little woven mat which lies on the flat raked expanse of gravel. The virginia creeper hangs over the *persiennes*. Opposite him across the gravelled space is Mr Gladstone's visage, composed and leonine, while in the background sits the old professor. These points are here recalled, for John Acton had now entered that age of burgeoning material ease which was to characterize the middle and later portions of the reign of Queen Victoria. It was a period of facilities which he accepted, comforts which were in the background of his swift mental activity, and a social ritual which he observed. It is easier to picture Acton in his later manhood if we recall the actual facilities and amenities which built up the physical surroundings of that clear-cut personality.

A few details may be mentioned merely to establish the position. Galoshes had been introduced some years ago; the Inverness cape was still in fashion; phosphorous matches he had known since boyhood. These were the days of carriage exercise in the afternoon and the rite of the dinner party. It was a period of shooting in the Highlands and summer holidays in Brittany and Normandy. This was the beginning of the English discovery of the French Riviera. Railway travel was satisfactory for daylight journeys; at night a gentleman did not attempt it. The early morning train from the Gare de Lyon would reach the Mediterranean the same evening. This equally applied to Scottish journeys. Reeve on his summer visits to the deer forest, which his friends had leased, was accustomed to take a stateroom in the steamship sailing from London to Aberdeen. On the railroad the well-packed luncheon hamper, the grouse, the flask of brandy against the cold, sustained the traveller. The fog closed in past the massive archway before that station which was still known as Euston Square. The travelling valet with the folded rug borne on his left arm stood waiting beside the door of the first-class railway coach with its grey and swiftly soiled upholstery.

In this country lamps were universal, lit by paraffin and burning in a globe of white ground glass. There had now been some time in fashion striped wallpapers, royal-blue curtains, gilt pelmets, inner curtains of Nottingham lace, Brussels carpets with their thick sharp pattern and Berlin woolwork enriched with beads. The naming of magenta was fairly recent; this was the period of shades and dyes. On the tables stood silver tureens, epergnes and bread baskets. Beside the hostess would be placed the tea equipage. In the dining-room wine-coolers rose beneath the sideboard under the family portraits in heavy oils. The bell-pulls were of woolwork in subdued colours. Knick-knacks were dusted lightly with a feathered brush. In the reception-rooms the great fires roared, and in the bedrooms firelight played about the whitewashed ceilings and the new beds without curtains, and lay on the large china jugs and basins and the shining soap-dishes and sponge-trays.

Into this world Lord Acton returned when he came to take up residence again in London and at Aldenham. A chapter entitled 'Aldenham Chapel' sets out his last relations, cordial if a trifle distant, with his chaplains in Shropshire. His controversy, if that is not too sharp an expression, with Mr Gladstone in *The Times* brought on a correspondence with Archbishop Manning, which is given in some detail. It seems that at one period Acton envisaged himself as in danger of excommunication and with this was bound up an acerbity in regard to the Roman Church in his letters to Gladstone's daughter. With the passage of years the danger, real or alleged, would pass away, and when he reached Cambridge his relations became cordial with the Catholic authorities in England.

A series of chapters sets out Lord Acton's final penetration into the intimacies of Mr Gladstone's family life at Hawarden Castle. For various reasons and chiefly on account of the great mass of published comment, it is easier to obtain an impression of the precise detail of the Hawarden household than that of any other so remote in time. In all the chapters until that on 'Gladstone's resignation' Lord Acton is seen as a very close friend of the Liberal leader. The various diplomatic posts which were considered for him are passed in review and the gradual contacts which he made with the professional world of English historians from whom as a young man he had been so isolated. A fairly detailed examination of Lord Morley throws a light on Acton's true position in the Gladstone circle.

At the same time three personal studies in some detail of Bishop Samuel Wilberforce, Bishop Creighton and Professor York Powell help to build up Acton's situation in his later life. It is important in considering these years to give due weight to the Anglican position. Acton was at this period remote from his co-religionists and he gave advice to the prime minister on Anglican appointments. Whether this was a wise procedure on his part may be considered an open question. Several aspects of his outlook will become clear in setting out his relationship with Mr Gladstone.

This eventually led on during the Liberal Administration to his appointment at Court, for which he was in some ways so uniquely suited. The Court life is a facet of his career which previous writers have tended to neglect. At this time, too, those events were taking place which rendered him a candidate for one of the major history chairs. The reasons why he was invited to Cambridge and not to Oxford are suggested.

The last portion of the book deals with his life at Cambridge, with the founding of the *English Historical Review* and with his work as the chosen editor of the *Cambridge Modern History*. The degree to which this great work, so characteristic of its period, reflected Lord Acton's own idea is considered. We can trace through the years at Cambridge the use to which he put his own vast knowledge.

I

The Gladstone Controversy

Four years had passed in which Lord Acton did not touch in print upon religious subjects. It was only in 1874 that the correspondence in *The Times* opened. During this period it had become clear that the Temporal Power of the Papacy had gone beyond recall. The Italian kingdom with Rome as its capital was a settled factor in the life of Europe. This had a tranquillizing effect upon Lord Acton.

Linked with the effect produced on Acton's outlook by the events of the Vatican Council and by the political destruction of the States of the Church there is the matter of the letters sent to *The Times* by Mr Gladstone and himself. A charge has been brought against Lord Acton to the effect that he acted insincerely in not abandoning Catholicism after the Vatican decrees and that his comments on the Papacy cannot be squared with the formal letters which he exchanged in 1874 with Dr Manning. It does not seem that this question ever posed itself to Mr Gladstone or to Lord Acton's other intimates who dwelt upon the phrases of the enlightened Roman Catholic *savant*. Nevertheless, it was vividly present with Acton's outlook, to Dr Figgis and Mr Laurence, and to some extent to Mr Herbert Paul. It is a matter of crucial significance for there are few men whose whole reputation turns to such a great extent on the satisfactory proof of their sincerity. The markedly ethical content of Acton's thought was on his own declaration linked with an integrity of outlook which he was not afraid to declare as the touchstone of his acceptance or aversion. A convinced integrity of thought was, as Acton said in another connection, his whole Capital.

The four years which followed upon the prorogation of the Vatican Council in July 1870 had been for Acton comparatively uneventful. They had witnessed the foundation of the Old Catholic body, the excommunication of Döllinger and the establishment of the latter in the position of an excommunicated Catholic, who refused assent to the Vatican decrees but gave no adherence to schismatic movements. The next development in Acton's position was the result of the fall of the first Gladstone Administration in November 1874, an event which set the Liberal leader free for controversy. In the same month there came Mr Gladstone's letter to *The Times*, followed by Lord Acton's reply in the same organ.

This was a lengthy document printed on 8 November and followed on 21 and 29 November and 12 December by letters containing supporting evidence for his contentions. The second of these contributions was concerned principally with the attitude of St Pius V to the Ridolfi conspiracy and that of Gregory XIII to the massacre of St Bartholomew. The fourth letter dealt in detail with Fénelon's public and private attitude towards the papal condemnation of *Les Maximes des Saints*.

It seems simplest to concentrate here on certain general propositions contained in Acton's first letter. The specific historical charges can be related more easily to the general canons of judgment which the historian came to adopt. An advantage of following this method arises from the fact that the subsequent exchange of letters between Acton and Archbishop Manning turned solely on the line of thought expressed and not on the detailed historical cases. Acton's letter is long and extensive quotation unavoidable.

In the first place Gladstone had stated that the Catholic Emancipation had been passed in 1829 because the vicars apostolic had declared that Papal Infallibility was not a dogma.

Your indictment[1] [Acton replied in this connection] would be more just if it was more complete. If you pursue the inquiry further, you will find graver matter than all you have enumerated, established by higher and more ancient authority than a meeting of bishops half a century ago. And then I think that you will admit that your Catholic countrymen cannot fairly be called to account for every article of a system which has never

[1] This letter from Lord Acton, dated from the Athenaeum on 8 November 1874, addressed to Mr Gladstone and forwarded to the Editor of *The Times* for publication, is printed in *Correspondence*, pp. 119–24.

come before them in its integrity, or for opinions whose existence among divines they would be exceedingly reluctant to believe.

There is waste of power by friction [Acton continued, using a metaphor that appealed to him] even in well-constructed machines, and no machine can enforce that degree of unity and harmony which you apprehend. Little fellowship and confidence is possible between a man who recognises the common principles of morality as we find them in the overwhelming mass of the writers of our Church and one, who on learning that the murder of a Protestant sovereign has been inculcated by a saint, or the slaughter of Protestant subjects approved by a Pope sets himself to find a new interpretation of the Decalogue.

It is worth examining the attitude of the English Protestant Liberals towards this letter. Far from the preoccupations of Dr Manning, the sedate English Liberalism of the period knew how to give an appreciative welcome to the new thinker. The grave men with the spade beards sat in their armed chairs; the atmosphere of the great club rooms a little heavy; the windows sealed against the fog; a hint of the smell of oil from the shaded lamps. *The Times* with its thick imposing print would lie folded before them on the book rest as they scrutinized Lord Acton's letter. All that he said was very welcome. For that Liberal world possessed a clear antipathy for the Church of Rome welded to a hearty and a frank suspicion. The soft lamplight fell on the austere spectacles of the 1870s through which they perused Lord Acton's paragraphs as they sat ensconced in the warm leather. The letter went on:

There is little to apprehend from combinations between men divided by such a gulf as this, or from the unity of a body composed of such antagonistic materials. But where there is not union of an active or aggressive kind, there may be unity of defence; and it is possible, in making provisions against the one, to promote and confirm the other.

There has been, and I believe there is still, some exaggeration in the idea men form of the agreement in thought and deed which authority can accomplish. As far as decrees, censures and persecution could commit the Court of Rome, it was committed to the denial of the Copernican System. Nevertheless, the history of astronomy shows a whole catena of distinguished Jesuits.

There now comes a sentence which seems to lie at the core of Lord Acton's thought. 'It is not the unpropitious times only, but the very nature of things, that protect Catholicism from the consequences of some theories that have grown up within it.'

The standpoint is resumed in a peroration of some length. He concludes:

That opinions likely to injure our position as loyal subjects of a Protestant sovereign, as citizens of a free State, as members of a community divided in religion, have flourished in various times, and in various degrees, that they can claim high sanction, that they are often uttered in the exasperation of controversy, and are most strongly urged at a time when there is no possibility of putting them into practice – this all men must concede. But I affirm that, in the fiercest conflict of the Reformation, when the rulers of the Church had almost lost heart in the struggle for existence, and exhausted every resource of their authority, both political and spiritual, the bulk of the English Catholics retained the spirit of a better time. You do not, I am glad to say, deny that this continues to be true. But you think that we ought to be compelled to demonstrate one or two things – that the Pope cannot by virtue of powers asserted by the late Council, make a claim which he was perfectly able to make before: or that he would be resisted if he did. The first is superfluous. The second is not capable of receiving a written demonstration. Therefore, neither of the alternatives you propose to the Catholics opens to us a way of escaping from the reproach we have incurred.

The publication of this letter was the signal for action by the Archbishop of Westminster. The first approach appears to have been in the nature of a formal enquiry and on November 12 the Archbishop wrote again. To this letter he received from Lord Acton a reply which gave him some satisfaction and the following exchange at once took place. It must be said for Dr Manning that he had been long patient and that his talent is as manifest in this matter as his heavy and insensitive courtesy. His mind had indeed the virtue of iron and its smoothness.

My dear Lord Acton,[1] I have to thank you for your letter dated yesterday [November 15]: from which I gather, with much satisfaction, that your answer to my first question, whether in your letter to *The Times* you intended to repudiate the Vatican Decrees, is in the negative.

I am not, however, able to gather what answer you desire to give to the second question, namely, whether you adhere to the doctrines defined in the Vatican Council: unless you intend to describe yourself as one of 'those who adopt a less severe and more conciliatory construction' of those decrees.

If I am right in this inference, I would still ask you to enable me to understand what that construction is.

I see with great pleasure in your note that you had written an emphatic repudiation of the statements of *The Times*: and I regret much that any advice should have defeated your judgment of what is at this moment urgently needed for your own sake. Let me therefore ask you to enable me to reassure the minds of a multitude of those who at this time believe of you what *The Times* has sent all over the world.

Believe me, my dear Lord, yours faithfully,

Henry E., Archbishop of Westminster.

PS. I must ask you to forgive the omission of date in my last letter. It was written on Thursday 12.

H. E., Abp.

The dilemma in which this letter placed Lord Acton should be noted before consideration is given to the terms of his reply. A draft letter to Archbishop Manning composed by the historian at this period has been preserved and is now given. The words in brackets represent alternative suggested phrases.

My dear Lord, I gave no answer to the question, which did not seem to me to arise out of the terms or the spirit of my letter to Mr Gladstone.

But I must decline the inference which a passage in my letter of this last Sunday has suggested to you. I have no private gloss or special interpretation for the decrees of the Vatican Council. [Trent].

The acts of the Council are the law which I obey. I am not

[1] This and the draft reply and the letter which follows were printed in *Correspondence*, pp. 151–3.

concerned [bound] to follow the comments of divines or to supply their place from [with] private judgments of my own. I am content to adhere implicitly with an absolute reliance on God's Government of his Church to the construction she herself shall adopt in her own time.

Command. Submit accept.

It is already clear which way his mind was moving and on November 18 the following letter was despatched to Archbishop Manning from the Aethnaeum.

My dear Lord, I could not answer your question without seeming to admit that which I was writing expressly to deny, namely, that it could be founded on anything but a misconception of the terms or the spirit of my letter to Mr Gladstone.

In reply to the question which you put with reference to a passage in my letter of Sunday, I can only say that I have no private gloss or favourite interpretation for the Vatican decrees. The acts of the Council alone constitute the law which I recognise. I have not felt it my duty as a layman to pursue the comments of divines, still less to attempt to supersede them by private judgments of my own. I am content to rest in absolute reliance on God's providence in His Government of the Church.

I remain, my dear Lord, yours faithfully,

Acton.

A phrase in this letter seems to reflect a particular quality of Acton's thought: 'I have not felt it my duty as a layman to pursue the comments of divines.'

Another letter, written while this mood was on him, was despatched to his own bishop. Aldenham Park was in the parish of Bridgnorth, which since 1851 had formed a part of the Shrewsbury diocese. Further, his private chapel at Aldenham was supplied by secular priests, who belonged to this jurisdiction. On 16 December 1874 Lord Acton wrote[1] to Bishop Brown of Shrewsbury in these terms.

To your doubt whether I am a real or a pretended Catholic I must reply that, believing all the Catholic Church believes,

---

[1] Printed in Leslie's *Cardinal Manning*, p. 233. It would appear to have been this letter which was regarded as acceptable by the episcopate.

and seeking to occupy myself with no studies that do not help religion, I am, in spite of sins and errors, a true Catholic, and I protest that I have given you no foundation for your doubt. If you speak of the Council because you supposed that I have separated myself in any degree from the Bishops whose friendship I enjoyed at Rome, who opposed the Decrees during the discussion, but accept them now that it is over, you have entirely misapprehended my position. I have yielded obedience to the Apostolic Constitution which embodied those decrees, and I have not transgressed, and certainly do not consciously transgress, obligations imposed under the supreme sanction of the Church. I do not believe that there is a word in my public or private letters that contradicts any doctrine of the Council; but if there is it is not my meaning, and I wish to blot it out.

In a letter[1] written from Aldenham on a Monday in this same December Acton had made a comment to Lady Blennerhassett. *Voici mon évêque qui perd patience à ma politesse, et fait la même demande que son metropolitain. Vous voyez que ça chauffe.* Acton's approach to Archbishop Manning and Bishop Brown was very different. The first was and had been for many years a declared enemy and the second an acquaintance of long standing of whose intellectual capacity he did not have a good opinion. A letter written much later to Lord Emly bears on this point. 'I know,'[2] explained Lord Acton, 'that Dr Grant [Bishop of Southwark] was among those whom Newman's theory of development repelled, who thought it undermined Tradition, and who were therefore rather uncomfortable with him. It was the same with my own Bishop Brown, of Shrewsbury; but he did not count.'

There is, however, another aspect under which this letter can be examined. I gain the impression that Acton had lost the power of writing a natural letter to a Catholic bishop. The reference to 'the Bishops whose friendship I enjoyed at Rome' will bear this out. Acton's relations with these 'friends' were now extinguished. His mind was turned away from every bishop and his *entourage*.

---

[1] *Correspondence*, p. 153.
[2] Letter dated at Munich, 10 February 1892, preserved in Lord Emly's MSS, communicated through the kindness of Sir Shane Leslie.

There is a sense in which both the letters to Archbishop Manning and to Bishop Brown appear to be an exercise.

There is some further light on Acton's attitude in a letter sent to Lady Blennerhassett a few months later.

It is clear[1] there has been some hesitation lately as to pushing things to extremity, and it has delayed any critical and decisive proceedings. The German bishops have repudiated the Vatican doctrine that the Pope absorbs the authority of bishops in every diocese; and they have not only been approved by the Pope, but he has declared that there is nothing new or changed in the Church. Stated in this connection his words are a virtual acknowledgment of the rule of faith, and preclude all interpretations that are inconsistent with tradition. Newman's declaration on the authority of conscience necessarily implies that one may not build up one's system on forgeries, or omissions, or forced constructions, and the results that can be obtained subject to this rule are such as none can quarrel about.

If this letter is examined carefully it clearly suggests a certain lack of interest.

A letter from Dr Newman, written about this time to a correspondent who had attacked Lord Acton's character, provides a view of the estimate formed of him in the more sympathetic Catholic circles. 'I do not think,' wrote Newman,[2] 'you should say what you say about Lord Acton. He has ever been a religious, well-conducted, conscientious Catholic from a boy.' These are the significant words, but a point is added relating to the correspondence in *The Times*. 'In saying this,' Newman went on, 'I do not at all imply that I can approve those letters to which you refer. I heartily wish that they had never been written.'

The general background of Catholicism had been through all his life among the commonplaces of Acton's thought. It was not the elements in the Vatican decrees which would be unacceptable to the Protestant mind that were likely to give him pause. The words of the Tridentine profession of Faith had been for so long familiar: *Sanctam catholicam et apostolicam Romanam Ecclesiam omnium*

---

[1] Letter dated at Torquay, 21 April (1875), *Correspondence*, p. 154.
[2] Letter dated from the Birmingham Oratory, 13 April 1874, p. 155.

ecclesiarum matrem et magistram agnosco; Romanoque Pontifici, beatri Petri Apostolorum principis successori ac Jesu Christi vicario, veram obedientiam spondeo ac iuro. Acton was a Liberal and not a Gallican. He would not, therefore, like a Gallican of the extremer school contest the Vatican interpretation word by word and give his qualified assent or his denial to each succeeding phrase and sentence. There was a further factor in the situation. The historian's waning interest in theology was in the last stage of replacement by historico-political preoccupations arising from an ethical basis. This reading of the position may help to explain a phrase in a letter written by Lord Acton[1] to Lady Blennerhassett in which he states that 'Newman's conditions would make it possible, technically, to accept the whole of the decrees'.

Yet there is another aspect of this personal history. In a statement made in 1874, and quoted[2] in the Introduction to Lord Acton's letters to Mrs Drew, the historian declared that 'Communion with Rome is dearer to me than life'. He could not envisage himself as cut away from that setting of the European Catholic life in which the Actons and the Arcos were embedded. If even Döllinger, from whom he became increasingly remote, had never joined the Old Catholics, it was perhaps improbable that Acton himself was ever tempted to go out into that parochial wilderness, where he would consort with men without his range who were pre-occupied with ultra-Gallican theology. The fabric of Catholic life was so familiar to him and by his middle years inevitable. Mass and a frequentation of the Sacraments took their place in his life whether he was in London or at Aldenham or, later, at Tegernsee or at Mentone. He withdrew his interest from theology, but his devotional customs were unchanged. It was on another plane that he was moved to testify to the Truth. Here, where his enthusiasm was engaged, he gave his mind to the construction of the Liberal doctrine.

It is difficult to decide these questions. Still, this is the theory which seems best to cover the documents in the case. If this is correct, or if some similar reading of the situation is correct, the main point is made. Without straining honesty, but with a dis-

---

[1] P. 155.
[2] *Introductory Memoir*, iii.

H*

heartened and uninterested mind, Acton was able to satisfy Manning's juridical enquiries.

Meanwhile, he waited for the blow of excommunication apparently unwilling to understand how completely this danger had been staved off by his own action. The blow never fell; the *dénouement*, which his Liberal supporters had expected, did not materialize. Throughout life his views on Ultramontanism remained severe. There was no moderation in this quarter. These, however, belong more precisely to his later years. In some respects Acton had been keyed up to face the persecutors as he conceived them, and now he found himself in quite a different situation. It may perhaps be best defined as the unfriendly calm of nonpersecution.

2

Aldenham Chapel

There was another factor which would have caused Rome to pause before taking action. The Bishop of Shrewsbury's judgment had the greater weight because Lord Acton was a Catholic landowner, who maintained throughout these years a chaplain at Aldenham. All through his most troubled period this Catholic life went forward; the chapel with its round of 'obits', the regular Masses for his friends and family.[1] Among the archives of the diocese of Shrewsbury there are the answers given to the bishop's visitation in 1871 and 1880. The second series is the more complete and they are worth setting down in some detail for the impression they give of the position.

The chaplain begins with a record of his own career and then sets down the facts about the mission. 'My name,' he begins in commencing the visitation sheet for 1880, 'is Thomas Green (otherwise Thomas Louis Green). My age is eighty-one years and ten months; the date of my ordination was the twenty-fifth day of February A.D. 1825.' He stated that he remained at Oscott for three years after his ordination for the Midland District and then 'I was at Norwich about two years, at Tixall somewhat more than fourteen years'. He had set down the next part of his career in his answer to the visitation questions in 1871. From Tixall he had gone to Mawley, where he had spent ten years and a half, and then to Madeley. It was after a year and a quarter in this latter place that he had gone to Aldenham. He came of a middle-class

---

[1] The *Liber Missarum* made up at Aldenham in 1863 includes the names of the following relatives: Elizabeth Throckmorton, *Baronettissa*; Robert Charles Courtenay Throckmorton, Almeric, Duke of Dalberg; Andrea de Ferrari; Anne Marie d'Eltz; Granville Fullerton and all the deceased members of the families of Dalberg, Acton, Brignole Sala and Pange. The friends mentioned include Laurette de Gramont, all deceased members of the La Ferronays family, Matilda von Degenfeld, Antonin de Noailles, Walburga Mauracher, David Chapman, Peter Ostrowski.

family in the neighbourhood of Birmingham. His closest relative appears to have been William Green of Victoria Place, Cragoe Street, Birmingham, a retired tradesman.[1] The details of Dr Green's career make it plain that he had passed a long life in the chaplaincies and rural parishes maintained by the surviving Catholic squires in Shropshire and in Staffordshire. He set down in 1880, 'I have been upon my present mission nineteen years and nearly eight months'. He then gave the salient details.[2]

The church is dedicated to the Blessed Virgin, under the title of her Assumption. The church property, viz., church, sacristy, garden etc. does not belong to the mission. It is the private property of the patron, Lord Acton. There is a tribune for the accommodation of the patron and his friends. I believe that the church is insured against fire; but inasmuch as the property does not belong to the mission, I have not deemed it requisite to enquire.

There is one Mass said in my church on Sundays at eleven o'clock. I have also one afternoon English service at half past three. One Mass is usually said on week days, when the patron is at home at nine o'clock; at other times in the summer at eight o'clock, and in the winter at half past eight. Benediction has not been given within the last two years; and I am doubtful if, when the patron returns, there will be a sufficient number of singers.

Hitherto when the patron has been at Aldenham, I have had Mass on the Thursday in Holy Week and the Mass of the Presanctified on Good Friday; and in the afternoon of Wednesday, Thursday and Friday the devotion of the *Via Crucis*. The whole of the church furniture is the private property of the patron. My salary as chaplain is £140 *per annum*.

A few points may be added from the briefer visitation answers for 1871. It was noted that the Stations of the Cross had been erected by the present pastor on Sexagesima Sunday 1864 and that Mass was said on week days at nine o'clock when the patron was at home.

---

[1] He received an annuity from Dr Green and acted as his executor.

[2] The quotations that follow are from the Visitation for 1880 and that for 1871 among the Shrewsbury Diocese MSS. The report of the Visitation is not printed *in extenso*.

These details throw light from another angle upon Lord Acton's religious outlook. It is always difficult to assess the nature of the sacramental practice of the Josephists and this term must be used in regard to Acton with much caution. During the later part of the eighteenth century it had been a standpoint which tended to become hereditary among the male members of certain families; but Acton did not bring up his children in any way that could be described as anti-clerical. In fact they were educated and brought up along strict Catholic lines. It was one of Lord Acton's links with Mr Gladstone that both men were at the head of such God-fearing households attached to the rites of their two Communions.

It may be hazarded that Acton never lost the regular worship of his childhood days, nor is there any evidence that he criticized the pronouncements of the Church which related to Christ or to the Blessed Virgin. It seems he felt that the elucidation of the Christian mysteries was indeed the proper field for all churchmen's activities. Thus it is noticeable that he never criticized the proclamation of the dogma of the Immaculate Conception in 1854. It was only when the secular field appeared to be invaded that he rose in opposition. Thus as the years went past the Encyclical on the *Syllabus Errorum* seems to have come to his mind as the transient pronouncement of an earlier Pontiff. It appears to have been central to his position that the events of 1870 had given this Encyclical no greater and no fresh authority. Such an attitude gave him a rather solitary standpoint among his co-religionists, although it was both sympathetic and explicable to the High Anglican Gladstonian circle. His attitude towards the priesthood mellowed as is seen in the support that he afforded in his later years to the work of Dom Aidan Gasquet. He remained attached to sacramental life and to religious practice.

In some respects there is a faint resemblance to the nature of Friedrich von Hügel's thought. Both men had certain Anglican affinities and yet remained securely anchored in the full devotional practice of the Church of Rome. It occurred to neither to break the ties that held them to the Holy See. At the same time they both found difficulty in what they regarded as the contemporary policies of the Roman Court. As the years passed they

were both grateful for the forbearance with which they were left
unmolested by their own authorities.

This background helps to explain Lord Acton's next letter to
his own Bishop. Dr Brown had been failing since an attack of
diphtheria in 1877 from which he never really recovered. At his
death in 1881 he was succeeded by his Auxiliary Bishop, Dr
Edmund Knight. This episcopal change had led the aged Dr
Green to consider resignation and the prelate had written to the
patron on the matter. It will be useful to give Acton's reply in full.
It may be mentioned that the feud to which he refers relates to
Dr Green's difficulty in regard to the school for both Catholic and
Protestant children founded originally by Lady Granville.[1]

> My dear Lord[2] [Acton wrote in a letter dated at Cannes on
> 13 December 1882]: I regret exceedingly to say that your letter,
> sent to me in Austria, has not reached me and I beg you to
> accept my apologies for having left it unanswered. I learned
> from Dr Green that he was about to leave us, as he said, on
> account of increasing deafness.
>
> We shall all regret him, and regret that it should not be
> possible for him to close his long career amongst us, on the
> mission where he has been longest. The isolation already too
> great in consequence of our absence from home will be made
> worse by his infirmity and so I hope that better arrangements
> can be made for the comfort of his remaining years and that a
> certain feud will not be remembered to his detriment. There
> were few people with whom he became intimate, but he is held
> in great respect by the whole neighbourhood and others
> besides ourselves will feel his loss.
>
> I have only to beg that you will make such arrangements for
> the future as you consider best for the diocese as well as for our
> humble mission. It has long been in my thought that whenever
> this critical moment should arise I should have to submit a
> request, a negative, but very urgent request to our late Bishop
> or to Your Lordship, such as used sometimes to be made in
> conclaves. But I learn that a change has occurred coincident,
> I presume, with your coming to Shrewsbury which removes the

---

[1] 'The school was finally closed to Dr Green's great delight about two years ago.
This school had been begun by Lady Granville', note on the history of Aldenham
mission compiled by the Rev. David Williams on 4 May 1884.

[2] Shrewsbury Diocese MSS.

occasion and leads me to think that it would have been superfluous to say a word to you about it.

There appears to be no reference in the Archives to the name of
the priest he wished to veto. Acton continues:

Aldenham cannot be an important mission worthy of one of
your most vigorous subjects, and as we live very quietly in the
family circle when we are at home, it is not a matter of great
importance that the chaplain should be selected among those
most accustomed to Protestant society. If he chances to be a
studious man, he will of course be *Bibliothecarius natus* and will
use my books exactly as his own.

If it should suit convenience that Dr Green should leave
before a successor is ready, there will be little hardship caused
by a slight interregnum.

Wishing to facilitate your choice, and not at all to cause
difficulty or trouble, I may add that we have had two priests at
Aldenham, who know this district and are well-known there.
Perhaps it would be disrespectful to them if I did not mention
their names, in order to say that they left in good report, and
that, if circumstances brought them back, they would find
themselves at once among friends. One of them, Father Darnell
is in his own country now, but I do not know how far he has
taken root there. I have very little hope that he would care to
come, if it could otherwise be managed. The other is Mr O'Neill
of whom I once heard that he would not dislike to follow Dr
Green, but I have no knowledge about it. . . .

I should wish to have an opportunity of enquiring after those
of your brothers who were my school fellows, one of them the
model of all schoolfellows, whom I have lost sight of for a whole
generation.

With every good wish for your prosperity, personal and
official, I remain, My dear Lord, very faithfully yours,

Acton.

Meanwhile, Bishop Knight had written to Dr Green, who took
his stand on Lord Acton's position as the patron. 'In the first
place,' he replied, 'as a matter of course, I at once resign the
deanery. I am sorry that I misunderstood you concerning the
coming of my successor, though it appeared to me strange, inas-

much as I could not suppose that you had corresponded with Lord Acton. His address is "St Martin – Ried – Haute Autriche." I have written to him.' In another letter, this time undated,[1] Dr Green explained to the new Bishop that when he arranged to come he could meet him at Bridgnorth Station 'with a wagonette which Lord Acton leaves at my service'. In another hand there is written on the envelope to this note '*ob*. 27 February 1883'. Remote as the aged priest was from his patron he had been a helpful influence for him in the bad times.

The next and last chaplain at Aldenham in Lord Acton's period was the Rev. David Williams, a Welshman of energetic character, who later became the first secular priest in charge of St David's, Cardiff. He was one of those priests who maintain a cosy correspondence with their own Bishop and it is clear that he was never happy at Aldenham.[2] During his seven years in residence he only appears to have met the patron once, although he had a helpful exchange of letters with Lady Acton. He started to compile a history of the Aldenham mission and noted[3] down the evidence of Thomas Massey, then seventy-six years of age and residing at Much Wenlock, that he used to come with his grandfather to Mass at Aldenham, the chapel being a room on the top floor of the Hall, which was now used to keep old books in. Two references to the Library at Aldenham, both made in letters to the Bishop, are worth recording. 'Respecting[4] the Library of My Lord, one so active in body and mind as I am must make work so that on wet days like to-day, when I cannot go out, I spend my time in the Library. It is a dangerous library if not used with great care and prudence. Lying on the table on entering the library is the 2nd vol. Oct. of a parody of the lives of the Saints by Baring Gould.' He had also made an earlier comment.[5] 'I could say a great deal about the library here, which I prefer not to write. It is easy to trace a particular line of reading. The marks left are

[1] This letter is merely headed 'Aldenham, Saturday'. The other letter was dated at Aldenham, 22 September 1882, *ibid*.

[2] He had occasional hopes of a Catholic tenant. Thus he wrote to the Bishop that on Holy Thursday 1885 Mr Joseph Radcliffe and his wife had come to view the Hall, but that it was rather too large for them.

[3] Notes compiled on 4 May 1884, Shrewsbury Diocese MSS.

[4] Letter dated 19 February 1884, *ibid*.

[5] Letter dated 10 February 1883, *ibid*.

very numerous – Against the Jesuits – The Temporal Power – *Crimen Sacerdotium* etc. etc.'

The years after 1880 were in any case a financially difficult period in Acton's life, but he retained a chaplain for the care of the flock around Aldenham as long as the Hall remained in his hands. A letter[1] from Bishop Knight to Fr Williams gives the position from the angle of the diocese. 'I wish it were possible to get at Lord Acton's ultimate intentions. Can you get me his Lordship's present address? Writing has not hitherto been a very successful mode of communication, but if his Lordship contemplates closing the mission I must try it once more.'

Finally the Bishop heard from Lord Acton in a letter dated at the Grand Hotel, Brussels on 15 June 1890.

> My dear Lord,[2] I have been travelling in improbable places so that your letter, forwarded from Cannes, has only just reached me. For several years I have been strongly advised that it would not be possible to continue the mission at Aldenham. I was anxious to make every other economy and to keep it as long as I could. . . . I have no alternative but to take the course recommended to me and to confirm what Freshfield [his agent] has written to you. . . . Mr Williams has the esteem of the neighbourhood and if not more than that, it is due to the disadvantage he has had of our absence all the time of his stay. He is a man whose strength and vigour will be useful, I hope, in a more active and a more important place.

Five days later a letter was sent from Aldenham to Bishop Knight by Fr Williams. 'After Mass about an hour I was thinking over Lord A's treatment & indifference etc.' He had had seven years of loneliness and an ever-doubtful future. He had been cosseted at Mawley before he came to the chaplain's quarters at Aldenham, and he had a warm emotional nature. All the same Lord Acton showed a very generous attitude towards his chaplain.

By 1880 the family was complete. Lord Acton's youngest child, a daughter Jeanne, was born in April 1876. He had lost his second son in early childhood. One son remained, Richard, who had

---

[1] Copy of a letter dated at Avondale, Claughton, Birkenhead, on 22 March 1886, *ibid.*
[2] *Ibid.*

been born in Bavaria in 1870, that ill-starred year. There were three other daughters; the youngest of these, Elizabeth, was very delicate.

There was a certain resemblance between the outlook of Friedrich von Hügel's wife Lady Mary and that of Lady Acton. Neither woman had anything in common with nor perhaps much understanding of her husband's tensions. But here the resemblance ended. Lady Mary von Hügel was a daughter of Lady Herbert of Lea and had been brought up in the emotional and aggressive warmth of her mother's interpretation of religion. In the Bavarian world to which Lady Acton belonged, piety was held to be a feminine virtue. It was *outré* when displayed by a man of standing. It was only that her husband was rather more unorthodox in his private views and also more interested in religion than the male members of her own stock. There is evidence that Lady Acton realized that at this time of his life her husband was a little formidable towards the clergy. Her letters to their rather awkward chaplain were kind and full of helpfulness.

It seems likely that Gladstone came slowly to appreciate Acton's deep attachment to his own children. This was a link between Hawarden and Aldenham. Children of friends were seldom in evidence at Hawarden. At this time the younger members of the family only went to stay with their own relations. Acton was ripe to be received into the Gladstone world.

3

Hawarden Castle

Hawarden Castle was essentially the setting of Mr Gladstone's private life. It was a considerable building, a large rather heavy house, with two round towers attached to the centre block, balanced at the ends by two lesser towers, the whole completely castellated. Above the machicolations rose the stone chimneys and the chimney pots. The colouring of the stone was grey and rather sad. This on the garden front was relieved by the large windows, showing a nineteenth-century appreciation of the need to catch the North Welsh sunshine. The Glynnes were devoted to this house,[1] which they inherited, and had spent their lives there. They were of old Welsh stock, cadets of the Glynnes of Glynllifon, but completely anglicized. By ancestry and nature a true towns-man, Mr Gladstone was something of a caretaker in the Castle. For long the nominal owner was his brother-in-law, Sir Stephen Glynne, and his own wife had had the practical management since her childhood.

To this house on the sloping land beyond the ridge above the estuary of the Dee in Flintshire there came Mr Gladstone's some-times curious friends, but not the leaders of the great Whig world. There was a constant coming and going of his wife's nephews and nieces, the Lytteltons. These and his wife's family, the Glynnes, had their own Whig affiliations, thus Lord Lyttelton's mother had been a Spencer. All the Whig world would understand Mrs Glad-stone, it was Mr Gladstone with whom they were not at ease. G. W. E. Russell, speaking from the standpoint of the Bedford family, explains the feeling that the Whig magnates had towards him. 'For many years,' he writes,[2] 'after Mr Gladstone had come

---

[1] The residential castle at Hawarden was built in 1752 and extended in 1809.
[2] *Sketches and snapshots*, p. 42.

over, *via* Peelism, to Liberalism, he was "suspect" in the eyes of the Whigs. They believed that a good deal of his early Toryism still clung to him, and in particular they dreaded his devoted and eager Churchmanship.' Of the great peers among his Party it was only the Duke of Argyll who came to Hawarden, and he was not an English Whig, he was a Scotsman.

By this time Mr Gladstone was in late middle life. He had given up shooting in 1870 and had blown off the index finger of his left hand as long ago as 1842 as the result of not uncocking the un-discharged barrel.[1] He had recently begun the practice of cutting down trees in his own policies. This was not an accustomed exer-cise for the rich; it built up the picture of the People's William. The limes, planted to the west of the house below the bank on which Hawarden Old Castle stood, were growing up and the lawns had now obliterated the line of the ancient road from Chester to Holyhead, whose course Sir Stephen Glynne had changed in his young manhood. The house was now approached by a short drive which entered under the frowning new port-cullis, which stood among the straggling houses of Hawarden village.

This appears to have been an Anglican oasis; there is little reference to Welsh nonconformists. There was a close relationship between the parson and the squire; the patronage of the advowson went with Hawarden Castle. When the Glynnes were young the rector had been their cousin, the Rev. and Hon. George Neville, who lived at Hawarden Rectory with his wife Lady Charlotte. Bishop Heber had been a visitor. In 1874 the two neighbouring bishops were both Liberals. Joshua Hughes of St Asaph was in fact one of Mr Gladstone's own appointments and William Jacobson of Chester had been chairman of his Oxford election committee. In the case of the latter prelate his scholarly approach and his old-fashioned High Church views were most congenial.

There is little evidence of much contact with the surrounding gentry, who would all in any case have been of a different political complexion. With Eaton Hall, where the Marquess of Westminster received a dukedom on his proposition, he always maintained a certain rather faint relation. This was about the farthest distance

[1] Cf. *After Thirty Years* by the Viscount Gladstone (1928), p. 59.

that his carriage horses could manage. He approved and shared the Anglo-Catholic outlook of Lady Grosvenor.

Mr Gladstone had lately given up his tenancy in Carlton House Terrace. His life was for the moment centred upon Hawarden. He was back[1] 'again in the old room, at the old table, among the old brown hollands'. Most of his day was spent in reading and writing in that room which he called the Temple of Peace. In the afternoons he took his exercise and in the evenings after dinner he played 'Commerce' with his family. On the dressing-table in his bedroom lay the big Bible always open, which he read daily[2] while dressing and undressing.

Mr Gladstone seems to have had in his heart a very simple belief in the permanence of the social order. One comment, although made much later, seems to reflect his permanent attitude to one side of Lord Acton's life. There is a brief exchange which is recorded in Mr Tollemache's description[3] of his table talk.

Mr Gladstone: 'Lord Acton is writing a history of Liberty, and I shall be glad to see how he will treat the question of the Jews.'
Mr Tollemache: 'In writing such a work is he not likely to get into trouble with the Roman Authorities?'
Mr Gladstone: 'His work may be put on the *Index*; but that is all. They will never excommunicate an English peer.'

There was from an early date a certain amount of travel that involved the Acton and Gladstone families. Thus in September 1879 Acton met the Gladstones at Munich station on their way to the Arco-Valley chalet[4] on the lake at Tegernsee. The main purpose of this journey was Mr Gladstone's meeting with Dr Döllinger. The Gladstone children rowed their father and his friends across the lake. In early October both families went southward to Venice, the Actons staying at Danieli's. A note[5] describes

---

[1] Entry dated 17 May 1875, *Gladstone to his Wife*, ed. A. Tilney Bassett (1936), p. 215.
[2] Cf. for these details of his family life, *After Thirty Years* by Viscount Gladstone, pp. 11, 15, 16.
[3] *Talks with Mr Gladstone* by the Hon. Lionel A. Tollemache, third revised edition (1903), p. 103. The entry belongs to a later date in Gladstone's life but reflects an unchanging attitude.
[4] For an account of this journey, cf. *Mary Gladstone, Her diaries and letters*, ed. Lucy Masterman, pp. 165-8.
[5] *Ibid.*, pp. 171-2.

their occupations. 'With Lord A. and children all day. . . . They were supremely happy gathering shells, and we sat on the grass looking over the sea towards Turkey, a great, blue, sunny stretch with ships and coloured sails.'

At Venice Acton gave to the Gladstone children a sketch of the History of Liberty. 'It is extraordinary the way he tingles with it to his fingers' ends and yet can sit quiet over wife and children and wait and wait another year before he writes it.' The Gladstones left in a reserved carriage and went to Innsbruck and then over the Kuefstein Pass into Bavaria and so to Munich. They sat in the train eating Venetian figs. On occasion they joined the Actons during their winter visits to the Riviera, driving up to Gourdon and having luncheon by the roadside on the edge of an olive wood. The Gladstones in their turn took Lord Acton with them on a journey to Oxford in 1884. It is a mistake to conceive their contacts as being confined to meetings in London and visits to Hawarden.

There is very little in Acton's various letters that suggests regret for Aldenham. I can only recall a single note[1] in which it seems possible to detect this. Acton is speaking of Shakespeare's Sonnets. 'A dear friend of mine, now dead,[2] devoted himself to the study of the Sonnets, as the real key to Shakespeare, being the form of his own ideas, not what he gave to his characters. We discussed them much together in the long evenings at Aldenham.'

Throughout his life Acton remained faithful to the laymen who had shared his position at the Council. Thus in 1881 he made a special journey to Nice to see Harry von Arnim Suckow, who was dying there. He had been Prussian ambassador to the Holy See. He gradually brought each contact that he wished to keep within the Gladstone circle. Thus letters were exchanged between Bishop Strossmayer, the one prelate of the Minority with whom Lord Acton maintained a form of correspondence, and the Liberal statesman. Acton is seen at Hawarden translating the German letter to Mr Gladstone, while the recipient composes a French reply.

Curiously enough the difficulty in dealing with this period of Acton's life is the great mass of documentation that surrounds the

[1] *Letters of Lord Acton to Mary Gladstone*, p. 42.
[2] Richard Simpson (1820–1876).

life at Hawarden. This is of more importance because the only lengthy printed series of Acton's correspondence is that with Mr Gladstone's second daughter. For various reasons, and in particular to prevent an imbalance in the picture, it is essential to consider this matter very carefully. There is certainly a great mass of papers in the University Library at Cambridge, but these deal for the most part with his ideas on history and politics and with his historical projects. Men with interests similar to his own were very naturally accustomed to keep his correspondence as in the case of the body of letters addressed to Sir Peter Renouf, now preserved at Pembroke College, Oxford, and those covering a shorter period sent to Mr Reginald Lane Poole. At the same time what is not provided is an insight into his private character.

A few of Acton's letters sent to his mother in his boyhood have been printed, as well as a number of letters, dealing with matters of religion, scholarship and politics, written to Lady Blennerhassett. The letters to Mary Gladstone might be given a disproportionate importance in the assessment of Acton's character since they contain the only intimate correspondence, apparently complete for the period with which it deals, that we can now examine.

It seems that Acton's capacity for friendship tended to merge in the easy social relationship which he knew well how to develop. A didactic element appealed to him. He once stated that he had no contemporaries and there runs through so many of his letters the suggestion that he is dealing with colleagues and collaborators, with his one master, Gladstone, and with disciples. The letters to Mary Gladstone suggest that through all his middle life Acton was essentially a teacher.

The two principal influences during the period of his early manhood and the years which followed appear to have been those of Countess Marescalchi and Lady Blennerhassett. From Countess Marescalchi he obtained that worldly poise which enabled him to play his part so perfectly as a Lord-in-Waiting. Lady Blennerhassett's influence was of a different significance since, among other benefits, she was the recipient of his confidences in regard to his relations with ecclesiastics. It is evident that he had a great trust in her judgment, a reliance on her deep concern for him and a happiness in her company.

It was, perhaps partly, the teacher in him that made his sympathy veer towards women much younger than himself and from 1878 there began his friendship for Gladstone's daughter. This was a quasi-paternal relationship, although Acton was forty-six and Miss Gladstone thirty at its commencement. Like so many friendships with an emotional element it does not seem effectively to have survived her marriage to the Reverend Henry Drew[1] in 1886. Lady Blennerhassett's friendship for Lord Acton never regained its former intimacy after the development of this close Hawarden relationship.

It has always seemed to me that there is in Lord Acton's correspondence a desire to please the woman who received his letters. He also appears very conscious of the interests and degree of knowledge of his correspondents. A teacher should always be aware of the limitations of those whom he instructs. To understand the correspondence requires a brief *excursus* on Mary Gladstone.

Lord Acton's approach to intimacy was gradual and it does not seem that he made his first visit to Hawarden until 1876. The children of the family, the eight Gladstones and eleven Lytteltons, whose mother, Mrs Gladstone's sister, had died long ago, were now for the most part scattered. That tiresome private language called *Glynnese*, invented by the Lytteltons, was therefore less in use. Mr Gladstone was approaching seventy; the customs of his old age were slowly forming.

Two of his children were still at home, Herbert and Mary. The latter was now twenty-nine. She had had a half-fanciful love affair in Rome some ten years since with the young Marquess of Lorne. Her own contemporaries were all now married. She had had her periods of warm lavish admiration for elder women, the three beautiful Talbot sisters, Lady Brownlow, Lady Pembroke and Lady Lothian. She seems to have felt that she was now past the period for a love affair; she settled down to give her admiration to older men. Her general education had been sketchy; she had good French and enough Italian to read her Dante. She was quick and picked up information from the air about her. She almost worshipped her father's judgment.

---

[1] Canon Drew died in 1910 and his widow died at Hawarden in 1927. Mrs Drew's book *Acton, Gladstone and Others* was published in 1924.

In appearance she had a touch of the pre-Raphaelites, those wide-open candid eyes of the Burne-Jones drawing. Her tastes were of her sex and period. She spoke of a big picture by Burne-ones: 'Cupid dragging a maiden through all the meshes and mazes of Love.' She noted that[1] 'he has got a glory of little birds, so pretty'. And of a project for a window by the same artist in Mr Gladstone's study 'the City of Troy, and all the pattern near it little flames'. She wrote[2] of a picture by Millais, 'three girls at Whist with an azalea background, beautifully done'.

Her whole life was centred on her father, but when she was quite young she showed no concern about domestic politics. She took interest in local happenings and in matters of national excite-ment, the Bravo murder case, the Tichborne Trial, and the trial of Constance Kent, which had special interest because of Miss Kent's Anglican confession. Mary Gladstone was always deeply religious. Her father had a broad outlook and her delightful mother much detachment; but Mary had the reinforced opinions of innumerable clergymen. It is worth noting, when considering the letters that Acton wrote to her, that she always had a deep and built-in anti-Romanism. Not that she did not criticize her own clergy. When staying at Belton with her friend Lady Brownlow she made this note[3] in her diary on the evening of Easter Sunday 1872. 'Went to Church by myself. The clergyman preached an odd sermon. Said the Devil laid eggs in us. An unpleasant idea.'

She had a hero-worship for Sister Dora: her allowance was small and was given wholly to good works, except what she re-quired for boots and gloves. She was ready to open herself to any influence that gained her admiration, as can be seen in the disas-trous visits of Mr Ruskin. Mary Gladstone knew nothing of the Church of Rome. In all her diaries there is only one reference to the Roman clergy. 'Father Mulooly [sic] an Irish priest.' She seems to have had no contact with the old Catholic families.

Such social connections as she had with Catholics seem to have sprung from her admiration for the Talbot sisters, some of the

[1] Entry dated 14 February 1875, *Mary Gladstone, her Diaries and Letters*, ed. Lucy Masterman, p. 94.
[2] Entry dated 4 March 1872, *ibid.*, p. 77.
[3] *Ibid.*, p. 77.

family at Newbattle 'with its gorgeous trees', Lord Ralph Kerr and his sister Lady Alice Gaisford, and Lady Herbert of Lea. There was an occasional friend who became a Catholic in later life, like Lady Mary Herbert who married Friedrich von Hügel, and Meriel Lady Howard-Stepney. All these, however, had been born in that Anglican world in which she was embedded. They had failed to follow the line laid down by Dr Pusey.

It was part of Lord Acton's social gifts that he could easily gain the interest of women. He had a didactic turn and therefore did not need a conversation of equals. He loved to *teach*, whether it was Mary Gladstone or his own daughters. In his later years he would explain to his children, walking about the roads of Cambridge, the story of Marie Antoinette and the Diamond Necklace. In another form it was this impulse which directed his relations with Queen Victoria to whom he would respectfully answer points about the Saxon genealogies.

This is set down as the prelude to Lord Acton's account of the Inquisition and the place which this to his mind filled in the Roman system. He wrote to Mary Gladstone in 1884:

> The Inquisition[1] is peculiarly the weapon and the work of the Popes. It stands out from all those things in which they co-operated, followed, or assented as the distinctive feature of papal Rome. It was set up renewed and perfected by a long series of acts emanating from the supreme authority in the Church. No other institution, no doctrine, no ceremony is as distinctly the individual creation of the papacy, except the Dispensing power. It is the principal thing with which the papacy is identified, and by which it must be judged.

And now we come to a passage which was one aspect of the thought processes of his later life:

> The principle of the Inquisition is the Pope's sovereign power over life and death. Whoever disobeys should be tried and tortured and burnt. If that cannot be done, formalities may be dispensed with, and the culprit may be killed like an outlaw. That is to say that the principle of the Inquisition is murderous, and a man's opinion of the papacy is regulated and determined by his opinion about religious assassination.

[1] *Letters of Lord Acton to Mary Gladstone*, pp. 185–6.

The historian had had a conversation on this subject with Dr Döllinger two years earlier.[1] 'In a great number of men,' explains Acton, 'he [Dr Döllinger] sees virtue where I see vice – Gerson, Arnauld, Luther, Bossuet, Pius VII, St Bernard, Lacordaire.'

It is worth quoting Professor Butterfield's judgment upon this matter. 'It was,' he writes,[2] 'his [Lord Acton's] great anxiety to decide by pontifical decrees whether an historical character was "good" or "bad". He explicitly states in his notes that the judgment should depend on the lowest point a man ever reached, and that "you cannot judge until you have said the worst". And it was a curious form of morality that was in question, for he could write repeatedly, "Do not so much mind the sins of private life". This is the key to very much of Acton's thought.'

It will not be surprising to find that he gave his severest comments on Ultramontanism[3] to Mary Gladstone. His viewpoint on this subject must have been strange and, indeed, repellent to his English co-religionists. It does not even seem that Richard Simpson shared it; he was a straight old-fashioned anti-Clerical. On the other hand it would have been understood in Germany as a notion that belonged essentially to the eighteenth century, to the world of Joseph II and Kaunitz and their followers. It implied something that Acton shared with that past generation, a desire that the Papacy should stay inactive. This carried with it a deep lack of respect for the Holy See.

What Professor Butterfield describes as Acton's 'great anxiety to decide by pontifical decrees' is a different question. It can be seen in germ in early life. Its growth was a consequence of his misfortune that he did not know the English professional historians until his mind was set and he could no longer learn from them.

We now return to his approach to Mary Gladstone. 'Therefore,' he wrote,[4] 'the most aweful imputation in the catalogue of crimes

---

[1] Notes on an important conversation dated 16 July 1882.

[2] *Lord Acton* by Professor H. Butterfield, Historical Association, 1948, p. 14.

[3] It is only fair to set down the most hostile comment on the Papacy which Lord Acton ever made. This occurs in a letter to Lady Blennerhassett dated February 1879. 'It is the fiend skulking behind the Crucifix. The corruption which comes from revolutionary or absolutist sympathies is far less subtle and expansive,' *Correspondence*. He wrote this while he still believed that he was about to suffer the 'injustice' of excommunication and the removal of the Sacrament from his private chapel.

[4] *Letters of Lord Acton to Mary Gladstone*, p. 186.

rests, according to their knowledge and their zeal, upon those whom we call Ultramontanes. The controversy, primarily, is not about problems in theology: it is about the spiritual state of a man's soul, who is the defender, the promoter, the accomplice of murder.' Just as Acton's assessment of character oscillates, so he would use extreme expressions in building up his cases. He had a German dislike for shades of meaning. 'Every limitation,' he went on, 'of papal credit and authority which effectually dissociates it from that reproach, which breaks off its solidarity with assassins and washes away the guilt of blood, will solve most other problems. At least, it is enough for my present purpose to say, that blot is so large and foul that it precedes and eclipses all the rest, and claims the first attention.' This was a subject on which Acton's mind worked in its private world. His views were here addressed to warm, devoted Anglicans. In all these matters Mr Gladstone saw more clearly; but he was humble before Lord Acton's historical analyses. And there was after all no section of English life where antipathy to Rome was found so strong as among those political leaders who had come to Liberalism from the middle classes.

There was always in these years two levels in Acton's examination of the Church of Rome. A power of severe judgment was never distant when the conception of Ultramontanism was in question, and from another angle it is possible that the word murder had appeal to him, for it was the slamming of the door on many contacts. At another level, where the subject was purely antiquarian, the mood was different. The letters relating to Mr Shorthouse's novel display this second character.

An interesting example of Acton's approach to new books of a religious nature can be seen in his reactions to *John Inglesant* by J. H. Shorthouse, which was published in 1882. This was a book begun in 1866 and finished ten years later, the only serious literary work of the director of a chemical works in Birmingham who had never left this country. Shorthouse, who was of Quaker stock, had joined the Church of England as a young man. *John Inglesant* deals much with Rome at the time of the Conclave in 1656; it puts the condemnation of Molinos at this period when it really took place thirty years later.

Acton, in writing to Mary Gladstone about this book,[1] states accurately that 'Mysticism and High Church Anglicanism are so highly favoured that the hero . . . acquiesces in both'. He also remarks shrewdly[2] that 'Jansenism, odious, probably, to the author is not displayed'. A little later the historian provides a rare excursion into topography. It seems that Shorthouse had studied Rome in some guide book, perhaps in an old Murray's. He knew the ground plans, but not the elevations. Thus Acton remarks[3] 'there are no spires in Rome'. He also has a short discussion on the date of the Spanish Steps, which Shorthouse brings into his story. 'The date of the steps of the Trinità,' writes Acton,[4] might be discovered in the life of Cardinal Polignac (who held the title of Santissima Trinità *ai Monti*), or on the article on him in Michaud or Didot.[5] It matters not; but the correctness of local and chronological colour turns on such points as these.' It is worth noting that Acton's approach to architectural history was through biography.

The Spanish Steps were in fact constructed in 1723–25 according to De Sanctis' designs. In 1656 the slopes of the Pincian were not yet laid out, and the great block of the Palazzo di *Propaganda Fide* at the southern end of the Piazza di Spagna looked out across a wilderness of little streets. It was one of Acton's sympathetic traits that he was always impatient of inaccuracy.

[1] Letter dated at Cannes 20–22 March 1882, *Letters of Lord Acton to Mary Gladstone*, p. 134.
[2] *Ibid.*, p. 134.
[3] *Ibid.*, p. 147.
[4] *Ibid.*
[5] Didot is printed in the *Letters*. This may be a mistake for Diderot.

4

George Eliot

There is a considerable difference between Acton's attitude to the fiction of his day as a young man and that which he adopted in later life. The first example to be quoted occurs in a letter written to Richard Simpson in 1861. Here Acton set out in terms stronger than he would subsequently have used the errors of the naturalism that he saw around him.

> Certain Germans of the last century remind me of him [Boz] as to religion. They saw 'no divine part of Christianity', but divinified humanity, or humanised religion, and taught that man was perfectible, but childhood perfect. So they used to die full of benevolence and admiration of the sun and moon, and for their children and their dog and for their home. They hated intolerance, exclusiveness, positive religion, and with a comprehensive charity embraced all mankind and condemned alike differences of faith and distinctions of rank, as insurrection against the broad common humanity.

It is a clear expression of Acton's early views, and all the more so since it introduces the only discussion which the historian permitted himself at that time of Dickens and Thackeray.

'Their religion,' he continued[1] in this long stiff-jointed letter to Richard Simpson, 'was a sort of natural religion adorned with poetry and enthusiasm – quite above Christianity. Herder was a man of this stamp. Surely Dickens is very like them. He loves his neighbour for his neighbour's sake, and knows nothing of sin when it is not crime.' Here was something of Acton's determined judgment, but the analysis which follows belongs manifestly to his early

---

[1] Letter dated 8 December 1861, printed in Gasquet, *Lord Acton and his Circle*, pp. 241–2.

period. 'Our recent novel literature,' he declared, 'seems to me to be our great glory in literature since Bulwer's reformation. They are nearly all respectable except Currer Bell and Kingsley – but at least the masters, Neo-Bulwer, Thackeray, Dickens, Reade, Trollope.' It was now six years since Charlotte Brontë, who had used the pseudonym Currer Bell, had died. Charles Kingsley had published *Westward Ho!* in 1855: it is not difficult to see how this book and *Jane Eyre* would rile the young John Acton. He was always hostile to any emotional heightening of a situation. Bulwer Lytton's appeal is more difficult to fathom.

The letter dealing with his views on Thackeray was written more than two years later, in January 1864, just after the novelist had died. Acton explained to Simpson:

> I am sorry to say[1] I have neither his books nor any good ideas about him. His views of history are surely very superficial, and he is not in the first rank of literary critics, but he can go to the bottom of small minds in a way which is wonderful because he was not a first-rate judge of character among his acquaintances. Thackeray was extremely sensitive in the great world. I certainly did not think him *distingué*. The marvel is how he knew the ladies of the great world so, for that is his strongest department. *Esmond*, again and again I assure you, is a masterpiece for that sort of knowledge. Also, in the *Virginians* . . . Dickens is far below Thackeray in his characters.

These letters were written to an equal, a man of balanced if sometimes bitter judgment.

The next series are part of his instruction of Mary Gladstone. The first letter contains the judgment of his middle age on Dickens, who was now just ten years dead. 'It is,' he wrote,[2] 'beginning at the wrong end to read *David Copperfield* first, but he [Dickens] is worth anything to busy men, because his fun is so hearty and so easy, and he rouses the emotions by such direct and simple methods. I am ashamed to think how much more often I return to Dickens than to George Eliot.' But before coming to his estimate of this last-named writer, it is worth studying his

---

[1] Letter, *ibid.*, pp. 310–11.
[2] Dated 21 September 1880, *Letters of Lord Acton to Mary Gladstone*, p. 34.

references to other women novelists. '*Consuelo* is a very great novel. Afterwards she [George Sand] threw herself away on monographs.' Acton here means the tales of that remote and marshy countryside which stretched around her manor at Nohant-Vicq and spread southwards to the boundaries of the plain of Berri. 'I know,' he continues,[1] 'that I do not like her; but I don't think that I could ever have compared Miss Brontë or Miss Austen to her.'

With this is paralleled an account which in its criticism of the French seems to owe something to those walks with Dr Döllinger in the *Englischer Garten:*

> Until George Eliot I thought G. S. [George Sand] the greatest writer of her sex in all literature. I cannot read her now. But that is individual taste, not deliberate judgment. She is as eloquent as one can be in French – the unreal, unhealthy eloquence that Rousseau brought in, that the Girondins spoke, that Chateaubriand, Lamennais, Lamartine made so popular, that nobody but Hugo strives after now, and that was modified in her case by Polish influences.
>
> Some of these Frenchmen live on nothing else, and if one plucks them, or puts their thought into one's own language, little remains. But she [George Sand] had passion and understood it, and deep sympathy, and speculative thought, and the power – in less degree – of creating character. She could rise very high, for a moment, and her best prose is like a passage from good poets. It is a splendid exhibition, diffuse, ill-regulated, fatiguing, monotonous. There is not the mastery, the measure, the repose one learns from Goethe and the Greeks. She scatters over twenty volumes the resources her English rival [George Eliot] concentrates into a chapter. There is beauty, but not wisdom; emotion, but not instruction; and, except in her wonderful eye for external nature, very little truth. I would call her a bad second – such as Swinburne is to Shelley, or Heine to Schiller – comparisons which involve a great deal of disparagement.[2]

The lack of value that Acton placed on Jane Austen's work is interesting. She wrote of the world that he knew well, for her baronets and squires and clergymen were in the main derived from her Hampshire background. They cannot have been very

---

[1] Letter dated 25 March 1881, *ibid.*, p. 83.
[2] Letter dated 7 March 1881, *ibid.*, pp. 78–9.

different from their equals around Bridgnorth. The problem
perhaps lay in the fact that they lived half a century before John
Acton had reached manhood. It is difficult to appreciate novels in
which all the apparatus of social life is just fifty years out of date.

These comments on George Sand are, perhaps, of no great
consequence, but they serve to introduce his estimate of George
Eliot. Among the various literary and political figures upon whom
Lord Acton passed judgment, his praise of George Eliot remains
outstanding. It is to be noted that his writings were in each case
posthumous. The first dates from the news of her death:

> You cannot think[1] how much I owed to her [George Eliot]. Of
> eighteen or twenty writers by whom I am conscious that my
> mind has been formed, she was one. Of course I mean ways,
> not conclusions. In problems of life and thought, which
> baffled Shakespeare disgracefully, her touch was unfailing. No
> writer ever lived who had anything like her powers of manifold,
> but disinterested and impartially observant sympathy. If
> Sophocles or Cervantes had lived in the light of our culture, if
> Dante had prospered like Manzoni, George Eliot might have
> had a rival.

Later he returned to the same subject. 'It is hard,' he wrote,[2] 'to
say why I rate *Middlemarch* so high. There was a touch of failure in
the two preceding books, in *Felix Holt*, and even *Romola*. And it was
Middlemarch that revealed to me not only her grand serenity, but
her superiority to some of the greatest writers.' And again, 'those[3]
are not truisms about George Eliot. The reality of her characters
is generally perfect. They are not quite always vivid or consistent.
They degenerate sometimes into reminiscences. But they live a life
apart from hers and do not serve her purposes.'

This is in some ways a strange enthusiasm. She wrote in general
of a society with whom he had no contact; the life of the lawyers,
the lesser clergy, the small gentry and the farmers of thickly
populated rural neighbourhoods in Warwickshire and the
Eastern Midlands. True there are some exceptions among the
characters and he calls Dorothea Casaubon 'the heroine of my

---

[1] Letter dated 27 December 1880, *ibid.*, p. 57.
[2] Letter dated 21 January 1881, *ibid.*, p. 60.
[3] Letter dated 28 January 1881, *ibid.*, p. 62.

I

dreams'.[1] But there are other matters which aroused his sympathy. As a minor point Mary Anne Evans, to give George Eliot her real name, came from the Gladstone neighbourhood. Her grand-father had been born at Northop, a village seven miles from Hawarden along the St Asaph road. But the real line of contact with Lord Acton was her deep attraction for German studies; she had translated the *Das Leben Jesu* of David Friedrich Strauss. She entered into the extreme Liberal approach as seen by certain Lutheran theologians. Her old beliefs had withered at the roots. She had forsaken that English Methodism with which Acton had so little sympathy. Still it was not so much her religious approach as her deeply Teutonic method which made an appeal to him. When she went to Florence before writing *Romola*, she took a German view of her meticulous archaeological preparations. Lord Acton held very naturally that good historical fiction must depend on careful delving.

The principal works to which George Eliot addressed herself before settling down to write her novel were the lives of Savonarola by Villari and Burlamacchi and the books by Machiavelli and Sismondi. She was detained from writing 'by the necessity[2] of gathering particulars, first, about Lorenzo de Medici's death; secondly about the possible retardation of Easter; third, about Corpus Christi Day; fourthly, about Savonarola's preaching in the Quaresima of 1492'. She was exact about these details of liturgy with that heavy accuracy which she shared with the Ger-man post-Evangelicals who were her masters. At this time she also finished a second reading of *La Mandragola* for the sake of the Florentine expressions. It is worth noting Leslie Stephen's con-clusion in his study of this novel. 'Perhaps, too,' he writes, 'Rom-ola's sentiments show rather too clearly that she has been pre-maturely impressed by the Positivists' Religion of humanity.'[3] As far as Lord Acton was concerned, it would seem to be the method of construction of her books that had most appeal for him. After his warm appreciation of aspects of *John Inglesant* and *Romola*, he

[1] Cf. *ibid.*, p. 66.

[2] *George Eliot* by Leslie Stephen, p. 123.

[3] Cf. some of her earlier poems printed in 1840 in the *Christian Observer*. 'Blest Volume! whose clear truth-writ page once known Fades not before heaven's sunshine and hell's moan.'

does not seem to have shown much interest in later novels. His own world was remote from that absorption in the Old Testament in which George Eliot had been trained. It is on the whole not surprising that after a final note of praise he seems to have turned against her.

'George Eliot,' Acton had written in an earlier letter, 'seemed to me capable of . . . exposing scientifically and indifferently the souls of a Vestal, a Crusader, an Anabaptist, an Inquisitor, a Dervish, a Nihilist or a Cavalier without attraction, preference or caricature.' One wonders where Lord Acton found the attraction in the character of an Inquisitor, a Dervish or a Nihilist?

As the years went by his enthusiasm for this novelist's work would wane. George Eliot was passing into history and Lord Acton now reserved for her the judgment that he passed upon historical figures. 'I have said,' he wrote[1] to Mary Gladstone, 'that I am divided from G. Eliot by the widest of all political and religious differences and that political differences essentially depend on disagreement in moral principles. Therefore I cannot be suspected of blindness to her faults.' But this was only preliminary to the charge which he now brought against her. 'More particularly,' he went on, 'because I have insisted on another grave delinquency which has struck few persons, her tolerance of Mazzini. That is a criminal matter, independent of the laws of states and churches, which no variety of theological opinion can by any means affect.'

Giuseppe Mazzini, the Italian revolutionary, had died at Pisa just twelve years earlier. He was using an assumed name; he had lived a selfless life in poverty. George Eliot's 'tolerance' of this man was to him a criminal matter. Lord Acton was very much alone, not in his social life, but in his thought.

Towards the conclusion of the same letter he wrote as follows: 'To be truly impartial, that is, to be conscientious and sincere, we must be open equally to the good and evil of character'. How can we penetrate so far and reach these iron certitudes? Acton was very far from most historians. It was his misfortune in these Gladstone years not to be able to stretch his mind in company with those scholars who were his equals.

[1] Letter dated April 1885, *Letters of Lord Acton to Mary Gladstone*, p. 210.

5

Samuel Wilberforce

Samuel Wilberforce was the member of the Anglican episcopate whose general standpoint bore most resemblance to Mr Gladstone's, and it is essential to give an unbiased picture of this Anglican world because the succeeding chapter deals with Lord Acton's proposals to the prime minister in regard to his responsibility for filling bishoprics. Acton possessed only a superficial clubman's knowledge of the Anglican candidates and this, combined with the positiveness of his utterance, would give an unfair picture of an important field.

Wilberforce had been an intimate at Hawarden in the years before Lord Acton reached the Castle. He died in 1873 and it seems that his first meeting with Acton took place at breakfast at Mr Gladstone's house in London in 1861.

Another reason for choosing Wilberforce is the detailed excellence of the diaries which give their value to the three-volume biography by Canon Ashwell and his own eldest son. Just as one speculates as to what would have been the effect on Disraeli's biography if Buckle had finished the work instead of Monypenny, so also one wonders as to the result if Canon Ashwell could have finished the book on Wilberforce. His work has the delightful character of the affectionate Anglican friendship of the 1870s, but he died when the first volume was just completed. Mr Wilberforce had a family *pietas* which prevented him from discussing his father's failures, the breakdown of his influence at Court and the very long years when he was left in the Oxford diocese. Wilberforce was never a popular figure, perhaps because, like his brother-in-law Manning, he was too much attached to his own opinion. Like other men whose careers have somehow gone adrift, he did not have the imagination to test the effect of his actions on those around him.

The story of his life really begins in July 1828, towards the end of the reign of George IV, when, just down from Oriel, he married his distant cousin, Emily Sargent. She was the eldest daughter of the Rev. John Sargent, Rector of Lavington and Graffham in West Sussex, who was himself the eldest son of John Sargent of Lavington House, who had married the heiress of that estate. They were strict Evangelicals of the Simeon tradition; the bride's three sisters all married clergymen. She was twenty-one and the bridegroom twenty-three. He had loved her since she was fourteen and it was a perfect marriage of its period, the husband giving a guiding and protective love, the wife loving obedience. This was an important element in Wilberforce's life, a distant resemblance here to Coventry Patmore's experience.

Samuel was the favourite son of William Wilberforce, the Liberator of the Slaves. He had been educated by private tutors and his father always called him 'my lamb'. From the very beginning of his priesthood, Dr Sumner, the Bishop of Winchester, took him by the hand. He was in fact a distant cousin, although he only learned this fact in later life, but he and his brother owed a debt of gratitude to the Liberator for his help when they were young. While Samuel was still a deacon Sumner gave him charge of the living of Checkendon to be under his care, for he then still held from Eton the wealthy neighbouring rectory of Mapledurham. (Both the Sumners and John Sargent were at Eton.) On his appointment to the diocese of Winchester, Bishop Sumner ordained him in 1829 and immediately presented him to the living of Brightstone in the Isle of Wight. He never had a period of curacy.

Although not at that time wealthy, there was money in the background. The Wilberforce fortune had come from the Baltic trade. The elder John Sargent was the son of a Director of the Bank of England. His wife's ancestors the Gartons had built the original Elizabethan house at Lavington on a city fortune. Mrs Wilberforce's mother was a member of the great banking family, the Abel Smiths. There was nothing spectacular in Samuel Wilberforce's rise; he had the benefit of a flowing tide.

At his ordination he had become almost imperceptibly a High Churchman and a Tory. From his early days there was always something of a preacher's style about him and he was always positive. 'I hope,' he wrote[1] to his friend Patrick Boyle, 'that you will allow the justice of my often disputed character of "candied" Orange Peel, and allow that he has shown himself either a rogue or a poltroon.' He was devoted all his life to riding and to ornithology. In time he came to know very perfectly the English scene; he loved the elms beneath the white chalk downs at Brightstone. At a later stage he is describing a ride to Bagot's Park. '*There*,' he wrote,[2] 'are the noblest oaks in England, and I suppose therefore in the world.'

His religion was bound up with England and the English soil. He seldom travelled; he did not care for foreigners or speak their languages. His notes[3] show the tone of his early reading, Clarendon, Mosheim, Davison on Prophecy, the volumes of Archbishop Leighton's sermons and Richard Hooker. It is no surprise that he should state that he had read through the last-named writer for the second and third time. Later he declared that he belonged to no school, but he was in fact always a High Churchman.[4] Writing to his mother in 1835[5] he made this profession. 'I agree as far as I can with all those great lights whom God has given from time to time to his church, with Hooker and Bramhall and [Jeremy] Taylor, with Beveridge and Stillingfleet and with the primitive Church of the first three centuries.' There is missing from this list the name of Andrewes. Otherwise it represents the line of a High Churchman's descent from the great Anglican divine, Richard Hooker. It was a descent broadly conceived, for Stillingfleet was a Latitudinarian and Bramhall an adopted member of the Church of Ireland. Wilberforce was not a man who changed his positions and we find almost the same list in 1850.[6] 'I *was* a Church of England man of the school of Hooker, Beveridge and Andrewes

[1] *The Life of the Right Rev. Samuel Wilberforce*, vol. i, p. 45.
[2] *Ibid.*, vol. ii, p. 13.
[3] These include the *Institutiones Ecclesiasticae* by Johann Lorenz von Mosheim (1694–1755), *Discourses on Prophecy* by John Davison (1777–1834) and the Sermons of Archbishop Leighton (1611–1684) published posthumously.
[4] 'He was a High Churchman from the first,' *Life of Bishop Wilberforce*, i, p. 55.
[5] *Ibid.*, i, p. 90.
[6] Letter sent to Dr Dallas on 28 December 1850, *ibid.*, ii, p. 65.

and so I am now.' In a letter[1] sent to Dr Pusey in the previous month he had referred to doctrines 'wholly unlike the teaching of Hooker, Andrewes, Bramhall and Jackson', the last-named being the Dean of Peterborough under Charles I, the author of *Commentaries upon the Apostles Creed*. There was a link between Wilberforce's standpoint and that of the Evangelicals from whom both he and his wife had come. The Evangelicals and the old High Churchmen both had their heart-land in the Church of England. For various different reasons they were repelled from and without interest in the modern Church of Rome.

There are further notes[2] upon his reading, St Bernard's *Sermon on the Nativity* and St Chrysostom's *Homilies*, the latter more than once. There is a single reference[3] to a strictly historical subject 'Madame de Maintenon'. It seems almost certain that this was an article in some review. He showed no interest in the labyrinths of the religious history of her great country. There is also a further note[4] on how *Holy Living* struck him. 'Read some Jeremy Taylor. I shrink from the severe countenance of perfect devotion to God despicably. Lord have pity on my miserable weakness.' At no time in his life could Dr Wilberforce see any reason why John Henry Newman should have come to trouble the Church of England.

Wilberforce and Emily would stay with his patron and his wife at Farnham Castle or at Winchester House in St James's Square. The world went well with him. He notes[5] in his *Diary* that he had been one Sunday to St James's, Piccadilly. 'Heard Bp. of London. Good sermon, very; "Flee youthful lusts". He was affected to tears.' Two other comments[6] are worth inserting. 'You should over-drive yourself,' wrote Bishop Sumner, 'as little as you would your horses.' In writing to his brother Robert, Wilberforce referred to 'the internal heat and volcanic heat, which is always burning in my own mind'. One example of this should here be given. He was approached at Brightstone by two serious men,

[1] Letter to Dr Pusey on 2 November 1850, *ibid.*, ii, p. 61.
[2] List for 1838, *ibid.*, i, p. 124.
[3] Note in *Diary* for 23 March 1833, *ibid.*, i, p. 65.
[4] Note in *Diary* for 21 January 1838, *ibid.*, i, p. 113.
[5] Note in *Diary* for 24 March 1833, *ibid.*, i, p. 65.
[6] *Ibid.*, i, p. 81 and p. 86.

Captain Gambier and Brother Silent, who endeavoured to explain
to him the truth of the Irvingite Church. 'You are,'[1] replied
Wilberforce to the naval captain, 'one of those false prophets
mentioned in Jeremiah who say "The Lord sent me" when the
Lord hath not sent you, and you have much reason to fear the
burning fire of his offended jealousy.'

As a relief from this severity, there is an account of the Rector
when his mood was fanciful.[2] It should be explained that he
worked very hard for Missions in the Colonies. He imagines a
dinner in New Zealand, where he thought the Maoris had not yet
abandoned their ancient practices. 'And your man will add there
is *cold clergyman* on the side table.' There seems a touch of Archdeacon Grantly here.

Some comments on the general situation have their own interest. 'Things loom dark with us, I think, as a people, our navy
is almost dismantled and England has never prospered yet, when
either wooden walls are neglected or Popery encouraged.'[3]
Another aspect is suggested in a letter to Dr Hook.[4] 'The most
effectual engine of the Low Church batters a truly Catholic
opinion.' There had been a rumour that the Romanists wished to
purchase Buckden Palace, the ancient country house of the see of
Lincoln. 'I hate,' Wilberforce explained,[5] 'such buildings getting
into Roman hands.' There is a gleam of hope in a note to Mr
Gladstone[6] 'but still the coming year [1839] bears to my view an
aspect of gloom for the country – not for the Church, she is the
land of Goshen'.

While he was still at Brightstone, a great post was offered to
him, that of Vicar of Leeds, a growing northern town with several
Anglican churches but still one parish. 'You would govern Yorkshire,' his brother Robert told him;[7] but Bishop Sumner took
another view. 'I cannot,' he wrote,[8] 'repress the enquiry for how
long would your *lamp burn*? Not an hour. And just before or just

[1] *Ibid.*, i, p. 100.
[2] *Ibid.*, i, p. 203.
[3] *Ibid.*, i, p. 131.
[4] *Ibid.*, i, p. 132.
[5] *Ibid.*
[6] *Ibid.*, i, p. 135.
[7] *Ibid.*, i, p. 106.
[8] *Ibid.*, i, p. 104.

after your own [lamp] would expire that of Emily choked by coal dust.' He wished to keep him in that soft climate in which the Sumners had always lived.

And then he was promoted on the death of Lord Walsingham to the archdeaconry of Surrey, and with this went a transfer from Brightstone to Alverstoke. Shortly before, his wife had inherited the estate at Lavington. The Sargents were unfortunately riddled with consumption and the two sons had died as undergraduates. Landed property was a reassuring possession for a clergyman. He was only thirty-five; there was no post to which he might not expect to rise.

It was at this time that Archdeacon Wilberforce lost his wife, who died suddenly at Alverstoke. In a sense he never got over this disaster. He had the high Victorian ideal of marriage and did not re-marry. His mother-in-law, Mrs Sargent, came to live with him and helped to bring up the four young children. In his bedroom in his various homes he always kept a picture, presumably a water colour, of the corner of the churchyard at Lavington where his wife was buried. Beside her grave the mown grass covered the place where he would lie. He was a man without friends or, to be more exact, a man whose self-confidence made friendship difficult. He lost something of humanity when his wife died.

Like Dr Döllinger, the Archdeacon valued pictures for what they represented, not for their execution. There hung in his bedroom a big German lithograph described[1] as the Translation of Saint Catherine of Alexandria. The martyr was travelling after her death across the world of light; she was illuminated by the rays of Heaven. Below her lay a darkening territory, those still unsullied miles of sand between the Mediterranean and the Gulf of Akaba. Beyond her lay the amethystine hills. The Archdeacon had seldom been abroad; but he had a home-grown knowledge of Old Testament geography.

He had a healthy liking for Mr Landseer. We can almost see Archdeacon Wilberforce as he enumerates the merits of a large modern painting in his possession. 'Magnificent picture,' he writes,[2] 'by Landseer. A star-and-moonlight lake with a red deer

---

[1] Description, *ibid.*, i, p. 375.
[2] *Ibid.*, i, p. 238.

I*

swimming over, neck white and almost bright in the moonbeams.'
It does not seem imaginary to detect the same flavour in a letter
that Wilberforce wrote in later life about John Russell.[1] 'I believe
that Lord John will do nothing but try like a cunning little fellow
as he is, to puzzle the scent of his own trail by turning out Trac-
tarianism as his bagged fox.' There was no red deer and no
English fox across the Channel.

The Lavington estate lay on the northern slope of an outlying
spur of the South Downs. He spoke of riding over to his property
in later life.[2] 'Everything was in glory – horse chestnuts, oaks,
beech, elms. How I wish I could come and see my black-headed
gulls.' The Archdeacon built a wooden gazebo on the highest
point of his land and would go up and sweep West Sussex with
his telescope. Below him lay Lavington, with the rhododendrons
and the araucarias that he had planted, the place where he would
put the cedar of Lebanon that the Prince of Wales would give him.
On Chanctonbury Ring were the trees which old Mr Goring had
planted when a boy. The Archdeacon made a note of the chief
points.[3] Reigate Chalk Pit lay thirty-five miles to the north and
Beachy Head forty-two miles to the eastward. Southward the
view took in the sweep of sea and Spithead and the shores of the
Isle of Wight. This was that England in which his heart and
thought were anchored. Throughout his life his views and ideas
were quite selective. He makes no reference to the castle and the
woods of Arundel, which lay in the foreground from his gazebo.
Similarly his *Diaries* make no reference to Newman's *Apologia
pro vita sua*.

The Archdeacon was about to embark upon his great career.
From the early days of his ministry he had been growing in distinction as a preacher. The idea of a sermon came to him quite
spontaneously; he was the son of the only natural preacher in the
House of Commons. In William Wilberforce's life the practice of
prayer and preaching were intertwined. While his 'dear lamb'
was quite young, he had written[4] to him from Marden Park, his
rented house in Surrey. 'How constantly I shall pray for you to-

[1] *Ibid.*, ii, p. 55.
[2] *Ibid.*, iii, p. 415.
[3] *Ibid.*, ii, p. 242.
[4] *Ibid.*, i, p. 20.

morrow *inter silvas Mardeni* that you may be strengthened with might by the Spirit in the inner man.'

Samuel Wilberforce's reputation began at Brightstone: his Bishop had his charge sermon printed and he preached for the first time before the University of Oxford on 'The Prodigal Son' when he was thirty-three. All accounts agree as to his great self-confidence. He seems to have liked to watch the unfolding of his argument. He was very soon preaching to the Court. At Windsor Castle Chapel he spoke twice. On the second occasion Mrs Gladstone's sister, Lady Lyttelton, was in waiting. She wrote[1] of 'the golden sweetness of his language'. He preached twice at the Pavilion at Brighton before the Queen gave up her visits there. He nearly always found appreciation. In 1849 Lord Carlisle noted[2] in his *Diary* how admirably he preached upon 'The Barren Fig Tree'. This was not the period of fashionable preaching that would belong to London of the 1880s. The Queen, while her wishes still held sway, had a taste for religious observance at a rather low pressure. In these years it was men and women of a serious character who attended sermons.

It was at this time that Wilberforce was made a chaplain to the Prince Consort. The latter had a concern to study the British Constitution in which the bishops of the Church of England had their allotted sphere. The choice was prudent, for the Archdeacon had a respect for the Lutherans who had freed Northern Europe from the Roman yoke. Well-read in Church history, he regretted that the proposals made in Archbishop Tenison's time for providing the German Lutherans with an episcopate had then miscarried. There is little information as to the Prince Consort's conversations with the Archdeacon beyond the fact that he assured him that Lord Aberdeen, the Presbyterian prime minister, was possessed of all the virtues. There was one thing, however, that the prelate forgot that the Prince was almost doggedly attached to the Queen's rights and all her privileges.

The Archdeacon was absorbed to some extent in his life at Court; it was quite new to him. He refers[3] to the Duchess of Kent

---

[1] *Ibid.*, i, p. 221.
[2] *Ibid.*, ii, p. 16.
[3] *Ibid.*, ii, p. 169.

as a 'woman of great truth'. He liked the religious life of the Hohenzollerns. He describes the conversion of the Crown Princess of Prussia; the zealous Lutheranism of her father-in-law the King and her husband's reticence out of respect for her own Catholic upbringing; the joy of her new family when she accepted the Lutheran Faith. It is difficult to remember that in their psychological approach the Protestants and Catholics were then identical. The exact phrases with their warm undertones of sentiment would have been used by Father Faber; but the change would have been in the reverse direction.

It was evident that his career was going smoothly. In the early days of the New Year the Archdeacon came beneath the sliding observation of Charles Greville. They were both fellow-guests of Lord Ashburton at the Grange, near Alresford. 'I met,' wrote Greville,[1] 'Dr Buckland and Archdeacon Wilberforce, the latter a very quick, lively, agreeable man, who is in favour at Court.' That autumn of 1845 he was promoted to the post of lord high almoner. The deanery of Westminster was given to him and, before he was settled in, Sir Robert Peel had made the offer of the bishopric of Oxford. There was little doubt that this was aided by the royal favour.

It was a difficult moment to take over the diocese. Mr Newman had just submitted to the Roman Obedience and the Right Reverend and Honourable Richard Bagot had decided to take refuge from his troubles in the quieter atmosphere of Bath and Wells. He was a quiet aristocratic bishop of the old school, who had received a canonry of Windsor when he came of age; he had quite failed to control Dr Pusey. The new Bishop and his mother-in-law, Mrs Sargent, came down to Cuddesdon, where they were received by the Bishop and Lady Harriet. 'The house at Cuddesdon,' wrote Wilberforce,[2] 'stands near the top of a hill, sheltered from the north-east, but open except for elms around it (one hundred and fifty years old and noble fellows). The palace is not a bit of a palace. It is an old H-shaped house, a rambling sort of a country gentleman's house.' Beyond lies Shotover Hill,[3] 'one of the noblest terraces for riding or walking in all England'.

---

[1] *The Greville Memoirs*, vol. v, p. 197.
[2] *Life of Bishop Wilberforce*, vol. iii, p. 309.
[3] *Ibid.*, ii, p. 310.

There is a note made a little later at Cuddesdon Palace. 'The Abingdon Road station [later re-named Culham] and the Oxford station of the Great Western are nearly the same distance [from here], the Abingdon Road a little nearer.' The Bishop was always exact about all distances. He often wrote letters in the train. The farthest away was one that he composed when coming into Carmarthen in a train taking him to Tenby for a summer holiday with his mother-in-law and his three boys. It was his practice to ride down to Oxford without a groom. Across his lawn there lay the little parish church of Cuddesdon; he served this on the Sundays that he was not away on Confirmations. At home he made his lists of the number of attendances of labourers and their wives and children, mainly the latter.

This was the beginning of the long evening of the landed polity. Dr Pusey had a position in that grouping which Dr Newman, his predecessor as leader of the Tractarians, did not possess. Edward Bouverie Pusey belonged in the main line to the Radnor stock; his mother was a Sherard of Harborough – the family, the title, even the house itself, Fineshade Abbey in Northamptonshire, are all now vanished. His brother held the county seat for Berkshire and lived with his wife Lady Emily on his estate in the Vale of Pewsey. In the earlier troubles Pusey had been forbidden to preach for two years, and now Wilberforce privately inhibited him from exercising his functions except in his home village. An adroit solution does not suit the Church of England. Further, the mild Pusey now gained that influence over Wilberforce which the conquered sometimes gains over the only man who has been his conqueror. He knew, too, that the side on which Wilberforce was most vulnerable was that on which it could be said that he was not exercising his full rights as a bishop. This was the origin of the Hampden matter.

The bishopric of Oxford was erected several centuries after the constitution of the university and, considering that the Anglican Church was Established, the bishop had regrettably little power in academic questions. In November 1847 the bishopric of Hereford was offered by Lord John Russell, then prime minister, to Renn Dickson Hampden, who held the regius chair of divinity at Oxford. His opinions, as shown in his writings, had been condemned by convocation. Pusey was inevitably a leading member of the opposition. The regius chair was officially attached to the rectory of Ewelme in the Oxford diocese. Pusey considered this factor to be important. Three of his associates, all beneficed clergymen within this see, brought charges against Hampden's orthodoxy. Wilberforce issued letters of request to the Court of Arches.

The actual prosecution faltered and was unsuccessful, but Wilberforce had ruined his position with the Court. He had questioned the orthodoxy of the Queen's candidate. He was a solitary man without advisers and his imagination did not stretch far enough to envisage the reactions of the Prince Consort; for it was the Queen who in law appointed bishops and the prime minister's offer was in her name. By a single action Wilberforce's influence at Court was wholly broken. A certain haze envelopes all this matter in the biography, for the Bishop's son had by that time taken over. The *Greville Memoirs*, on the other hand, are quite explicit.[1] The Bishop's warm attitude towards the Queen dropped some degrees. He was still lord high almoner and in that capacity attended the christening of Prince Leopold. The Queen wore the great Koh-i-Noor diamond at this ceremony; 'theatrical' he called it.

At Oxford he went on with his work year after year. He had hoped for York and the chance to be the northern primate. Yorkshire had been his father's county. No offer would come to him from Lord Palmerston's administration. That jaunty premier did not take to him, and he certainly would not receive Lord Shaftesbury's suffrage. As time went on he had other troubles. At Lavington he had had a talk about religious issues with Archdeacon Manning.[2] This disagreement had not mattered; they were in essence two bishops-of-business, who had little in common save their profession. But then his three brothers, including the Archdeacon, his favourite, went to Rome.[3] Later in 1868 his only daughter and her husband followed suit. This mattered less,

[1] Cf. *The Greville Memoirs*, vol. vi, pp. 1, 3, 4 and 6. There is a curious episode of Wilberforce's offer of spiritual advice in vol. v, pp. 340–1.

[2] These changes of allegiance are described in detail with the use of hitherto unpublished Wilberforce MSS in David Newsome's *The Parting of Friends* (1966).

[3] The Bishop's mind was nourished on the Old Testament. In his agony he called that 'Roman Jezebel' a painted hag. These miseries prevented him from sleeping. He rose after a sleepless night and was like a hunted hare. *Life of Wilberforce*, ii, p. 213.

for a wife would naturally follow her husband, and as for the Reverend J. H. Pye, he had a mean opinion of that young man.

The Bishop belonged to that old High Church tradition which, unlike the new Tractarians, had no opening upon the Roman side. At heart he disliked the whole idea of foreign influences over England, the busy Italian priests making their cunning choices among his countrymen. Though some of the phrases of his last years were strong, he had a deep and sincere conviction that the God-protected English Church must be quite free. In 1869 he had received from Mr Gladstone the see of Winchester, which he accepted. It was burdened with a pension for old Charles Sumner. His new see carried with it the offices of chancellor and prelate of the Order of the Garter. He thus gave up his post as lord high almoner. 'I still retain,' he wrote,[1] 'the right of *Entrée* and of passing through Windsor Great Park.' He did a great work for his two dioceses, especially on the side of organization and finance; he obtained a reasoned share of patronage for the local bishop. He had revived the convocation of Canterbury and had worked for the Foreign Missions.

On 19 July 1873 he went riding with Lord Granville. The Bishop had slept the previous night at Winchester House and had then gone to the Athenaeum to write some letters. He had met Lord Granville at Waterloo and they had gone by train to Leatherhead. They then took a fly to Burford Bridge, where he mounted a hack hunter called 'Carrickbeg'. He broke into a gentle canter on a smooth stretch of turf. His horse put his foot in a gutter on the turf and threw him. The Bishop broke his neck. He was buried in Lavington churchyard beside his wife.

[1] *Ibid.*, iii, p. 306.

6

The Anglican Episcopate

An interesting element in the letters addressed to Mary Gladstone is the light thrown on Acton's attitude towards the Church of England of his day. It may appear strange that he should have used Miss Gladstone as a channel to press on the prime minister his suggestions in regard to the filling of Anglican bishoprics. There are, however, certain circumstances which may explain the line that he adopted. The effort on which Acton concentrated was the appointment of Canon Liddon to the see of London, and Liddon had an especial claim on his interest as a result of his sympathy for Döllinger. The two men had in fact first met at Tegernsee during one of Acton's summer visits to Bavaria.

There were, besides, two general considerations. An aspect of the situation of the Anglican episcopate that aroused Acton's sympathy was its complete powerlessness in the field of active politics. Under this head that episcopate must have seemed to the later Acton as the most innocuous of ecclesiastical bodies. The 'Church interest' had its strong supporters like Mr Gladstone and Lord Salisbury. These, however, supported where practicable existing privileges; there was no question of any open or occult intervention in the political sphere in its wider sense.

On the other hand there was one element in the position which Acton regarded with sustained disapprobation. He had a horror of the use of ecclesiastical patronage for political ends.[1] It is likely that he joined with Gladstone in this matter as a result of their profound dislike for Disraeli's methods. The views of Acton and Gladstone can hardly be appreciated without some consideration

[1] In a certain sense both political parties considered the side on which the future prelate would vote in the House of Lords. Cf. a letter from Gladstone to Lord Granville written at Fasque on 27 September 1869. 'Thanks for the report of Lord A. Compton. I am afraid the politics are fatal', *Correspondence*, i, p. 59.

of the policy pursued by the Tory leader. Disraeli's purpose was not the mere acquisition of a new supporter on the bench of bishops, it was rather an attempt to gain support from the various sections of the clergy and the lay voters associated with them. This was held to depend on the promotion of candidates congenial to the interests concerned. To explain this matter it is necessary to go back some time. The circumstances surrounding the translation of Archbishop Tait to the see of Canterbury[1] indicate the trend of Disraeli's mind during the months of his first short-lived administration.[2] The episode is significant since it contains in a brief compass so many judgments well calculated to exacerbate the ethical and Liberal outlook of the two friends.

'No human being,'[3] wrote Disraeli at Hughenden to Lord Stanley, 'can give anything like a precise estimate of the elections until the Registration is over. . . . What we want at this moment is a strong Protestant appointment in the Church. I have been expecting a bishop to die every day, but there's hardly a "good Protestant" strong enough to make a bishop.' Five days later, on 21 August 1868, he continued with the same theme.[4] 'Things are rapidly maturing here: the country, I am convinced is, almost to a man, against the High Ch[urch] party. It is not the townspeople merely, but the farmers universally, the greater portion of the gentry, all the professional classes: nay, I don't know who is for them, except some University dons, some youthful priests and some women: a great many, perhaps of the latter. But they do not have votes yet.'

A letter sent in the following month to the Queen, with a tactful reference to her own position, elaborates Disraeli's thought. 'Nevertheless,' he wrote,[5] 'the Church as an institution is so rooted, and the doctrine of the royal supremacy so wonderfully popular, that if the feeling of the country be guided with wisdom

---

[1] Archibald Campbell Tait was translated to Canterbury in 1868 and died on 1 December 1882. William Ewart Gladstone formed his second administration on 23 April 1880.

[2] Disraeli's first administration lasted from 27 February until 3 December 1868.

[3] Letter dated 16 August 1868, *The Life of Benjamin Disraeli Earl of Beaconsfield* by W. F. Monypenny and G. E. Buckle, 1929 ed., vol. ii, p. 401.

[4] *Ibid.*

[5] Letter dated 'end of August'. The Queen replied from Lucerne on 7 September, *ibid.*, ii, p. 402.

Mr Disraeli believes that the result of the impending struggle may be very advantangeous and even triumphant to the existing constitution of the country.' The reference to the 'impending struggle' refers to the forthcoming General Election.

On 27 October 1868 Archbishop Longley died of bronchitis at Addington Park. He was one of the last of the old prelates and had been ordained in the reign of George III. 'My Church policy,'[1] wrote Disraeli to Lord Derby on hearing of this event, 'was this: to induce, if possible, the two great and legitimate parties to cease their internecine strife, and to combine against the common enemies: Rits and Rats.' Very soon it appeared that the Queen favoured the promotion of Bishop Tait of London. Disraeli, although subsequently overborne, was opposed to the appointment of a Liberal and Broad Churchman. In his difficulties he turned again to Derby. 'Harold Browne,' he wrote,[2] 'is offered as a compromise. But what do I gain by Harold Browne?[3] While H.M. will only be annoyed. I could win if I had a man.' Later in the same letter he returned to his main point. 'I thought, last night, of . . . raising Jackson to London. He is orthodox and Protestant.'

Making allowance for Disraeli's manner, which was so uncongenial to both Gladstone and Acton, these comments deserve some study. They indicate an approach to Church questions which was profoundly distasteful to both men. Disraeli always saw his role romantically, he gave free rein to his imagination. In the spring of 1879, towards the end of his second term of office, he called one afternoon on Lady Salisbury and discussed his difficulties. 'And what have we got to offer,' he exclaimed, 'one Garter and the Bishopric of Durham.' This said, the Liddon episode can be treated in some detail.

Henry Parry Liddon was five years older than Acton, who had fairly recently made his acquaintance. He was at King's College School and then at Christ Church. He had been vice-president at Cuddesdon and at St Edmund's Hall; he held the Ireland chair

---

[1] Letter dated 2 November 1868, *ibid.*, ii, p. 408.

[2] Letter dated 12 November 1868, *ibid.*, ii, p. 409.

[3] A similar comment to that made on Bishop Edward Harold Browne of Ely occurs in a letter written to Montagu Corry from Balmoral on 21 September 1868, when the Queen was successfully pressing for the appointment of Dean Magee of Cork to the see of Peterborough. 'One objection to Magee is, that his appointment would give us nothing, and that is a great objection,' *ibid.*, ii, p. 406.

of exegesis. For some years he had been examining chaplain to Bishop Hamilton of Salisbury and had held the prebendal stall of Major Pars Altaris in that cathedral. One would have imagined that Lord Acton would have found Bishop Stubbs much more congenial, but then he was a Tory. Acton first met his candidate in June 1880. 'I have made Liddon's acquaintance at last,' he wrote[1] to Mary Gladstone, 'I found in him all that I love Oxford for and only a very little that I dislike in it.'

Four years later he is found proposing him for a bishopric. In the intervening period the new Oxford contacts, which Acton was then making, had brought the men together. In particular he had stayed at Keble with Liddon's friend and supporter Dr Talbot. Liddon, who had been Pusey's disciple and was now his biographer, lived at this time in Amen Corner as a Canon of St Paul's.

Early in 1884 Acton set out his views on Liddon's character. 'For,' he began,[2] 'I am not in harmony with Liddon, and scarcely in sympathy. He has weak points that nobody sees and resents as sharply as I do; and he has got over, or swallowed, such obstacles on the road to Rome that none remain which, as it seems to me, he ought logically or legitimately to strain at.' After this he settles down more cheerfully. 'But one might pick holes in any man, even in the new Bishop of Chester [Dr Stubbs]. Nothing steadies a ship like a mitre – and as to his soundness, his determination to work in and through the Church, and not on eccentric courses, I satisfied myself with the supreme authority of Dean Church, on my last night in town. One cannot help seeing that Liddon is a mighty force, not yet on its level.[3] He knows how to kindle and how to propel.' This letter was written from 18 Carlton House Terrace on 15 February 1884, and in the course of that year certain episcopal vacancies occurred which would have to be filled by Mr Gladstone.

---

[1] Letter dated at Tegernsee, 21 June 1880, *Letters of Lord Acton to Mary Gladstone*, p. 21.

[2] *Ibid.*, pp. 179–80.

[3] Another impression of Liddon is given by Sir Francis Burnand, who was a student at Cuddesdon during his vice-principalship. 'I was "in amazement lost" on being received at the college by an Italian-looking ecclesiastic, glittering-eyed, clean-shaven, and closely cropped, wearing a white band for a collar and a black cassock with a broad belt,' *Records and Reminiscences*, ed. 1917, p. 109. It must be admitted that Burnand was a hostile witness.

Four months later, in a letter to Mary Gladstone written from La Madeleine, Acton returned[1] to the same subject.

First as to the personal question. It was not my purpose to depreciate Canon Liddon. I came over with the highest opinion of him – an opinion higher than Dr Döllinger's, or even than Mr Gladstone's, whose ostensible preference for divines of less mark has sometimes set me thinking. Impressed by his greatness, not as a scholar to be pitted against Germans, but as a spiritual force, and also by a certain gracious nobleness of tone which ought to be congenial I tried, at Oxford and in London, to ascertain whether there is some element of weakness that escaped me.

Evidently Liddon is in no peril from the movement of modern Science. He has faced those problems and accounted for them. If he is out of the perpendicular, it is because he leans the other way. The question would rather be whether a man of his sentiments, rather inclined to rely on others, would be proof against the influence of Newman, or of foreign theologians like Newman.

We now come to an *excursus* on Liddon's stability in the Church of England.

On the road Bishops and Parliament were taking a few years since, there would be rocks ahead, and one might imagine a crisis in which it would be doubtful who would be for maintaining the National Church and who would not. I have chanced to be familiar with converts and with the raw material of which they are made, and cannot help knowing the distinct and dissimilar paths followed by men like Newman himself, Hope, Palmer, R. J. W. Wilberforce, Ward, Renouf, many of whom resembled Liddon in talent and fervour, and occupied a position outwardly not far from his own.

He once called the late Bishop of Brechin [Dr Forbes] the first divine in the Church. I knew the Bishop well, and am persuaded that the bond that held him in the Anglican Communion might easily have been snapped, under contingencies to which he was not exposed. Putting these questions not quite so crudely as they are stated here, I thought that I had obtained

---

[1] Letter dated 18 June 1884, *Letters of Lord Acton to Mary Gladstone*, pp. 182–4.

an answer. At any rate, I was assured that Liddon is made of sterner stuff than I fancied. . . .

Under this impression, I could not help wondering why Wilkinson, Stubbs, and Ridding are judged superior to Liddon. I could have felt and would have expressed no such wonder if I had not taken pains to discover that he has tried and has rejected the cause of Rome, and that neither home difficulties nor external influence are at all likely to shake him.

Far, therefore, from meaning disparagement, I rate him higher than any member of the English clergy I know; and touching the question of stability, I have the sufficient testimony of his friends, of men naturally vigilant on that point, of which I am not competent to judge or to speak. So little competent, indeed, that I should be at a loss to define his system, or to corroborate, of my own knowledge, the confidence which others have expressed. It seems to me necessary to indicate that, for myself, I could not speak without some qualification or reserve, such as perhaps would only occur to a close student of Roman pathology.

Lord Acton then goes on to indicate that he was troubled by Canon Liddon's attitude to evidence placed before him at the time when he was translating Rosmini's *Five Wounds of the Church*.

My real difficulty is that he [Liddon] speaks of his author with great respect, and evidently thinks his doctrine sound and profitable. Now Rosmini, allowing for some superficial proposals of reform, was a thorough believer in the Holy See. His book itself, by the nature of the reforms proposed, implies that no other defects of equal magnitude remain to be remedied. Apart from the five points he accepts the papacy as it stands; and he had no great objection to it, five points included.

After a consideration of Ultramontanism the historian returns to his particular objection. 'When,' it is explained, 'he [Liddon] speaks of an eminent and conspicuous Ultramontane divine with the respect he might show to Andrewes or Leighton, or to Grotius or Baxter, he ignores or is ignorant of the moral objection, and he surrenders so much that he has hardly a citadel to shelter him.' Only a part of this long letter is here reproduced, but it is characterized as were so many other lengthy and spontaneous Victorian

letters by a change of temper. The perspective alters with the
introduction of the words 'Roman pathology'.

Six months later Acton returned to the same subject of Canon
Liddon's qualities. He wrote[1] on 14 January 1885 from La
Madeleine:

> I have bored the P.M. to extinction with praise of Liddon,
> and as all I could say is obvious to others, I am not tempted to
> repeat the offence. But the death of that uninteresting, good
> Bishop Jackson[2] disturbs my rest. It is clear, very clear to me,
> that it would not be right to pass Liddon[3] over now that there
> are two important vacancies to fill; and one asks oneself why
> he should not be chosen for the more important of the two. The
> real answer, I suppose, is that his appointment will give great
> offence, and that he is a decided partisan, and a partisan of
> nearly the same opinions as the P.M. himself.
>
> No doubt there would be much irritation on the thorough
> Protestant side, and in many quarters very near Downing Street,
> and I feel myself, more strongly than many people, that
> partisanship in Liddon runs to partiality, to one-sidedness, to
> something very like prejudice. And with all that strong feeling,
> I cannot help being agitated with the hope that the great and
> providential opportunity will not be lost.

Certain aspects of this correspondence are rather curious.
Liddon was in effect an old-fashioned Conservative, a defender of
the Athanasian Creed and of the older practices in the University.
He was Dr Pusey's disciple and his biographer. Like Bishop
Wilberforce, he had preached his first university sermon very
early, at thirty-four. But, unlike the Bishop, he had studied
French oratory and there were traces in his manner of both
Bourdaloue and Lacordaire. 'He was,' wrote[4] Canon Scott
Holland, who knew him well, 'intensely Latin in mental structure;

---

[1] Letter dated 14 January 1885, *ibid.*, pp. 201–2.

[2] John Jackson, Bishop of London, died on 6 January 1885.

[3] Evidence of Acton's persistence in recommendation is provided from the following
sentence in a letter written to Mr Gladstone from Tegernsee on 24 August 1884. 'I
ought to add, because he wishes it, and not to tinkle the same bell always, that Strossmayer was very much impressed by Liddon', *Correspondence*, p. 237.

[4] *D.N.B.*, vol. xxxiii, p. 225.

he delighted in calling himself an ecclesiastic.' He had played at preaching, whilst a child. I admit that I do not find this picture attractive; but I can trace no evidence that there is the faintest sign that he would in later life have abandoned Dr Pusey's faith for Cardinal Newman's. It seems strange that Lord Acton should have considered that the opinions of either Dr Döllinger or Bishop Strossmayer would be of value in determining an appointment to the English Bench.

This aspect of the Gladstone *milieu* was profoundly ecclesiastical and it is curious to compare these letters with the comments Lord Acton made on other churchmen. It is of interest to make suggestions as to what may have caused the change. From one angle this letter may be viewed as belonging to the time of Acton's maximum absorption in the Hawarden vocabulary. It was also at this particular period desirable for him to share all Mr Gladstone's interests. A later portion of the same letter provides evidence which may tend in this direction. 'Who are conceivable candidates? Temple, Westcott, Wilkinson, Butler, Lightfoot?', wrote[1] Acton, with his mind still running on the see of London. 'Two of these are more learned and more indefinite theologians; but I can see no other point of rivalry.' He was writing through Mary Gladstone to the minister ultimately responsible. Perhaps the words 'more indefinite theologians' just hint a touch of scepticism in the historian's approach to the whole field.

That he had a genuine if temporary interest in these matters is shown in a letter to Lady Blennerhassett, who was in touch at this time with Dr Döllinger. 'King,' he writes,[2] 'who gets the mitre [Lincoln], is professor of pastoral theology, next to Liddon the greatest High Church influence at Christ Church, but quite without his magic power as *allumeur des âmes*.' This exchange may or may not be linked with a comment of Sir Rowland Blennerhassett's quoted in an unfortunately undated letter from Wilfrid Ward to his wife.[3] 'He [Acton] has been travelling. He considers (says B.) that at this crisis he is going to govern England through Gladstone.' In the whole spectrum of the Liberal leadership, from

---

[1] *Letters of Lord Acton to Mary Gladstone*, p. 203.
[2] Letter from La Madeleine, dated 31 January (1886?), *Correspondence*, p. 269.
[3] *The Wilfrid Wards and the Transition* by Maisie Ward, vol. i, p. 149.

Sir William Harcourt to Mr Morley, there were very few who shared Mr Gladstone's theological preoccupations.

The strangeness of the *terrain* may have had its appeal for Acton and he had a feeling for the making of a combination. 'And speaking on a lower level,' he had written in the same long document, 'the shock of Liddon's elevation might be blunted by the contemporaneous choice of Lincoln.' Perhaps there was for Acton some attraction in political manipulation in a field which his friend had made peculiarly his own. Throughout his approaches to the subject there appears a combination of sympathy and dissection. The latter quality is exemplified in the comment made on Frederick Temple, later Archbishop of Canterbury, who was at this time chosen for the London diocese. 'Temple is [1] vigorous and open; but he is not highly spiritual, or attractive, or impressive as a speaker; he has an arid mind, and a provincial note in speech and manner. But he also understands Science.'

An exchange between Mr Gladstone and Lord Acton concludes this matter of Canon Liddon's promotion. 'We must,' wrote[2] the prime minister from Hawarden Castle on 27 January 1885, 'have not one only, but two new Bishops.' He then stated that Liddon had refused preferment. Gladstone had then gone on to praise the religious spirit of Oxford, mentioning 'Mr Gore, head of the Pusey Institute' and his followers. 'I try to console myself,' wrote[3] the historian, 'for what seems a loss to religion by what you say of Oxford and the expanding sphere of action it promises to Liddon. On my last visit to Keble I obtained a glimpse of what is going on and of Gore and his doings; and I saw that there are good men there, and opportunities that would be available and inviting if Liddon's temper was not curiously unacademic.'

Throughout this correspondence the reader is impressed by Lord Acton's capacity for identifying himself with Mr Gladstone's interests. These letters reflect his friend's vocabulary. It may be surmised that it was a happiness to be the mentor of the prime minister of England and to move forward over ground which his rivals could not occupy. These particular exchanges depended on

[1] *Letters of Lord Acton to Mary Gladstone*, p. 204.
[2] *Correspondence*, p. 196.
[3] *Ibid.*, pp. 197–8.

Gladstone remaining in power and his Government was defeated on 8 June 1885. There do not appear to be traces of a similar intervention, where ecclesiastical appointments were concerned, when Gladstone was again in office. Archbishop Tait, whom both friends disliked,[1] had been succeeded at Lambeth by Edward White Benson, who was the only primate to have a place in the Hawarden circle. It is noticeable that Acton hardly ever mentions him.

A more important factor was Mrs Drew's marriage, which brought to an end the experience of emotional sympathy with a religious bias which marked Acton's correspondence with her before that time. Although he judges various bishops, it would seem that Acton had only met them in London at the Athenaeum or in society. He visited Oxford for the first time in February 1884 and Cambridge a little later. The first of these visits perhaps aroused a sympathy with the Anglican traditions then represented in the University, but Acton's knowledge of the clergy of the Church of England was very limited. They were a group who had hardly been on social terms in the great Whig houses where he passed his youth. These points are borne out by a comment made in a letter written to Mary Gladstone from La Madeleine. 'Yesterday,' Acton explains,[2] 'I chanced to see, at Mentone, the best of the Anglican clergy that I have ever known, a Mr Sidebotham.' This hardly suggests a wide experience.

It is worth drawing attention at this point to the few comments that Lord Acton made about the Papacy during these years. He seems to have made no remark when Pius IX died in 1878; but in the spring of 1881 he was on a brief visit to Rome to bring his mother-in-law, who had fallen ill, home to Bavaria. He occupied himself with conversations with Minghetti, his now ageing relative. His letters contain two references to Leo XIII, whose policy towards France had aroused his interest.

The Pope[3] probably had no clear view of policy. If he had, he would hardly be Pope. But he sees that the old spells have lost

---

[1] In a letter to Gladstone, dated at Tegernsee, 9 June 1891, Acton wrote, 'You must have been much interested in the life of the late Primate [Tait]. I never succeeded in liking him much, but a certain strength he manifestly had.' *Ibid.*, p. 194.

[2] Letter dated 22 January 1885, *Letters of Lord Acton to Mary Gladstone*, p. 204.

[3] Letter dated at Cannes, 2 April 1881, *ibid.*, p. 86.

their power over men, and so he gives them up. . . . The attempt to disengage himself from the crash of the Legitimists is the most remarkable instance of the change. He [the Pope] explains that the Church must not be so committed to any political party as to stand or fall with it. But that has been, since 1849, the entirely unvarying policy of Rome, and has forced all the enemies of absolute power to turn their forces against Catholicism. If one of the two are separated, there will be a great change in the position of things in Europe. If the Pope does not maintain Legitimacy, he gives up the temporal power. He has no legal or political claim to Rome that Chambord has not to France, for arguments derived from Canon Law are without validity in politics. By weakening his one resource, he shows that he thinks the game is up. And then there is no insuperable obstacle to reconciliation with the Powers. . . . To surrender it [temporal sovereignty] implies such a conversion that I shall not believe in it till I see clearer signs; for his chief confidant is the Archbishop of Capua, an old friend of mine, who is what Newman would be without his genius, his eloquence, and his instruction. I don't know where to stop. Capua is a bad stopping place.

An earlier comment will build up the picture. 'I remained,' he wrote,[1] '[at the Hôtel d'Angleterre in Rome] a week, very ill with sunshine and south wind.' He occupied himself with reading Illingworth's *Sermons*. 'The bewildered Girondin at the Vatican, who stands so well with Dublin Castle, I did not see, but heard much of his moderation, patience and despair. I think he is the first Pope who has been wise enough to despair, and has felt that he must begin a new part, and steer by strange stars over an unknown sea.'

The word 'despair' seems carefully chosen. It appears to chime well with Lord Acton's deep distrust for the summit of the Roman Hierarchy. And Leo XIII had been trained from childhood in the world of the *Curia*. This appears to be the only glimpse that we receive of Lord Acton's reaction to the twenty-five years of Vatican history covered by the reign of Leo XIII. At least it enabled the period of Pius IX to fade into the background. And there was no suggestion that in 1881 Acton would not have been

[1] *Ibid.*, p. 80.

received at the Papal Court. In fact he states in the earlier of these two letters that he himself decided not to pay his respects to the Reigning Pontiff.

There had been changes at the Vatican and these had been reflected in Acton's outlook if, not yet, in his mood. The last panel in the historian's religious life was thus set against the background of the reign of Leo XIII, who was to outlive him by some nine months. As time went by the memory of Pius IX and Cardinal Antonelli faded into the past.

7

The Liberals and Bulgaria

It was his association with Mr Gladstone and the exercise of Government patronage that seems first to have brought Lord Acton into contact with the official world of English History. As far back as 1878 he had been invited[1] by Sir George Jessel, the Master of the Rolls, to propose candidates for the post of deputy keeper of the Public Records. He had suggested the name of Samuel Rawson Gardiner, but this had not been accepted. Four years later it was at Acton's instigation that Mr Gladstone had conferred on him a civil list pension of £150 a year. Later he had much to do with Acton at the time of the foundation of the *English Historical Review*.

Although educated at Winchester and Christ Church, Gardiner had been kept out of the main stream of English life by his Irvingite[2] parents and his Irvingite first wife. He was until his middle life an active member of the Catholic Apostolic Church. A fellowship at Oxford was at that date and for this reason denied to him. A certain shyness limited his social life. It was his great work on early Stuart history that appealed to Acton. When he gave up his contacts with the church in Gordon Square, he lived at Sevenoaks very quietly. At this time he hardly came at all into Acton's world.

S. R. Gardiner's Liberalism was rather faint, although he was a strong supporter of Home Rule. Both E. A. Freeman and J. R. Green on the other hand were ardent Liberals. Both men belonged to that early Victorian middle class which did not then aspire to the public schools, which were in fact created so largely for them. Freeman had a private income and Green just sufficient funds for

[1] Cf. *Letters of Lord Acton to Mary Gladstone*, p. 149.
[2] Popular name for the members of the Catholic Apostolick Church, founded in 1832 by Edward Irving.

his education. They had won Oxford scholarships at Trinity College and Jesus College. Freeman had been for many years a figure in the Oxford history schools. He had obtained a fellowship at Trinity, which he had vacated after two years on his marriage. He was at various periods an examiner in history and a candidate for different Oxford chairs. He had lived since 1860 at Somerleaze, a smallish Victorian house with a restricted park in the neighbourhood of Wells. He was a gentleman of means, who had settled in the country. He was in no sense of the word a country gentleman. 'He detested,' explains Lord Bryce,[1] 'what are called field sports, knew nothing of natural history, and had neither taste nor talent for farming.'

Freeman was the only one of the three men here considered to occupy a history chair at the older universities. By his resemblances and his contrasts with Lord Acton one can gain some impression of what that generation then required. 'French was the only foreign language that he spoke with any ease.' He pushed about Europe with his portfolios full of rather inaccurate architectural drawings. He paced the different battlefields. 'His conception [of history],' we are told,[2] 'was one which belonged to the eighteenth century. It was to him not only primarily but almost exclusively a record of political events.' He had a singularly channelled mind. 'Among English poets his preference was for the old heroic ballads, such as the songs of Brunanburh and Maldon, and among recent writers for Macaulay's *Lays*. . . . He was wont to say that no one was a better model to follow in the choice of pure English, than Macaulay.' His favourite novels were Marryat's *Peter Simple* and Trollope's *The Warden* and *Barchester Towers*. Froude he heartily disliked because he thought him indifferent to truth.[3]

All his life he had been a devoted Liberal, contesting Cardiff in 1857 and one of the two seats for mid-Somerset in 1868. He was intensely English and Teutonic. His racial prejudices set him against all Frenchmen, Irishmen and Jews. In 1886 he espoused the Irish Home Rule scheme warmly and praised the removal from

---

[1] *Studies in Contemporary Biography* by Lord Bryce, p. 263.
[2] *Ibid.*, p. 268.
[3] He was fond of quoting the euphemism of an old Oxford professor of ecclesiastical history describing the reign of Henry VIII. 'The later years of this great monarch were clouded by domestic troubles.' *Ibid.*, p. 271.

Parliament of the Irish members. He wished the Gael to be left to settle, or fight over, their own affairs in their own island. It is not surprising with his Saxon views that Harold, son of Godwin, was one of his favourite heroes. He had a clear dislike for St Thomas of Canterbury; but then in general he did not care for Roman ecclesiastics. Freeman was in many ways an old-fashioned historian insisting in working in his own library and having a certain aversion to the employment of manuscript sources. All the same, unlike Acton, he produced seven thick volumes on the Norman Conquest and William Rufus, and a further four on Sicily.

It may seem surprising that he could not speak German, but he read that language. Like Lord Acton, he did not always bring his audience into focus. During his election campaign he gave the Somersetshire country people 'an eloquent description of the Landesgemeinde which existed in the thirteenth century in the Swiss canton of Uri'. There was an odd contrast between his fondness for describing wars and battles and that extreme aversion to militarism which made him appear to dislike the very existence of a British army and navy. The colonies he was ready to give away. It was something different that brought him into practical politics. 'The passion of his later years was his hatred of the Turk.'

Freeman was in fact the first to set on foot that anti-Turkish agitation which began as a support for the Serbian Christian rebels and was later transformed by Mr Gladstone into a humanitarian protest against the murders in Bulgaria. Freeman, who, together with Canon Liddon, was the only man in English public life to visit the frontiers of the Balkans at this time, had been in Dalmatia in 1876, while his son-in-law, Arthur Evans, was making an archaeological survey in Turkish territory. The latter, who in later life was celebrated for discovering the palace site of Knossos, was friendly to the Christians who had just begun a revolt in Herzegovina. It was on his return that Freeman first began to collect money to help fugitives and to trumpet his hatred of the Turkish tyranny.

Within the matrix of official Liberalism, Freeman gathered together a number of historians, including J. R. Green, Bryce, Thorold Rogers and Justin McCarthy. There was also on their side the consul at Trieste Richard Burton, whose Arab sympathies, which dated from the time of his consulate at Damascus, had prejudiced him against the Turks. In general support for the Christians against the Turks involved a clear application of Liberal principles. Thus Freeman was unable to convince his close friend Bishop Stubbs because he was by temperament a hearty Tory.

The peers, who supported the agitation, were for the most part convinced Liberals like Acton himself and Camoys, Cowper, Ripon, Shaftesbury and Russell. The case of Canon Liddon needs a brief examination. In company with Canon McColl he had recently journeyed through Slavonia to visit Bishop Strossmayer in his little cathedral city of Djakovo. That grand prelate, as a subject of the Emperor Francis Joseph, could take no part in the struggle that was developing. On their return Liddon and McColl made great play with the fact that they had found the body of a dead Bulgarian lying impaled on the banks of the Save. The whole course of that river, which crosses the plains flowing southeastwards from the Julian Alps, lay then in Austrian territory. It was far from Bulgaria. There was something insular in Liddon; he was not at his ease south of Bavaria. There was a double element in Canon Liddon's attitude, a sympathy with the Eastern Christians and a detestation of Islam. It is worth while to record a sentence from his correspondence. A clergyman, the Revd Mr Poole, wrote[1] to him: 'That most nauseous of all abominations, Mohammedanism.'

There were a few men of a Conservative temper of mind, who were brought into the movement by a sympathy for the Orthodox like the Roman Catholics Lord Bute and March Phillipps de Lisle. One of the members of the Catholic hierarchy, the Bishop of Clifton,[2] the brother of Lord Clifford of Chudleigh, a Liberal peer, supported Freeman's agitation. He was thus brought once again, as at the time of the Council, within reach of Acton. It would seem to have been the former's deep devotion to Newman which kept them separate.

The attitude of the Vatican was hostile to intervention in the

[1] Letter dated 4 February 1877, Liddon Papers.
[2] A good deal of private correspondence of Bishop Clifford remains uncalendared in the archives of Lord Clifford of Chudleigh at Ugbrooke Park.

Bulgarian Question. There were certain different strands of influence. This was one of the periods of uninterested coldness in the relations between the Holy See and the patriarchate at the Phanar. A feeling against public utterance on general questions affected the last years of the aged Pope. There was, further, the influence of the Sacred Congregation *de Propaganda Fide*, whose effort to detach the Bulgarian Church from its links with Constantinople by means of the French Lazarists had hopelessly miscarried. There was present also a certain tenderness towards the Porte on account of the scattered pockets of Catholics throughout the Empire. After all, it was at the request of Abdul Hamid that the letters i.p.c., *In partibus infidelium*, were omitted after the titles of titular sees in Turkish territory. Acton must have noted without surprise that on this point the Holy See was passive.

Two Turkish provinces would soon become the tsardom of Bulgaria. The southern region was known as Roumelia. They were about the size of Portugal, and, like her, in a rough sense rectangular. In 1888 the population would amount to rather over three million. The northern frontier ran along the Danube, flowing seawards and, when the great river turned northwards at Silistria, a straight artificial boundary line divided the marshes of the Dobrudja country from the desolate and almost empty slopes of the Deli Orman. The eastern frontier occupied some seventy miles of the low shelving coast of the Black Sea. The western frontier ran along the crest of Serbian mountains. The remaining boundary, which was soon to become the northern border of Turkey-in-Europe, extended both north and west of the small Turkish city of Adrianople. There was no British consular post within this territory. The two provinces were singularly bare of archaeological sites or of antiquities, except possibly the monastery of Saint John at Sila. No member of the House of Commons or the House of Lords had travelled there. This is a description of the setting on which there broke that great event in English politics, the murders in Bulgaria.

The little town of Batak lay far inland within the sanjak of Kiustendil and on the northern slopes of the Rhodope mountains. It was close to the then boundary of Turkish Macedonia. It stood within the land of the beech forests in a country occupied by

Bulgarians beyond the rice fields and the rose plantations of the river valley of the Maritza, where Moslem Circassians had been settled. To the eastward lay the administrative centre of Philippopolis, with its minarets and its Turkish and Jewish quarters. The wild lilac was out upon the hills. The area was very isolated. Twelve years would pass before the metals would be laid which would carry the Orient Express.

For fear that their little risings might synchronize with events in Serbia, a punitive expedition had been arranged to destroy the Bulgar villages and the small monasteries. The men of the Maritza valley looked down on the hill tribes. They were despised as Unbelievers, who still dwelt on what for four hundred years was Moslem soil. They lived in a barbarous fashion; there was no protection for the women, they wore no veil. In their mean tabernacles without a minaret the villagers would come to worship, but never heard the Truths which God had given to men through His Prophet.

Orders came for enlisting an irregular force, which was largely drawn from the settled Circassians. It is not suggested that it was unreasonable to place some check upon the Bulgars; but it was unfortunate that the soldiers' patriotism was inflamed by religious animus.

The administrative system of the Ottoman Empire was venerable and by this time disjointed. It is not clear that the details of local happenings were known at Yildiz Kiosk. The lines of authority, both military and civil, were centred upon the Grand Vizier. The diplomatic service, as an example, was rudimentary. Musurus Pasha, a swift and friendly Cretan Greek, had been ambassador in London for thirty years. The inner circle of the Osmanlis frequently relied upon such alien servants.

In 1876 the summer had been disturbed and the imperial palace of Yildiz was more than usually impenetrable. It was difficult to discern what was happening in that curious grouping of linked pavilions, which lay in their closely-guarded gardens along the northern shore of the Golden Horn. On 4 June, before any news came down from Batak, the Sultan Abdul Aziz had been murdered, and after six weeks' rule Murad V had been declared insane. It was a disaster to discover that the Commander of the

K

Faithful was an alcoholic. The last Sultan had been succeeded by his half-brother Abdul Hamid II.

He could be seen every Friday morning emerging from the gates of Yildiz Kiosk for the mid-day prayer, the Selamlik at the adjacent mosque, a little figure in a military uniform, a trifle shabby. He was said to be timid and parsimonious, the husband of one wife. In accordance with his predecessor's practice he would only cross the water to the City on two occasions in each year.

The British ambassador had retired to the summer embassy at Therapia across the Bosphorus. His was a somewhat closed society. Sir Henry Elliot had been for nine years in his present post; his health was wavering. He belonged to one of the old-established diplomatic families; his son was that Sir Francis Elliot described by Compton Mackenzie in *Athenian Memories*. His sister was the second wife of Lord John Russell.

Lord Salisbury might refer[1] in a private letter to his 'stupidity and caprices'; but in public both he and Granville gave him their support. The ambassadors of this period were not removed, their posts were changed. Elliot in fact went on to Vienna. The same applied to Lord Augustus Loftus, who at this time held the embassy at St Petersburg. He was known to Disraeli as 'that old Polonius'; he soldiered on.

The ambassador at Constantinople could not justly be described as pro-Turk, but he had a certain confidence in Midhat Pasha, the first of Abdul Hamid's Grand Viziers, whose policy was to modernize the ancient Ottoman administration. In general Sir Henry kept to himself, surrounded by his staff and by distinguished guests from England, and maintaining contact with those of his colleagues whose policies had proved congenial.

The commercial colony, the Whittalls and the journalists and the staff of the dragoman's office, were quite remote. The chief dragoman would report from time to time to the ambassador. It was his duty and that of his assistants to try to discern the trend of movement within Yildiz. This necessarily involved rather unsavoury contacts with the palace eunuchs. It was a particularly quiet summer, for the consul general was dying and the delicate

---

[1] Letter to Lord Carnarvon, dated 13 September 1876, Salisbury MSS at Christ Church.

situation of the dynasty would make for caution. It was almost somnolent at the summer embassy. Magnolia bushes lay below the house; there was a certain coolness from the water; the Bosphorus tides swept down towards the Golden Horn and the hot City.

The Times at this period was accustomed to receive foreign correspondents of doubtful character but highly recommended. At Paris, de Blowitz had been introduced by Thiers, and at Constantinople they had Antonio Gallenga, who had lived for many years under the name of Luigi Mariotti. He was a man of seventy and Sir Henry found him distasteful. By origin from Ivrea he was, like Russell, the celebrated correspondent in the Crimea, an ex-Catholic. He was somewhat lethargic and it was held at *The Times* office that his relations with the Italian legation were too close. These points are all set out to show the way that everything played into the hands of J. A. McGahan.

The special correspondent, who made the investigations at Batak, is better remembered in the United States than in Great Britain. Januarius Aloysius McGahan was a young Irish-American of vast experience.[1] He was only thirty-two, but he had already reported the Franco-Prussian war, the Commune and the *Alabama* tribunal. More recently he had covered the Russian campaign in Central Asia, the Carlist war in Spain and the Arctic expedition of the *Pandora*. It is interesting to note that his services had been rejected by *The Times*. To the correspondent in Greece the Manager had explained,[2] 'McGahan offered himself among others, but I dreaded his sensational proclivities.' In the event he was sent out by the *Daily News*, and this was significant for the outcome since Mr Gladstone perused with care the columns of that Liberal newspaper.

When he reached the frontiers of Eastern Roumelia, McGahan found that six thousand Bulgars had been killed at Batak after surrender to the Turkish commander and about the same number in various other parts of the region. His telegraphic despatch, which appeared in the *Daily News* on 7 August, described how the women and children had been sealed up in the church and burned

---

[1] There is an interesting analysis of his career in R. T. Shannon's *Gladstone and the Bulgarian Atrocities 1876*, pp. 41–2.
[2] *The History of the Times*, vol. ii, p. 465.

to death. A less clearly substantiated report also stated that young Christian girls were being sold in the market at Philippopolis for three or four *lire* a head.

Mr Gladstone was not at this time Leader of the Opposition, but he had retained his seat on the front bench. On 29 August he began his pamphlet, which was based on McGahan and other sources. He was at Hawarden and racked by lumbago, and finished it on 5 September. Mr Gladstone then gave to the world *Bulgarian Horrors and the Question of the East*. It was published within two days by Murray's, and before the end of the year two hundred thousand copies had been purchased.

It was only late in life that the Liberal leader discovered his power to move great masses of men. The Midlothian election was to prove this clear capacity. What he appears most deeply to have enjoyed, whether consciously or not, was a political operation in an ethical setting. There was nothing graceful in the pamphlet that he now gave forth; it was the prophet in an hieratic mood speaking heart-to-heart to his people. The constituency that he addressed in England and in Wales was the great body of the lower middle class and the more highly-paid sections of the working class, those elements of the nation which were still the strongholds of Old Nonconformity. He spoke to men who could read and whose main reading was their Bible. The situation was presented as a modern example of Old Testament iniquity. It would seem that, as in Holy Writ, the case had little contact with geography. Above all, his words were red-hot with an impassioned sincerity.

Mr Gladstone described scenes at which, as he explained, 'Hell itself might almost blush'. He drew attention to the 'heaps and heaps of dead'. He explained how women and children had been violated, roasted and impaled. His peroration was terrific. 'There is not a criminal in a European gaol; there is not a cannibal in the South Sea Islands, whose indignation would not arise and over-boil at the recital of that which had been done.' As the head of the family sat studying the literature of the Methodist missions, he may well have felt that all the cannibals had been converted. There does not seem to be much reason to suppose that those cannibals who remained attached to their former habits would in fact agree at all with Mr Gladstone.

Such trade union leaders as Joseph Arch, himself a Primitive Methodist, were always in support of Mr Gladstone, and he brought in the National Union of agricultural labourers. In general and of necessity the appeal did not reach to that section of the working class which still remained illiterate. This was, however, a matter of small concern to either party. Even in 1884, by the Franchise Act of that year, the electorate of the United Kingdom was only raised from roughly three to about five million voters. This new tactic of Mr Gladstone brought over for a time to his side the mass of the lower-paid sections of the English constituencies.

This episode has been described in some detail, for it is of interest in regard to Acton's life in politics. To me it seems that it served to show his keen determination to support his leader. He was a good Liberal and Mr Gladstone had brought in the nation's votes to his own party. In these years, too, he was getting closer and closer to Mr Gladstone. On the Irish Question they would be as one. But what were Acton's real views on Balkan politics? There seems little reason to suppose that he had interest in such topics beyond his decision to give his leader full support. He was determined to back the policy of Mr Gladstone.

A few years later, in 1894, when Acton held the Cambridge chair, there occurred the outbreak of the Armenian massacres carried out by the Turks in Asia Minor. The victims were in this case also Christians, members of the Armenian Gregorian Church. As far as I am aware these massacres did not impinge on Acton's life, nor does it seem that they were reflected in his correspondence. He was in essence a man of the Continent, his interests channelled upon Western Europe. The Liberal historians, who supported Gladstone over the Bulgarian atrocities, were for the most part deeply insular. Their position was very far apart from that of Acton. This contact did not bring him into touch with the official teachers of English history.

8

The Estimate of Gladstone

In the long friendship between Mr Gladstone and Lord Acton there is no lack of material for forming a judgment on the historian's views. It is true that the opinions are expressed to Gladstone's daughter and are therefore couched in as acceptable a fashion as the writer could manage. They are written out at great length with a kind of festive gaiety and with *aplomb*; to build up a balanced impression extensive quotation is necessary. Miss Gladstone had enquired the view that posterity would take of her father.

> The generation you consult [wrote[1] Acton from Cannes on 14 December 1880] will be more democratic and better instructed than our own; for the progress of democracy, though not constant, is certain, and the progress of knowledge is both constant and certain. It will be more severe in literary judgments, and more generous in political. With this prospect before me I ought to have answered that hereafter, when our descendants shall stand before the slab that is not yet laid among the monuments of famous Englishmen, they will say that Chatham knew how to inspire a nation with his energy, but was poorly furnished with knowledge and ideas; that the capacity of Fox was never proved in office, though he was the first of debaters; that Pitt, the strongest of ministers, was among the weakest of legislators; that no Foreign Secretary has equalled Canning, but that he showed no other administrative ability; that Peel, who excelled as an administrator, a debater and a tactician, fell everywhere short of genius: and that the highest merits of the five without their drawbacks were united in Mr Gladstone.

[1] *Letters of Lord Acton to Mary Gladstone*, pp. 44–7.

Possibly they may remember that his only rival in depth, and wealth, and force of mind was neither admitted to the Cabinet nor buried in the Abbey. They will not say of him, as of Burke, that his writing equalled his speaking, or surpassed it like Macaulay's. For though his books manifest the range of his powers, if they do not establish a distinct and substantive reputation, they will breed regret that he suffered anything to divert him from that career in which his supremacy was undisputed among the men of his time. People who suspect that he sometimes disparaged himself by not recognising the secret of his own superiority will incline to believe that he fell into another error of wise and good men, who are not ashamed to fail in the rigid estimate of characters and talents.

This will serve them to explain his lofty unfitness to deal with sordid motives, and to control that undignified but necessary work, his inability to sway certain kinds of men, and that strange property of his influence, which is greatest with multitudes, less in society – and least at home. And it will help them to understand a mystery that is becoming very prominent, that he formed no school, and left no disciples who were to him what Windham, Grenville, Wellesley, Canning, Castlereagh were to Pitt; that his colleagues followed him because he had the nation at his back, by force more than by persuasion, and chafed as he did by the side of Palmerston.

The document is interesting. Some allowance must be made for the paternal rhetoric which the historian allowed himself to employ. At times one senses that this is Gladstone as Acton would have him act, a Liberal made in his own fastidious image. The last sentences were written under the effect of the Midlothian campaign, when Gladstone in his later years for the first time swept away the mass of the poorer Christian voters by his own fervour. A tendency is also discernible in which Acton portrays himself as one of the few genuine friends of the great statesman. The note soon changes and Acton's dislike brings back his realism.

Some keys, I imagine [he continued], will be lost, and some finer lines will yield to the effacing fingers: the impress left by early friendship with men who died young, like Hallam, or from whom he was parted, like Hope Scott; the ceremonious deference to authorities that reigned in college days under a system heavily weighted with tradition; the microscopic subtlety and care in the choice of words, in guarding against misinterpretation and in correcting it, which belonged to the Oxford training, which is a growth of no other school, which even in such eminent men as Newman and Liddon is nearly a vice, and is a perpetual stumbling-block and a snare for lesser men – these are points appreciable by those who know him that must be obscure to those who come after us. They will wonder how it was that an intellect remarkable for originality and independence, matchless in vigour, fertility, and clearness, continued so long shrouded in convictions imbibed so early as to be akin to prejudices, and was outstripped in the process of emancipation by inferior minds. The pride of democratic consistency will aim its shafts at those lingering footsteps, as a scientific age will resent the familiarity and sympathy with Italian thought to the detriment of more perfect instruments of knowledge and of power, and that inadequate estimate of the French and German genius which has been unfortunately reciprocal.

The passage that follows has praise of Mr Gladstone's oratory in which the easy phrases link themselves together. Behind this there does not appear that stringent thought which Acton had bestowed on the preceding paragraphs. 'But that illustrious chain of English eloquence,' explained[1] the writer, 'that begins in the Walpolean battles, ends with Mr Gladstone. His rivals divide his gifts like the generals of Alexander. . . . C'est la grandeur de Berryer avec la souplesse de Thiers, was the judgment of the ablest of the Ultramontanes in his speech on Charities.'

The following sentences have a sharper interest.

His other pre-eminent characteristic is the union of theory and policy. Bonaparte must have possessed the same mastery of infinite detail; and the best democrats, Jefferson, Sieyès, and Mill, were firm and faithful in their grasp of speculative principle. But in democracy that doctrinal fidelity is neither difficult nor very desirable of attainment. . . . We always know what is coming. We know that the doctrine of equality leads by steps

[1] *Ibid.*, pp. 47–8.

not only logical, but almost mechanical, to sacrifice the principle of liberty to the principle of quantity; that, being unable to abdicate responsibility and power, it attacks genuine representation, and, as there is no limit where there is no control, invades, sooner or later, both property and religion. In a doctrine so simple consistency is no merit. But in Mr Gladstone there is all the resource and policy of the heroes of Carlyle's worship, and yet he moves scrupulously along the lines of the science of statesmanship.

These statements have their own perfection, but here again the historian's thought is tinged with rhetoric as he builds up a comparison with Burke. He goes on[1]

Those who deem that Burke was the first political genius until now, must at this point admit his inferiority. He loved to evade the arbitration of principle. He was prolific of arguments that were admirable but not decisive. He dreaded two-edged weapons and maxims that faced both ways. Through his inconsistencies we can perceive that his mind stood in a brighter light than his language; but he refused to apply in America reasons which might be fitted to Ireland, lest he should become odious to the great families and impossible with the King. Half of his genius was spent in masking the secret that hampered it. Goldsmith's cruel 'And to party gave up what was meant for mankind' is literally true.

The end of this estimate is in fact, as in form, a peroration.

Looking abroad beyond the walls of Westminster, for objects worthy of comparison, they will say that other men, such as Hamilton and Cavour, accomplished work as great; that Turgot and Roon were unsurpassed in administrative craft; that Clay and Thiers were as dexterous in parliamentary management; that Berryer and Webster resembled him in gifts of speech, Guizot and Radowitz in fullness of thought; but that in the three elements of greatness combined, the man, the power, and the result – character, genius, and success – none reached his level.

[1] *Ibid.*, p. 49.

K*

The same series of letters contains two further considerations of Burke and Gladstone. In a parenthesis in a long letter written from Cannes on 25 March 1881 there occur[1] these sentences. 'I admit no comparison [of Mr Gladstone], except with the Burke of 1770–80. That early Burke would have made the peace with the Africanders, which is the noblest work of the Ministry.' Nearly a year previously, in a somewhat didactic letter, Acton had set out[2] some further comments.

> In reality, they [the Bristol electioneering speeches] are an epoch in constitutional history. Burke there laid down, for ever, the law of the relations between members and constituencies, which is the innermost barrier against the reign of democratic force. Charles Sumner once said to me: 'Mr Burke legislated from those hustings.' It is impossible not to be struck by the many points of resemblance between Burke and your father – the only two men of that stature in our political history – but I have no idea whether they would have been friends or bitter enemies.

Extracts from two other letters will complete the picture. In the first the historian's view of Mr Gladstone's relation to the Liberal Party is given shape. In a long paper written from La Madeleine, he begins:[3]

> Has Mr Gladstone fairly faced the question, What will the party do without him? I may quote my own sentiment, because I grew up among Russells, Ellices, Byngs; and though I am very suspicious of early impressions and of doctrines unaccounted for, I know I am much more favourable to the great Whig connection, to the tradition of Locke and Somers, Adam Smith and Burke and Macaulay, than Mr Gladstone would like. Yet it would seem dust and ashes but for him.
>
> The idea that politics is an affair of principle, that it is an affair of morality, that it touches eternal interests as much as vices and virtues do in private life, that idea will not live in the [Liberal] party.

[1] *Ibid.*, p. 81.
[2] Letter dated at Mentone, 15 March 1880, *ibid.*, p. 5.
[3] Letter dated 27 October 1881, *ibid.*, p. 107.

This quotation marks the change that had taken place in the political scene in England since the Whig heyday. At this time Acton was only forty-seven, but the figures of his youth, 'Poodle' Byng and 'Bear' Ellice, seem almost to belong to another world. This section may be concluded by a general defence of Gladstone's statesmanship that his friend embarked upon during a leisurely stay at Cannes in the spring of 1881. He is found writing[1] to Mary Gladstone:

> I am not sure that there is any quite available and com-pendious answer to the two reproaches of setting the poor against the rich, and of giving power to those least fit for it. . . . Assuming the first objection culminates in Midlothian: it was necessary to bring home to the constituencies, to needy and ignorant men, the fact that Society, the wealthy ruling class, that supported our late Mazarin in clubs and drawing-rooms, was ready to spend the treasure and blood of the people in defence of an infamous tyranny (in Turkey), to gratify pride, the love of authority, and the lust of power. Nearly the same situation arose in Ireland, and in other questions not so urgent.
>
> Secondly, as to Democracy, it is true that masses of new electors are utterly ignorant, that they are easily deceived by appeals to prejudices and passion, and are consequently un-stable, and that the difficulty of explaining economic questions to them, and of linking their interests with those of the State, may become a danger to the public credit, if not to the security of private property. A true Liberal, as distinguished from a Democrat, keeps this peril always before him.

This gives a singularly balanced view of Acton's thought on cur-rent politics. On the other hand Mazarin was, perhaps, the most sympathetic name with which he endowed the Earl of Beacons-field. He went on:[2]

> We are forced in equity to share the government with the working class by considerations which were made supreme by the awakening of political economy. Adam Smith set up two propositions – that contracts ought to be free between capital and labour, and that labour is the source, he sometimes says

[1] Letter dated 24 April 1881, *ibid.*, pp. 90–2.
[2] *Ibid.*, p. 92.

the only source, of wealth. If the last sentence, in its exclusive form, was true, it was difficult to resist the conclusion that the class on which national prosperity depends ought to control the wealth it supplies, that is, ought to govern instead of the useless unproductive class, and that the class which earns the increment ought to enjoy it. That is the foreign effect of Adam Smith – French Revolution and Socialism.

We, who reject that extreme proposition, cannot resist the logical pressure of the other. If there is a free contract, in open market, between capital and labour, it cannot be right that one of the two contracting parties should have the making of the laws, the management of the conditions, the keeping of the peace, the administration of justice, the distribution of taxes, the control of expenditure, in its own hands exclusively.

After some historical comparisons Acton deals with the objections that the ignorant classes cannot understand affairs of state.[1]

The danger is not that a particular class is unfit to govern. Every class is unfit to govern. The law of liberty tends to abolish the reign of race over race, of faith over faith, of class over class. It is not the realisation of a political ideal: it is the discharge of a moral obligation.

Acton then goes on to examine the contention that Mr Gladstone aroused class animosities.

No doubt the[2] line has not always been broadly marked between Liberalism where it borders on Radicalism, and Radicalism where it borders on the Charter. Some reproach may visit Bright and Mill, but not Mr Gladstone. If there were no Tories, I am afraid he would invent them. He has professed himself a decided Inequalitarian. I cannot discover that he has ever caressed the notion of progressive taxation. Until last year I don't think he ever admitted that we have to legislate not quite impartially for the whole nation, but for a class so numerous as to be virtually equal to the whole. He dispels the conflict of classes by cherishing the landed aristocracy, and making the most of it in office. He has granted the Irish landlords an absolution ampler than they deserve. Therefore, though

[1] *Ibid.*, p. 93.
[2] *Ibid.*, pp. 94–5.

I admit that the condition of English society tends in some measure to make the poor regard the rich as their enemies, and that the one inveterate obstacle to the welfare of the masses is the House of Lords, yet I must add that he whose mission it is to overcome that interested resistance has been scrupulous not to excite passionate resentment, and to preserve what he cannot correct. And I do not say it altogether in his praise.

This passage, in itself a trifle verbose, throws a light upon the nature of Acton's Gladstonian championship. In a sense he appears to have come to see himself as the old prime minister's one discerning friend.

The following paragraph, which is near the conclusion of this long letter, tends to bear out the same contention.

But I am not surprised[1] at the complaint you heard. To many people the idea is repugnant that there is a moral question at the bottom of politics. They think that it is only by great effort and the employment of every resource that property and religion can be maintained. If you embarrass their defence with unnecessary rules and scruples, you risk defeat, and set up a rather arbitrary and unsanctioned standard above the interest of their class or of their church. Such men are not at ease with the Prime Minister, especially if he is against them, and even when they are on his side. I am thinking of Argyll in Lytton's first debate; of Kimberley always; of soldiers and diplomatists generally.

It is true that Gladstone's contacts with the members of his Cabinet diminished in his later years. At Hawarden he very seldom invited wives, the husbands came alone. Neither Lady Acton nor the Duchess of Argyll appear to have penetrated to this retreat. He knew the men, but only in a very general way their families. His associates in his later life, like Sir Donald Currie and Mr George Armitstead, were close supporters, but hardly operated in the field of national politics. For this reason within the inner circles of the Liberal Party attention was gradually concentrated on Lord Acton, who, with John Morley as a runner-up, was his one private friend in all that grouping.

---

[1] *Ibid.*, p. 96. This letter of 24 April 1881 fills pages 90–7 of the printed volume.

9

John Morley's Place

The Right Honourable the Viscount Morley of Blackburn died in the early autumn of 1923 full of years and honours at the small house 'Flowermead' at Wimbledon Park, where he lived with his old wife. Longevity had served him well. In his retirement he had written a highly selective book of recollections and there were the two massive volumes containing, in the 1905 edition, 1,974 pages, dealing with the life of Mr Gladstone. This was less attractive in its layout and rather long, but Mr Gladstone would carry any biographer. John Morley had been a delicate young man with a high ethical seriousness which perhaps masked for him his clear ambition. How did he come into the Hawarden world?

John Morley was born in Blackburn amid the high hills of Eastern Lancashire in the last week of 1838. It was then a fast-growing industrial town, the population mainly engaged in weaving cotton, with iron and coal in the vicinity. A new tram-line ran to Darwen to the South and on the other side the cottages stretched up the hill to Four Lane Ends. It was in those days very isolated. 'The district [around Blackburn],' wrote[1] Morley in his *Recollections*, 'was the centre of the almost countless divisions and subdivisions of the puritan nonconformity of Lancashire, just as Catholicism prevailed without movement in another area of the same county.' This was inner Lancashire before the Irish came to it.

My father was a surgeon of good professional repute. He came of homely stock (from Mytholmroyd) in one of the Yorkshire valleys near Halifax and my mother was a Northumbrian. He had taught himself a working knowledge of Latin and French, and I long possessed the pocket Virgil, Racine and

[1] *Recollections* by John Viscount Morley (1905), vol. i, p. 4.

Byron, that he used to carry with him as he walked to houses of handloom workers on the hillsides around. Born a Wesleyan (for he came of a family of small clothiers), he turned, though without any formality that I know of, from chapel to church, but he was negligent of its ordinances, critical of the local clergy and impatient as of some personal affront of either Puseyites on the one hand or German infidels on the other.

And this was very far from Hawarden Castle.

At the time, before Jonathan Morley took up his practice, a chief firm in the neighbourhood had been Haworth, Peel and Yates, the calico printers; but the first Sir Robert Peel had moved from Blackburn to the Midlands fearing, it is said, that the handloom workers might be provoked to wreck his new machinery.

In the late middle part of the reign of Queen Victoria the deepest social cleavage was that between the upper and the lower sections of the English middle class. In fact the upper middle class of this period was peculiar to England; there was no exact parallel on the Continent, nor was it found in Scotland. It was, broadly speaking, the class which had reaped the greatest profit from the industrial revolution; but it was also a group whose sons had had their education at the more expensive public schools. This class had shared from early boyhood the life of the aristocratic world and of the greater gentry; but always with the assurance that unlike these other groupings even the younger sons would have their share of capital. At the summit of English politics this grouping would include the dynasties of the Gladstones and the Peels.

Behind the Gladstones lay the shipping of Liverpool and the slave trade, and behind the Peels the firm of Haworth, Peel and Yates. The statesmen in these families had been respectively to Eton and Harrow; they had married into the landed squirearchy, the Glynnes and Floyds. Everything was arranged for their entry into politics; it was different for those who came from the lower middle class.

John Morley had neither influence, nor money. He came into the pipe-line which led to the literary side of public life when he won a scholarship at Lincoln College, Oxford. There he found an ebullient friend, James Cotter Morison. This young man was an enthusiastic student and toyed with the idea of a great work, based on Gibbon's example, with as its subject *The Decline and Fall of the Church of Rome.* He had the kind of liturgical interests which at that time led to Positivism. He was an orphan with a good private income derived from his father's invention and manufacture of vegetable pills.

Cotter Morison was all his life a *littérateur*. After various attempts to make a living in London as a weekly journalist Morley was appointed, through Morison's influence, as editor of *The Fortnightly Review*, which the latter had helped to purchase. Here he was in some ways almost in touch with Acton, for both revered George Eliot, who Morley approached from her Positivist side. He was in those days an Agnostic and a Radical. Mr F. W. Hirst explains his position quite succinctly. 'One,' he writes,[1] 'of his essays . . . arrested the attention of John Stuart Mill, and brought Morley into personal contact and lasting friendship with the great teacher and philosopher of Liberalism. After this, until Mill's death in 1873, Morley was a constant visitor at Blackheath; and never in after life forgot his debt to the "saint of rationalism".' This is set out to show how very far he was from Mr Gladstone.

Morley wrote a *Life of Cobden*. He was now a married man living a quiet middle-class existence at 'Pitfield', a small converted farm on the Hog's Back. On occasion he would stroll to Guildford station where he met Mill coming off the London train. 'We walked,' he explains[2] in a letter, 'in a leisurely way and through roundabout tracks for some four hours along the ancient green road that you know, over the high grassy downs, into old chalk pits picturesque with juniper and yew, across heaths and commons and so up to our windy promontory.' Morley was also linked with his guest as he was a reader for Macmillan's.

It should be made clear that Morley was in no sense an academic. He was a literary man devoted to *belles lettres*. He wrote essays on Turgot and Condorcet, whom he admired, and on De Maistre, whom he did not really understand. He had two assets for his contact with Mr Gladstone. He had a wide knowledge of the works of Edmund Burke and a liking, which he did not lose

[1] *D.N.B., 1922–1930*, p. 617.
[2] *Ibid.*, i, p. 65.

till middle life, for hearing sermons. He would compare the Bishop of Oxford and Mr Spurgeon; but Wilberforce 'excelled any man I ever heard in the taking gift of unction'. The phrasing makes one pause; John Morley was truly of his time.

I have tried to describe what Morley had in his portmanteau, when he came to Hawarden Castle and his new world. It was a change for him and he left his wife behind, but in this case quite completely. She is a shadowy figure and never comes into his Gladstone story.[1]

In 1883 Morley was elected as a Radical for the second of the two seats at Newcastle-on-Tyne. He was a supporter of Home Rule for Ireland. He had the Irish Catholic voters at his command, and among these was to be found the Garvin family. He had been a supporter, though hardly a close friend, of Joseph Chamberlain. It seems that once he was a member of the House it was his not very well articulated moral fire that captivated Mr Gladstone. Was Morley's Radical support for the Irish cause really a sufficient reason for his appointment to the great post of Chief Secretary for Ireland? Once he had acquired the contact he never gave up his place in Gladstone's household. It was necessary for all those close to the prime minister to accept him: he became a part of his *impedimenta*. It is possible that this may be one of the reasons why Acton was less at Hawarden with the old statesman. Morley went on his way through what to him was hitherto an unknown country.

In the writings of his last years Lord Morley gave an account of Acton.

It was about this time [1885] . . . that I had the privilege of becoming acquainted with Lord Acton. Friendship[2] as a relation has many types. On none did I presume to set a more special value than on my intercourse with this observant, powerful, reflective, marvellously full mind. He saw both past

[1] She is described in the *D.N.B.* as Mary, daughter of Thomas Ayling, of Abbey Road, London, and in *The Complete Peerage* as Mary the widow of – Ayling. The date of the marriage is given in the *D.N.B.* as May 1870. He was credited by rumour with several children, possibly these were born to him and his wife before their marriage. He was an Ethicist and as such little interested in religious ceremonies. At any rate it is clear that he had no legitimate children living when he was raised to a viscounty of the United Kingdom.

[2] *Recollections*, i, pp. 229–30.

history as a whole and modern politics as a whole. He was a profound master of all the lights and shades of ecclesiastical system; a passionately interested master of the bonds between moral truth and the action of political systems; an eager explorer of the ideas that help to govern the rise and fall of States; and a scrupulous student of the march of fact, circumstance, and personality in which such ideas worked themselves through. He was comprehensive as an encyclopaedia, but profound and rich, not tabulated and dry. He was a man who even on your busiest day could seldom come amiss, so deep and unexpected was he in thought, so impressive without empty pomp of words, so copious, exact, and ready in his knowledge. Once, after a great political gathering in a country town, owing to some accident of missing carriages, he and I had to walk home three or four miles along a moonlit road. I mentioned that I had engaged to make a discourse at Edinburgh on Aphorisms. This fired him. . . .

It should be remembered that this account is lightly powdered with sugar. It was written from Lord Morley's stance as an elder statesman and Acton's widow and his children were still alive.

He was fond[1] of society, but had a talent for silence that was sometimes provoking. He was not without some intellectual difficulties for us to reconcile. The union of devoted faith in liberty with devoted adherence to the Church of authority was a standing riddle. His conception of history as a business of wide general forces did not easily fit in with his untiring hunt for incidents on the political backstairs, as the historian's most precious and decisive prizes. He was sometimes fatally addicted to the oblique and the allusive, as if he might enjoy playing hide-and-seek with the well-meaning reader.

There is in this long book one phrase about Acton that is remembered.[2] 'Somebody said of Hallam that he was the magistrate of history. In a far deeper sense it was true of Acton.'

[1] *Ibid.*, i, pp. 230–1.
[2] Cf. for another opinion on this same subject 'Acton's introduction [to the edition of Machiavelli], as I [John Morley] said to Mr G., is as hard reading as a corrupt bit of Thucydides. French, German, Italian, Latin, Spanish etc etc., all in a single page – citation after citation – no grouping; you never know where you are, nor what he is at. The exact opposite to Acton's style is Maine's; one all-detailed and over abundant quotation, the other all generality and thoroughly well-digested novelty of thought.' *Ibid.*, i, p. 291.

As he went through life Morley grew in stature as a literary figure, although perhaps hardly as a politician. His account of Parnell, for instance, is as a character sketch one of the best that we have of that strange man. Up to his point we have been giving an account of John Morley as presented by himself. The comments made upon him were very different, and it is worth considering them for he was a considerable figure in Lord Acton's later life.

Sir Philip Magnus states[1] that he was 'sensitive . . . and thought to be fussy and old-maidish'. He was known to his colleagues as Priscilla. 'Gladstone,' he declares,[2] 'overvalued Morley because [he] tended to say smooth things to him and to give him the support and comfort which he liked.' And then there was the perhaps not unbiased judgment[3] of John Redmond. 'Morley has no courage, you can't depend upon him. Yes, he is a wretched fellow.' A recent review puts the hostile case quite strongly.[4] 'The winner,' the writer is describing the negotiations between Gladstone, Chamberlain and Hartington about Home Rule, 'from any such transaction would have to be mean, petty, jealous, vindictive, and dishonest; and surely enough it was John Morley. Morley won in every direction; he kept Chamberlain, a man who could "gobble him up for breakfast", safely in the outer darkness; he established himself unshakably as Gladstone's principal and most assiduous claque-leader; and he did it all with the warm moral glow of standing up for principle.'

How can we reconcile the various contrasts?

Morley had all those literary interests, the wide reading of a man of education, which pleased Mr Gladstone in his old age. He never really understood the tough world of politics, nor in fact the nature of his actions in that strange *milieu*. He was happy at 'Pitfield' and again at 'Flowermead' with his wife. He was an Ethicist and guarded by his own high standards. The gift of self-ridicule had passed him by; he was in a sense a solitary figure. He was not discontented with the management of his life; it was too close to him to see it clearly.

---

[1] Magnus, *Gladstone, a Biography*, p. 401.
[2] *Ibid.*, p. 381.
[3] Wilfred Scawen Blunt, *Diaries*, p. 548.
[4] *Times Literary Supplement* issue of 22 June 1967.

10

Acton and Office

Lord Acton had received his peerage in 1869 partly in recognition of his then status and partly as an earnest of the services which he would render. It was inevitable that in any question of promotion he should look to the Liberal Party; nothing would come to him during the years from 1874 to 1880, which were occupied by Mr Disraeli's administration. There were three types of appointment which at one period or another were in view, the first diplomatic, the second political and the third, to which he came in time, the Cambridge chair of history.

Curiously enough the most important of the earlier posts in question was also that for which Lord Acton was most suited. The ambassadorship in Berlin seems to have been brought forward[1] in 1873 and was then rejected on the grounds of the unwisdom of appointing someone who was not a member of the Diplomatic Service. There is, however, the difficulty that the embassy was not vacant in this year. The matter was certainly raised in 1884, a few months before the fall of the second Gladstone administration. The embassy was then available through the death of Lord Odo Russell, who had recently been raised to the peerage as Lord Ampthill. He had held this post for fourteen years and had received it as a reward for his services at the Vatican.

Lord Acton's name was proposed[2] in a letter from the Crown Princess to her mother Queen Victoria. As an alternative to Acton she also mentioned Lord Arthur Russell, then M.P. for

[1] According to Herbert Paul, who quotes the *Edinburgh Review*, No. 404, p. 528, the idea of sending Acton as ambassador to Berlin was seriously entertained in 1873, introductory memoir to the *Letters of Lord Acton to Mary Gladstone*, p. 1.

[2] Letter dated 30 August 1884, printed in *Letters of the Empress Frederick*, ed. Sir Frederick Ponsonby, pp. 192-3.

Tavistock, the late ambassador's elder brother. Neither of these men was a career diplomat.

Acton had a number of assets for this post. He was now fifty-two years of age. He had a perfect knowledge of the German language and his Dalberg connections would have been appreciated. The lands of the ecclesiastical electorates had been absorbed into the Prussian kingdom and there was much good will towards one who under other circumstances might himself have been a Prussian subject. His wife, even if a Bavarian, was a German, who had been brought up until her marriage in Germany. In Berlin she would have made a perfect ambassadress.

Lord Acton's difficulties with the Vatican would be sympathetic to the creator of the *Kulturkampf*. It was not surprising that the Gladstone administration should send a Liberal. The fact that he had been recommended by Bismarck's enemy the Crown Princess would probably not have been known in Berlin. He already had friends in the northern capital. Prince Hohenlohe would have welcomed him.

On the side of his work he had unusual advantages. His understanding of the complex movements of German politics was unrivalled. He was, it is true, not skilled as a negotiator, but such work would not fall to him in the peaceful years when the new German Empire was neither an ally nor an enemy of Great Britain. But Lord Granville was still foreign secretary; his long experience of Johnny Acton was sufficient to block any idea of such promotion. The appointment was to be kept within the circle of the diplomats, and Sir Edward Malet was transferred from Brussels, where he was minister. Malet had proved ability and was Lord Lyon's intimate *protégé*. Before taking up his post he married Lady Ermyntrude Russell, a spinster who was daughter to the Duke of Bedford and a niece of Ampthill's. There was something to be said at the Court of Prussia for keeping to the *hochwohlgeboren*. In these high posts fairly long spells were customary and Malet remained at Berlin till 1895. Acton's relations with the Crown Princess, who became the Empress Frederick, will be considered later. His chance of promotion to the post of ambassador vanished away.

There is, however, a further note to be added in regard to

possibilities for Acton in the diplomatic field. In Gladstone's fourth administration the foreign office was entrusted to the Earl of Rosebery. This might have seemed to offer a chance of posting which Lord Granville's opposition had long blocked.

Acton had maintained a quite intimate contact[1] with Robert Morier, who had had charge of the legation at Munich before he was promoted to be minister at Lisbon. It was Munich that the historian first thought of as a sphere of action. In this letter to Gladstone on this subject he began with a half-humorous manner of approach. 'I may of course,' he wrote[2] on 1 October 1892, 'fairly say that there are no complications between this country and Bavaria that would give me any opportunity for mismanagement; and I not only know Germany pretty well, but I enjoy a measure of favour with the Royal Family. You will laugh, but it is a fact due to family and social connexions.' The wording is not wholly clear, but he is surely referring to the House of Wittelsbach. This was the first period of the long regency of Prince Leopold for the two mad Kings, the brothers Louis II and Otto. The point now made is just a speculation, but it seems likely that Acton had developed a relationship with Prince Louis, who eventually became the last King of Bavaria. He was the Prince Regent's elder son, a man of forty-seven and living at Leutstetten.[3] At least this is the most that I can make of Acton's comment.

It also seems that he proposed about this time that he should be sent as minister to Stuttgart.[4] Württemberg had a Lutheran dynasty and William II, who would be its last sovereign, had just come to the throne. It was peaceful, and politically an outpost of Prussia. Bavaria lay along its eastern frontier. In this post Acton could not have used his own great knowledge. With certain reservations, this applies likewise to the Legation at Munich. It is not surprising that these suggestions were not taken up. Unlike Berlin, there were no particular services that he could have rendered in either of the South German States. There is, perhaps,

---

[1] Cf. an intimate letter from Acton dated 16 November 1874, Aldenham MSS.

[2] British Museum, Add. MSS 44094. Cf. Lionel Kochan, *Acton on History*, p. 30.

[3] This branch of the royal stock was closely associated with the Leydens. Carola Blennerhassett was in childhood the intimate friend of the third daughter of this family, the Princess Mathilde (1877–1906, later Princess Louis of Saxe-Coburg).

[4] This statement is made without giving an authority by Herbert Paul in his introductory memoir to the *Letters of Lord Acton to Mary Gladstone*, p. lxvi.

another aspect to this question. In these later years he might have valued an appointment which would have provided him with a house and income.

The next set of possibilities were within the field of English politics and were opened up when Mr Gladstone formed his last administration in August 1892. The growth of Lord Acton's intimacy had been very gradual and it is not surprising that this question was not raised in 1880; nor is there evidence that it arose in 1885. (These were the years of the formation of Mr Gladstone's two previous Governments.) By now the Liberal Unionists were in opposition as a result of Gladstone's Home Rule policy, to which Acton had always given his support. The prime minister was at this time eighty-two. He was beginning to suffer from a cataract and his hearing was much diminished. He made new ministers, Asquith and Grey are both examples; he did not make new friends. He felt the need of Acton as a councillor. From this rose the idea, the rather vague and tentative idea of introducing him into the Cabinet. One gets the impression that it was a matter about which the old gentleman was hardly very serious.

Our information on this and kindred subjects depends for the most part on the diaries of Sir Algernon West, who had once been Gladstone's private secretary and was now his unofficial *aide*. The chancellorship of the Duchy of Lancaster was the post which was proposed[1] for Acton; but this involved the appointment to a certain number of Anglican advowsons. There appears to have been no alternative suggestion. Meanwhile, the idea of Lord Acton in the Cabinet had met with opposition[2] from Sir William Harcourt, Lord Spencer and John Morley. It was natural that Harcourt and Spencer should have opposed the introduction of Mr Gladstone's private friend. The case of John Morley is more complex. He was an avowed admirer of Lord Acton, but was in the process of climbing towards the old statesman's intimacy. It seems that, as far as Acton was concerned, his good will was shot through by jealousy. It would appear that Gladstone had raised or indeed planted Lord Acton's hopes. Sir Algernon had to go and explain[3] that there was no place vacant for him in the Cabinet.

[1] *Private Diaries* compiled by Sir Algernon West, ed. Horace G. Hutchinson, p. 41.
[2] *Ibid.*, pp. 38 and 43.
[3] *Ibid.* p. 36

We now come to the more realistic search for minor office. It
has always seemed strange to me that Acton was not considered
for the post of under-secretary at the foreign office under Lord
Rosebery. Perhaps it was held that at fifty-eight he was too old
for an appointment that was subordinate. Two posts were independent; they were of small significance and teetering on the
verge of extinction. The first, the mastership of the Buckhounds,
had a certain decorative charm: it was offered[1] to Lord Brassey,
who refused it, and was asked for by Cyril Flower. The Buckhounds were then given[2] very appropriately to Lord Ribblesdale.
The second was the captaincy of the Yeomen of the Guard. This
was offered to Lord Acton; but Sir Algernon persuaded[3] him of
the absurdity of his wearing a big helmet and a sword. Lord
Kensington accepted the post instead and Acton took over the
vacant lordship-in-waiting which Kensington had held in the last
Liberal administration. He was given the responsibility of answer-
ing for the Government on questions relating to Ireland in the
House of Lords.

This was by chance for one side of Acton's interests an excellent
appointment. He served, however, the Court and not the Party.
Except for his rare official interventions in the upper house, this
marked the end of his effective interest in Liberal politics. He had
still his personal loyalty to Mr Gladstone.

The question of Acton's relations with the Queen will be considered in a later chapter, for he continued to hold the post at
Court for eighteen months after Mr Gladstone's resignation. This
final period was a difficult time, with the prime minister gradually
growing weaker and, as far as Home Rule was concerned, quite
dedicated to a hopeless task. Although he could steer a Bill dealing
with this subject through the House of Commons, it was bound to
be defeated in the House of Lords. For the final months of this his
last administration Mr Gladstone was seeking for a reason to lay
down his office.

---

[1] *Ibid.*, p. 40.
[2] *Ibid.*, pp. 46, 55.
[3] *Ibid.*, p. 56.

II

Gladstone's Resignation

The light from the swinging oil lamps in the board room of the Admiralty illuminated the Corinthian pilasters and the high oaken panelling. It fell on the stiff white collars of the naval lords as they perused with satisfaction the document which was to become known as the Spencer programme. The French naval building was entering on one of those spectacular but brief phases which the great wealth of England could so easily over-pass. In this case it was the need to out-distance the French construction in new battleships. *Bouvet, Gaulois, Charlemagne* and *St Louis*, the names suggesting one of the more traditional periods of the Third Republic, had all been ordered in the previous January. The naval lords were conscious that not a single British keel had been laid down in 1893; this was not a matter likely to trouble Mr Gladstone. Earl Spencer, who had become first Lord of the Admiralty at the beginning of the present administration, shared the pre-occupations of his professional advisers. He instructed the director of naval construction, Sir William White, to prepare an estimate of ship-building which would be completed within five years.

The Board at the moment was a strong one, strength was in fact its most marked feature. Admiral Sir Frederick Richards had taken over as senior naval lord in the previous September when Sir Anthony Hoskins had retired on reaching the age of sixty-five. Sir Frederick had commanded the *Devastation* for a three-year commission; he had known, as had all around that table, the slow, unhandy battleships with their low freeboard that old Sir Nathaniel Barnaby had designed for the Royal Navy. They were unsuited for ocean voyages; they came in pairs and driblets. And here Sir William had set out a series of six first-class battleships, all sister ships. They would, in fact, prove to be the first of the almost annual classes of great warships which the British and German navies would construct until the end of the first German war.

The list also included two armoured cruisers, first, second and third class cruisers, torpedo gunboats, sloops, torpedo boats and a torpedo boat depot ship. The estimated cost came to £31 million over a five-year period. Sir Frederick's mind worked slowly, but with power and great tenacity. Except for Rear Admiral Sir John Fisher, who was a volcano, these flag officers were silent and rather taciturn, Sir Frederick Richards, Lord Walter Kerr and Gerard Noel. There was that in Lord Spencer, the Red Earl, which chimed with them, great rectitude, a shining honesty, a bradawl mind. They soon were indivisible.

The plans of the fine battleships of the *Majestic* class lay on the drawing boards – the central citadel, the Hervey belt amidships, the high side armour. They were in part most modern and in some ways old-fashioned. The coal bunkers protected the ships' vitals. They had great reciprocating engines; the last of the fire-tube boilers; wire-wound twelve inch guns for the main armament, with the new hydraulic hoists. The upper fore-top and the after lower-top were fitted for fire control. It was clear that there would be no other squadron which could engage them. It has been justly stated[1] of these ships when completed that 'their magnificent masting offered a truly noble profile'. At last the new British Fleet began to shape itself before the eyes of the four naval lords.

Mr Gladstone spoke of the admirals, using a collective noun. They were on the edge of his horizon; he did not differentiate them. They were a disturbing factor in the political scene, as bulls might prove to be in the fields round Hawarden. There was a reason for this; their shade of politics was never Liberal. They were marked by a staid and sober Toryism, all save Fisher whose politics were his own career in action. They were not, outside the Service, an united grouping. Thus Fisher disliked Lord Walter, for he distrusted all Roman Catholics who attained to great positions. Lady Amabel Kerr, formerly Amabel Cowper, was very different from other naval wives, leading a deeply Evangelical life within the limits of her own Communion, living with her family

[1] Oscar Parkes, *British Battleships*, p. 383.

in that tall barrack in the Cromwell Road that she had bought for them. This was all very far from Lady Richards. Still, these flag officers were all Tories. Two of them were associated with the country peerage, and Noel was born into a Norfolk vicarage. Admirals Richards and Hoskins both belonged to that higher *stratum* of the clerical grouping which was allied to the squire-archy and were equally determined in their support of Tory principles. The admirals were inaccessible to Mr Gladstone and it was for this reason that the problem came to him in terms of figures. During December the prime minister had his first discussions with Lord Spencer. Public opinion, which had been affected by the loss of Sir George Tryon in the *Victoria* in the previous summer, was sympathetic towards the new proposals.

Mr Gladstone, who had just celebrated his eighty-fourth birthday, was of course moving towards resignation. His hearing was impaired and a cataract was forming in his right eye. He seems to have been much affected by the fact that Lord Spencer, twenty-five years his junior and one of the few peers whom he trusted, should move against him. He was never very good at assessing men and as he grew older his range was always narrowing. There was much in Spencer's normal country life which was very far from him. It is probable that Gladstone did not remember what Spencer never forgot, that the third Earl Spencer had been at the head of the Admiralty in Nelson's day.

On 13 January 1894 Mr Gladstone had gone with his family, Mr Armitstead and Lord Acton to Biarritz. He had found this place in his old age and liked it greatly. It was in these years very English, with the Avenue de la Reine Victoria and the Anglican church in the Rue Bacquedis. He would first consider all the precedents; his memory was best for the further details. He admitted that he had made limited concessions in 1860 and in 1884, but he had never accepted a whole new burden. His mind went back to July 1860 when the plan was set out for the naval forts. 'The demand,' he noted down,[1] 'was reduced from nine millions to about five (has this been done now?). I acted in concert with my old friend and colleague, Sir James Graham. We were entirely agreed.' There came the rub. Lord Spencer had given in to the

[1] John Morley, *Life of Gladstone*, iii, p. 563.

admirals. He was a man in whom Mr Gladstone placed great
confidence. He had stood by him in the Home Rule crisis; he had
offered him the use of Spencer House. The problem came to him
in terms of money. He hardly seems to have been aware of naval
changes. He had been chancellor of the exchequer in the days of
the wooden fleets of the Crimean War.

Few statesmen have had less feeling for the naval life. He had
taken two cruises at Sir Donald Currie's suggestion and by his
arrangement in British waters. The policies of Hawarden looked
inland; it was only on his visits to the Church on Sundays that
Mr Gladstone would look down upon the sands of Dee. He had
the landsman's pleasure[1] in a suitable storm. 'Down the pier,' it is
noted in a record of an earlier visit to Biarritz, 'and found all the
party watching the breakers and superb they were.' Later on this
same journey they went out to see Bayonne. 'Mr G. who has a
dizzy head did not venture on the jetty.'

A passage from his translation of Manzoni's ode on the death of
Napoleon may be quoted here:[2]

> As on the shipwreck'd mariner
>   The weltering wave's descent
> The wave o'er which, a moment since
>   For distant shores he bent.

The ocean was outside his sphere of interest. He would return to
more congenial topics. 'By the way,' he asked, 'how is it that we
have no word, no respectable word for backbone?'

This was not a time when one could argue with Mr Gladstone.
He was searching for a reason to resign. Soon after his return from
Biarritz he called his last cabinet. The scene has often been
described, Mr Gladstone sitting[3] 'composed and still as marble'.
That afternoon he made what was in fact to be his last
speech in the House of Commons. The next day was spent in
packing papers, varied by spells of work on his translation of
Horace. Then he and his wife went down to Windsor to dine and
sleep. An expression of opinion[4] made to Sir Henry Ponsonby,

---

[1] *Ibid.*, iii, p. 478.
[2] *Ibid.*, iii, p. 481.
[3] *Ibid.*, iii, p. 511.
[4] *Ibid.*, iii, p. 513.

who had tried to pump him, was much in character. 'I replied to him that this [the succession to the premiership] was in my view a most serious matter. All my thoughts on it were absolutely at the command of the Queen, and I should be equally at his command if he enquired of me from her and in her name, but that otherwise my lips must be sealed.' The council train (so called for it was specially run for the Privy Council) came down and Mr Gladstone joined the ministers in the drawing room of the Castle.

The audience with the Queen took place between the council and the dinner. 'There was,' wrote[1] Mr Gladstone, 'not one syllable on the past, except a repetition, an emphatic repetition of the thanks she had long ago amply rendered for what I had done, a service of no great merit, in the matter of the Duke of Coburg.' The prime minister, had he been asked to suggest his successor, would have proposed Lord Spencer. The Queen did not raise the matter, but invited Lord Rosebery to form a government.

One point is, perhaps, worth making. As Mr Gladstone left Downing Street for the last time the *Majestic* and her six sister ships were already building or soon to be built. The *Magnificent* had been laid down at Chatham in the previous December and Lord Charles Beresford, as captain of the steam reserve in the Medway, was determined that she should be completed first. The *Majestic* had been begun at Portsmouth the month before Mr Gladstone's resignation. There was a slip waiting for the *Jupiter* on Clydebank and for the *Hannibal* at Pembroke, where it was important to keep naval vessels building for there was no civilian work for the dockyard hands. Conservative and naval opinion were alike behind the building of these battleships. They would each carry a complement of 750 naval officers and ratings. They were in full accord with the buoyant phase which was now approaching, the twin buff funnels, the high masts, the white cutters and upper works to catch the sun, the long black hulls. At Berlin, in the *Marineamt*, Captain, later Grand Admiral, von Tirpitz already held the post of secretary to the naval supreme command. Mr Gladstone had, perhaps, some reason for his opposition for the Anglo-German armaments race was now begun.

[1] *Ibid.*, iii, p. 514.

PART FOUR

THE LATER PERIOD

I

The Court

It was Acton's wealth of German interests and the German elements in his thought and manner which were of such service to him when he joined the old Queen's household. In fact as far as the Royal Family was concerned he was in close contact only with those who were conditioned by German background and a German feeling. Beyond a superficial social contact with the Prince of Wales, he had nothing to do with the royal princes. His interests were wholly civilian and there is no evidence that he had anything resembling a close acquaintance with any officer in either of the Services. In fact his serious contacts were confined, as far as the Royal Family is considered, to the Queen and to her eldest daughter the German Crown Princess. There had been one other member of the family who shared these preoccupations with German life, the Princess Alice, who had been the Prince Consort's favourite daughter; but she had died at Darmstadt in 1878.

It seems that the Queen always saw in her eldest daughter the reflections of the interests of her husband, who had been the one erudite Prince of the House of Saxe-Coburg. The Queen was always deeply conscious of her position as the heir general of the House of Brunswick-Lüneburg. Thus she was concerned about the future of the territory of Brunswick-Wolfenbüttel, which could by no stretch of the imagination be considered as a British interest. She was anxious that the eldest son of the blind King of Hanover, who had been deprived of his kingdom at the end of the Austro-Prussian war, should be recognized as the heir male.

She had a clear, even a protective, interest towards all the members of her husband's stock, the ducal House of Saxe-Coburg-Gotha. It was this that guided her concern for the Saxe-Coburg princes, who inherited the Crown of Portugal on the death of

Queen Maria da Gloria and for all the diverse members of the line of Saxe-Coburg-Kohary. None of her English courtiers had any interests in such concerns.

Under these circumstances it is strange that the Queen's visits to Germany were so infrequent – to Rosenau and Coburg, with her husband, and once, after his death, to Darmstadt, and a single visit to her eldest daughter at Charlottenburg during the short sad reign of the Emperor Frederick. Curiously enough she had no knowledge of the South German States, which she never visited. Her aunt, the Queen of Württemberg, had been childless, and it seems that the only member of the Bavarian House whom she ever met in Germany was the Grand Duchess of Hesse-Darmstadt. She never sought for marriages for her children and grandchildren among the princes and princesses of South Germany. She disapproved of the marriage that took place between her granddaughter and the Prince of Hohenzollern-Sigmaringen. The Teck family hardly counted; they were anglicized and in origin morganatic. All her life, and more especially in her long widowhood, her thoughts went back again and again to her husband's country, the *Thuringer Wald*. In that land and across North Germany there lay the little Lutheran Courts on which her interest was concentrated. And it was at this point that Lord Acton's exact knowledge was most useful.

The whole Saxon group of families were among the objects of the Queen's benevolent concern. They were divided into two sections, the Ernestine and Albertine dynastic lines, coming from the Elector Ernest and his brother Albert of Meissen, who lived in the middle of the fifteenth century. With the exception of the Kings of Saxony they were all Lutherans; but the royal Albertine line was in some danger of extinction, and were this to occur the kingdom would pass to the Grand Duke of Saxe-Weimar-Eisenach. There had further been the provisions of the *Nexus Gothanus* in 1826 by which the lands of Saxe-Gotha, Saxe-Coburg and Saxe-Meiningen were reapportioned. There was no one else at Court, except Lord Acton, who had any interest in or knowledge of that complex of Ernestine lines in which the good Prince Albert lay embedded.

Disraeli was dead, who would have entered with gusto if not

with knowledge, into everything. It is pathetic to watch the Queen trying to interest Mr Gladstone in the character of the Dowager Princess of Waldeck-und-Pyrmont. On the other hand Lord Acton was at home at Courts and knew how to convey respectful information to his ageing sovereign.

When Lord Acton began to take his place in the life at Court, the Queen was seventy-three years of age. She was shrewd, hardworking and immensely practical; she shared the instinctive judgments of the great bulk of the middle class among her subjects. With her lace and the colour of her dresses, which varied from black to a deep purple silk, and her old-fashioned bonnet, she seemed *outrée* to the younger generation[1] of the world of fashion; but she was serene and confident.

It seems that she was unaware of her lack of literary or artistic taste. In these matters she merely reflected the ideas of the members of her Court. She had a clear idea of anything relating to her right or her prerogative. This appears in a brief exchange about the status of Admiral Hobart Pasha, who had entered the Turkish service. Lady Ely had said that he was an Englishman, but denationalized. 'But, my dear Jane,' replied[2] the Queen, 'he couldn't be.' It must be said that she possessed a deep quality of personal compassion. This instinctive sympathy with others was something which the loss of her husband had given to her.

It was an attractive quality that she endured much from boredom. A note sent[3] to Sir Henry Ponsonby on 31 January 1886 in the course of Mr Gladstone's second administration makes this point plain. 'People she [the Queen] is very anxious not to have as Lords [in-Waiting] are Ld. Sudeley and Ld. Wrottesley – both insufferable bores. The Queen would like young Lord Camoys.'

The Household was a more formidable element in the daily life of royal palaces in Great Britain than at other Courts. The Queen was often out of the capital at Windsor, Osborne and Balmoral. Compared to Berlin or Vienna or St Petersburg there were more Courtiers in actual residence. Lady Ponsonby describes a dinner of the Household waited on by fourteen footmen, all in red. There

---

[1] Cf. The correspondence between Everard Primrose and Lady Ponsonby in *Mary Ponsonby*, p. 167 and *passim*.

[2] Letter from Sir Henry Ponsonby, dated 20 May 1877, *ibid.*, p. 136.

[3] *Sir Henry Ponsonby* by Frederick Ponsonby, p. 207.

was also at the Victorian Court an element which reflected that of Louis XIV. The royal family were more intimate with those who did them real service, the palace servants, than with those whose service was mainly ceremonial.

The best evidence for this is Mary Bulteel, who was at first a maid-of-honour to the Queen and then the wife of her private secretary, Sir Henry Ponsonby. She was a Liberal and artistic in the fashion of her times; her views on religion fluctuated, but they were not those of the Court. She was a perfectly independent witness.

She always had an air of poised maturity. This resulted from the fact that her memoirs of her first period of service were composed in later life. Two references to the experience of her early days have bearing on the later situation. The first is an account of the Prince Consort. 'As for his sense of fun,' she wrote,[1] 'which has been so much talked of in the journals, I never could discover it. He went into immoderate fits of laughter at anything like a practical joke; for instance, if anyone caught his foot in a mat, or nearly fell into the fire or out of the window, the mirth of the whole Royal Family, headed by the Prince, knew no bounds. His original jokes were heavy and lumbering, like all German jokes I have ever known.' This particular form of pleasure affected the members of the family of both sexes until the end of the nineteenth century. The Queen herself was quite exempt from it.

There is a pleasant reference to the old royal yacht, the first *Victoria and Albert*. 'It is,' she explained[2] in a letter to her mother, 'a most glorious ship, fitted up in brass and mahogany like a huge toy. . . . Princess Royal is disporting on the deck, and I am supposed to be amusing her, but having letters to write, retired behind the paddle box.' This will serve to introduce the other member of the family, who played a certain part in Acton's life.

The Empress Frederick, as she had now become, had, when German Crown Princess, proposed that he should be sent to Berlin as ambassador. She was a remote, unhappy woman and it is not suggested that she had the same links with Acton as Queen

---

[1] *Mary Ponsonby, a memoir, some letters and a journal*, p. 5.
[2] *Ibid.*, p. 20.

Victoria. Wholly Teutonic in tastes and character, though of the Coburg mould, she had the misfortune to be regarded in her husband's country as the *Engländerin*. 'I don't think,' writes[1] Lady Ponsonby in describing her, 'many people could apprehend in England the sort of character and intelligence that the Empress Frederick had, because she was really not at all like an English woman. She had a keenly analytical mind like her father, and divided everything into . . . heads.' It was the English palaces to which she looked back; this was all that she ever knew of her mother's realm. 'Small things[2] got on her nerves like heavy German boots and the thin silver plate,' with its tendency to blacken. She read with a great speed and devoured reviews, including each monthly issue of the *Journal of Mining and Metallurgy*. In religious questions she followed closely David Friedrich Strauss. 'Faith,' she wrote[3] to Lady Ponsonby, 'is a frame of mind and nothing else.' She was a Liberal, as Acton would have put it, on the German model, although her thought was placed within an English framework. 'The European Concert seems[4] all out of tune to me when England does not play the first fiddle.'

She was professorial and hence could make no friendships within the circle of the Hohenzollern Court. Bismarck found her and her husband quite inexperienced opponents. She suffered from both loneliness and cold in the palace of Charlottenburg, while the snow-laden winds blew from the North across the Mark of Brandenburg. She did not move beyond her father's orbit. In these days she was at Cronberg and outside the world of politics. Lady Ponsonby comments[5] on 'how like it [Cronberg] is to Windsor years ago and the impossibility of any service being done – no bells and, if there were, no one to answer them.' Lord Acton was more at home with his own Queen.

There remain two other aspects of this time in waiting, first the reactions of the Queen and then those of Lord Acton. With the departure of Gladstone, the Queen's relations with her ministers would henceforth be tranquil. She had been taught in childhood

---

[1] *Ibid.*, p. 242.
[2] *Ibid.*, p. 241.
[3] *Ibid.*, p. 253.
[4] *Ibid.*, pp. 246–7.
[5] *Ibid.*, p. 238.

by Fräulein Lehzen the Lutheran doctrine of a God, all-seeing and
beneficent. In middle life she had come to disbelieve[1] in a personal
Devil, a modern outlook for that period. In the result she reposed
on a strong and comfortable religious faith.

She had a slight tinge of superstition; she disliked the number
fourteen.[2] There was the occasional heavy dosage of sorrow self-
administered, as on the death[3] of the Grand Duke of Hesse
Darmstadt, the widower of Princess Alice. Dizzy had gone and
his heady interests lay well behind her. Now she was concerned
in her grandchildren's marriages, a less exacting sphere than
English politics. Connected with these interests, she welcomed
each foreign bride[4] as she became a Princess of Saxe Coburg.

There are various references to Acton in the Queen's *Journals*,
but one relating to a visit to the Empress Eugénie will suffice to
give the general impression.[5] '1 December 1892, Windsor Castle.
Left at a quarter to one for Farnborough Hill. . . . The Empress
was all kindness and wonderfully well. The cure at Bath has made
her quite active again. If only I could become so too. But unfortunately I cannot stand baths. We lunched with the Empress
and Princess Murat, and I sat with her, whilst the others went to
see the Chapel. We left at a quarter to four and got back to
Windsor in about an hour. Jane C[hurchill], Ina McNeill, Lord
Acton, who is a charming person with such pleasant manners
(rather foreign) very like his mother the late Lady Granville (a
widow, daughter of the last Duke of Dalberg) who was so agreeable and clever, Count Steinbach and Captain Campbell dined.'
The Queen's life went forward very tranquilly, a little old-
fashioned and with nothing of the unexpected. The Court was
quiet and managed to her liking.

It is worth considering also how life at Windsor Castle struck
Lord Acton. There are three letters to James Bryce upon this sub-

---

[1] Statement of Princess Louise quoted in *Sir Henry Ponsonby, His Life and Letters*,
p. 119.

[2] Because the Prince Consort died on 14 December 1861.

[3] The Queen's Journal entry under 13 March 1892, *Letters of Queen Victoria*, third
series, ed. G. E. Buckle, vol. ii, p. 105.

[4] Letter from Marie-Louise de Bourbon-Parme, first wife of Ferdinand of Bulgaria
(of the line of Saxe-Coburg-Kohary) married at Schwarzau-am-Stansfeld, 26 February
1893, *ibid.*, p. 235.

[5] *Ibid.*, p. 188.

ject. 'It will be impossible,' Acton wrote[1] on 5 December 1892, 'for me to come to you on Sunday, to my great regret, my turn of service will not be over. It is not a difficult office until I dine with the Queen. There is nothing to do but to cajole your friends the maids of honour. I spend my days in the library to the amusement of everybody, especially of the Queen.' A little later he made[2] this comment. 'I don't remember the passage in Schiller and there is no copy here. Bear with me for being so useless, but this is not an intellectual place.'

Six days later he wrote[3] again. 'Duties here come to an end on Tuesday. They have been as you foretold altogether pleasant, with a want of intellectual stimulus quite astonishing. Here is the young Hohenzollern, who is an old friend of mine, and his bride[4] is charming, and that facilitates the Courtier's human functions. I have found much good literature, but a very bad library.' Acton twice refers to the Court as unintellectual, how could he have supposed that it was not?

The third letter was written some eighteen months later. 'I am very sorry,' explained Acton,[5] 'to fail you on Wednesday, but I shall be on duty here [at Windsor Castle]. These ancient walls re-echo much idle gossip, but not as much as one expected. The Queen spoke to me twice last night about Mr G[ladstone]'s eyesight, once in the presence of the Empress and again emphatically when we were alone. She had vaguely heard of incipient cataract, but knew no particulars. I told her none.' He was burdened by the state of the health of the prime minister. 'Asquith,' he went[6] on, 'has told his bride everything and her sister betrayed her knowledge to me at Spencer House on Wednesday. Lady Fanny[7] has evidently been indiscreet and I fear Lady Freddy.'[8] The historian here broke out into his social manner.

Another letter has some bearing on Acton as a courtier. It was

---

[1] *Bryce MSS*, Acton Letter Book, No. 72.
[2] *Ibid.*, No. 74.
[3] Letter dated 11 December 1892, *ibid*.
[4] Presumably the Queen's grandchildren, Prince Henry of Prussia and Princess Irene of Hesse-Darmstadt.
[5] Letter dated 23 February 1894, No. 84.
[6] *Ibid.*, No. 85.
[7] Lady Fanny Marjoribanks, *née* Spencer-Churchill.
[8] Lady Frederick Cavendish.

an enquiry from James Bryce about one of the archdukes, and the reply indicates how far Acton still remained aloof from the Court life of Vienna. 'My belongings,' he wrote[1] from the Grand Hôtel at Paris, and here he refers to the Arco-Valleys, 'know of your Balearic Archduke, chiefly I think as a collector and a faddist.' This comment refers to one of the more eccentric members of the Imperial House, the Archduke Ludwig Salvator of Austria-Tuscany. Together with his brother, the Archduke Johann-Nepomuk Salvator, better known as 'Johann Orth', who had disappeared some two years earlier while in command of the *Santa Margherita*, he was one of the children of the second marriage of the old Grand Duke. Apart from certain comments on the Emperor of Austria, considered as a political figure, this appears to be the historian's only reference to the Hapsburg family. He would soon be removed from all these preoccupations. Still the principal memory of these years is of Lord Acton working silently in the library at Windsor Castle.

[1]Letter dated 12 November 1893, Acton Letter Book, No. 81.

2

The English Historical Review

It was during these years at Court that Lord Acton's reputation as a historian began to burgeon. In 1888 he had received the honorary degree of LL.D. from Cambridge University, and in the following year a similar degree, in this case a D.C.L., from Oxford. It was one of Mr Gladstone's last kindnesses towards him that had resulted in his election in 1891 as an honorary fellow of All Souls. But perhaps his appointment to a university chair depended less upon these honours, which were to a great extent a recognition of his status as a historian than upon the very solid work that he had done for the *English Historical Review*.

Before describing the *E.H.R.* it is well to portray Dr Mandell Creighton, who was joined with him in this foundation. Creighton was a clergyman, quite out of touch with the Hawarden grouping, who at the time of his first contact with Acton was vicar of Embleton on the coast of Northumberland. His academic background was wholly Oxford and in fact Merton; he had been a fellow of that college and held a Merton living. He was quite unconnected with the old Church families and had been born in Carlisle over the shop where his father was a furnisher and decorator. His mother was of yeoman stock from the Cumberland countryside and her family, the Mandells, had contacts with St John's College, Cambridge. Her background resembles that of the neighbours around Richmond, across the Pennines, described[1] by Mark Pattison in the account of his own childhood. There was that same tendency to look towards the universities. Besides, Creighton had from an early age that contact with the members of the governing class which came so easily to the clergy of the Establishment. Among his friends at Embleton were Sir George and Lady

---

[1] Cf. Mark Pattison, *Memoirs*, pp. 1–9.

Grey of Fallodon, and he acted as tutor to their grandson Edward Grey, the future statesman.

Creighton had had High Church tendencies in his undergraduate days, but he grew out of these and also gave up his early Liberalism. He was born in 1843 and was therefore nine years Lord Acton's junior; a tall thin man, with blue-grey eyes behind his gold-rimmed spectacles, and a pale auburn beard. As an undergraduate he had rowed; but he never fired a gun or visited a race-course in his life. His Oxford friendships included Saintsbury; Copleston, later Bishop of Calcutta; and Stafford Northcote. Each of these three possessed his serious side. Andrew Lang was another friend that Merton gave him.

He married, when he was twenty-eight, Louise von Glehn, the daughter of a Baltic merchant from Reval, of Rhineland stock, who lived at Peak Hill Lodge, Sydenham. He enjoyed walking in Switzerland, later in North Italy. 'He always said,' recounts[1] his widow, 'that above the line where the chestnuts grow, the mountains began to lose their charm for him.' After his marriage and before he went to Embleton, he lived in a house at Oxford in St Giles' Road East, which he called 'Middlemarch' – in memory of the novel. He was interested in those days in Renaissance painting and began a collection of photographs. He was in some ways a perfect Oxford figure of the 1870s, established at 'Middlemarch' with his wife and family and his white Persian cat.

This background was very far from Lord Acton's then experience. At Embleton Creighton's *History of the Popes* went forward; the results of his former Renaissance studies were poured into this new enterprise. His first contact with Acton occurred in December 1882, a letter of thanks when the latter had reviewed the first two volumes of his book on the Papacy for the *Academy*. We have the exact date of their first meeting, for Creighton wrote[2] on 2 December 1884: 'To-morrow I am going to London to meet at dinner Lord Acton, whom I have been long pining to see. He is a Roman Catholick and the most learned of Englishmen now alive, but he never writes anything.'

---

[1] *Life and Letters of Mandell Creighton D.D.* by his wife, i, p. 70. The other personal details come from this biography.

[2] *Ibid.*, i, p. 275.

One does not gain the impression that these two men had much in common. Creighton was a very devoted clergyman, a trifle insular. He was a calm student and never heated. Rome was far away and of no interest to his English pastoral outlook. He had a warm Victorian concept of friendship. With children, his own and other people's, he was delightful. He would entrance the children of Dr Hodgkin, the author of *Italy and her Invaders*, by going about the floor pretending to be an animal. All his life he enjoyed walking with his wife in Northern Italy, discovering Lake Orta, going from village to village in the high hills.

On the side of historical studies the major work of his life was the *History of the Popes*, extending roughly from the end of the Avignon period to the eve of the Reformation. The attraction of the work lies in its approach and not its style. This was heavy and at times careless. For instance, he would frequently use the expression the Cardinal College when he was speaking of the Sacred College of Cardinals. On the other hand his judgments were essentially moderate and often tentative; he weighed up the authorities by then available; he left much to the reader. Even now, after eighty years, the absence of harsh and determined judgment leaves his work readable. He was always anxious not to exclude the various possibilities; he left room for different interpretations. It is curious that he did not perceive how his completed book would be judged by German standards and how it would infuriate John Acton.

At this time there was a plan for launching the *English Historical Review*, and a meeting had been held at James Bryce's rooms where Acton and Creighton had both been present. Longmans were suggested as the publishers and York Powell as editor. In fact Creighton emerged as editor and R. L. Poole as secretary. Acton's contribution to the *E.H.R.*, both in article form and in reviews, will be considered later; it is his attitude to Creighton's work that I now want to discuss. Creighton had a character of marked simplicity; he had moved in the clerical sphere, always protected. He was sure that Acton 'would' be most helpful through his learning.'

Early in 1887 the third and fourth volumes of the *History of the*

[1] *Ibid.*, i, p. 334.

Popes, which had as their sub-title 'The Italian Princes 1464-1518', were at length ready. Creighton asked Acton to review them for the *English Historical Review*. Acton agreed to do so and accepted the books, but made his position clear in a covering note. It is worth noting the terms and the tone of his reply. Both were very different from that calm which he would come to when he was settled in the Cambridge chair. 'You must understand,' he explained,[1] 'that it [the review] is the work of an enemy. . . . I need not explain, what you partly know, the width of yawning difference between your view of history and mine.' In general, and perhaps especially in the Victorian age, letters to third parties throw much more light upon the scene than those exchanged between the principals. In this particular correspondence two of Creighton's letters to R. L. Poole give the precise effect of Acton's onslaught.

The first letter is dated 29 March 1887. 'I am rather perplexed,' wrote[2] Creighton, 'about a matter in which it seems to me that the humour of the situation is great. I asked Lord Acton to review my *Papacy* and he graciously consented. Now he sends me a review which reads to me like the utterance of a man who is in a furious passion, but is incapable of clear expression. He differs *toto caelo* from my conception of the time, apparently on some concealed grounds of polemics esoteric to a Liberal Roman, who fought against Infallibility. That is all right if he would say so.' In reality, of course it was not all right at all. It seems very unlikely that Acton ever became aware of Creighton's judgment. Long letters of explanation passed between the principals in which occur Acton's celebrated phrase 'Power tends[3] to corrupt and absolute power corrupts absolutely' and also the doctrinal statement 'Great men are almost always bad men'.

The review itself was some fifteen pages in length. 'The author,' Acton writes,[4] 'prefers the larger public that take history in the shape of literature, to scholars whose souls are vexed with the insolubility of problems and take their meals in the kitchen.' The

---

[1] *Ibid.,* i, p. 372.
[2] *Ibid.,* i, p. 369.
[3] *Ibid.,* i, p. 372.
[4] *English Historical Review*, vol. ii, p. 372.

general charge is superficiality. Thus 'Burckhardt,[1] the most instructive of all writers on the Renaissance, is missed where he is wanted, though there is a trace of him in the description of Caterina Sforza.' The review contains quite lengthy quotations from diarists and chroniclers in Italian. There are of course some pleasant passages. 'Aretino relates[2] that an ape was caught in the apartments of Alexander VI, who exclaimed "*Lasolo, lasolo, che il diavolo*".'

Creighton is taken severely to task because he makes only a passing reference to the fact that Sixtus IV sanctioned the Spanish Inquisition. 'He is,' wrote[3] Acton, 'not striving to prove a case, or burrowing towards a conclusion, but wishes to pass through scenes of raging controversy and passion, with a serene curiosity, a divided Judgment, and a pair of white gloves.' This may strike the modern reader as hardly fair, and on a later page the full Actonian doctrine stands revealed. 'And[4] it is the office of historical science to maintain morality as the sole impartial criterion of men and things and the only one on which honest minds can be made to agree.'

It is worth noting a second letter from the historian of the Popes to R. L. Poole upon this subject. '*Mentem mortalia tangunt* is my motto,' wrote[5] Creighton on 12 April 1887. 'I try to put myself in their places, to see their limitations, and leave the course of events to pronounce the verdict upon system and men alike. No doubt Acton is more logical, but his view would reduce history to a dreary record of crimes to which I am unequal.'[6]

There was not much in common between the two historians. Creighton was deeply English; he had a sympathy for English Nonconformity; he was devoted to his many Quaker friends, the Fox family at Falmouth, the Peases, Dr Hodgkin. English Roman

---

[1] *Ibid.*
[2] *Ibid.*, ii, p. 376.
[3] *Ibid.*
[4] *Ibid.*, ii, p. 378.
[5] *Life and Letters of Mandell Creighton*, i, p. 376.
[6] Lord Acton's comment in a letter to Bryce, dated 8 January 1885, has its own interest. 'There has been no opportunity to thank you for making me meet Creighton, who I was very anxious to know face to face, and liked greatly in spite of a lurking desire, which he betrayed, to make the best of a bad case and to depreciate our friend Villari', Bryce MSS, vol. i, p. 10.

Catholics he seldom cared for, but that was very natural. There were none in the circle in which he was brought up. He loved to travel; he was not interested in his food and was always contented with the provincial inns in the Italian kingdom. He travelled in August inured to all discomfort. He also went at other seasons, climbing up to Olevano in the spring. On these travels he always used *Gsell-Fels*, a German guidebook, which he found admirable. We have the record of his journeys, Milan, Piacenza, Modena, Pistoja, Lucca, Pisa, Siena, Florence, and in another year Florence, Cortona, Arezzo, Perugia, Assisi, Ancona, Loreto, Rimini, Ravenna, Bologna. These were stations where the *diretto* stopped on the new railway lines. He would climb the hill to Orvieto with rug and spirit-lamp, accompanied always by Ella, his beloved wife, an English clergyman who saw the best in people. The whole scene was very far away from John Emerich Edward Dalberg-Acton.

Creighton's undertaking the editorship of the *English Historical Review* had been made possible by his move south from Northumberland. In 1884 he had agreed to become the first holder of the Dixie chair of ecclesiastical history at Cambridge. From the beginning he had the help of R. L. Poole, who soon became assistant editor. At the same time Lord Acton played the part of what may be called a 'founder member'. He had here no editorial responsibility such as he had shouldered in the case of the *Home and Foreign* in bygone days. There seems to have been no desire, or at least no effective desire, to curb him in any way. It was in one sense a help to Lord Acton to come to the English historians in his full maturity. His statements were still positive and now they were accepted with respect.

It is worth giving a brief list of those with whom he found himself. Nearly all the first reviewers in the *E.H.R.* were distinguished in their field, T. F. Tout, E. Warde Fowler, E. Maunde Thompson, C. H. Firth and H. C. Lea. Except for Charles Firth, who was born in 1857, these historians were already in middle life. Edward Armstrong was, perhaps, a figure of lesser weight. He had been born in 1846 and had undertaken the history teaching at Queen's College, Oxford, in 1883. Only one name introduces a slight jar, that of Oscar Browning, who was then a Fellow of King's College.

In this first number of the *English Historical Review*, forty-eight pages were devoted to Acton's 'German Schools of History'. His reviews also were fairly lengthy. In 1887 sixteen pages were given to *A short history of Napoleon I* by John Robert Seeley, a brief book expanded from an article in the *Encyclopaedia Britannica*. In the next year the same length was accorded to a notice of the last volume of *The History of England*, produced by James Franck Bright. I gain the impression that Lord Acton had chosen books which gave him an opportunity to lay down his general notions. In 1887 he had given just the same length to the third and fourth volumes of Creighton's *History of the Papacy*, a much more serious work. In 1888 Acton contributed a rather brief review of Emmanuel de Broglie's *Mabillon*, and four years later a short notice of H. Morse Stephens' *History of the French Revolution*.

In the course of the first six years of the *E.H.R.* the list of reviewers had been expanded to include R. L. Poole, J. B. Bury, Sidney Lee, H. Rashdall and Ugo Balzani. Among others were Wolfgang Michael, who was already examining German sources for the reigns of the Hanoverian sovereigns. It seems possible that he may have been introduced by Acton to this list. Included as representatives of the younger generation were D. G. Hogarth, Charles Oman and H. A. L. Fisher. In 1890 there had been printed in the *E.H.R.* an obituary notice of Wilhelm von Giesebrecht. This, with one exception, completes the list of Lord Acton's contributions before he was appointed to the Cambridge chair.

3

The Oxford Chair

The resignation of Mr Gladstone had a marked effect on Lord Acton's life. His influence on politics had depended on his constant presence in the prime minister's private councils. There was no such link with the Earl of Rosebery, who now took office. Acton remained for the present a Lord-in-Waiting.

By this time his contacts with the English universities had gradually been strengthening. These and his work for the *English Historical Review* had gradually built up for him a new position. It so happened that both the regius professorships of modern history were to fall vacant during the fifteen months of Rosebery's administration. Both these appointments lay with the prime minister. At Gladstone's resignation these chairs were held by Mr Froude and Sir John Seely respectively. The latter was Acton's exact contemporary, in fact a few months his junior; but Froude was already seventy-six, now lecturing with difficulty in failing health.

James Anthony Froude was an isolated figure in the closely integrated group of Oxford historians, so long dominated by his two great predecessors, Stubbs and Freeman. He had come back into the Oxford world when Lord Salisbury had appointed him to the chair in 1892. It had been more than forty years since he had resigned his Devon fellowship at Exeter College on the day when his book *The Nemesis of Belief* had been publicly burned by a fellow-member of the senior common room because it was in the possession of an undergraduate. His life as the son of Archdeacon Froude of Totnes, his connection with the Established Church and his broken friendship with Dr Newman were far away. I do not myself find him very likeable. He placed such a value on worldly success: this was, perhaps, something that sprang from one element of early Barchester.

In these forty years he had lived remote from the universities. He was linked with the upper *intelligentsia* of the capital; the Athenaeum, the Club, the Breakfast Club. He was thus in contact with Acton, but quite apart from him. His journeys were to Highclere, Lord Carnarvon's country seat, and to Hatfield, not to Hawarden. He was a frock-coated politician who placed value on his judgments in that field. In outlook he is best described as a Protestant Conservative. His first marriage had been with one of the daughters of Pascoe Grenfell, M.P., of Belgrave Square, the head of a house of merchants dealing in tin and copper ores. This was the world of new Victorian prosperity. The eldest son of this family, the younger Pascoe Grenfell, and his wife, Lady Charlotte, were laying out the terracing at Taplow Court; the daughters had made advantageous marriages except for the one, who had married a parson, young Charles Kingsley. Froude's first wife died and he married again in the same circle. His second wife was Henrietta Warre, a cousin of Dr Warre, the headmaster of Eton, and her stepmother was another Grenfell.

Froude edited *Fraser's Magazine* with the help of Sir Theodore Martin; both men were far away from academic history. And then he had his contact with Lord Carnarvon and made under his official auspices a journey to South Africa. It seems less characteristic that he should have acted as Carlyle's executor and carried out his long work as that historian's biographer. It was Professor Freeman's death that brought him back into Oxford history. The latter had been journeying in the Mediterranean countries in May during the summer term. He died of smallpox in the south of Spain and was buried in the Protestant cemetery at Alicante.

Froude had had many feuds. He had earned Freeman's disapproval. He was as far away from Acton as from all the others. He was now an old man, twice a widower. He had won a great popular success with his *History of England*; this was bound up with his patriotic feeling, his sense of the West Country, his eulogy of the Reformation. It seems reasonably exact to state that he and Kingsley between them told the public what English sentiment recognized as true.

He never answered the criticisms made by his academic colleagues. In one way Froude was remarkable; he had a lovely style. His skill in presentation was unusual, his arrangements and his settings. As a consequence his *Divorce of Catherine of Aragon*, for instance, can still be read with pleasure, but who reads Freeman? Froude was of small importance in Acton's life. His career is traced here briefly because his work was a subject on which Acton and the professional historians were in agreement.

It has always seemed to me strange that Acton was not offered the Oxford chair when Froude died in October 1894. The candidate expected at that time was S. R. Gardiner, the seventeenth-century historian, and when he refused the appointment went to young York Powell. Within three months the Cambridge chair was vacant. Perhaps in the preliminary enquiries Cambridge proved more welcoming to the stranger; there was something of a closed corporation in the Oxford colleges. Lord Acton took over rooms in Neville's Court and gave his inaugural lecture at Trinity in the summer term of 1895.

Here, before considering Acton's Cambridge work, seems the place to give an impression of his colleague in the Oxford history chair, a singularly appealing figure.

Frederick York Powell had had in some ways a conventional education; but he had only spent two years in Jex Blake's house at Rugby and had then travelled to Spain.[1] An acquaintanceship with the political characters of the last years of Isabel II was an unexpected trait in him. He came up to Oxford, aged eighteen, in 1868, already a Socialist and an Agnostic. Dean Kitchin describes[2] his first arrival: 'He came up for the matriculation examination, and in his Divinity papers, I do not know how, scared the tender susceptibilities of the Master [of Univ.].' He became a non-collegiate student and was then accepted into Christ Church. At the House he wore a velvet coat and pince-nez; he had as yet no beard. He was the only son of a commissariat merchant in Mincing Lane of Welsh extraction. He admired Swinburne.

In 1872, after obtaining a first class in the Law and History

[1] Cf. Wilfred Scawen Blunt, *My Diaries*, p. 513.
[2] *Frederick York Powell* by Oliver Elton, vol. i, p. 14.

school, he left Oxford and for the next two years lived in his father's house in Lancaster Gate. Although his father seems to have been prosperous, he left no money. In 1874, through Liddon's influence, York Powell gained a lectureship in Law at Christ Church and married Mrs Batten, a young widow, to whom he was devoted. He was really at home in London and with his contacts there; he never seems to have been at the high table of Christ Church on a Sunday. It was at this period of his life that he composed his literary work. In 1875 he had begun his partnership in Icelandic studies with Gudbrand Vigfusson, who had settled in Oxford; they published together the *Corpus Poeticum Boreale*. He continued with the *Origines Icelandicae*; these Icelandic studies made his reputation, but they were rather far outside Lord Acton's field.

At this time he was living in Norman Shaw's new suburb, Bedford Park. His wife had died in 1888 and Dr Vigfusson in the next year. These losses made him solitary; he was left with one small daughter, Mariella. He was, however, a much more unusual character than this *curriculum vitae* would suggest. When he came to the Oxford chair in 1894, he was a heavy man in a reefer jacket with a thick luxuriant beard. There was something of the sea about him and he was devoted to the fishermen at Sandgate. He knew the Channel well and those waters going northward from the Downs to Reykjavik. He did not travel far for he was always hampered by his poverty. He was superbly natural. 'Get married soon,' he told[1] an undergraduate, 'I have never repented marrying, so I don't speak as the fox with a cut tail.' He never greatly cared for Oxford life. 'The place,' he wrote,[2] 'is full of howling jackals and crocodiles, a sort of Nile valley with evil spirits walking up and down it.' As was to be expected, he was trenchant about politics. 'It is,' he used to say,[3] 'the love of Mammon and party motives of the "jumping cat", which run our political system.' It is not surprising that in 1880 he expressed[4] himself as glad to have got rid of 'that old hypocrite Disraeli'. In a sense he never took himself very seriously. When he came in the end to live in

[1] *Ibid.*, i, p. 73.
[2] *Ibid.*, i, p. 91.
[3] *Ibid.*, i, p. 66.
[4] *Ibid.*, i, p. 63.

the Banbury Road, he wrote[1] 'here in the north like Lucifer I have set my throne'.

He was the only one of his professorial generation who had the confidence of working men. This was helped by his Socialism, which he knew he should not live to see in office, by his constant lack of money and by his clearly-expressed Agnostic views. 'He read[2] anything in any tongue that made him laugh, and that had wit and humour.' He liked Casanova. He had all his life a tremendous interest in boxing. 'He knew the successes and burial places of the great English pugilists.' His room at Christ Church in Meadow Buildings reflected all these interests. There was usually a two-days' old evening paper in one corner. On his desk were copies of the *Licensed Victuallers Gazette* in which he studied the boxing reports. Stacks of the *Pink'un* were found in his room after death. 'I have a friend,' he wrote[3] to Kuno Meyer, 'who was knocked out by an Irishwoman in the Birmingham riots with a ginger-beer bottle in the toe end of a stocking.' He would like to chant out simple ballads:[4]

> Of Jonah living in the belly of the whale:
> But that was better than the County Jail.

With his beard and his old tall hat and the round serge jacket, and the sailor's silver ring on his fingers, he looked very like some shore-bound seaman.

There was of course another side to him. He had an enthusiasm, now so difficult to understand, for all Meredith's novels. 'Balzac and Meredith,' he wrote[5] in 1896, 'will represent their century. Do not mention such a person as George Eliot, let her lie.' He had a real affection for William Morris and a great feeling for *The Defence of Guinevere*. He liked sketches and short journeys abroad, to a hotel full of English people at Ambleteuse in the Pas de Calais. But these narrow limits were bound up with his poverty. In his last years he would devour the novels of Conrad, set in those seas that he had never seen. He had a sense of scenery

[1] *Ibid.*, i, p. 357.
[2] *Ibid.*, cf., i, p. 459.
[3] *Ibid.*, i, p. 376.
[4] *Ibid.*, i, p. 124.
[5] *Ibid.*, i, p. 229.

and liked the eighteenth-century English school. 'I have seen,' he wrote[1] in 1895, 'Sandwich and Richborough, however, and they are worth seeing. Beautiful Cotman view, or old Crome, from the Roman camp west over the flat.'

He was most generous to all who came to him, and to his colleagues. 'Liddon,' he once explained,[2] 'used to walk round and round the quad to get rid of insomnia, and I often came across him then.' As a neutral subject they then stuck to Dante. York Powell was a champion of Freeman, his dead friend. As a consequence he had no relations with Froude during his professorship. He did not know him personally, nor did he call upon him.

As a lecturer York Powell was unco-ordinated but rich in veins. His style of writing, as indicated in his reviews, tended to be stilted and of his period. 'Death,' he wrote in a review of Pasolini's *Catherine Sforza*, 'was ever lurking behind the pictured arras or in the silver cup.' In his letters he was much more natural. 'My garden[3] is full of marigolds, and the grass copper-green after the rain.' Rather surprisingly in his later life he supported the Boer war very strongly; he was always in tune with what the people thought. In his life cheerfulness came breaking out as in his song about the undergraduates of the old days, *Regnante Carolo*[4].

> The Provost, Dean and Dons likewise
> Sometimes desired to know
> What was the meaning of their cries
> That sometimes woke the midnight skies
> *Regnante Carolo* . . .

He was the most generous and unself-seeking of men. He loved the poor. He was one of the founders of Ruskin College. 'I have,' he wrote,[5] 'just ordered a lovely glass ball, perfectly turned. I have a passion for them. I have longed for years for one and now I hope to have it.' This was presumably the fruit of his professor's salary. 'I got,' he went on, 'one imperfectly turned, with a flat

---

[1] *Ibid.*, i, p. 223.
[2] *Ibid.*, i, p. 129.
[3] *Ibid.*, ii, p. 107.
[4] *Ibid.*, ii, p. 394.
[5] *Ibid.*, i, p. 335.

piece to stand on, 2/6 the other day.' There is something appealing in his low scale of expenditure. He wrote also in the same letter: 'Work *looms* ahead enormous like a monster of the deep, or an iceberg of appalling height and depth and weight and chill. It has got to be collared somehow.'

4

The End of Dollinger

During all the Gladstone years Döllinger had been in the background of Acton's life. Since his excommunication in 1871 he had lived quietly in Munich, giving an external support to the Old Catholic grouping, whose body he never joined. He died in that city on 14 December 1890 when approaching his ninety-first birthday; he was attended on his deathbed by his friend Dr Friedrich, who was one of the leaders of the Old Catholic communion.

Lord Acton at once settled down to write a long article, which was printed in the *English Historical Review* and was intended to take its place in a biographical study. It was entitled 'Döllinger's Historical Work'. Curiously enough it makes no reference at all to the Old Catholics. It appears to have been the only part of the book which was ever completed. Its particular interest depends upon its date; it belongs to that later period of Acton's life in which it can be said that his judgment had been settled. He was by now far from his period of discipleship and his views can be held to be objective. The chief value of this article is not so much for its account of Döllinger, but rather as an indication of the standpoint which Acton had by this time reached. He was now nearing sixty and it seems unlikely that his opinions on the historical questions which he treated were liable to any further change.

Fairly extensive quotation is required to bring out the flavour. It has in many ways the quality of the writings of a *revenant*.[1]

It was an epoch in which the layman and the *dilettante* prevailed. . . . The best traditions of western scholarship had died

[1] 'Döllinger's Historical Work', *Essays on Liberty*, p. 375.

away when the young Franconian obtained a chair in the re-organised university of Munich. His own country, Bavaria, his time, the third decade of the century, furnished no guide, no master, and no model to the young professor. Exempt, by date and position, from the discipline of a theological party, he so continued and never turned elsewhere for the dependence he escaped at home. No German theologian, of his own or other churches, bent his course.

Acton's style has an unusual simplicity as he records[1] his teacher's youth.

> Very young he knew modern languages well, though with a defective ear, and having no local or contemporary attachments he devoted himself systematically to the study of foreign divines. The characteristic universality of his later years was not the mere result of untiring energy and an unlimited command of books. His international habit sprang from the inadequacy of the national supply, and the search for truth in every century naturally became a lecturer whose function it was to unfold from first to last the entire life of the Church, whose range extended over all Christian ages, and who felt the inferiority of his own.

After a short comment[2] on the influence of Savigny, the account continues:[3]

> The first eminent thinker whom he saw and heard was Baader, the poorest of writers, but the most instructive and impressive talker in Germany, and the one who appears to have influenced the direction of his mind. . . . He probably owed to him his persistent disparagement of Hegel, and more certainly that familiarity with the abstruse literature of mysticism which made him as clear and sure of vision in the twilight of Petrucci and St Martin as in the congenial company of Duperron. . . . When the ancient mystic welcomed his new friend, he was full

[1] *Ibid.*
[2] *Ibid.*, pp. 376–7.
[3] Georg Friedrich Wilhelm Hegel (1770–1831), Friedrich Karl von Savigny (1779–1861) and Franz Xavier von Baader (1765–1841) were roughly contemporaries. Joseph de Maistre (1753–1821) and Louis Claude de St Martin (1743–1803) belonged to the preceding generation. Pier Matteo Petrucci (d. 1701) and Cardinal du Perron (d. 1618) worked in the seventeenth century.

of the praises of De Maistre. He impressed upon his earnest listener the importance of the books on the Pope and on the Gallican church, and assured him that the spirit which animates them is the genuine Catholicism. These conversations were the origin of Döllinger's specific ultramontanism.

When one comes across this word 'ultramontanism' one must always be careful of the sense in which men use it, and from this care Acton is not exempt. What Mr Gladstone and Lord Granville meant by 'ultramontanism' was a certain political attitude closely linked to Vatican politics. This was very far at any time from Dr Döllinger's opinions. He was also deeply conservative[1] on every question dealing with the structure of modern Germany. He was as far as Acton from any interest in the great mystical tradition stemming from St Teresa and St John of the Cross. Petrucci, who was referred to, had been condemned for Molinism.

From his early reputation,[2] and his position at the outpost, confronting Protestant science, he was expected to make up his mind over a large area of unsettled thought and disputed fact, and to be provided with an opinion – a freehold opinion of his own – and a reasoned answer to every difficulty. People had a right to know what he knew about the end of the sixteenth chapter of St Mark, and the beginning of the eighth chapter of St John, the lives of St Patrick and the sources of Erigena, the author of the *Imitation* and of the *Twelve Articles*, the *Nag's Head* and the *Casket Letters*.

It is remarkable how many of these problems belonged to the English-speaking world. St Patrick and Erigena were of Irish *provenance*. The *Casket Letters* related to the Queen of Scots and the *Nag's Head* was a very specialized subject, th libels relating to the consecration of Archbishop Parker.

The suspense and poise of the mind [it is explained in reference to Döllinger], which is the pride and privilege of the

---

[1] Cf. a comment by Alexander Dru in *The Church in the Nineteenth Century: Germany 1800–1918*, p. 89. 'Döllinger had begun his career as an ultramontane and a conservative, and had never, except on a quite superficial level, belonged to the romantic school with which he had grown up.'

[2] 'Döllinger's Historical Work', *Essays on Liberty*, pp. 382–3.

unprofessional scholar, was forbidden him. Students could not wait for the master to complete his studies; they flocked for the dry light of knowledge, for something defined and final, to their keen, grave, unemotional professor, who said sometimes more than he could be sure of, but who was not likely to abridge thought by oracular responses, or to give aphorism for argument.

The following passage is in a sense the key to this whole long article.[1] 'As an historian, Döllinger regarded Christianity as a force more than a doctrine, and displayed it as it expanded and became the soul of later history. It was the mission and occupation of his life to discover and to disclose how this was accomplished, and to understand the history of civilised Europe, religious and profane, mental and political, by the aid of sources which, being original and authentic, yielded certainty.' Two phrases are worth a longer consideration. It is clear that Döllinger regarded Christianity as a force rather than a series of doctrines, and the reference to the aid of sources yielding certainty is characteristic of the positive cast of Acton's mind. A historian who gives such weight to moral judgment should have a greater power of understanding different types, the men and women of the Renaissance for example, than Acton had.

The account[2] of Döllinger's early published work is exact and brief. 'The four volumes of *Church History* which gave him a name in literature appeared between 1833 and 1838, and stopped short of the Reformation. In writing mainly for the horizon of seminaries, it was desirable to eschew voyages of discovery and the pathless border-land. The materials were all in print, and were the daily bread of scholars.'

Acton then refers[3] to an illuminating episode. 'Döllinger, who had in youth acted as secretary to Hohenlohe,[4] was always reserved in his use of the supernatural.' This member of that great family was a priest of hectic and unbalanced judgment given to the idea of miracles and their multiplication. It is not surprising that

[1] *Ibid.*, p. 383.
[2] *Ibid.*, p. 384.
[3] *Ibid.*, p. 385.
[4] Prince Alexander of Hohenlohe/W/S (1794–1849), for the last five years of his life Bishop of Sardica.

he offended Döllinger's granite thought. It comes natural to us to read that 'he deplored the uncriticial credulity of the author of the *Monks of the West.*'[1]

We are then given certain elements of our subject's background. 'He was moved,' we are told,[2] 'not by the gleam of reform after the conclave of Pius IX, but by Pius VII. The impression made upon him by the character of that Pope, and his resistance to Napoleon, had much to do with his resolution to become a priest. He took orders in the Church in the days of revival, as it issued from oppression and the eclipse of hierarchy; and he entered its service in the spirit of Sailer, Cheverus, and Doyle. The mark of that time never left him.'

And again,[3] 'it was natural to associate him [Döllinger] with the men whom the early promise of a reforming Pope inspired to identify the cause of free societies with the Papacy which had Rosmini for an adviser, Ventura for a preacher, and Gioberti for a prophet, and to conclude that he thus became a trusted representative, until the revolving years found him the champion of a vanished cause, and the *Syllabus* exposed the illusion and bore away his ideal.'

The third passage[4] is rather different. 'Döllinger used to commemorate his visit to Rome in 1857 as an epoch of emancipation. He had occasionally been denounced; and a keen eye had detected latent pantheism in his *Vorhalle*, but he had not been formally censured. If he had once asserted the value of nationality in the Church, he was vehement against it in religion; and if he had joined in deprecating the dogmatic decree[5] in 1854, he was silent afterwards.' This was rather far from what Acton had said in his early Roman journeys. As he looked back in his late maturity, a *couleur de rose* spread over the situation.

The references to Döllinger's interest in English life and thought are many. 'After his last visit to the Marciana,[6] he thought more favourably of Father Paul [Sarpi], sharing the admiration which

---

[1] Montalembert.
[2] 'Döllinger's Historical Work', *Essays on Liberty*, p. 402.
[3] *Ibid.*, pp. 397–8.
[4] *Ibid.*, p. 410.
[5] The dogma of the Immaculate Conception.
[6] 'Döllinger's Historical Work', *Essays on Liberty*, p. 432.

Venetians feel for the greatest writer of the Republic. . . . The intermediate seekers, who seem to skirt the borders, such as Grotius, Ussher, Praetorius, and the other celebrated Venetian, De Dominis, interested him deeply in connection with the subject of Irenics.' In regard to Döllinger's reading we are told[1] that 'he possessed the English divines in perfection, at least down to Whitby,[2] and the non-jurors'. There are two other passages,[3] which are rather similar. 'He held to the epistles of St Ignatius with the tenacity of a Caroline prelate, and was grateful to De Rossi for a chronological point in their favour.' On the same page it is explained that 'his censure of the Reformation had been not as that of Bossuet, but as that of Baxter and Bull.'

There are valuable points on his attitude towards the Lutherans. It is simplest, perhaps, to place these together.[4] 'He believed so far in the providential mission of Protestantism, that it was idle to talk of reconciliation until it had borne all its fruit.' And again 'in cases of collision with the Church, he said that a man should seek the error in himself: but he spoke of the doctrine of the universal Church, and it did not appear that he thought of any living voice or present instructor'. From Harnack he received the greatest praise.

There is an interesting comment[5] in the work of his old age. 'When,' Acton writes, 'he began to fix his mind on the constitutional history of the Church, he proposed to write, first, on the times of Innocent XI. It was the age he knew best, in which there was most interest, most material, most ability, when divines were national classics, and presented many distinct types of religious thought, when biblical and historical science was founded, and Catholicism was presented in its most winning guise. The character of Odescalchi impressed him, by his earnestness in sustaining a strict morality. Fragments of this projected work reappeared in his lectures on Louis XIV, and in his last publication on the Casuists. The lectures betray the decline of the tranquil idealism which had been the admiration and despair of friends.'

---

[1] *Ibid.*, p. 388.
[2] Daniel Whitby (1638–1726), prebendary of Salisbury.
[3] 'Döllinger's Historical Work', *Essays on Liberty*, p. 416.
[4] *Ibid.*, pp. 416, 422 and 434.
[5] *Ibid.*, p. 433.

These passages are printed rather for the light that they throw on Acton than for an assessment of his former teacher. The article has another interest since it gives the final form of Acton's doctrine on moral responsibility. 'The study,' so this paragraph begins,[1] 'of intricate and subtle character was not habitual with Döllinger, and the result was an extreme dread of unnecessary condemnation. He resented being told that Ferdinand I and II, that Henry III and Louis XIII, were, in the coarse terms of modern life, assassins; that Elizabeth tried to have Mary made away with, and that Mary, in matters of that kind, had no greater scruples; that William III ordered the extirpation of a clan, and rewarded the murderers as he had rewarded those of De Witt; that Louis XIV sent a man to kill him, and James II was privy to the Assassination Plot.'

Acton lived in the peaceful years of the late nineteenth century, in the heyday of the *Pax Britannica*. He used the term 'assassins' and condemned men equally. He did not distinguish between the different periods and made no allowance for that reason of state which had an influence on the three Renaissance Queens, Catherine de Medicis, Elizabeth I and Mary Stuart. He makes no allowance for the circumstances in which that motive died away. He judged always by those standards which the Victorian Age had taken over from the eighteenth century. Among all the cases cited the only one which could be judged in such a way was the responsibility for the massacre of the Macdonalds of Glencoe; presumably this could be apportioned between the Master of Stair and his Dutch sovereign. If these judgments are, perhaps, less complete than in his earlier notes and writings, they are for that reason more defensible. This comment on Döllinger was similar to that which Acton made in regard to Mandell Creighton's work. As a purely personal judgment my sympathies are with Döllinger and Creighton and not with Acton. It has always seemed to me that this need to judge was the fruit of too much solitude or to put it more exactly the result of a vigorous social life in which he had had no contact with contemporary historians.

This whole article, however, has a calm which is absent from Acton's earlier writings. It is fresh and in no way overloaded.

[1] *Ibid.*, p. 410.

Perhaps this was because he was writing about an old man from whom he had grown apart. He looked back with a tranquillity, which was very rare in him, to the days when he himself had been a pupil. It seems to carry in its peaceful phrasing the essence of what Acton brought to Cambridge.

5

Cambridge

It was at the beginning of the summer term in 1895 that Lord Acton came to Cambridge to take up his position as regius professor of modern history. The chair carried with it a fellowship at Trinity, and he was allocated a set of rooms in that college in Neville's Court. He also took a large house in Cambridge called 'Birnam' and there installed his family.

The most recent change in the life of the university in Victorian times had been occasioned by the passing in 1878 of the *Revised Statutes*. These allowed fellows to marry and still retain their college fellowships. Year by year new roads developed in the former open lands across the Cam. The large families of the period already provided a growing population of children, and among the little girls was Rose Macaulay. Sedgwick Avenue was being made and called the New Road. In this area there arose the new buildings of Newnham College. We can obtain an impression of the life of Cambridge families from the memoirs of Gwen Raverat,[1] who gives an account of the house of her childhood, the garden stretching to the river by Silver Street bridge and Foster's Mill. Inside the house a new bathroom was installed with a large bath cased in mahogany. There was gas-light in the corridors and bedrooms, and a Colza oil lamp in the drawing-room. The dining room was still lit by candle light.

The Cambridge cattle market was held on Mondays. The corn sacks came in from the country in great yellow carts; the barges came upstream to Foster's Mill. The Great Eastern railway services were good and there was an occasional Great Northern train whose advantages were canvassed. Outside Cambridge station stood the lines of slow four-wheelers.

[1] *Period Piece, A Cambridge Childhood* by Gwen Raverat (1952).

Lord Acton had had one friend at Cambridge in his middle life, the great jurist Sir Henry Maine, with whom he had been brought into contact by Sir M. Grant Duff. Acton's first letter[1] from him that survives was written in 1877, the year that Maine returned to Cambridge as Master of Trinity Hall. There is evidence that Acton was invited with his daughter to visit the Lodgings there in 1884; but it is not clear whether he accepted. Maine had, however, died in 1888.

When Lord Acton came to take over the regius chair, it was not the first time that a Cambridge professorship had been proposed to him. Just four years earlier the newly-founded Dixie chair of ecclesiastical history had been rendered vacant by the promotion of Canon Creighton, the first holder, to the see of Peterborough. Oscar Browning, a tormented character, who had been settled at King's College since his dismissal from Eton by Dr Hornby some twenty years before, busied himself about the matter. He wrote[2] to Acton and the letter, like everything from Browning's pen, was hardly tactful. He explained that he had already approached S. R. Gardiner, an extraordinary choice for an ecclesiastical professorship, and had been refused. 'The stipend,' wrote Browning, 'is £500 a year besides a fellowship at Emmanuel, which I suppose would be £300 more.' He admitted that there was a local candidate, H. M. Gwatkin, then lecturer in theology at St John's, but stated that 'he was felt not to be the right man'. He had been passed over when Dr Creighton had been appointed.

There is some evidence that the Bishop of Peterborough felt that Acton might like it; but prudently he refused to stand. He would have been corralled in the special field of ecclesiastical history and he would have had Professor Seeley as the head of his department. When he came in 1895 he was quite free.

Acton was pursued by letters from Oscar Browning throughout his years at Cambridge. Twenty-three letters and a postcard from Stralsund still survive. Wherever he was, whether in England or abroad, Browning always wrote on King's College notepaper with the college arms upon the envelope. He belonged to a generation

[1] The letters are in the ninth bundle of Lord Acton's correspondence, now in the custody of Douglas Woodruff.
[2] Letter dated 4 March 1891 in the sixth bundle of correspondence addressed to Lord Acton.

which did not yet conceal its taste for aristocracy; he liked asking favours from a lord. He was perfectly uninhibited and carried on a running feud against Professor Gwatkin, who had been appointed to the Dixie chair. He tried without success to involve Acton in his feuds. Then he sought for his judgment on the relations (if any) between Sieyès and Robespierre. One of his notes has a quite lush account of how he met a Hohenzollern prince. He shows no understanding of Lord Acton.

Acton was particularly fortunate in his two fellow-professors, who dealt with aspects of historical study in the University. Frederic William Maitland, although still a young man,[1] had held the Downing chair of the Laws of England since 1888 and was in process of completing his *magnum opus* on the history of English Law before the time of Edward I, which was published in the next year as the widely-known 'Pollock and Maitland'. Belonging to the Law School he was quite independent of Lord Acton; but they had throughout these years a perfectly harmonious relationship of mutual respect. With the holder of the Dixie chair his links were naturally much closer.

Henry Melvill Gwatkin was born in 1844 and was thus just ten years Lord Acton's junior. He was the son of the Rector of Barrow-on-Soar, a living in the East Midlands. He had come up to St John's College as a schoolboy in 1863 and had lived there ever since. He had taken holy orders when appointed to the Dixie chair; but all his life he had been deeply Evangelical. His favourite work was his readings in the Greek Testament, which he gave to a group of undergraduates. There was a certain resemblance here to Dr Coulton. His principal publication was his *Studies in Arianism*, which had been issued a good many years previously. He had a very happy marriage with a delicate and ailing wife. His chief recreation was the study of conchology. In his later life he divided the summer vacation between supplying in some country vicarage to enable the incumbent to take a holiday and examining the south coast between Lyme Regis and Land's End, searching for shells.

It is probable that because of the grapevine in the life of the University he knew how Acton had refused to act when Browning

[1] He was born in 1850.

M

tried to exclude him from the Dixie chair. This would have left him prejudiced in Acton's favour. At any rate their relations were set fair and were full of kindness until the end.

Gwatkin in his first surviving letter[1] applauded Lord Acton's decision not 'to lecture (except Inaugural) before October'. He and his wife were always inviting Acton to their house at 8 Scrope Terrace. He had a close personal care for the new professor. Thus he wrote in the next year. 'Sorry to hear *teste idonea gypissa tua* – on the evidence of your "gyp" – that you have been out of order.'

The letters were naturally more frequent during the vacations. There were the usual questions as to the University régime, the normal difficulties about the frontiers between the Classical and History Schools. A letter from Gwatkin written from Brantham Rectory near Manningtree in the Easter vacation of 1897 bears on this matter. 'I am anxious,' he wrote,[2] 'also to get at the post-classical part of the Ancient History. It is my walk, if anything is: and there is no small risk that it may be properly done by a classical man . . .[then apparently on some proposed lectures] I lean to declining it, for Edward VI is not a very specially strong subject of mine. I do not suppose I know of it a quarter of what Mullinger knows of Mary. . . .' The final sentence suggests a peaceful scene. 'I get into the quiet away here, alone in the house, with no definite occupation but the Sunday duty.'

There is a letter in the next year in the summer term. 'How,' he wrote[3] from 8 Scrope Terrace, 'to hook on John of Salisbury, by the tail, I fear is the only way. Mullinger knows that ground in a way that I do not, so he will be the best counsellor. . . . Cram full of work. Heaviest bit of the year. I hope the Council will like *our* statement [on History School requirements].' The summer term was barely ended and Professor Gwatkin wrote[4] again from a house that he had taken, 'Fairlight' at Paignton. 'Beasts for ever,' he began in reference to his collection of *radulae*, 'and the University and all its works be anathema. I got dead tired on the rocks this morning and had a fine haul of beasts. I could hardly crawl back.' He was a cheerful man.

[1] Letter dated 26 February 1895.
[2] Letter dated 31 March 1897.
[3] Letter dated 2 May 1898.
[4] Letter dated 20 June 1898.

This friendship, full of concern and care, lasted all through the Cambridge years. A letter during the autumn[1] of 1900 bears this out. 'What do you say to coming here [to 8 Scrope Terrace] for Tuesday night.' It is clear that 'Birnam' was for the moment closed. 'You would be further from your work, but you would be better looked after than in college. We would be very glad to have you.'

Much of Lord Acton's life in the University was dominated by the development of the project of the *Cambridge Modern History*; but before dealing with this subject we should touch on certain other aspects of his professorship on which light is thrown by his correspondence. He was clearly a supporter of women's education at Cambridge. Three letters survive[2] from the principal of Newnham College. In one Lord Acton is invited to join the council of the college, and it is pointed out that the commitment is not heavy, involving only five meetings in each academic year. On a more homely level he was asked to judge the essays which the Newnham students doing History could send in for an annual prize.

Lord Acton had in these years full play for the exercise of his erudition. Two examples will describe this situation. Towards the end of his term of office Adolphus Ward asked for his judgment on a series of letters between Count Konigsmarck and the Princess of Hanover which had just been discovered. Acton took the view that the letters from Konigsmarck were in the Count's own handwriting 'and [that] those from Sophie-Dorothée were more doubtful'. A question of more importance had been submitted to him in 1893 by Hastings Rashdall, a young Fellow of Hertford College, Oxford, who was hardly known to him. This scholar had been working for ten years on *The Universities of Europe in the Middle Ages*. Rashdall explained that in his opinion the accepted view that the sympathies of the University of Paris in the 1420s were Burgundian was not correct. He, on the other hand, had come to

[1] Letter dated 3 November 1900.
[2] These are in the first bundle and were dated 27 October 1896 and 15 January 1898. There was also a third note from the Principal dated 5 March 1896. 'Miss Gladstone and I have attended [at your lectures] regularly. I do not think that any others of the staff go.' The reference to Mr Gladstone's daughter Helen perhaps indicates how this contact first began.

hold that the secular clergy at the University were on the whole Orleanist rather than Burgundian. He sought for Acton's judgment on this point.

These Cambridge years were also the time when Acton's attendance at his London breakfast and dining clubs became more regular. He belonged both to Grillion's and the Dilettanti, but according to Sir M. Grant Duff's notes he was most regular at the Club and Breakfast Club. The latter was the more informal type of gathering. The members came together in the house of one of their number whose family were allowed to take part in the proceedings. During the Cambridge years Acton was present at meetings which took place at Herbert's, Herschell's and Courtney's houses and on two occasions at Lord Reay's. For the most part these took place in term-time and Acton probably passed the previous night at the Athenaeum.

The meetings of the Club had fluctuating numbers. On one occasion there were only four, Acton, Trevelyan, Grant Duff and Lord Carlisle. Grant Duff, in his *Diaries*, gives examples of Lord Acton's phrases culled from both these quarters. 'At this meeting,' he writes in connection with a gathering of the Breakfast Club, 'Acton quoted a saying of Moltke's as containing a very magnificent boast within an expression of self-depreciation. "Oh! don't think of comparing me to Napoleon: I never had to retrieve a disaster." ' This is paralleled by another phrase from a Club meeting. 'Acton said that he had undoubted authority for Flahaut's statement when leaving Waterloo. "*Ça a toujours été arrivé depuis Crécy.*" '

It seems that there were only two other historians at these Club meetings, the Bishop of Peterborough and Lecky. Acton and his contemporaries were now ageing; they thought back on their own pasts. Acton spoke of an article by the King of Roumania throwing light on the origins of the Franco-Prussian war as seen from the Hohenzollern *schloss* at Sigmaringen. Sir Henry Elliot spoke of the personage known as Garibaldi's Englishman, who had been heard saying 'And to think that I should have come out from England to serve under a mad attorney'. Lacaita had said that Ferdinand of Naples knew 78,000 men in his army by name; the King's power of gaining over and fascinating people was quite extraordinary. Acton was growing old and his mind went back to the days of conflict.[1] There are many reasons for concluding that these years at Cambridge were the happiest of his life.

[1] All these details come from the *Diaries* of Sir Mountstuart Grant Duff. Of course they only record the meetings which Grant Duff himself attended and also those stories which were told in his presence. Before Acton went to Cambridge the Breakfast Club met in his house in London on 12 June 1887. His attendance is noted most frequently in 1896 and 1897. The last dates on which Lord Acton's presence was noted were 13 May and 25 May, meetings of the Breakfast Club and Grillion's; and 26 June 1900, a dinner at the Club.

6

The Cambridge Modern History

The years that Acton spent at the University were dominated by the planning of the *Cambridge Modern History*. This formidable series has always lain across the background of the historical studies of the Englishmen of the older generation who gave themselves to the work of Modern History. Looking back now it seems to have had many of the qualities of an ironclad; the workmanship was really excellent. It has an especial interest in Lord Acton's life, for the completion of the first volume, which was launched on 1 November 1902, marks the final period of his career; but the series itself now bears the lasting imprint of Adolphus Ward. Nor did the idea of the *Cambridge Modern History* originate in Acton's mind. It was a project of the Syndics of the University Press, the body charged with publications, and was conceived in the first place as a universal history.

The idea had been pared down to a series of volumes carrying the history of Europe and also of the United States from the time of the Renaissance until the close of the nineteenth century. The conception of the Renaissance as a turning-point was at that date dominated by the work of Burckhardt.[1] Acton's responsibilities lay in planning and in the selection of contributors. It is of interest that he made it clear he wished these to be chosen wherever possible 'from among British historians'.

Before coming to the complex of writers of history linked for the most part with either British or American universities, it is perhaps best to begin with Acton's contact and correspondence with the only proposed English contributor who was outside their circle, Dom Aidan Gasquet.

[1] Jacob Burckhardt (1818–1897), the Basle historian, the first edition of whose *Die Kultur der Renaissance in Italien* had been printed in 1860.

358

The first letter to Lord Acton deals with quite a different subject and is in some ways rather unexpected. It is a courageous remonstrance from someone who did not know his correspondent very well. It dealt with the annual liquefaction of the blood of St Januarius at Naples. 'Twice since I have been in Rome,' Dom Gasquet wrote[1] from San Silvestro *in Capite* on 20 April 1896, 'I have heard people speak about the Miracle of St Januarius' blood, as being a "well ascertained mystification practised on people". The second time I heard you given as the authority for the statement. I said that I was quite certain that there was some mistake and that I felt sure you never could have spoken of any deliberate fraud practised by the clergy of Naples in this matter.'

So far the question was clear enough. A belief in the miracle of the liquefaction of the blood of the principal patron of the city was one of the many things that linked the Bourbon princes with the *Lazzaroni*. The two phials had been present in their chapel since 1497 and it will be remembered that the Duchess of Dalberg had expressed her belief in the miraculous character of the event.

The circumstances behind the story are described by Gasquet in these terms. 'As far as I have been able,' he wrote, 'to trace the story, it is that Mrs Renouf states that her brother Professor Franz Brentano had said that he was assured by Lord Acton that when the pious Countess Arco-Valley was in Naples the priest who exhibited the relic of St Januarius' blood to her explains how the mystification was practised on the people and how the reliquary was handled to produce the effect.' The phrase 'the pious' has a jarring note, and would a priest have given himself away to a Bavarian *grande dame*, who was a stranger to him?

The letter ends as follows. 'The question of the miracle is to my mind altogether a different one from the question of ecclesiastical fraud in the matter and I shall be very glad if you will let me say – as I feel absolutely sure must be the case – that you have been represented altogether wrongly. I am, as you perhaps know, here on the very dreary question of Anglican orders and so cannot find the time I should like to work in the archives.' Lord Acton, it appears, was not alleged to have attacked the *Curia* of the arch-

---

[1] This and the subsequent letters are in the first bundle of Lord Acton's correspondence.

diocese of Naples. He had passed his time with the anti-clerical exiles of the *intelligentsia* of that city, who had come to England. What he had actually said we do not know. He was always admirably courteous to Father Gasquet.

Francis Aidan (later Cardinal) Gasquet seems always to have been devoted to serving the interests of his Church. His historical studies were invariably undertaken for some ulterior purpose. The conception of pure history was unknown to him. He had a quality of charm, but without humility. He gained and retained the shy affection and devoted service of Edmund Bishop, that self-effacing scholar. Acton he never really understood or he would not have 'tailored' his correspondence, when he was dead.

Gasquet's regular monastic life in England had ended in 1885 and the three remaining letters in this collection were all written at 4 Great Ormond Street. They were sent at two years' intervals and the first was despatched on 9 December 1896. 'Your idea,' Dom Gasquet wrote, 'for my contribution to your proposed first volume [of the *Cambridge Modern History*] would I think "suit me down to the ground" as they say. I have often thought over and sketched in my imagination some such study of Catholic England, just before the Reformation.' In the next letter[1] he pointed out that the great difficulty was the small space that was allowed him. By October 1900 it is clear that some draft had been submitted. 'I do not,' wrote Gasquet, 'really understand what you have done. If you could cross out the passages which seem to you to have "the note of contention" the thing would be done.' In fact his contribution was never published and it seems unlikely that it was completed. The subject in the first volume was dealt with by Canon Barry.

From about this time Gasquet's historical work was gradually becoming crowded out. He always had a dulled imagination and he was soon, surely unconsciously, engaged in building up his kingdoms in this world. His interest in Vatican-British politics engaged him. He always had a great effect on ladies of position and, more surprisingly, on the members of the Howard family. His funeral took place in Santa Maria *in Trastevere*. The church was packed with members of religious orders and by the English-

---

[1] Letter dated 18 March 1898.

speaking Roman a colony; group of the Sacred College were mourning behind their *grille*. There we may leave the Cardinal of Santa Maria in Portico *in Campitelli*.

Acton also made an offer to his old friend Peter Renouf, who had retired from the keepership of the department of Egyptian and Assyrian antiquities at the British Museum in 1891 on reaching seventy. The proposal, like the one to Gasquet, did not materialize, but Pembroke College library contains letters which are marked by Lord Acton's flowing ideas on history. Renouf had gained distinction as an Egyptologist and Oriental scholar but Acton looked back to the ideas that both had held at the time of the Council.

Acton wrote[1] from Munich in an *excursus* on the *Cambridge Modern History*:

> My plan is to break through the mere juxtaposition of national histories and to take in, as far as may be, what is extra-territorial and universal. So there is a chapter on the Suppression of the Jesuits. It requires an understanding of their great standing controversies and the part they had played in the Church, in society, in literature, and their missions and the disputes that arose out of their then kingdom in Paraguay. [He then continued with his catalogue] . . . their attempted conversion of China; the uprising against them in Southern Europe; Pombal, Spain, France expelling them, the suppression and the fortunes of the suppressed. Would you undertake to tell this story?

This was a coherent plan, but one which in the end was not accepted. The next proposition seems to me less carful. 'It is my plan,' he went on, 'to define chapters not by a limit of years, but by some salient point and catchword. So on Lewis XIV, a chapter on Nimwegen and what pertains to it, and then on 1688 and the Grand Alliance. Then ten years later one (chapter) called in my setting the Gallican System, that is to say the growth thereof, the Jansenist intrusion, the 4 articles, the (English) Revolution, the strange picture of the Pope who preferred Jansenists to Jesuits and a Protestant Revolution to legitimate Catholicism.' It must be said that this is hardly a balanced judgment on Pope Innocent XI.

[1] Letter from the Renouf MSS at Pembroke College, Oxford.

M*

The next phrases deal with theological opinions, not one of Lord Acton's favourite subjects. 'The parallel movement in theology,' he went on, 'after Holden and Davenport to Dupin,[1] the corresponding advance of Leibniz, and the shock administered to the whole by Lewis and Bossuet, in consequence the quarrel with Rome and with the Emperor.

'Here also there is much unwritten history to write and new and absorbing material. Which would you prefer for yourself and when could it be done? For the second part [the French chapter] my second choice would be Duchesne.[2] But I want as few foreigners as possible and he is almost certain to refuse.'

Acton returned to England and wrote[3] again from Trinity College. 'I have just finished my lectures and my examinations, and am able to devote my time to all that relates to the work in which I am to have the happiness of being aided and abetted by you. . . . Of course it all [the contribution] centres round the years 1760–1775. The rest is summary. The discussion of tyrannicide, and what pertains thereto, comes elsewhere in a chapter on the theories of the time of the *Ligue* and need not trouble you as a substantial topic.'

All this was evanescent. The chapter was never written, for Acton was dead before the later volumes were even arranged. His successors adopted a system that was strictly chronological. Renouf had been knighted in 1896 and he died four months after receiving this second letter. One reflection crosses the mind. Was he a competent historian for dealing with either of the periods which were offered to him?

The lives of these two non-contributors lay well outside the stream of academic history. The same may be said of de Blowitz,[4] *The Times* correspondent in Paris, who was asked to contribute without success. I am, however, not aware of any evidence that Acton was concerned in this venture.[5] The rest of the surviving

[1] Henry Holden (1596–1662), professor at the Sorbonne, Christopher Davenport (1597–1680), F. Franciscus a Sancta Clara, and Louis Ellies Du Pin (1657–1719).

[2] Louis-Marie-Olivier Duchesne (1843–1922), Director of the French School in Rome from 1895.

[3] Letter dated 8 June 1897.

[4] Henry-Georges-Stephen-Adolphe Opper de Blowitz (1825–1903), who adopted his name from his birthplace, Blowitz in Bohemia.

[5] Cf. 'The origins of the *Cambridge Modern History*' by G. N. Clark, the *Cambridge Historical Journal*, vol. viii, no. 2, 1965, p. 63.

correspondence relates to those within the academic stream. The final entry relating to the establishment of this project was made in the minutes[1] of the Syndics of the University Press on 13 March 1896. It is curious to find Acton writing[2] to R. L. Poole that 'there is no real difficulty about time', when time and space were to prove the two main problems.

The whole correspondence was carried on in an atmosphere of calm and sunny weather. Acton was at last appreciated by his equals and returned their cordial friendliness. This spirit may be compared with that of a letter written some twenty years earlier from St Martin in Austria to Renouf. It dealt with defects in the British Museum library;[3] but all such exacerbation was now behind him.

There were two main sections of the *History* which benefited from Acton's planning. These were the first volume called *The Renaissance* and with this went certain projects that overflowed into the second and third volumes, and then that called *The United States*. This was the seventh in the series, but the third in order of appearance; it had, besides other new matter, two chapters on the early history of Canada which Acton had not envisaged; he had, however, made the contracts with five of the authors of this volume.

It should be mentioned that at the beginning of his editorship Acton ranged over the whole scope of the *History*. He had been appointed as editor for the whole series and from time to time he would make suggestions to contributors that they should undertake chapters in the volumes dealing with the eighteenth and even the nineteenth centuries. This was particularly the case in the proposals that James Franck Bright, the Master of University College, should write on the Empress Maria Theresa and that Charles Oman should undertake a detailed study of the Peninsular Wars; the latter work in fact eventuated.

There remains a section of the correspondence with some of the contributors to the first two volumes. Acton himself proposed to

---

[1] Cf. *ibid.*

[2] MS. Corespondence of Acton to Poole.

[3] '1. Works of Bellarmine, Mohler, Niebuhr, Ranke missing. 2. English Catholic bibliography in Dodd shows hundreds of books missing. 3. Glaring defects in French section,' Acton's letter in Renouf MSS.

treat the Council of Trent, but he did not live even to begin this section. He did, however, compile a bibliography on this subject, and this he circulated as a specimen to his contributors. The letters on this subject throw a sharp light on Acton's outlook; but the subject is treated in great detail and most of the contemporary foreign historians, whom he mentions, are now forgotten in this country.

The choice among British historians for the sections on Venetian history was fore-ordained. Since 1862 the work of calendaring the State Papers relating to England in the archives at Venice had been carried out by two historians who had the same surname, but were not related. The elder, Rawdon Brown, had died in 1883 and had been replaced by the better-known Horatio Brown, then a young man.[1] He received Lord Acton's invitation. The letter in reply Brown wrote[2] from his house Ca' Torresella on the Zattere was full of warmth.

> Pray excuse me for not having answered your letter sooner. I am rather busy just now. I telegraphed a 'Yes' to Your most kind and flattering proposal, & I hope you received the telegram before you left Cambridge. I like the idea very much and will do my best to draw a full & coloured sketch of the Republic. As regards the first chapter I suppose I shall not be strictly bound to begin with the date of Lorenzo's death. 1492 is, I think, a little late. The reigns of Tommaso Mocenigo & Francesco Foscari 1414–1457 more nearly coincide with the highest point of Venetian development. But I imagine that in this first chapter I am to give a retrospect and a summing up. I have a letter to-day from Armstrong about the wars of the League of Cambray, & we must settle some definite line about them.
>
> The second chapter I think I understand about, though it will require some handling to weave the Turkish Wars, Father Paul (Sarpi) and the Valtelline into a consecutive narrative.... I am very much obliged to you for asking me to undertake it.

One pauses on the 'coloured'. What exactly does he mean? In fact Horatio Brown contributed two chapters to the *Cambridge*

[1] Horatio Forbes Brown (1854–1926). He was at this time occupied in covering the years 1581 to 1613.

[2] Fifth bundle among the Acton MSS.

Modern History. The first in the first volume on 'Venice' only took the story down to 1479. Later, after Acton's death, he wrote a chapter for the fourth volume on 'The Valtelline 1603–39'. The episode of Paolo Sarpi was treated in 'Papal Policy 1590–1648' by Moritz Busch.

The next letter linked with the same first period came from Edward Armstrong[1] at Queen's College, Oxford. It was a vague suggestion[2] that he might deal with the Medici Popes. Nearly three years passed and he is found writing again, this time on the bibliography of Savonarola. 'Here at last[3] is the Savonarola bibliography & a nasty fidgetty thing it is. . . . Of course there are heaps of biographies which I have not mentioned e.g. Bussante of the eighteenth century & Aquarone which was almost simultaneous with Villari and died still-born.' This letter was followed by another just three weeks later.[4]

I am most grateful for your suggestions as to Savonarola's bibliography.[5] I deliberately rejected Cantu's history because the account of Savonarola was very slight & Capponi[6] superseded him *ad hoc*. But I think that the essay in Cantu C. *Italiani Ilustri*, vol. iii, 1874, is well worth adding as Cantu is so representative an Italian. I hardly think that either Dr Herzog's *Real Encyclopadie* or Hergenrother's *Handbuch*, vol. ii, 1886 need be mentioned as they add nothing and their bibliography is of course not up to date –but if you think it might be convenient for Germans please throw them in. I have not been able to get Ferrari, nor the Venetian *Memorie* etc – but I almost think that I should have seen them quoted if at all important. Döllinger's account is, indeed, very slight, but on a topic as

---

[1] Edward Armstrong (1846–1928), Fellow of Queen's College from 1869. Pro-Provost 1911–22.

[2] Letter dated 15 November 1896, sixth bundle of the Acton MSS.

[3] Letter dated 23 February 1899, *ibid.*

[4] Letter dated 13 March 1899, *ibid.* Armstrong explained that it was his practice to lunch at the Red House and dine at Queen's. Acton on his visit stayed at the *Mitre*.

[5] Armstrong had his idea of the treatment of this chapter a little earlier. 'My idea,' he wrote on 17 March 1898, 'rather was to start him (Savonarola) as Prior of S. Marco with a few introductory lines. I then rattle along to 1494, then show his influence on Florentine & Italian politics, & his difficulties temporal and ecclesiastical & then kill him.'

[6] Capponi (1792–1876) and Cantu (1804–1895) were contemporaries.

essentially controversial people like to read the views of such a thinker.

It was natural that Martin Hume, who was making calendars from the archives of the Crown of Castile at Simancas, should also be asked to contribute to the *History*. This whole group was in constant contact and Armstrong, as an example, would go and stay in Venice with Horatio Brown.

We now come to the correspondence with Dr J. B. Bury, who then held the Erasmus Smith chair of Modern History at Trinity College, Dublin, and who was to become in time Lord Acton's successor. Acton proposed that Bury should come to Cambridge as professor of Ancient History; but Bury felt that he could not afford this. There was at that time always a difficulty about the salaries of the lesser chairs. On 5 April 1900 he wrote[1] to Acton about his chapter for the *History* which was now ready.

My chapter on the Ottomans (what is to be the title?), which I forward by this post runs to something more than the prescribed thirty pages – I think nearly to thirty-four. As it stands it is more compendious than I should have wished, and I don't well see how I can cut it down further without making it unreadable. Thirty pages is a small allowance for 75 years crowded with important events; especially as I have to set in some account of Ottoman Institutions. At the other end I have left my successor to tell of the Ottoman Navy & the sea expansions; Solyman's lordship in the western Mediterranean did not begin till after 1529, though the way was being prepared for it.

J. B. Bury's 'Ottoman Conquest' ends with the Battle of Mohacs in 1526. It seems to have been printed as he delivered it to Lord Acton.

It is now that the massive figure of Dr Adolphus Ward appears on the scene. It seems best to begin with the description given by Sir George Clark in his essay on 'The origin of the *Cambridge Modern History*'.[2]

From his earliest weeks he [Acton] had consulted a remarkable man, three years his junior, Adolphus William Ward.

[1] Sixth bundle among the Acton MSS in the custody of Douglas Woodruff.
[2] *Op. cit.*

Ward was a grand-nephew of Thomas Arnold of Rugby, and he had something of Arnold's driving force. An enthusiastic teacher and a conspicuously successful academic organiser, he always worked punctually and quickly. The son of a diplomatist and educated partly in Germany (at Leipzig where his father was consul general), he had a wide knowledge of modern history and had been strongly influenced by German historians, indeed in his literary style too strongly. Gradually Acton's enterprise came under the influence of Ward.

In 1897 Dr Ward resigned from his headship of Owens College, Manchester; but it appears that he made this move too soon, for it was not until 1900 that he was elected to the mastership of Peterhouse. During part of this time he acted as assistant editor of the *History*. But he found both the salary and influence inadequate and in time resigned. With the breakdown of Acton's health he took over from him. It is his mind that lies behind the *Cambridge Modern History*.

At the same time we cannot draw too sharp a line. Ward was the supporter of the idea of many chapters being contributed by a single worker and in the end he himself wrote eighteen chapters.

It would be attractive if Lord Acton could be presented as the defender of the idea of short contributions each written by a historian with a unique knowledge of the special field. He certainly played with this idea at times; but in 1897 he is found writing to James Ford Rhodes, the American historian, inviting[1] him to contribute three hundred pages, that is to say about a dozen chapters, on the history of the United States, for the seventh volume. The invitation was, however, not accepted.

In some ways Lord Acton's work on the *Cambridge Modern History* gives evidence that his habit of solitary thought was now unbreakable; he seems to have lost the power of consultation. During the Council and through the Gladstone years he had been in essence so much alone. He seems to have desired to finish what he had begun. Perhaps his age precluded him from the approach

[1] Letter from James Ford Rhodes (1840–1902) dated 7 January 1897 from 176 Newbury Street, Boston, in the fifth bundle of the Acton MSS. At about this period there is a letter from Captain Alfred Thayer Mahan, U.S.N. (1840–1914), agreeing to write chapters on U.S. Naval History from 1812 to 1865 inclusive. These were to contain 15,000 words; but they were apparently never completed.

of the quiet planner. In so many cases he had given an early date for the conclusion of a chapter, even one which would come quite late in the great series. He seems to have thought that the *History* would be completed some years before 1911. His concentration on the bibliographies was intensive; but he does not seem to have grasped the fact that, while the manuscript materials and the list of early printed books would remain of permanent value, the secondary modern sources would soon pass out of date.

Adolphus Ward should not be underestimated. He had a calm and balanced judgment and his chapters (the first serious historical work that I ever read) were smooth and competent. He was necessarily limited to the ideas of his time; but he brought his heavy task to a conclusion.

7

The Final Phase

This was the last period of the domination of the old political history, the varying appreciations of the cabinets of princes. The modern world was still encased in the old monarchies. In Europe the French Republic was the only exception among the Great Powers, which consisted at this time of the three empires and all the kingdoms. With the history of kingdoms there went the history of their treaties. The State Papers, which were in course of publication, were in great part a record of the reports of ambassadors.

Economic history and agrarian study were in their infancy. There is little evidence that they occupied Lord Acton's mind. Thorold Rogers, who till recently had held the Drummond chair of political economy at Oxford, had concluded in 1887 his six volumes of the *History of Agriculture and Prices*; but the understanding of their significance lay in the future. The history of Art had not yet come to occupy its territory. There was a marked interest in the characters of kings and their great ministers. This is, perhaps, only a way of saying that Lord Acton's detailed interests were of his time.

As his sickness[1] increased his mind went back to Tegernsee, where his wife was living. In his correspondence with James Bryce there is an account of his Bavarian home. In an undated letter he describes Tegernsee.[2]

In the Bavarian Alps there are seldom reasonably good inns at an Engadine elevation. If you will be content with two thousand five hundred feet above sea level, Tegernsee is the place for you. There is a decently good inn by the side of a

[1] Acton had high blood pressure leading to a stroke.
[2] Bryce MSS, volume of Acton Papers.

beautiful lake, with splendid mountains of six or seven thousand feet to scale, and endless walks in the forest. There is a villa there belonging to my kinsfolk [the Arcos], in which I have three or four thousand volumes at your service. It is only two hours from Munich.

This appears to have been written about 1884, because on 6 September of that year there is a note[1] from Acton, then at St Martin. 'I enclose a card which will induce the *Hausmeister* [at Tegernsee] to take you upstairs where my books are.' A brief note to help the traveller is much in character. 'Roberts, chemist in New Bond Street, nearly opposite Daniell's china shop, will sell you a little bottle of Dr Davidson of Florence's remedy for sea sickness. It is infallible.' In a sense his appointment to Cambridge strengthened again his links with Tegernsee. There was less opportunity for visits to the Riviera because of the autumn and spring terms, but there was time for Tegernsee in the long summers.

These years had also seen the failing health and death of Mr Gladstone. This must have had a very deep effect upon a Liberal of Acton's colour. There were certain elements in the Cambridge life which helped to render Acton less *political*. A Conservative Government was now in power and would continue so throughout the years which still remained to him. He had little contact with the new leaders of the Liberal Opposition. Gladstone's whole life had been bound up with the other seat of learning, 'the God-fearing and God-sustaining University of Oxford'. There was very little in his life at Cambridge to remind Acton of his old leader.

In 1897 had come the Diamond Jubilee, which in its various emphases seemed to mark the burial of the Gladstonian era. Lord Acton was still well thought of at the Court and received a knighthood of the Victorian Order (K.C.V.O.) on this occasion. Mr Gladstone was now dependent upon his family and on the friends of his old age, Lord Rendel and Mr Armitstead. That phalanx of Whig peers, which had for long stood round him in uneasy support, had disappeared; they had followed Hartington, now Duke of Devonshire, into opposition over the question of Home

[1] *Ibid.*

Rule. He was out of touch with the young ministers of his last Cabinet, like Grey and Asquith. Acton was one of the small number of Liberals still left in the House of Lords.

When Michaelmas term was over in that year he went out to Cannes, where the aged leader was staying with Lord Rendel in what Gladstone called his *palazzetta*, using once again the Italian or rather the Italianate phrases[1] of his years in Italy long ago. Acton and Gladstone did not meet again. The latter returned to England and went to Bournemouth, and then back to his own home. Mr Gladstone died in his big bedroom on the Castle's upper floors. The morning sun had just touched the policies of Hawarden; it was the feast of the Ascension.

He was buried in the Abbey and the Prince of Wales and Duke of York were among the pall bearers. This honour had been foreseen some ten years previously. When the Prince of Wales failed to come up from Sandringham to the funeral of Lord Iddesleigh, who had died while surrendering the seals of foreign secretary, Lady Geraldine Somerset, then in waiting to the Duchess of Cambridge, made an entry in her *Diary*. She expressed[2] her anger at 'the knowledge that had Heaven in mercy delivered us from the curse of Gladstone's existence, the Prince of Wales would have run, with ten special trains and twenty extra engines, and enveloped in yards and folds of crepe, to do honour to his funeral and curry favour with the plebs.' Mr Gladstone never knew how certain people hated him.

In these years Lord Acton turned back for the last time towards the Prussian world of scholarship. There survives a long letter[3] to James Bryce, dated at Cambridge on 18 January 1898, which is full of interesting details. 'Bamberger,[4] 18 Margaretenstrasse, Berlin,' he explained to Bryce, 'is one of the men you ought to meet. He was long in public life and is not only a German Liberal, which is nothing, but an English Liberal and a most independent witness of men and things in his own country. If you see him, pray mention to him how very sorry I am that he will not write my

---

1 *Palazzina* is the only diminutive of *palazzo* found in the dictionary.
2 The *Royal George* by Giles St Aubyn, p. 268.
3 *Bryce MSS*, Acton Letter Book, no. 100.
4 Ludwig Bamberger (1823–1899).

chapter on the German Empire since 1870. . . . Hans Delbruck[1] is the very opposite. . . . He was the Emperor's tutor, knows the inside of things and is a professing Liberal, but Imperialist and colonially expansive. He speaks perfect English.'

There was also a reference to the holder of the Berlin chair, 'my friend Max Lenz,[2] whose studies are chiefly modern and who represents the tradition of Ranke',[3] who had died recently at a great age. In conclusion Acton made this panegyric 'Harnack,[4] the foremost divine in the world, seeing divine things from the standpoint of critical erudition and somewhat indifferent to modern times, but unsurpassed in the Middle Ages and surpassing all men in earlier centuries.' This was, curiously enough, almost the last of Acton's positive judgments. The old historian's life was drawing to a close.

By this time Lord Acton's formal position as a leading English Catholic had been re-established. This was the work of Herbert Cardinal Vaughan, who had succeeded to the see of Westminster when Manning died in 1892. He had written to congratulate him on attaining the Cambridge history chair. The Cardinal had done a great work for the establishment of the foreign missions; but this was outside Lord Acton's field. Vaughan had in the first place a deep and simple charity. He was an outdoor-man; reading was a hardship to him and was confined to where his duty lay, to Catholic devotion and polemics. He had a sympathy for a fellow-owner of a Catholic estate. Aldenham lay some fifty-five miles to the north of Courtfield across the Herefordshire apple orchards just beyond the edge of a friendly horizon. He had known it as a Catholic house through all his boyhood.[5] These considerations appear to have been the motives for the Cardinal's action. He was also for various reasons not unwilling to take a different line from Cardinal Manning. Lord Acton was invited and agreed to take a leading part in the ceremonies of the laying of the foundation stone of Westminster Cathedral.

His daughters were grown up, but not yet married. His only

[1] Hans Delbruck (1848–1929).
[2] Max Lenz (1850–1932).
[3] Leopold von Ranke (1795–1886).
[4] Adolf von Harnack (1851–1930).
[5] The Cardinal was just eighteen months Lord Acton's senior.

son after education in Bavaria by private tutors and a spell at Magdalen had entered the diplomatic service and was now abroad. The Empress Frederick had died at Friedrichshof in the Taunus, and the Queen of England's reign was now drawing to a close. His contemporaries in the world of English history were thinning out. Samuel Rawson Gardiner and Mandell Creighton, who had been translated from Peterborough to the London diocese, both died in 1901, and York Powell was in his last stages with acute heart disease. Acton's generation was now passing.

He went for a few months to Meran and then to Tegernsee. In the autumn of 1901 his eldest daughter married Edward Bleiddian Herbert, a young Catholic neighbour of the Vaughans of Court- field and within their cousinage.[1] All those many links between England and Germany on which Acton's life had prospered could not survive the old Queen's time. He had never been concerned with the French or British colonies, still less the German. The Boer War, which filled his later days, meant nothing to him. The politics of the German Empire were slowly changing. Bismarck was dead, his successor Caprivi had retired, and his second suc- cessor, Prince Hohenlohe, who had been with Acton long ago in 1870, was now dead likewise. In South Germany the old ways continued; even now there was not yet adult male suffrage in Bavaria and Württemberg. As Acton lay dying at Tegernsee there was enacted one of the last pageants of the old Empires, the funeral of the King of Saxony.

On the evening of Acton's death in the Silesian summer Albrecht-Friedrich-August, the old King of Saxony, died at his country palace of Sybillenort beyond the eastern frontiers of the Saxon kingdom. He had reigned at Dresden for thirty years. These were the last days of the great royal trains before the age of motor cars. The imperial landaus with their escort of mounted guards set out from the Neue Palais at Potsdam for the Anhalt Station and from the Hofburg for the Franz Josef Terminus. A mass of German princes, and those aged rulers the Emperor of Austria, the Prince Regent of Bavaria, the last Grand Duke of Tuscany, all gathered upon Dresden. This was the old world of which Acton

---

[1] The two surviving Catholic families among the squirearchy in Monmouthshire were the Herberts, formerly Jones, of Llanarth, and the Vaughans of Courtfield.

was in some ways sceptical, the peaceful nineteenth century coming slowly to its close.

The same night, 19 June 1902, Lord Acton died at Tegernsee, fortified by the rites of the Catholic Church administered by the local priest who belonged to one of the parishes of the archdiocese of Munich. He was buried in the churchyard beside the lake. Thus ended the great historian's last peaceful years.

Bibliography

PRINTED PRIVATE CORRESPONDENCE OF LORD ACTON

Letters of Lord Acton to Mary Gladstone, ed. Herbert Paul (1904)
Lord Acton and his Circle, ed. Abbot later Cardinal Gasquet (1906)
Selections from the Correspondence of the first Lord Acton, ed. Figgis and Laurence (1917)
Acton-Döllinger Correspondence, ed. Viktor Conzemius (1963)

SELECT BIBLIOGRAPHY

These books are arranged according to the sections of Lord Acton's life to which they are relevant

I. THE EARLY PERIOD

a. The Catholic background

The Life of the Rt. Rev. Mgr Weedall by Frederick Charles Husenbeth (1860)
The Life of the Rt. Rev. John Milner, Bishop of Castabala by Frederick Charles Husenbeth (1862)
The Sequel to Catholic Emancipation by Bernard Ward (1915)
The Life and Times of Cardinal Wiseman by Wilfrid Ward (1897)
Nicholas Wiseman by Brian Fothergill (1963)
Letters and Correspondence of J. H. Newman, ed. Anne Mozley (1891)
The Life of John Henry Cardinal Newman by Wilfrid Ward (1912)
The Letters and Diaries of John Henry Newman, ed. C. S. Dessain (1961)
Newman by Meriol Trevor (1962)
Father Faber by Ronald Chapman (1961)
The Life and Times of Bishop Ullathorne by Abbot Cuthbert Butler, O.S.B. (1926)
Catholicism in England by David Mathew (1936)

b. The general background

Acton. The Formative Years by David Mathew (1946)
Conversations of Dr Döllinger by Luise von Kobell (1892)
The Age of Reform 1815–1870 by E. L. Woodward (1938)

375

Foundations of British Foreign Policy by H. Temperley and L. M. Penson (1938)

The Greville Memoirs, ed. Lytton Strachey and Roger Fulford (1938)

The Spanish Marriages by E. Parry Jones (1936)

The Life of Granville George Leveson Gower, second Earl Granville by Lord Edmond Fitzmaurice (1905)

Life of Lady Georgiana Fullerton by Mrs Augustus Craven (1888)

The Life, Letters and Literary Remains of Edward Bulwer, Lord Lytton by Edward 1st Earl of Lytton (1883)

A Vanished Victorian (Life of the 4th Earl of Clarendon) by George Villiers (1938)

The Later Correspondence of Lord John Russell, ed. G. P. Gooch (1925)

Autobiography by John Stuart Mill (1873)

The History of 'The Times', vol. ii. 1841–1884 (1939)

II. THE ROMAN SCENE

The Roman Journals of Ferdinand Gregorovius 1852–1874, ed. Friedrich Althaus, trans. by Mrs Gustavus Hamilton (1911)

The Roman Question (Extracts from the despatches of Odo Russell from Rome 1858–1870), ed. Noël Blakiston (1962)

Leopardi by Iris Origo (new ed. 1953)

Italy in the Making 1846–8 by G. F.-H. and J. Berkerley (1940–2)

Le Comte de Cavour by W. de la Rive (1862)

The Last Bourbons of Naples by Harold Acton (1961)

Baron Ward and the Dukes of Parma by Jesse Myers (1938)

The Vatican Council by Abbot Cuthbert Butler, O.S.B. (ed. of 1962)

Diario del Concilio Vaticano I by Léon Dehon (1962)

Letters of 'Quirinus' from Rome on the Council, English trans. (1870)

Memoirs of Francis Kerril Amherst, Bishop of Northampton, ed. Dame Mary Francis Roskell, O.S.B. (1903)

Henry Edward Manning, his life and letters by Shane Leslie (1923)

Pio Nono by E. E. Y. Hales (1954)

III. THE GLADSTONE YEARS

England 1870–1914 by R. C. K. Ensor (1936)

The Life of Gladstone by John Morley (1903)

Gladstone, a Biography by Philip Magnus (1954)

Mr Gladstone by Sir E. W. Hamilton (1898)

The Queen and Mr Gladstone by A. Tilney Bassett (1933)

Disraeli, Gladstone and the Eastern Question by R. W. Seton-Watson (1935)

Gladstone and the Irish Nation by J. L. Hammond (1938)

Gladstone to his Wife, ed. A. Tilney Bassett (1936)

Gladstone and Liberalism by J. L. Hammond and M. R. D. Foote (1952)

Catherine Gladstone by Mrs Drew (1919)

Mrs Gladstone by Esther Battiscombe (1956)

After Thirty Years by Herbert Viscount Gladstone (1928)
Acton, Gladstone and Others by Mrs Drew (1924)
Memoirs of J. R. Hope-Scott by Robert Ornsby (1884)
Memoirs of an ex-Minister by James 3rd Earl of Malmesbury (1884)
Reminiscences by Lord Kilbracken (1931)
Life of Disraeli by W. F. Monypenny and G. E. Buckle (ed. of 1929)
Disraeli by Robert Blake (1966)
The Political Correspondence of Mr Gladstone and Lord Granville, vol. i,
    1868–71, and vol. ii, 1871–76, both edited by Agatha Ramm (1952)
The Life of Granville George Leveson Gower, second Earl Granville, vol. ii,
    by Lord Edmond Fitzmaurice (1905)
Lord Lyons by Lord Newton (1913)
Recollections by John Viscount Morley (1917)
John Morley, Early Life and Letters by F. W. Hirst (1928)
Life of Sir William Harcourt by A. G. Gardiner (1923)
An Italian Englishman: Sir James Lacaita by Charles Lacaita (1933)
Prince of Librarians, Life and Times of Antonio Panizzi, by Edward
    Miller (1967)
Antonio Panizzi by Constance Brooks (1938)
Memoirs and Letters of the Rt. Hon. Sir Robert Morier 1826–76 (1911)
Life of the Rt. Rev. Samuel Wilberforce, first volume by Canon A. R.
    Ashwell, second and third by R. G. Wilberforce (1880–2)
The Parting of Friends by David Newsome (1966)

IV. THE LATER PERIOD

The Letters of Queen Victoria, second series, ed. G. E. Buckle (1926)
Mary Elizabeth, Lady Ponsonby, a memoir, some letters, and a journal, ed.
    M. Ponsonby (1927)
Victoria R.I. by Elizabeth Longford (1964)
Letters of the Empress Frederick, ed. Frederick Ponsonby (1928)
Life and Letters of Mandell Creighton D.D. by Louise Creighton (1904)
Life and Letters of Edward A. Freeman by Dean Stephens (1895)
The Life of Froude by Herbert Paul (1905)
Memoirs by Mark Pattison (1885)
A Victorian Childhood by Gwen Raverat (1952)
Frederick York Powell by Oliver Elton (1906)
James Bryce by H. A. L. Fisher (1927)
Notes from a Diary, 1851–1901 by Sir Mountstuart Grant Duff (1897–
    1905)

BOOKS COVERING LORD ACTON'S LIFE

As Lord Acton says by F. E. Lally (1942)
Lord Acton. A study in conscience and politics by Gertrude Himmelfarb
    (1952)
Acton on History by Lionel Kochan (1954)

A LIST OF THE DATES OF THE PRINCIPAL EVENTS
OF LORD ACTON'S LIFE

1834, 10 January. John Emerich Edward, only son of Sir Ferdinand Richard Edward Acton, born at Palazzo Acton all'Chiaja in Naples

1837, 31 January. John Acton inherits as eighth baronet of Aldenham Park in Shropshire on his father's death

1840, 25 July. His mother, Lady Acton, marries Lord Leveson, later Earl Granville

1843. Sir John Acton goes to St Mary's College, Oscott

1847, 23 June. His uncle, Charles Januarius Edward Acton, Cardinal of Santa Maria della Pace, dies in Naples

1848. Sir John Acton goes to Edinburgh for private tuition under Mr Logan

1850. He goes to Munich to study under Dr Döllinger

1855, 10 January. He comes of age and enters into possession of Aldenham Park. He accompanies Lord Ellesmere as A.D.C. on his visit to the United States

1856. He is attached to Lord Granville's mission to Russia to the coronation of the Tsar Alexander II

1857. He visits Italy and Rome with Dr Döllinger and makes the acquaintance of his connection Marco Minghetti (1818–1886)

1859. He becomes co-proprietor of *The Rambler*

1859. He is elected as Whig M.P. for the borough of Carlow and undertakes the editorship of *The Rambler*

1860. Death of Lady Granville. On her death-bed Acton promises to marry his cousin Countess Marie Arco-Valley. He inherits Schloss Herrnsheim in the Rhineland from his mother

1862. Sir John changes the monthly *Rambler* into a quarterly *The Home and Foreign Review*, of which he is both proprietor and editor

1864. He attends the Congress at Munich. He decides to close down *The Home and Foreign Review*. In December the Pope issues the Encyclical *Syllabus Errorum*

1865, 1 August. Sir John Acton marries the Countess Marie Anna Ludomilla Euphrosyne Arco-Valley (she died 1923)

1866, 15 August. His eldest daughter Mary Elizabeth born (died 1955)

1867. He begins contributing to the weekly *Chronicle* (ceased at the end of 1868) and then to the quarterly *North British Review* (begun 1869 and ceased 1872)

1868. His parliamentary career comes to an end. He had given up his seat at Carlow to contest Bridgnorth in 1865, where he won by a single vote and was unseated on petition. Three years later he again contested the seat without success

1868, 26 September. His second daughter Annie born (died 1917)

1869. Sir John, who had also made visits in the previous years, estab-

lishes himself at Rome at 74 Via della Croce to watch the Council.
In December he moves to the Palazzo Chigi. During these and the
succeeding months he contributes his share to the letters of Quirinus
printed in the *Allegemeine Zeitung*

1869, 11 December. He is created Baron Acton of Aldenham

1870, July. Lord Acton leaves Rome for Florence *en route* for Tegernsee

1870, 7 August. His elder son Richard Maximilian born (died 1924)

1872. Lord Acton receives an honorary doctorate from the University
of Munich

1873, 15 March. His grandmother Mary Anne Lady Acton died
16 April. His younger son John died aged ten months

1874, November and December. His correspondence in *The Times*
addressed to Mr Gladstone

1876, 12 March. His youngest daughter Jeanne Marie born (died
1919)

1877. His last lectures at Bridgnorth on 'The History of Freedom in
Antiquity and in Christianity'

1878, January. His article in the *Quarterly* on Sir Erskine May's
'Democracy in Europe'

1879. Lord Acton lets Aldenham Park and sells Schloss Herrnsheim
and his estates in the Rhineland

1881, 1 October. His third daughter Elizabeth dies aged seven

1886. Lord Acton helps to found the *English Historical Review*

1888. He is made Hon. LL.D., Cambridge

1889. He is made Hon. D.C.L., Oxford

1891. He is appointed a Lord-in-Waiting to the Queen

1895. He resigns this post on appointment as Regius Professor of
modern history at Cambridge

1898, 19 May. Mr Gladstone dies

1899. Lord Acton settles down to his work of organizing the *Cambridge
Modern History*

1902, 19 June. Lord Acton dies at Tegernsee

Index